Europe
Through the
Back Door

Europe Through the Back Door

Ninth Edition

Rick Steves

John Muir Publications
Santa Fe, New Mexico

Thanks to Gene Openshaw, Dave Hoerlein, Steve Smith, and Anne Steves for research assistance. And to Carl, Ruth, Gene, Greg, Patty, Dave, Mike, the mini-bus tours, my parents, and my wife Anne for sharing with me the excitement of European travel.

Rick Steves's lecture and travel seminar schedules are available from Europe Through the Back Door, 120 4th North, Edmonds, WA 98020 (telephone: 206-771-8303).

John Muir Publications, P.O. Box 613, Santa Fe, NM 87504

Library of Congress Cataloging-in-Publication Data
Steves, Rick, 1955-
    Europe through the back door / Rick Steves: [illustrations, Melissa Meir; maps, David Hoerlein]. — 9th ed.
        p. cm.
    ISBN 0-945465-42-4
    1. Europe—Description and travel—1971- —Guide-books.
I. Title.
D909.S93854   1990
914'.04558—dc20   89-13737
                                                              CIP
Distributed to the book trade by:
W. W. Norton & Company, Inc.
New York, NY

Cover: Jennifer Dewey
Illustrations: Melissa Meier
Maps: David Hoerlein
Typography: Copygraphics, Inc., Santa Fe, NM
Printer: McNaughton & Gunn

**To
the People
of Europe**

Contents

Part Two: Forty Back Doors

Contents

What Is a Back Door, and How Can I Find One of My Own?

Undiscovered Towns

Natural Nooks and Undiscovered Crannies

Back Door Travel Philosophy

Travel is intensified living—maximum thrills per minute. It's one of the last great sources of legal adventure. It's recess, and we need it.

Affording travel is a matter of priorities. Many people who "can't afford a trip" could sell their car and travel for a year. A friend marvels at my ability to fund my travels as we sit on $2,000 worth of his living room furniture. I read my journal on a $60 sofa and spend my free time and money exploring the world.

You can travel simply, safely, and comfortably anywhere in Europe for $40 a day plus transportation costs. In many ways, spending more money only builds a thicker wall between you and what you came to see.

A tight budget forces you to travel "close to the ground," meeting and communicating with the people, not relying on your bucks to do the talking. Never sacrifice sleep, nutrition, safety, or cleanliness in the name of budget. Simply enjoy the local-style alternatives to expensive hotels and restaurants.

To really experience Europe, you have to catch it by surprise. A "Sound and Light" show at the Acropolis with six busloads of tourists is OK, but you'll find the real Greece down the street, playing backgammon in an Athens taverna. Rome has plenty of temples and monuments to the dead. After your tour of the Forum, liven things up by crossing the river for a stroll through Trastevere, today's village Rome. Europe is a cultural carnival, and time after time, you'll find that its best acts are free.

Traditional travel writing teaches tourism, not travel. This book gives you universal travel skills that will prepare and encourage you to experience Europe—as well as the world—from Walla Walla to Bora Bora. You'll enjoy Europe as a temporary local—seeing a living Europe, not just making a quick appraisal from the roof garden of the Inter-Continental Hotel and collecting cultural clichés kept alive only for tourists.

Americans are generally too things-oriented to travel well. Travel like Gandhi—with simple clothes, open eyes, and an uncluttered mind. It's a gift to be simple. If things aren't to your liking, don't change the things; change your liking.

Extroverts have more fun. If your trip is low on magic moments, kick yourself and start making things happen. Dignity and good travel don't mix. Leave your beeper at home. Let your hair down.

If you don't enjoy a place, it's often because you don't know enough about it. Seek out the truth. Recognize tourist traps.

A culture is legitimized by its existence. Give a people the benefit of your open mind. Think of things as different but not better or worse. Wise travelers don't see a world as a pyramid with us on top and everyone else trying to get there.

Of course, travel, like the world, is a series of hills and valleys. Be fanatically positive and militantly optimistic.

Travel is addicting. It can make you a happier American as well as a citizen of the world. Our Earth is home to five billion equally important people. That's wonderfully humbling.

Globe-trotting destroys ethnocentricity. It encourages the understanding and appreciation of various cultures. Travel changes people. It broadens perspectives and teaches new ways to measure quality of life. Many travelers toss aside their hometown blinders. Their prized souvenirs are the strands of different cultures they decide to knit into their own character.

The world is a cultural yarn shop. And Back Door travelers are weaving the ultimate tapestry. Come on . . . join in!

—Rick Steves

Preface

The average American traveler enters Europe through the front door. This Europe greets you with open cash registers, $5 cups of coffee, and service with a purchased smile.

Make your trip special. Come with me, through the back door where a warm, relaxed, personable Europe welcomes us as intimate friends. Through the back door, we become temporary Europeans, part of the family—approaching Europe on its level, accepting and appreciating its unique ways of life. We'll demand nothing, except that no fuss be made over us.

Spending money has very little to do with enjoying your trip. In fact, spending less money brings you closer to Europe. A lot of money forces you through Europe's grand front entrance, where people in uniforms greet you with formal, polite, and often stuffy smiles. But through the back door—well, that's my kind of Europe.

I've spent twenty years exploring Europe through the back door. This book, which has evolved over nine editions, is my report to you after a virtual lifetime in the travelers' school of hard knocks. Experience is a great teacher. These are my notes, taken in the hope that you'll learn from my mistakes rather than your own and have the best possible trip.

The character and cost of your trip depends on which door you decide to enter and what travel skills you take with you. If you're looking to really immerse yourself in Europe—footloose, fancy-free, and on a budget—the back door is your door.

The first half of this book covers the skills of Back Door European travel—packing, planning an itinerary, finding good hotels, getting around, and so on. The second half gives you keys to my favorite discoveries, places I call "Back Doors," where you can dirty your fingers in pure Europe—feeling its fjords and caressing its castles. Happy travels!

Part One:
Basic Travel Skills

1
Planning

A European adventure is a major investment of time and money. Those who think of the planning stage as part of the experience invest wisely and enjoy tremendous returns. A well-planned trip is more fun, less expensive, and not necessarily more structured. Planning means understanding your alternatives, preparing to be spontaneous.

Tour versus Independent Travel

One of the first big decisions to make is whether to travel independently or with a group tour. Consider the pros and cons of each. Do you want the security of knowing that all your rooms are reserved and that a trained guide will take you smoothly from one hotel to the next? Do you require consistently good hotels and restaurant meals, wishing at the same time to be as economical as possible? Will you forgo adventure, independence, and the challenge of doing it on your own in order to take the worry and bother out of traveling? Is sitting on a bus with the same group of tourists an acceptable way to spend your vacation? If the answer to these questions is "yes," then you need a good European tour company. There's a tour for just about every travel dream. Your travel agent can help you.

For many people with limited time and money, tours are the most efficient way to see Europe. Without a tour, three restaurant meals a day and a big, modern hotel are very expensive. Large tour companies book thousands of rooms and meals year-round and can, with their tremendous economic clout, get prices that no individual tourist could even come close to. For instance, on a recent "Cosmos" tour (one of the largest and cheapest tour companies in Europe), I got fine rooms (with private bath), three hot meals a day, bus transportation, and the services of a European guide—all for $60 a day. Considering that each hotel room alone would have cost the tourist off the street at least $60, that all-inclusive tour price per day was great. Such comfort without a tour is very expensive.

Eight and forty tourists baked in a bus

There are cheaper ways to see Europe than from the tinted windows of a tour bus. The cheapest and—for me—the best way to see Europe is to travel independently. If you've read this far, you've got what it takes intellectually to handle Europe on your own. To the independent traveler, Europe can be a rewarding challenge and adventure as well as an enjoyable vacation. The tour groups that unload on Europe's quaintest towns are treated as an entity, a mob to be fed, shown around, profited from, and moved out. They drink at Europe while the individual traveler drinks with Europe.

This book focuses on the skills necessary for do-it-yourself European travel. If you're destined for a tour, read on anyway (especially the section on bus tour self-defense). Even on a bus with fifty other people, you can and should be in control, equipped with a guidebook and thinking as an independent traveler. Your trip's too important for you to blindly trust an overworked and underpaid tour guide.

Alone or with a Friend?

The independent traveler must decide whether to travel alone or with a friend. Here are some pros and cons.

Traveling alone gives you complete freedom and independence. You never have to wait for your partner to pack up; you never need to consider what the partner wants to see, where he wants to go, how fast he wants to travel, when he's tired, how much he wants to spend; you go where you want to, when you want to, and you can get the heck out of that stuffy museum when all the Monets start looking alike.

You meet more people when you travel alone because you're more approachable in the eyes of a European, and loneliness will drive you to reach out and make friends. When you travel with someone, it's easy to focus on your partner and forget about meeting Europeans.

Solo travel is intensely personal. Without the comfortable crutch of a friend, you're more likely to know the joys of self-discovery and the pleasures found in the kindness of strangers. You'll be exploring yourself as well as a new city or country.

But traveling alone can be very lonely. Hotel rooms become lifeless cells, and meals are served in a puddle of silence. Big cities can be cold and ugly when the only person you have to talk to is yourself. Being sick and alone in a country where no one even knows you exist is, even in retrospect, a miserable experience.

Europe is full of lonely travelers, and there are a some natural meeting places. You're likely to find a vaga-buddy in youth hostels, museums (offer to share your _Mona Winks_ chapter), on one-day bus tours, and on trains. Eurailers buddy up on the trains. If you're carrying a Cook Timetable, leave it lying around, and you'll become the most popular kid on the train. Travel as a student, whatever your age: they have more fun, make more friends, and spend less money than most travelers.

Traveling on your own, you'll have the locals dancing with you — not for you.

Board the train with a little too much of a picnic—and share it with others. Bring a Walkman headphone with a Y-jack (or just the Y-jack) and a couple of good tapes. Be bold; if you're lonely, others are, too. **Traveling with a partner** overcomes many of these problems. Shared experiences are more fun, and for the rest of your life, there will be a special bond between you. The confident, uninhibited extrovert is better at making things happen and is more likely to run into exciting and memorable events. And when I travel with a partner, it's easier for me to be that kind of "wild and crazy guy."

Traveling with a partner is cheaper. Rarely does a double room cost as much as two singles. If a single room costs $20, a double room will generally be around $30, a savings of $5 per night per person. Picnicking is cheaper and easier when you share costs, as are travel guides, banking, maps, magazines, taxis, storage lockers, and much more. Besides expenses, partners can share the burden of time-consuming hassles, such as standing in lines at trains stations, banks, and post offices.

Remember, traveling together greatly accelerates a relationship—especially a romantic one. You see each other constantly, making endless decisions. The niceties go out the window. Everything becomes very real, and you are in an adventure, a struggle, a hot air balloon for two. You can jam the experiences of years into one summer.

I'd highly recommend a little premarital travel. A mutual travel experience is a good test of a relationship—often revealing its ultimate course. It's the greatest way to get to know somebody, in every conceivable sense.

Your choice of a travel partner is critical. It can make or break a trip. Traveling with the wrong partner can be like a two-month computer date. I'd rather do it alone. Analyze your travel styles and goals for compatibility. Consider a trial weekend together before merging your dream trips.

Choose a partner carefully. One summer I went to Europe to speed up life, to dive into as many cultures and adventures as possible. The trip was a challenge, and I planned to rest when I got home. My partner wanted to slow life down, to get away from it all, relax and escape the pressures of the business world. Our ideas of acceptable hotels and good meals were quite different. The trip was a near disaster.

Many people already have their partner—for better or for worse. In the case of married couples, minimize the stress of traveling together by recognizing one another's needs for independence. Too many people do Europe as a three-legged race, tied together from start to finish. Have an explicit understanding that there's absolutely nothing selfish, dangerous, insulting, or wrong with splitting up occasionally. This is a freedom too few travel partners allow themselves. Doing your own thing for a few hours or days breathes fresh air into your togetherness. Traveling in a threesome or foursome is usually troublesome. With all the exciting choices Europe has to offer, it's often hard for even a twosome to reach a consensus. Without a clear group leader, the "split and be independent" strategy is particularly valuable here.

Another way to minimize travel partnership stress is to go communal with your money. Separate checks, double bank charges, and long lists of petty IOUs in six different currencies are a pain. Pool your resources, noting how much each person contributes, and just assume everything equals out in the long run. Keep track of major individual expenses, but don't worry who got an extra postcard or gelato. Enjoy treating each other to taxis and dinner out of your "kitty," and after the trip divvy up the remains. If one person consumed $25 or $30 more, that's a small price to pay for the convenience of communal money.

Many single travelers pick up a partner in Europe.

Our Travel Industry

Travel is a huge business. Most of what the industry promotes is decadence: lie on the beach and be catered to; hedonize those precious two weeks to make up for the other fifty; see if you can eat five meals a day and still snorkel when you get into port. That's where the money is, and that's where most of the interest is. You (anyone who's read this far in this book) are just a fringe that fits the industry like a snowshoe in Mazatlán.

As a newspaper travel columnist, I've learned a lot about the politics of tourism. Advertising makes your newspaper's travel section possible. If you ever want to be a successful travel columnist, write articles that enthuse prospective travelers while furthering the myths that scare people into the arms of organized travel. Tales of Ugly Americanism, high costs, language barriers, theft, and sickness help fill the cruise ships and tour buses with would-be independent adventurers. Practical consumer information does not sell cruises. In other words, it doesn't attract advertisers. Typically, a travel editor's job performance is measured by ads sold. My cynicism is based on experience. For instance, travel agencies that advertise in the travel section of one of the newspapers for which I write organized a kind of boycott, telling the travel editor they wouldn't advertise as long as he ran my column called "The Budget Traveler." I met with the editor, and, to save the column, we changed the name to "The Practical Traveler"—same subversive information but with a more palatable title.

Most travel agents don't understand travel "through the Back Door." The typical attitude I get when I hobnob with bigwigs from the industry in Hilton Hotel ballrooms is, "If you can't afford first class, save up and go next year." I'll never forget the bewilderment I caused when I turned down a free room in Bangkok's most elegant Western-style hotel in favor of a $10 room in a Thai-style hotel.

Of course, these comments are generalizations; there are many great travelers in the travel industry. These people will understand my frustration because they've also dealt with it.

Travel can mean rich people flaunting their affluence, taking pictures of black kids jumping off white ships for small change. Or it can

Their travel agent recommended this tour.

promote understanding, turning our American perspective into a human perspective and making our world more comfortable in its smallness. What the industry promotes is up to all of us—writers, editors, agents, and consumers.

Why You Need a Travel Agent, and How to Choose One

How do you find a travel agent? When do you use one? And which of their services is necessary? I start every trip by visiting my agent. So should you.

What do I need from an agent? Travel agents are, or should be, experts on the logistics of travel—getting there, getting around over there, and tour options. For independent budget international travel, I use an agent only for my plane ticket, train pass, or car rental, nothing else.

Although many agents can give you tips on Irish B&Bs and sporadic advice on the best biking in Holland, you'll generally do better if you use your travel agent to get you to your destination and, after that, rely on a good guidebook.

It takes a full-time and aggressive travel professional to keep up with the constantly changing airline industry these days. You won't save money by going directly to the airlines. Most airline representatives barely know what they're charging, much less their competitors' rates and schedules. And only your agent would remind you that leaving two days earlier would get you in on the end of shoulder season—and save you $50.

Agents charge you nothing. They make their money from commissions paid by the airlines, not by marking up your tickets. Take advantage of their expertise. A good agent understands that there's no free lunch in the airline industry. Normally, for every dollar you save, you're losing a dollar's worth of comfort, flexibility, or reliability. Rather than grab the cheapest ticket to Europe, I go with my agent's recommendation for the best combination of reliability, economy, and flexibility for my travel needs.

Car rentals are cheaper when arranged before departure through your agent. Eurail, Francerail, and Britrail passes must be purchased before you leave home. To get good service on small, tedious items like these, do all your trip business through the agent who made a good commission on your air ticket.

When do I buy? Survey the ticket situation with your agent as soon as you know where you're going. Buy your plane tickets as soon as you're ready to firmly commit yourself to flight dates and ports. As you

Know Thy Travel Agent—A Quiz

One way to be sure your travel agent is properly suited to help-ing you with your trip is to ask him or her a few questions. Here's a little quiz—complete with answers.

1. **What is "open jaws"?**
   a) Yet another shark movie sequel.
   b) A tourist in awe of the Mannekin Pis.
   c) A special-interest tour of Czechoslovakia's dental clinics.
   d) An airline ticket that allows you to fly into one city and out of another.
2. **Which international boat rides are covered by the Eurailpass?**
   a) Poland to Switzerland.
   b) All of them.
   c) Ireland to France, Sweden to Finland, Italy to Greece, Germany to Denmark, and Sweden to Denmark.
3. **What's the Youth Hostel membership age limit?**
   a) Five.
   b) As high as 30 if you like Michael Jackson.
   c) There is none, except in Bavaria where it's 26.
4. **What is the most economical way to get from London's Heathrow Airport into London?**
   a) Walk.
   b) In a Youth Hostel.
   c) Don't. Spend your whole vacation at Heathrow.
   d) By subway or airbus.
5. **What is an ISIC card?**
   a) A universal way to tell foreigners you're not feeling well.
   b) It beats three-of-a-kind.
   c) The International Student Identity Card, good for many discounts at sights and museums.
6. **Is there a problem getting a "bed and breakfast" in England's small towns without a reservation?**
   a) Not if you live there.
   b) Yes. Carry No-Doze in England.
   c) No.
7. **How much does a Yugoslavian visa cost?**
   a)"How much you have, comrade?"
   b) You can just charge it on your Visa card.
   c) More than a Grecian urn.
   d) It's free and can be obtained easily at the border.

Answers: The last answer to each question is the correct one.

delay, dates sell out and prices may rise. Once you buy your ticket, you fix the price. Remember, cheap tickets are very expensive to change. **From whom do I buy?** If people would spend as much energy finding the right agent and cultivating a loyal relationship with him or her as they do shopping around for the cheapest ticket, they'd be much better off. A good agent can get you almost any ticket, and dumping your agent for a $30 savings from a discount agent down the street is a bad move. (See chapter 3, Transportation, for flight information.)

These days, people are milking every good agent for all they're worth and then buying tickets from their sister's friend's agency around the corner. Because of this trend, it's tough to get good advice over the phone, and "browsers" usually get no respect. I thoroughly enjoy the luxury of sitting down with my agent, explaining travel plans, getting a thorough briefing on my options, and choosing the best flight. I don't have time to sort through all the frustrating, seemingly too-good-to-be-true ads that fill many Sunday mornings with shouts of "Come on!"

If you have a travel specialty, find an agency with the same focus. In the fast-paced and deregulated airline industry, your agency should be computerized. Big or specializing agencies have more clout with the airlines and can often exercise a little more flexibility with airline rules and prices. Big-city agencies have a closer working relationship with airlines and, therefore, a slight advantage. But a hardworking smaller agency might give you more personal attention and be less distracted. The travel agency chains are best suited to help the business traveler. Often, but not always, the discounting agencies make too little per ticket to properly serve their masses. I'd choose a no-frills flight, not a no-frills agency. Travel agency recommendations from other travelers provide excellent leads.

But the right agency doesn't guarantee the right agent. You need a particular person—someone whose definition of "good travel" matches yours. Consider his or her attitude and experience. Are you a Love Boat, shuffleboard-and-bad-magic-acts-after-dinner traveler? Or do you travel to leave behind rather than flaunt your Americanness? Quiz your agent.

Once you find the right agent, nurture your alliance. Be loyal, keep your traveling eggs together in the correct basket, and travel with this expert on your side.

Travel Insurance—To Insure or Not to Insure

Travel insurance is a way to buy off the considerable financial risks of traveling. These risks include accidents, illness, missed flights, canceled or interrupted tours, lost baggage, and emergency evacuation. Each traveler's risk and potential loss varies, depending on how much of the trip is prepaid, the kind of air ticket purchased, you and your loved ones' health, value of your luggage, where you're traveling, what health coverage you already have, and the financial health of the tour company or airline. For some, insurance is a good deal; for others, it's not.

Travel agents will recommend travel insurance because they make a commission off of it, because they can be held liable for your losses if they don't explain insurance options to you—and maybe because it's right for you. But the final decision is yours. What are the chances of needing it, how able are you to take the risks, and what's peace of mind worth to you?

You can design your own coverage by ordering à la carte through a policy like Access America's or Mutual of Omaha's. This insurance menu includes four sections: medical, baggage, trip cancellation, and flight insurance. Tailor it to your needs, then compare it with the package deal explained below.

Medical insurance might be unnecessary. Most health insurance policies (such as Blue Cross, Group Health, and Blue Shield) cover emergency medical expenses wherever you break your toe. Before your trip, check your coverage and know what information to collect to be properly reimbursed when you get back home.

Baggage insurance costs about $2 or $3 per day per $1,000 coverage, occasionally with some serious limitations on coverage of items such as cash, eye wear, and photographic equipment. If you've left your valuables either in your money belt or at home, this coverage is unnecessary.

Trip cancellation or interruption insurance covers your losses if: (1) your travel partner or a family member cannot travel due to sickness or a list of other acceptable reasons; (2) your tour company or airline goes out of business or can't perform as promised; (3) a family member at home gets sick, causing you to cancel; or (4) for a good reason, you miss a flight or need an emergency one. In other words, if, one day before your trip, you or your travel partner breaks a leg, you can both bail out and neither of you will lose a penny. And if, one day into the tour, you have an accident, both of you will be flown home, and you'll be reimbursed for the emergency one-way return flight (which usually costs far more than your economy round-trip fare) and whatever portion of the tour you haven't used. This insurance costs about 5 ½ percent of the amount you want covered (for example, $1,500 tour and $500 airfare can be fully insured for $110). This is a good deal if you figure there's a better than 1-in-20 chance you'll need it. The rugged, healthy, unattached, and gung-ho traveler will probably skip this coverage. Someone with questionable health taking an organized tour (which is very expensive to cancel) should get this coverage.

Flight insurance (crash coverage) is a statistical rip-off that heirs love. More than 60,000 airplanes take off and land safely every day. The chances of being in an airplane crash are minuscule.

There are **package insurance** deals (such as Travel Guard's) that give you everything but the kitchen sink for 7 percent of your prepaid trip cost (airfare, car rental, Eurail ticket, tour cost, etc.). This can be a better deal for travelers with less of the trip prepaid (those without tours) because coverage is the same regardless of the premium you pay. This covers any deductible expense your existing medical insurance plan doesn't cover. And it also gives you a supplemental collision damage waiver (CDW) on rental cars. (See below.)

The problem with a Travel Guard-type package is that you must take the whole works—dental care, hotel overbooking, CDW supplement and all—whether you need it or not. It's comprehensive but not necessarily the cheapest coverage.

Your travel agent has insurance brochures. Ask your agent which he or she recommends for your travels and why. Study the brochures. Consider how insurance fits your travel and personal needs, compare the likelihood of your using it and your potential loss to its cost—and then decide. Every traveler can and should make an informed decision on whether to travel insured.

The Collision Damage Waiver Racket

In the past, the insurance on a rental car normally had a $1,000 deductible clause. Car companies charged a ridiculous fee to waive this deductible, so travel insurance companies and credit card companies were offering more reasonable CDW supplement deals to persons renting cars. Lately, car rental companies have raised their "deductible" to as much as the entire value of the car, far beyond the CDW coverage offered by the more reasonable alternatives. And the car renter has one way to drive without this huge deductible hanging over his or her head: pay the roughly $10 a day the car rental companies charge for CDW. Ask your travel agent about ways to avoid this fee. If you have to pay the car company, remember that the rental rates are so competitive that, to make a reasonable profit, these companies have had to make a killing on the CDW. If it's any consolation, think of your CDW fee as half for CDW and half money that you should have paid on the rental fee.

Regardless of how tough CDW is on the pocketbook, I get it for the peace of mind. It's so much more fun to hold your own on the road

Luckily, he paid extra for full insurance.

with Europe's skilled maniac drivers, knowing you can turn in your car in an unrecognizable shambles with an apologetic shrug, saying, "S·s·s·sorry," and lose no money.

Red Tape—Passports, Visas, Shots, and Such

The only document a U.S. citizen needs to travel through Western Europe is a passport. For most travelers, the only complicated border crossing and the only time any customs official will look at you seriously is at the airport as you reenter the United States. Most European border crossings are a wave-through for U.S. citizens.

Passports, good for 10 years, cost $42 ($35 for a renewal). Apply for one at the U.S. Passport Agency, any federal or state courthouse, or some post offices. For a recording with complete details, look up an information number in your phone book. Although they say applications take several weeks (and you should be prepared for delays), most passports are processed within a few days. If you can prove you're in an emergency situation and go in person, they'll do it while you wait.

Losing your passport while traveling is a major headache. Contact the police and the nearest U.S. consulate or embassy right away. You can get a short-term replacement, but you'll earn it. A photocopy of your lost passport helps.

As you travel, keep a tight grip on your passport. But that's not always possible. As you cross some Eastern European borders by train, a usually unofficial-looking character will come down the aisle picking up all the passports. Relax, you'll get it back later. When you sleep in a couchette (night train sleeping car) that crosses a border, the car attendant will take your passport so you won't be disturbed when the train crosses the border at 3:00 a.m. And hotels routinely take your passport "for the night" so they can register you with the police. This bookwork must be done for foreign guests throughout Europe. Receptionists like to gather passports and register them together when things are quiet. Although it's unreasonable to expect them to drop whatever they're doing to register you right now, I politely ask if I can pick up my passport in two hours. I just don't like my passport in the top drawer all night long. A passport works well for collateral in cases when you don't have the cash right now (hefty deposits on bike rentals, hotels that don't trust you, and so on).

Visas are not required for Americans traveling in Western Europe. A visa is a stamp placed on your passport by a government, allowing you to enter their country. A few countries (such as Yugoslavia) technically require a visa, but they stamp it in without delay as you enter. Although things can change, I'd expect that through the 1990s only Warsaw Pact countries will require visas for traveling Americans, and as the Iron Curtain melts, these restrictions should too. For up-to-date information on visa requirements, ask your travel agent or the U.S. Department of State.

If you do need to get a visa, it's usually best to get it at home before you leave. Remember that every European country has an embassy or consulate (which can issue visas) in the capital of every other European country. Paris is a great place to get visas in person and (for a $10-$20 speed fee) without a wait.

At this time, shots are not required for travel in Europe. But this can change, so check the inoculation requirements before you leave home. Remember that countries "require" shots in order to protect their citizens from you and "recommend" shots to protect you from them. If any shots are recommended, take that advice seriously.

Customs is not a concern unless you plan to buy more than $1,400 worth of souvenirs. Your first $400 worth are duty-free, and the next $1,000 worth are dutied at a flat 10 percent rate. If you buy less than $400 worth of goods, you simply say so as you reenter the United States.

The ISIC card, the only internationally recognized student ID card, will get you lots of discounts on transportation, entertainment, and sightseeing throughout Western Europe. If you are a full-time student or have been recently before your travels (and can prove it), get one. (The cost is $10 from your CIEE student travel agency or university foreign study office.)

Information Sources

Books

Too many people spend their vacations stranded on a Paris street corner. You need a good directory-type guidebook. Those who get the best trip for the least expense and with minimal headaches not only have a good guidebook, they use it. I can step off the plane for my first time in Bangkok and travel like an old pro by taking full advantage of a good guidebook.

Before buying a book, study it. How old is the information? The cheapest books are often the oldest—no bargain. Who wrote it? What's his or her experience? Does it promote the tourist industry or smart travel? To whom is it written? Is it readable? Many guidebooks are practical only as a powerful sedative. It should have personality without chattiness.

Don't believe everything you read. The power of the printed word is scary. Most books are peppered with information that is simply wrong. Incredibly enough, even this book may have an error (but I could be wrong). Many "writers" succumb to the temptation to write guidebooks based on hearsay, travel brochures, and other books.

There are many handy books. Bookstores that specialize in travel books have knowledgeable salespeople (take advantage of their expertise) and the best selection. Browse—guidebooks are $10 tools for $2,000 trips. If your city lacks a good travel bookstore, call Book Passage in California for their excellent free catalog (1-800-321-9785).

Here's a rundown of my favorite guidebooks:

Let's Go: Europe. Aptly subtitled "The Bible of the Budget Traveler," I wouldn't travel without it. *Let's Go* covers the big cities, towns, and countryside of all European countries as well as North Africa and the USSR. You'll find listings of budget accommodations and restaurants, information on public transportation, capsule social, political, and historical rundowns, and a refreshingly opinionated look at sights and tourist activities. It doesn't teach "Ugly Americanism," as do many prominent Europe guidebooks.

Although written by Harvard students for young train travelers on tight budgets, it's the best book available for anyone wanting to travel as a temporary European in search of cultural intimacy on a budget. It is updated each year and hard to find in Europe. Always use the current edition. If you've got more money, stick to its higher-priced listings. The only problem with _Let's Go_ is that every young traveler has it, and the flood of American business can change the character of places listed.

Let's Go also publishes books covering these countries individually: Britain/Ireland, Spain/Portugal/Morocco, France, Greece, Italy, and Israel/Egypt. If you'll be spending two weeks in any of these areas and like _Let's Go_'s style, these editions are for you. With ten times the information and a tenth the readership of _Let's Go: Europe_, these are easily the best guides available for these countries.

Arthur Frommer's classic guide, _Europe on $30 a Day_, is the best around for the big cities but totally ignores everything else (and there's so much more!). It is full of reliable and handy listings of budget hotels, restaurants, and sightseeing ideas compiled by the father of budget independent travel himself. I take along only the chapters on the cities I plan to visit as supplemental information. This book is attuned to the needs of older travelers.

Frommer books on specific countries are good, offering yet more coverage of each country—regions, towns, and villages as well as cities. But Arthur is only one man, and although his name is on the cover, the research and writing is farmed out and listings are inconsistent. Some are wordy at the expense of practical help, and most overemphasize hotel and restaurant listings, neglecting sights and culture. I hate to see 80 percent of a book's pages spent listing places to eat and sleep when any B&B will do. This conditions readers to think that 80 percent of their concern will be on finding room and board. Frommer's $X a Day books have a budget focus, whereas his _Dollarwise_ guides are for pricier travel.

Discovery Trips in Europe. This Sunset guide is great pretrip reading, offering "Discovery Trips" (their "Back Doors") to every corner of Europe. It's a snatch-here-and-snippet-there approach that can give you some unique ideas for your itinerary. Well written and worth studying. Take applicable photocopies or notes with you.

The Council on International Educational Exchange's (CIEE's) _Whole World Handbook_ is the best source book for work or study in Europe. CIEE is the biggest and most energetic student travel service in the United States—worth taking advantage of. (For a catalog, send $1 to CIEE, 205 E. 42nd St., New York, NY 10017. CIEE's telephone number is 212/661-1414. The CIEE travel agency, Council Travel, has offices in over 20 major U.S. cities. Call 1-800-223-7402 for flight information.)

Michelin Green Guides. These famous tall green books, available in dryly translated English all over Europe, ignore hotels and eating but are a gold mine of solid, practical information on what to see, covering many regions in Europe. English editions I've used are Paris, London, southwest England, Scotland, Italy, Spain, Portugal, Greece, Germany, Austria, Switzerland, the Loire Valley, Normandy, Brittany, the French Riviera, and Provence. Each book includes chapters on history, life-styles, art, culture, customs, and economy. My favorite feature is the large map with places listed according to their touristic importance rather than their population. Take advantage of this feature, where an exciting village appears bolder on the map than a big, dull city. These books are filled with good maps and designed for drivers, ideally on Michelin tires.

Real Guides is a series by Englishman Mark Ellingham (formerly the *Rough Guides*) which includes books about Germany, Spain, Portugal, Morocco, Greece, Yugoslavia, Eastern Europe, and Holland. They have been great sources of hard-core go-local-on-a-tight-budget information. Recently gobbled into the big-time American book world and slicked up, it remains to be seen if their rough soul has survived.

The *Blue Guides* series (which has nothing to do with European brothels) takes a very dry and scholarly approach to the countries of Europe. *Blue Guides* are ideal if you want to learn as much history, art, and culture as you possibly can about each country. With the *Blue Guide to Greece*, I had all the information I would ever need about any sight in Greece. There was never a need to hire a guide.

There are excellent books specifically for hikers, bikers, campers, motorcycle travelers, lovers of hill towns, wine snobs, hitchhikers, hedonists, those camping Europe by train, drivers, pilgrims, the terminally ill with a fortune to blow in a hurry, bird-watchers, children traveling with parents, gay people, gray people—you name it. If you have a focus, there's a book written just for you. Find it and use it.

Rick Steves's Books

22 Days in Europe, 5th ed. (Santa Fe, N.M.: John Muir Publications, 1990). This book offers Europe's best three weeks—in recipe form. It lays out the most efficient and exciting mix of "must see" sights, intimate "Back Door" nooks and offbeat crannies, with lots of great budget places to eat and sleep. It's a step-by-step handbook complete with city maps, day plans, train schedules, and everything you need to know to be your own tour guide.

Also available (from John Muir Publications): *22 Days in Great Britain, 22 Days in France, 22 Days in Spain and Portugal, 22 Days in Germany, Austria, and Switzerland, 22 Days in Norway, Sweden, and Denmark. (See Appendix for itineraries.)*

~Europe 101: History and Art for the Traveler, by Gene Openshaw and
Rick Steves (4th ed.; John Muir Publications), is the first and only fun
travelers' guide to Europe's history and art, full of boiled-down, practical information to make your sightseeing more meaningful and
enjoyable. The perfect companion to all the survival guides, _Europe 101_
is your passport to culture in a practical and easy-to-read manual.

~_Mona Winks: Self-Guided Tours of Europe's Top Museums_, by Rick Steves
and Gene Openshaw (John Muir Publications). Don't assume you can
buy good English guidebooks on the spot for Europe's sights and
museums. Those that are available are so dry that if you read them out
loud your lips would chap. _Mona Winks_ is a breezy, step-by-step,
painting-by-sculpture walk through the best two hours or so of
Europe's twenty most overwhelming and exhausting museums and cultural obligations including the Louvre, the Uffizi, Renaissance Florence, the British Museum, Classical Rome, the Vatican, and the Prado.
Essential for those who know a lot about everything but art. (See the
back of this book to order Rick Steves's books.)

Although adequate travel information keeps you afloat, too much
information can sink the ship. You can always find good travel books
in English in Europe. Rip up your books, bringing with you only the
applicable chapters. There's no point in carrying 120 pages of information on Scandinavia to dinner in Barcelona. When I finish seeing a
country, I give my stapled-together chapter on that area to another
traveler or leave it at my last hotel.

Your public library has a lifetime of valuable reading on European culture. Look under Dewey Decimal #914 for plenty of books on your destination. The *Newsweek* book on the court of Louis XIV brings Versailles to life. If travel partners divide up their studying, they can take turns being "guide" and do a better job.

Maps

Drivers need top-quality maps. Buy them in Europe. It's important to get up-to-date maps with the European place-names spelled as you'll see them in your travels. Excellent maps are on sale throughout Europe. The Michelin 920 Europe map is a handy overall planning map. Michelin maps for each region (1/200,000) are good and cost only $3 or $4. Consider the popular and inexpensive road atlases for each country available at freeway gas stations. Learn the key. Very handy sightseeing information (such as scenic roads and towns, costs and opening schedules of remote roads, ruined castles, youth hostels, mountain huts, and viewpoints) can be found on any good map.

By train, you can pretty much wing it with the free Eurail map that comes with your pass and free or very cheap little maps of each town that you'll pick up at the local tourist offices as you go.

Talk with Other Travelers

Both in Europe and here at home, travelers love to share the lessons they've learned. Grab every opportunity you can to learn from other tourists. Firsthand, fresh information is the best kind anywhere. Keep in mind, however, that all assessments of a place's touristic merit (including my own) are a product of that person's time there and his personality. It could have rained, he could have shared an elevator with the town jerk, or he may have been sick in "that lousy, overrated city." Or he might have fallen in love in that "wonderful" village. Every year, I find travelers hell bent on following miserable travel advice from friends at home. All opinions are just that—opinions.

As you travel, remember that many great guidebooks are not sold in the United States. Take advantage of every opportunity (train or bus rides, etc.) to swap information with travelers you meet from other parts of the English-speaking world. This is particularly important when traveling beyond Western Europe.

Classes

The more you understand something, the longer it stays interesting. For instance, travelers enjoy their first Gothic cathedral. But those with no background in medieval architecture are the first to get "cathedraled out." Whether you like it or not, you'll be spending lots of time browsing through historic buildings and museums. Trust me, you'll have more fun sightseeing in Europe if you prepare by doing some reading or taking some classes beforehand.

There are plenty of worthwhile classes on many aspects of Europe. Although you can get by with English, a foreign language—even a few phrases—can only make Europe more fun. History makes Europe come alive. A basic modern European history course turns a dull museum into a trip highlight. An Eastern European studies class will bring a little order to that demographic chaos.

Art history is probably the most valuable course for the prospective tourist. Please don't go to Europe—especially Italy or Greece— without at least having read something on art and architecture.

Travel Videos

The world is anxiously waiting for good travel videos. So far, most travel videos are uninspired destination picture books or cheesy promos sponsored by tourist boards or hotel groups. I'm doing my best to change all this. My first television venture, a three-part series filmed over six weeks in Europe on Back Door travel, is now available as a 75-minute video (see Back Door Catalog).

National Tourist Offices

Tourism is an important part of Europe's economy. Each country has a National Tourist Office in the United States with a healthy promotional budget. They are happy to send you a free package of promotional information on their country. Just send the office of each country you plan to visit a postcard. If you ask for specific information (such as brochures on hiking in Austria or castles in Germany, maps, a calendar of festivals), you might get more than the general packet. I get answers to specific questions best by telephone.

Europe

Austrian National Tourist Office, 11601 Wilshire Blvd. #2480, Los Angeles, CA 90025, tel. (213) 477-3332. 500 Fifth Ave., #2009-2022, New York, NY 10110, tel. (212) 944-6880.

British Tourist Authority, 40 W. 57th St. 3rd floor, New York, NY 10019, (212) 581-4700. BTA World Trade Center, 350 S. Figueroa St. #450, Los Angeles, CA 90071, tel. (213) 628-3525.

Belgian National Tourist Office, 745 5th Ave., New York, NY 10151, (212) 758-8130.

Bulgaria—Balkan Holidays, 161 E. 86th St., New York, NY 10028, (212) 722-1110.

Czechoslovakia Travel Bureau, 10 East 40th St. #1902, New York, NY 10016, (212) 689-9720.

Denmark (see Scandinavia)

Finland (see Scandinavia)

French Tourist Office, 610 Fifth Ave., New York, NY 10020-2452, (212) 757-1125. 9454 Wilshire Blvd., #303, Beverly Hills, CA 90212-2967, tel. (213) 271-6665.

German National Tourist Office, 747 Third Ave., 33rd floor, New York, NY 10017, (212) 308-3300. 444 S. Flower St., Los Angeles, CA 90071.

Greek National Tourist Organization, 645 Fifth Ave., 5th floor, New York, NY 10022, (212) 421-5777. 611 West 6th St., Los Angeles, CA 90017.

Hungarian Travel Bureau IBUSZ, 1 Parker Plaza, #1104, Fort Lee, NJ 07024, (201) 5922-8585.

Irish Tourist Board, 757 3rd Ave., New York, NY 10017, (212) 418-0800.

Italian Government Travel Office, 630 Fifth Ave., #1565, New York, NY 10111, (212) 245-4822. 360 Post St. #801, San Francisco, CA 94108.

Luxembourg National Tourist Office, 801 Second Ave., New York, NY 10017, (212) 370-9850.

Netherlands National Tourist Office, 355 Lexington Ave., 21st floor, New York, NY 10017, (212) 370-7367.

Norway (see Scandinavia)

Polish Travel Bureau, ORBIS, 342 Madison Ave., #1512, New York, NY 10173, (212) 867-5011.

Portuguese National Tourist Office, 590 Fifth Ave., New York, NY 10036, (212) 354-4403.

Romanian National Tourist Office, 573 Third Ave., New York, NY 10016, (212) 697-6971.

Scandinavian National Office, 655 3rd Ave., 18th floor, New York, NY 10017, (212) 949-2333.

Spanish National Tourist Office, 665 Fifth Ave., New York, NY 10022, (212) 759-8822. San Vicente Plaza Bldg., 8383 Wilshire Blvd. #960, Beverly Hills, CA 90211, (213) 658-7188.

Sweden (see Scandinavia)

Swiss National Tourist Office, 608 Fifth Ave., New York, NY 10020, (212) 757-5944. 260 Stockton St., San Francisco, CA 94108, (415) 362-2260.

Turkish Tourism Office, 821 United Nations Plaza, New York, NY 10017, (212) 687-2194.

USSR: Intourist, 630 Fifth Ave., #868, New York, NY 10111, (212) 757-3884.

Yugoslavia National Tourist Office, 630 Fifth Ave., #280, New York, NY 10111, (212) 757-2801.

Middle East and North Africa

Egyptian Tourist Office, 630 Fifth Ave., New York, NY 10111, (212) 246-6960.

Israel Government Tourist Office, 350 Fifth Ave., New York, NY 10118, (212) 560-0650.

Moroccan National Tourist Office, 20 East 46th St., #1201, New York, NY 10017, (212) 557-2520.

Pack Light Pack Light Pack Light

The importance of packing light cannot be overemphasized, but for your own good, I'll try. You'll never meet a traveler who, after several trips, brags, "Every year I pack heavier." The measure of a good traveler is how light he or she travels. You can't travel heavy, happy, and cheap. Pick two.

Limit yourself to 20 pounds in a carryon-size bag. A bag of 9″ × 22″ × 14″ dimensions fits under most airplane seats. You're probably muttering, "Impossible," but believe me, it can be done, and after you enjoy that sweet mobility and freedom, you'll never go any other way. I've taken several hundred people of all ages and styles to Europe in minigroups. Only one carryon bag was allowed, and now these former nonbelievers are the fanatical nucleus of my pack-light cult.

You'll walk with your luggage more than you think you will. Before leaving home, give yourself a test. Pack up completely, go into your hometown, and be a tourist for an hour. Fully loaded, you should enjoy window shopping. If you can't, go home and thin things out.

When you carry your own luggage, it's less likely to get lost, broken, or stolen. It sits on your lap or under your seat on the bus, taxi, and airplane. You don't have to worry about it, and when you arrive, you leave—immediately. It's a good feeling. When I land in London, I am virtually downtown while everyone else still stares anxiously at the luggage carousel.

Older travelers photographed while traveling like college kids—light, mobile, footloose and fancy-free, wearing their convertible suitcase rucksacks.

Too much luggage marks you as a typical tourist. It slams the Back Door shut. Serendipity suffers and changing locations becomes a major operation. Porters are only a problem to those who need them. With one bag hanging on your back, you're mobile. Take this advice seriously.

Backpackademia—What to Bring?

How do you fit a whole trip's worth of luggage into a small suitcase or rucksack? The answer is simple: bring very little.

Spread out everything you think you'll need on the living room floor. Pick up each item one at a time and scrutinize it. Look at it critically. Ask yourself, "Will I really use this snorkel and fins enough to justify carrying them around all summer?" Not "will I use them?" but "will I use them enough?" I'd buy them in Greece before I'd carry that extra weight through the Alps.

Think in terms of what you can do without—not what will be handy on your trip. When in doubt, leave it out. I've seen people pack a whole summer's supply of deodorant, nylons, or razors, thinking you can't get it there. The world's getting awfully small; you can buy Dial soap in Sicily. Tourist shops in major international hotels are a sure bet whenever you have difficulty finding some personal item.

Whether I'm traveling for three weeks or three months, I pack exactly the same things. Rather than take a whole trip's supply of toiletries, I take enough to get started and look forward to running out of toothpaste in Bulgaria. Then I have the perfect excuse to go into a Bulgarian department store, shop around, pick up something I think might be toothpaste. . .then go back when I find out it's itch ointment.

Rucksack or Suitcase?

Whether you take a small suitcase with a shoulder strap (wheels are silly for independent international travel) or rucksack is up to you. Packing light applies equally to suitcase or rucksack travelers.

Most young-at-heart travelers go the rucksack route. If you are a suitcase person who would like the ease of a rucksack without forgoing the "respectability" of a suitcase, use the new and popular convertible suitcase/rucksacks with zip-away shoulder straps. These carryon-size bags give you the best of both worlds. I live out of one of these for three months at a time—and even take it with me when I travel. (See the Back Door Catalog at the back of this book.)

I used to carry a frame pack because I had a sleeping bag. Unless you plan to camp or sleep out a lot, a sleeping bag is a bulky security blanket. Even on a low budget, bedding will be provided. I'd rather risk being cold one or two nights out of the summer than carry a sleeping bag just in case I might need it. Don't pack to camp unless you're going to camp.

Without a sleeping bag, a medium-size rucksack is plenty big. Start your trip with it only two-thirds full to leave room for picnic food, things you'll pick up, and the inefficiency of a messy bag on the road. Sturdy stitching, front and side pouches, padded shoulder straps, and a low-profile color are rucksack virtues. Many travelers figure an interior frame and a weight distribution belt are worth the extra

The popular new carry-on-the-plane size (9 x 22 x 14 inch) convertible suitcase/rucksack.

money and get a more high-tech bag for around $120. Those packing very light manage fine without the extra weight and expense of these fancier bags.

There are entire books written on how to pack. It's really quite simple: use nylon stuff bags (color coded, one each for toiletries, underwear and socks, bigger clothing items and towel, camera gear and film, and miscellaneous stuff such as a first-aid kit, stationery, and sewing kit). Be careful to choose clothes that either don't wrinkle or look good wrinkled. (Experiment by hand-washing and drying at home.) Roll and rubberband clothes to minimize bulk and wrinkles.

Clothing

The bulk of your luggage is clothing. Minimize by bringing less and washing more often. Every night you'll spend two minutes doing a little wash. This doesn't mean more washing, it just means doing it little by little as you go.

Bring dark clothes that wash and dry quickly and easily. You should have no trouble drying clothing overnight in your hotel room. I know this sounds barbaric, but my body dries out a damp pair of socks or shirt in a jiffy. It's fun to buy clothes as you travel—another reason to start with less.

For winter travel, I pack just about as light. The only difference is a down coat, long johns, mittens, and an extra pair of socks and underwear since things dry slower. Pack with the help of a climate chart. (See the Appendix.)

Europe is casual. I have never felt out of place at symphonies, operas, or plays wearing a decent pair of slacks and a good-looking sweater. Cultural events seem to be more formal outside of the tourist season. Of course, there are situations where more formal attire would be in order, but the casual tourist rarely encounters these. Wear color-coordinated clothes and layer it for warmth.

Many travelers are concerned about appropriate dress. European women wear dresses more often than pants. American women will generally feel fine in pants, but in certain rural and traditional areas, they'll fit in better and more comfortably in their skirt or dress. Tennis shoes and jeans mark you as an American. Frankly, so what? Europeans will know anyway. I fit in and am culturally sensitive by watching my manners, not the cut of my pants.

Recommended Clothing (for summer travel)

Two pairs of long pants; one lightweight cotton and another super lightweight.

Walking shorts with plenty of pockets—doubles as a swimsuit.

Two T-shirts or short-sleeved shirts, cotton/polyester blend.

Two long-sleeved shirts, same blend.

Dark, warm sweater—for warmth and for dressing up; it never looks wrinkled and is always dark, no matter how dirty it is.

Light, waterproof windbreaker jacket—folds up into pocket; Gortex is good.

Underwear and socks—four sets, quick-dry.

One pair of shoes—sturdy vibram-type sole, good traction, well broken in, light, cool. I like Rockports. Sturdy, low-profile-colored tennis shoes with a good tread are fine, too.

A tie (instant respectability), cheap necklace, colorful scarf, pair of lime-green socks and suspenders. Anything light-weight that can break the monotony and make you look snazzy.

Especially for women—summer dress or skirt, swimsuit, sandals, robe or nightshirt.

A handful of sacred places, mostly in southern Europe, have modest dress requirements: basically, no short pants or bare shoulders. Although these dress codes deserve respect, they are rarely enforced. If necessary, it's usually easy to improvise some modesty (even a hairy-legged man can wear a nearby tablecloth as a kilt in order to be allowed in).

Go casual, simple, and very light. Remember, in your travels, you'll meet two kinds of tourists—those who pack light and those who wish they had.

Other Things to Pack

Hostel sheet. Youth hostels require one. You can bring your own or rent a sheet there for about $2 per night. If you plan to do a lot of hosteling, bring your own regular bed sheet or buy a regulation hostel sheet (basically, a normal bed sheet sewn together like a sleeping bag, $14) at the first hostel you visit. This sheet can double as a beach or picnic blanket, is handy on overnight train rides, and will save you money in other dorm-type accommodations, which often charge extra for linen.

Poncho or parka. Hard-core vagabonds will want a plastic poncho, large enough to protect you and your pack in a rainstorm, that can open flat to serve as a ground cloth for sleeping on or for a beach or picnic blanket. Otherwise, a good weatherproof parka is your best bet. In southern Europe, I wing it without rain gear. But I plan for lots of rain in Britain.

Small day pack. A small nylon rucksack is great for carrying your sweater, camera, literature, food, and so on, while you leave most of your large bag at the hotel or train station. The little rucksack folds into a pocket-size pouch when not in use. Fanny-packs (small bags with gypsy-risky zippers on a belt) are a popular alternative.

A good paperback. There's plenty of empty time on a trip to either be bored or enjoy some good reading. Books such as *Iberia* for Spain and Portugal, *The Agony and the Ecstasy* for Italy, or *Trinity* for Ireland are a real trip bonus.

European map. An overall map best suited to your trip's needs. Get maps for specific local areas as you go.

Money belt. Essential for the peace of mind it brings; you could lose everything except your money belt, and the trip could still go on. Light-weight, beige, and water-resistant is best. (See the Back Door Catalog at the back of this book.)

Cash. Bring American dollars (Europeans get a kick out of seeing George Washington fold up into a mushroom) for situations when you want to change only a few bucks and not a whole traveler's check. I bring twenty ones and a few $10 and $20 bills. And bring one bill worth about $30 for each country you plan to visit so you can function easily until you can get to a bank. (See chapter 5, Finances and Money, for details.)

Picnic supplies. A small tablecloth to give your meal some extra class (and to wipe the knife on), a small can opener, salt and pepper, a col-lapsible cup, a damp facecloth in a baggie for cleaning up, and a Swiss army-type knife with a corkscrew.

Water bottle. Small. The plastic reusable mineral water bottles sold throughout Europe work great. Also a small syrup bottle with an up-down top fits easily in your purse or daybag. (Sanitary sharing, bota bag-style, is a great way to start a conversation and a friendship. Anyone who's just climbed St. Peter's dome would love you for a squirt.)

Earplugs. If night noises bother you, you'll grow to love a good set of plugs such as Sleep-well. Europe has more than its share of night noises.

Zip-lock baggies. 1,001 uses; great for leftover picnic food, containing wetness, and bagging potential leaks before they happen. Bring a variety of sizes.

First-aid kit. (See chapter 7, Health.)

Medicine. In original containers with legible prescriptions.

Wristwatch. A built-in alarm is handy. Otherwise, pack a small travel alarm clock, too.

Extra eyeglasses, contact lenses, and prescriptions. Many find their otherwise-comfortable contacts don't work in Europe. Bring your glasses just in case.

Toiletries. In a small, easy-to-hang-on-a-hook stuff bag. Minimal. Put all squeeze bottles in zip-lock baggies since pressure changes in flight cause even good bottles to leak. Consider a vacation from cosmetics. Bring a little toilet paper.

Soap. Not all hotels provide soap. A plastic squeeze bottle of concentrated, multipurpose biodegradable liquid soap (such as REI's Biosuds or Dr. Bronner's) is handy for laundry and much more.

Nothing electrical. Although there are good adapters available, every year some American plugs his Universal adapter into my hotel and the whole place goes universally black.

Clothesline. For hanging up clothes to dry in your hotel room. The handy twist kind needs no clips.

Small towel. You'll find small bath towels at all moderate hotels, most cheap hotels, and no youth hostels. Although $25-a-day travelers will often need to bring their own towel, $50-a-day folks won't. I bring a thin hand towel or fast-drying cotton dish towel for the occasional need. Face towels are very rare in Europe.

Sewing kit. Clothes age rapidly while traveling.

Travel information (minimal). Rip out appropriate chapters, staple them together, store in a zip-lock baggie. When you are done, give them away.

Postcards or small picture book from your hometown and family pictures. A zip-lock baggie of show-and-tell things is always a great conversation piece with Europeans you may meet.

Address list. For sending postcards home and collecting new addresses. Taking a whole address book is not packing light. Consider typing your mail list onto a sheet of gummed address labels before you leave. You'll know exactly who you've written to, and the labels will be perfectly legible.

Journal. An "empty book" filled with the experiences of your trip will be your most treasured souvenir. I guarantee it. Use a hardbound type designed to last a lifetime rather than a spiral notebook.

Sony Walkman-type recorder. Partners bring one, with Y-jacks for two sets of earphones. Many travelers enjoy a microcassette recorder to record things such as pipe organs, tours, and journal entries. And some recorders have radios, which add a whole new dimension to your experience.

Small notepad and pen. Carry in back pocket—great organizer, reminder, and communication aid.

Camera (film, protective and polarizing lens, midrange zoom lens, cleaning tissue, all stored not in a camera bag but in a nylon stuff bag).

And consider these options: a pillow case (cleaner and possibly more comfortable to stuff your own), inflatable pillows for sun-snoozing, light warm-up suit (for pajamas, evening lounge outfit, street wear, going down the hall), stronger light bulbs (get in Europe to give your cheap hotel room more brightness than the 25- to 40-watt norm), an envelope of envelopes, paper, tiny miscellaneous office supplies, safety pins, sunglasses. Little gifts (local kids love T-shirts and baseball cards; gardeners appreciate flower seeds).

2
Designing an Itinerary

If you have any goals at all for your trip, make an itinerary. I never start a trip without having every day planned out. Your reaction to an itinerary may be, "That shackles me to a rigid plan at the expense of spontaneity and freedom!" Although I always begin a trip with a well thought out plan, I maintain my flexibility and make plenty of changes. An itinerary forces you to see the consequences of any spontaneous change you make while in Europe. For instance, if you spend two extra days in the sunny Alps, you'll see that you won't make it to, say, the Greek Isles. With the help of an itinerary, you can lay out your goals, maximize their potential, avoid regrettable changes, and impress your friends.

By planning an itinerary, you can deal thoughtfully with issues like weather, crowds, culture shock, health maintenance, fatigue, festivals, and inefficient transportation. The result is a more enjoyable trip.

An Efficient Plan

1. Establish a logical flight plan. You can avoid needless travel time and expense by flying "open jaws." With open jaws, you fly into one port and out of another at no extra expense. You just pay half the round-trip fare for each port. For example, you could fly into Oslo, travel south through whatever interests you in Europe, and fly home from Lisbon, eliminating the costly and time-consuming return to Oslo. Your travel agent will know where flying open jaws is economical.

2. Moderate the weather conditions you'll encounter. Match the coolest month of your trip with the warmest area, and vice versa. For example, for a spring and early summer trip, enjoy comfortable temperatures throughout by starting in the southern countries and working your way north. If possible, avoid the midsummer Mediterranean heat. Spend those weeks in Scandinavia or the Alps. (See the Appendix for climate charts.)

A romantic stroll through St. Mark's Square in July. Venice is sinking under its peak season crowds.

3. Avoid tourist crowds. Europe is most crowded in July and August. Try to avoid this peak season crush by scooting your trip into the more relaxed shoulder months (May, early June, and September). Or arrange your activities to minimize crowds.

Consider, for instance, a six-week European trip beginning June 1, half with a Eurailpass to see the famous sights and half visiting relatives in Scotland. It would be wise to do the Eurail section first, enjoying those precious last three weeks of relatively uncrowded shoulder season, and then spend time with the family during the last half of your vacation, when Florence and Salzburg are teeming with tourists. Salzburg on June 10 and Salzburg on July 10 are two very different cities.

Although the tourist crowds can generally be plotted on a bell-shaped curve peaking in July and August, there are odd glitches that individual country guidebooks normally explain. For instance, Paris is empty and easy during its July and August holiday season, while a busy convention schedule packs it out in September.

In much of Europe (especially Italy and France), cities are partially shut down in July and August when local urbanites take their beach break. You'll hear that these are terrible times to travel. You can't get a dentist and many laundromats are shut down, but the tourist is basically unaffected by Europe's mass holidays unless he or she happens to be caught on the wrong road on the 1st or 15th of the month or is crazy enough to compete with all of Europe for a piece of Riviera beach.

4. Punctuate a long trip with rest periods. Constant sightseeing is grueling. Schedule a peaceful period every two weeks. If your trip is a long one, schedule a vacation from your vacation in the middle of it. Most people need several days in a place where they couldn't see a museum or take a tour even if they wanted to. A stop in the mountains or on an island, in a friendly rural town, or a visit with a relative is a great way to revitalize your tourist spirit. Alternate intense big cities with villages and countryside (for example, don't do Venice, Florence, and Rome in rapid succession).

5. Leave some slack in your itinerary. Don't schedule yourself too tightly (a common tendency). Everyday chores, small business matters, transportation problems, constipation, and planning mistakes deserve about one day of slack per week in your itinerary.

6. Don't overestimate your powers of absorption. Especially on your first trip, European travel can be intense, bombarding your senses from all sides day after day. Each day is packed with experiences and memories. It may be thrilling, but you can only take so much. You have a saturation point. Rare is the tourist who doesn't become somewhat jaded after several weeks of travel. At the start of my trip, I'll seek out every great painting and cathedral I can. After two months, I find myself "seeing" cathedrals with a sweep of my head from the doorway, and I probably wouldn't cross the street for a Rembrandt. Don't burn out on mediocre castles, palaces, and museums. Sightsee selectively. Look ahead on your itinerary. Save your energy for the biggies.

7. See countries in order of cultural hairiness. For instance, if you plan to see Britain, the Alps, Greece, and Egypt, do it in that order so you'll grow steadily into the more intense and crazy travel. In reverse order, even if you do survive the culture shock of Egypt, England's culture will seem like a wet noodle compared with Egypt's.

8. Save your good health. Visit countries that may be hazardous to your health (North Africa or the Middle East) at the end of your trip so you won't needlessly jeopardize your healthy enjoyment of the safer countries. If you're going to get sick, do it at the end of your trip so you can recover at home, missing more work—not vacation.

9. Assume you will return. This Douglas MacArthur approach is a key to touristic happiness. You can't really see Europe in one trip. Don't try to. Enjoy what you're seeing. Forget what you won't get to on this trip. If you worry about things that are just out of reach, you won't appreciate what's in your hand. I'm planning my twentieth three-month European vacation, and I still need more time. I'm happy about what I can't get to. It's a blessing that we can never see all of Europe.

The nine factors listed above must be weighed and thoughtfully juggled until you arrive at a plan that best fits your needs. There are several trade-offs (for instance, you may have to choose between optimal weather and minimal crowds). You can't have the best of each point.

Your Best Itinerary in Eight Steps

1. Read up on Europe, talk to travelers, study. You must have some friends who'd love to show you their slides. What you want to see is determined by what you know (or don't know). Identify your personal interests. World War II buffs will study up on battle sites, and McGregors will locate their clan in Scotland.

2. List all the places you want to see, keeping these factors in mind:
(a) Minimize redundancy. On a quick trip, focus on only one part of the Alps. Oxford and Cambridge are redundant. Choose one.

(b) Have a reason for every stop. Don't go to Casablanca just because it's famous.

(c) Minimize travel time required. When you must cut something, cut to save the most mileage. For instance, if Amsterdam and Berlin are equally important to you and you don't have time for both, cut the more distant destination, Berlin.

(d) Minimize clutter. A so-so sight or breaking a convenient night train into two half-day journeys is clutter. Once you've settled on a list, be satisfied with your efficient plan and focus any more study and preparation only on places that fall along your proposed route.

Step 2 example: Places I want to see:

London	*Alps*	*Bavaria*	*Florence*	*Paris*
Amsterdam	*Rhine*	*Rome*	*Venice*	*Greece*

3. Establish a general structure or framework. Decide on the length of your trip and where you'll fly into and out of. Research flights for cheapest and most convenient dates and ports.

Step 3 example: I can escape for 23 days. Cheapest places to fly to: London, Frankfurt, Amsterdam.

4. Determine mode of transportation. Do this not solely on economical terms but by analyzing what is best for the trip you envision.

Step 4 example: Since I'm traveling alone, going so many miles, and will spend the majority of my time in big cities, I'd rather not mess with a car. I'll use a Eurailpass.

5. List the sights you want to see in a logical geographic order. Consider minimizing miles, an open-jaws flight plan, your mode of transportation, getting maximum overnight train rides (if you want them), weather, and crowds. Pin down any places that you have to be on a certain date (and ask yourself if it's really worth the stifle).

6. Write in the number of days you'd like to stay in each place, considering transportation time. Eurailers often use night trains (NT) to save time and money whenever possible.

Steps 5 and 6 example: Logical order and desired time in each place:

Days	
3	London
1	English Channel crossing
5	Paris (NT)
3	Alps (NT)
2	Florence
3	Rome (NT)
7	Greece (NT)
2	Venice (NT)
3	Munich/Bavaria
3	Romantic Road/Rhine Cruise
4	Amsterdam
—	
36	_Notes: If I eliminate Greece, I'll still need to cut six days. Open jaws into London and out of Amsterdam is economical. "Logical" order may be affected by night train possibilities._

7. Add up the number of days. Adjust by cutting, streamlining, or adding to fit or fill your time limitations. Consider economizing on car rental or Eurailpass. For instance, try to manage a 23-day trip on a 15-day train pass by doing London, Paris, and Amsterdam outside of its validity.

Step 7 example: Itinerary adjusted to time limitations:

Days

4	*London (NT)*
3	*Paris (NT)*
3	*Alps (NT)*
1	*Florence*
2	*Rome (NT)*
2	*Venice (NT)*
3	*Munich/Bavaria*
2	*Romantic Road/Rhine Cruise*
3	*Amsterdam*
—	
23	*Twenty-three days with a 15-day Eurailpass from last day in Paris until first day in Amsterdam.*

8. Fine tune. Study guidebooks. Be sure crucial sights are open the day you'll be in town. Maximize festival and market days. Ask your travel agent which flight departure days are cheapest. Write out a day-by-day itinerary.

Step 8 example: According to my guidebook, I must keep these points in mind as I plan my trip. London: theaters closed on Sundays, Speaker's Corner is Sunday only. Paris: most museums are closed on Tuesdays, Versailles and the Orsay Museum closed on Mondays. Florence: museums closed Mondays. Rome: Forum closed Tuesdays, Pantheon closed Mondays. Dachau: closed Mondays. Amsterdam: museums closed on Mondays and most shops closed on Monday mornings.

S	1	*Leave home. (You'll always arrive the next day in Europe.)*
S	2	*Arrive in **London**. Buy train ticket to Paris and a Tuesday eve theater ticket at Victoria Station. See Speaker's Corner. Take orientation bus tour.*
M	3	*Sightsee all day London.*
T	4	*Sightsee all day London. Leave bags at station. See play. NT.*
W	5	*Arrive early in **Paris**. Find hotel. Explore Latin Quarter, Louvre, Champs-Elysées, take bus orientation tour.*

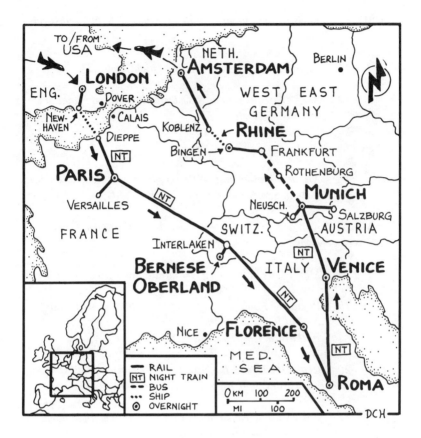

T	6	Sightsee all day Paris, Orsay museum, Notre-Dame; Eve: Montmartre.
F	7	Early side trip to Versailles. Afternoon in Paris. NT.
S	8	Arrive early in Interlaken. All day **Alps** hike (Back Door).
S	9	Free in Alps, Lauterbrunnen, Gimmelwald, Schilthorn.
M	10	Cruise Swiss lakes, afternoon and evening in Bern. NT.
T	11	**Florence.** Check museum hours carefully. David closes at 1:00, Uffizi open all day.

W 12   *Early train to* **Rome.** *Set up near station. Explore classical Rome.*

T 13   *Visit Vatican, St. Peter's, famous night spots. NT.*

F 14   *Arrive early in* **Venice.** *Slow boat down Grand Canal to St. Mark's. All day free.*

S 15   *All day free in Venice. NT.*

S 16   *Arrive early in* **Munich.** *Reserve Romantic Road bus tour at station. Sightsee all day. Evening beer hall.*

M 17   *All-day side trip to Neuschwanstein ("Castle Day" Back Door).*

T 18   *Most of day in Salzburg (90-minute train from Munich).*

W 19   **Romantic Road** *bus tour from Munich to Frankfurt, stopping at Rothenburg and Dinkelsbühl. Short train to Bacharach. Check boat schedule.*

T 20   *Cruise the* **Rhine,** *Bacharach to St. Goar (one hour) for the best castles. Tour Rheinfels.*

F 21   *Early train to* **Amsterdam.** *Call to reconfirm flight home. Orientation canal tour, nightlife.*

S 22   *All day free in Amsterdam for museums, shopping, or bike ride into countryside.*

S 23   *Catch plane, Amsterdam—U.S.A. (Note: my* 22 Days in Europe *is a 192-page blueprint for this basic plan in reverse order.)*

Itinerary Miscellany

Hit as many festivals, national holidays, and arts seasons as you can. This takes some study. Ask the national tourist office of each country you'll visit for a calendar of events (see the festival listing in the Appendix). An effort to hit the right places at the right time will drape your trip with festive tinsel.

Carefully consider travel time. Driving, except on super freeways, is slower than in the United States. Borrow a Thomas Cook Continental Timetable from your travel agent and get an idea of how long various train journeys will take (see the Appendix). Learn which trains are fast, and avoid minor lines in southern countries.

Remember that most cities close many of their major tourist attractions for one day during the week. It would be a shame to be in Milan only on a Monday, for instance, when Leonardo da Vinci's *Last Supper* is out to lunch. Mondays are closed days for tourist sights in many cities, including Amsterdam, Brussels, Munich, Vienna, Lisbon, Florence, Milan, Rome, and Naples. Paris closes the Louvre and many other sights on Tuesdays.

Minimize "mail stops." Arrange mail pickups before you leave. Some American Express offices offer a free clients' mail service for those who have an AmExCo card or traveler's checks (even just one). Have mail marked "Clients' Mail." They'll hold for five days unless the envelope instructs otherwise. For the "Travelers' Companion" booklet listing participating AmExCo offices, call 1-800-528-4800. Friends or relatives are fine for mail stops. Every city has a general delivery service. Pick a small town where there is only one post office and no crowds. Have letters sent to you in care of General Delivery (or Poste Restante in French-speaking cities). Tell your friends to print your surname in capitals, underline it, and omit your middle name. If possible, avoid the Italian mail.

Don't design your trip around stale mail. Every year my mail stops are farther apart. Once a month is comfortable. If you get homesick, mail just teases you, stirring those emotions and aggravating the problem. The best remedy for homesickness is to think of Europe as your home. Wherever you go, there you are.

High Speed Town-hopping

When I tell people that I saw three or four towns in one day, many either say or think, "That guy must be crazy! Nobody can really see several towns in a day!" Of course, it's folly to go too fast, but many stopworthy towns take only an hour or two to cover. Don't let guilt feelings tell you to slow down and stay longer if you really are finished with a town. There's so much more to see in the rest of Europe! Going too slow is as bad as going too fast.

If you're efficient and use the high-speed town-hopping method, you'll amaze yourself at what you can see in a day. Let me explain with an example.

You wake up early in Town A. Checking out of your hotel, you have two sights to cover before your 10:00 train. (You checked the train schedule the night before.) Before getting to the station, you visit the open-air market and buy the ingredients for your brunch and pick up a brochure on Town B at Town A's tourist office.

From 10:00 to 11:00, you travel by train to Town B. During that hour you'll have a restful brunch, enjoy the passing scenery, and prepare for Town B by reading your literature and deciding what you want to see. Just before your arrival, you put the items you need (camera, jacket, tourist information) into your small daypack and, on arrival, check the rest of your luggage in a locker. Every station has storage lockers or a baggage check desk.

Before leaving Town B's station, write down on a scrap of paper the departure times of the next few trains to Town C. Now you can sightsee as much or as little as you want and still know when to comfortably catch your train. You're ready to go. You know what you want to see. You aren't burdened by your luggage. And you know when the trains are leaving.

Town B is great. After a snack in the park, you catch the 2:30 train. By 3:00, you're in Town C, where you repeat the same procedure you followed in Town B. Town C just isn't what it was cracked up to be, so after a walk along the waterfront and a look at the church, you catch the first train out.

By 5:30, you arrive in D, the last town on the day's agenda. The man in the station directs you to a good budget pension just two blocks down the street. You're checked in and unpacked in no time, and after a few moments of horizontal silence, it's time to find a good restaurant and eat dinner. After a meal and an evening stroll, you're ready to call it a day. Thinking back, it really was quite a day: you spent it high speed town-hopping.

The Home Base Strategy

The home base strategy is a clever way to make your trip itinerary smoother, simpler, and more efficient. Set yourself up in a central location and use that place as a base for day trips to nearby attractions.

The advantages of this approach are:

1. The home base approach minimizes set-up time (usually an hour). Searching for a good hotel can be exhausting, frustrating, and time-consuming. And hotels often give a better price, or at least more smiles, for longer stays.

2. You are freed from your luggage. Being able to leave your luggage in the hotel enhances your mobility. You'll enjoy yourself more without luggage and with the peace of mind that you are set up for the night.

3. You feel comfortable and "at home" in your home base town. This feeling takes more than a day to get, and when you are changing locations every day or two, you may never enjoy this important rootedness.
4. The home base approach allows you to spend the evening in a city, where there is some exciting nightlife. Most small countryside towns die after 9:00 p.m. If you're not dead by 9:00, you'll enjoy more action in a larger city.

Europe's generally frequent and punctual train and bus systems make this home base strategy very practical. With a train pass, the round-trips are free; otherwise, the transportation is reasonable, often with reductions offered for round-trip tickets. Use train time productively.

Here are some of my favorite home base cities and some of their best day trips:

Madrid	Toledo, Segovia, El Escorial
Amsterdam	Alkmaar, the Arnhem Folk Museum, Hoge Veluwe Park with its Kroller-Muller Museum, Scheveningen, Delft, most of the Netherlands
Copenhagen	Lund, Malmo, Roskilde, Helsingor, Odense
Paris	Reims, Versailles, Chartres, Fontainebleau, Chantilly
Bregenz, Austria	Lake Constance (Bodensee) area: Lindau, Meersburg, Vorarlberg, Bregenzerwald, Feldkirch
London	Oxford, Stratford, Cambridge, Salisbury (Stonehenge), Bath, and 50 others as explained in a handy guidebook called _Day Trips from London_ (Hastings House)
Avignon	Nimes, Arles, the Rhone Valley
Florence	Pisa, Siena, San Gimignano, Arezzo, many small towns

| Munich | Salzburg: Berchtesgaden, Augsburg, Neu-schwanstein, Linderhof, and Herrenchiemsee (three of King Ludwig's castles), many small Bavarian towns including Oberammergau, Wies Church. |

Minimizing Peak Season Crowds

If you must travel in July and August, here are a few crowd-minimizing tips that I've learned over many peak seasons in Europe.

Get off the beaten path. So many people energetically jockey themselves into the most crowded square of the most crowded city in the most crowded month (St. Mark's Square, Venice, in July) and complain about the crowds. You could be in Venice in July and walk six blocks behind St. Mark's Basilica, step into a café and be greeted by Venetians who act as though they've never seen another tourist.

Be an early bird. Walk around Rothenburg's ancient wall before breakfast. Joggers and crack-of-dawn walkers enjoy a special look at wonderfully medieval cities as they yawn and stretch and prepare for the daily onslaught of the twentieth century.

Arrive at the most popular sights early or late in the day to avoid tour groups. I'd rather rush my visit starting an hour before closing than fight the midday tour mobs.

See how the locals live. Residential neighborhoods rarely see a tourist, much less a crowd of them. Browse through a department store. Buy a local home magazine and use it to explore that particular culture. Dance with the locals while your pizza cooks.

Spend the night. Popular places near big cities and resorts like Toledo (near Madrid), San Marino (near huge Italian beach resorts), and Rothenburg (near Frankfurt) take on a more peaceful and enjoyable atmosphere at night when the legions of day-trippers return to their home bases. Small towns normally lack tour-worthy hotels and are often inaccessible to large buses. So they will experience, at worst, midday crowds.

Study. Keep in mind that accessibility and promotional budgets determine a place's fame and popularity just as much as its worthiness as a tourist attraction. For example, Zurich is big and famous—with nothing special to offer the visitor. The beaches of Greece's Peloponnesian Peninsula offer the same weather and water as the highly promoted isles of Mykonos and Ios but are out of the way, not promoted, and have none of the crowds.

Develop a minimize-the-crowd mentality. Avoid museums on their weekly free days when they're most crowded. And because nearly all

Smart travelers avoid these lines. (Versailles on a Tuesday when Paris' museums are closed.)

Parisian museums are closed on Tuesday, nearby Versailles, which is open, is predictably crowded—very crowded. And it follows that Parisian museums are especially crowded on Mondays and Wednesdays. While crowds at the Louvre can't be avoided altogether, some thought before you start your trip can help. If you're traveling by car or bike, take advantage of your mobility by leaving the well-worn tourist routes. The Europe away from the train tracks seems more peaceful and relaxed. It's one step behind the modern parade and overlooked by the Eurail mobs.

Off-Season Europe? The Pros and Cons

Each summer, Europe greets a stampede of sightseers and shoppers with open cash registers. Before jumping into the peak season pigpile, consider an off-season trip.

In travel industry jargon, the year is divided into peak season (late June, July, and August), shoulder season (May, early June, September, early October), and off-season (the rest of the year). Each time has its pros and cons. While shoulder season is the best mix of decent weather and minimal crowds, off-season (November through February) is worth considering.

The advantages of winter travel are many. Off-season airfares are much cheaper. With fewer crowds in Europe, you'll sleep cheaper. Off-season adventurers wander all alone through Leonardo's home, sit quietly in Rome's Forum, stroll desolate beaches, and enjoy log fires and a cup of coffee with the guards in French chateaus. Lines in tourist offices and at bank exchange desks will be gone. Although Europe won't be geared up for you and many popular tourist-oriented parks, shows, and tours will be closed, the real arts seasons, such as the Vienna Opera's, will be rolling, and the people you deal with will be more relaxed.

But winter travel has serious problems. Because much of Europe is in Canadian latitudes, the days are very short. It's dark by 5:00. The weather can be miserable—cold, windy, and drizzly—and then turn worse. But just as summer can be wet and gray, winter can be crisp and blue, and even into mid-November, hillsides blaze with colorful leaves.

Off-season hours are limited. Some sights close down entirely, and most operate on shorter hours (such as 10:00-5:00 rather than 9:00-7:00), with darkness often determining the closing time. Winter sightseeing is fine in big cities, which bustle year-round, but it's more frustrating in small tourist towns, which often shut down entirely. In December, many beach resorts remind me of canned hams. Europe's wonderful outdoor evening ambience, a fair weather phenomenon, hibernates each winter, especially in the north. English-language tours, common in the summer, are quite rare off-season, when most visitors are natives. Tourist information offices normally stay open year-round but with shorter hours in the winter. A final disadvantage with winter travel is loneliness. The solo traveler won't have the built-in camaraderie of other travelers which he or she would find in peak season.

To thrive in the winter, you'll need to get the most out of your limited daylight hours. Start early, eat a quick lunch, and telephone the tourist offices before they close (usually 5:00 p.m.) to double-check hours and confirm your plans. Pack for the cold and wet—layers, rainproof parka, gloves, wool hat, long johns, waterproof shoes, and an umbrella. Remember, cold weather is colder when you're outdoors trying to enjoy yourself all day long. Use undershirts to limit the washing of slow-drying heavy shirts.

Accommodations will be easy to find—but not always heated. I conducted an 18-day November tour of Germany, Italy, and France with 22 people and no room reservations. We'd amble into town around 5:00 p.m. and always found 22 beds with breakfast for our $15 per bed budget.

Most hotels charge less in the winter. To save some money, arrive late, notice how many empty rooms they have (keys on the rack), let them know you're a hosteler (student, senior, honeymooner, or whatever) with a particular price limit, and bargain from there. Big city business centers are busiest and most expensive outside of summer holiday time.

Italy, so crowded in peak season, is back to normal; its hill towns are brisk and glorious. The Alps are crowded with skiers. It's easy to rent gear, but the snow often comes late. Off-season hiking is disappointing. Travel north of the Alps suffers more in the winter.

A Few Itinerary Problems

An efficient overall plan for a six-week introduction to Europe is as follows. Fly into London. Spend four days there. Rent a car for a week in England (Bath, Cotswolds, Oxford, Blenheim, Warwick, Iron Bridge Gorge, North Wales). Drop it in North Wales. Boat to Dublin, and take a look at West Ireland. Begin your 21-day Eurailpass to catch the included 20-hour boat ride from southeast Ireland to France. Spend three weeks touring central Europe (Paris, Benelux, Rhine, Romantic Road, Bavaria, Swiss Alps, Italy, boat to Athens where train pass expires). Relax in the Greek Isles before flying home from Athens.

To Greece or Not to Greece?

Many itineraries are really stressed out by people who underestimate the travel time involved and wrongly plug in Greece. It takes two days of solid travel—if all goes well—to get from Rome to Athens and two days to get back. If all you've got is a week for Greece, I question the sanity of traveling four days for a couple of days in huge, overrated, and polluted Athens and a quick trip to an island, especially when you consider that 500 years before Christ, southern Italy was called Magna Graecia (Greater Greece). You can find excellent Greek ruins just south of Naples. Greece is great, but it needs more time or an open-jaws plan that lets you fly out of Athens.

In the summer, Greece is the most-touristed, least-explored country in Europe. It seems that nearly all of its tourists are in a few places, while the rest of the country casually goes about in its traditional way.

Getting to Greece: The Brindisi (Italy)-Patras (Greece) Boat Connection

Brindisi, the spur on the Italian boot, is a funnel where thousands of Eurailers (who get to cross for free, except taxes and supplement) and backpackers fall out to catch the boat to Greece. Three boats make the

21-hour crossing each day in the summer, usually sailing in the evening. Getting on the boat is no problem without reservations except at peak-season time (Italy to Greece—July 22 to August 15; Greece to Italy—August 11 to September 3), when it's a mob scene.

Tickets cost about $40 for deck class (really on the deck, unless it rains and they open up the otherwise closed restaurant), $47 for an assigned airplane-type seat, $55 for a bed in a four-bed stateroom, and $90 for a bed in a double. During peak season, prices are $30 higher. Voyagers under 26 save about $10. Children who can pass for 2 to 12 go for half price. Cars cost $40 to $60. A Eurailpass gives you, in essence, a $30 discount on these prices. You get a free stopover halfway on the lush and popular island of Corfu if you have "S.O. Corfu" marked on your ticket.

For a summer crossing, make a reservation at least three days in advance from an Italian (or Greek) travel agency (easy but with a small service charge). On arrival in Brindisi, follow the mob on the half-mile stampede from the train station down the city's main drag to the dock. Stop at one of several agencies along the way which sell tickets and handle boat-related business such as reserving staterooms, collecting port taxes and Eurail supplements, and distributing boarding passes. Then, at the port, go through another round of customs-related bureaucracy and board your boat. The crossing from Patras to Brindisi features similar headaches. Off-season, I'd go to the port and bargain. Student discounts are often given to anyone who asks for them.

The Patras-to-Athens connection is a five-hour train ride or a frightening three-hour bus ride. (The fear welds some special friendships on the bus.) Buses meet the boat, and I'd buy the $8 bus ticket with the boat ticket. Consider taking the indirect route, hooking south through the fascinating Peloponnesian Peninsula. Start with the hour-long bus ride (leaving every two hours) to Olympia.

Brindisi is well connected by night trains from Rome, Milan, Florence (via Bologna), and Venice. If you have time to kill (boats leave in the evening, overnight trains arrive early), do it in Lecce, a hot, noble, but sleepy city of lovely baroque facades and Roman ruins; pick up a town map at the three-star hotel in front of the station (a $2, 40-minute train ride south, hourly departures) or at nearby beaches. Mobbed by transit tourists throughout the summer, Brindisi has arranged an hourly "Sea Bus Service" that shuttles those on their way to Greek beaches to one last Italian beach, either Punta Penne or Apani (the better, just 30 minutes north of town on the Adriatic coast). I'd rate the beaches as fair; the water is clean. Get information in Brindisi on the bus service (when you arrange for your boat trip).

How Much Italy?

Italy is Europe's richest cultural brew. Get out of the Venice-Florence-Rome crush and enjoy its hill towns and Riviera ports. Italy intensifies as you go south. If you like Italy as far south as Rome, go farther. It gets better. If Italy is getting on your nerves by the time you get to Rome, don't go farther south. It gets worse. For most first-timers, Switzerland starts looking really good after a week in Italy. The travelers I respect most count Italy as one of their favorite countries.

By train, you might consider seeing everything except Venice on your way south. Enjoy a last romantic late evening in Rome before catching the midnight train north, arriving in Venice at 8:00 a.m., when it's very easy to find a room.

Crossing the English Channel

Until the "Chunnel" (English Channel tunnel) is completed in 1992, we still need to sort through the various ways to cross the Channel. From London, consider it a train ride. Don't worry about which boat or which harbor, just buy a train ticket that says "London-Paris" or whatever. The boat is figured in. If the train is late, the boat will wait. Usually, the train is a nonstop express to the boat dock. Catch the train (the correct London station is listed on the ticket). When everyone gets out, follow them through customs and onto the boat. When you get to the Continent (the first and only boat stop), go through customs and find your train among the many that await the boat passengers to fan out to various points in Europe.

This train-boat-train trip is cheaper overnight but a miserable trip with the two tedious changes and border crossings. Still, this is my preferred way to arrive in Paris—inexpensively and in time to find a room. To get to Amsterdam, you can choose the longer boat ride (via the Hoek of Holland) or the longer train ride (via Oostende, Belgium). I sleep well on the longer boat ride. On any boat, you can normally buy a $25 stateroom from a staff person upon boarding. Anyone can wander downstairs and take a shower.

Many travelers get excited about the hovercraft or hydrofoil crossing. This pound-pound, stay-seated-please "flight" is a couple of hours faster but has none of the romance of the boat crossing and is around $10 more expensive. A little choppiness cancels the flight and you're back on the big slow boat standing in line for a refund. I don't mess with them and just enjoy the crossing.

In London, get information and tickets at the Sealink office in Victoria Station. If you're under 26, save money by getting a Transalpino ticket (office near Victoria Station). Reservations are rarely needed.

Paris to Amsterdam, Not Skipping Brussels

Anyone traveling from Paris to Amsterdam will stop in Brussels, but very few even consider getting out. Each train making the five-hour trip from Paris to Amsterdam stops in Brussels, which has three stations, Nord, Midi, and Central. There's always another train coming in an hour or so. Leave an hour early, arrive an hour late, and give yourself two hours in one of Europe's underrated cities. Luckily for the rushed tourist, Brussels Central Station has easy money-changing and baggage storage facilities and puts you two blocks (just walk downhill) from the local and helpful tourist office, a colorful pedestrian-only city core, Europe's greatest city square (Grand Place), and its most overrated and tacky sight, the Mannekin Pis (a much-photographed statue of a little boy being a fountain). Ask if your train stops at Central (middle) Station. If you have to get off at Nord or Midi, there are local subway-like connecting trains every few minutes. You'll have no trouble finding English-speaking help.

Cruising the Rhine

Every year, the Rhine steamer schedules changes slightly, but the one below (taken from the *Cook Continental Timetable*) should be close.

Rhine Cruise

Table 700   KÖLN-DÜSSELDORFER DEUTSCHE RHEINSCHIFFAHRT AG
KD GERMAN RHINE LINE

A— Daily, Apr. 20–30.
B— Suns., May 1–June 2.
C— Daily, May 1–Sept. 18.
D— Daily, April 20–Oct. 30.
E— Daily, June 12–Sept. 18.
F— April 21, 22 and daily April 25–Sept. 18.
G— Daily, Sept. 19–Oct. 30.
H— Daily, Sept. 19–Oct. 2.
J— Daily, Oct. 3–30.
K— Daily, April 20–Oct. 2.
L— Daily, May 1–Oct. 2.
M— Daily, June 12–Sept. 18 (not Koblenz-Boppard on Sats.).
N— Daily except Weds. May 1–Sept. 18.
O— Express service, daily except Mons., May 1–Oct. 2 by hydrofoil *Rheinpfeil*. Also runs Apr. 21, 22, 28, 29, Oct. 8, 9, 15, 16, 22, 23, 29, 30. Special fares apply.
P— Mons., Tues. and Thurs., July 11–Aug. 18 also June 13, 20, 27, July 4, Aug. 22, 29, Sept. 5, 12.

Q— Daily Sept. 19–Oct. 2, also Sats. and Suns. July 10–Aug
R— Daily, Oct. 3–9.
S— Daily, June 12–Sept. 18, except Aug. 27, Sept. 3, 10, 1;
T— Daily, Sept. 19–Oct. 9.
W— Daily, May 8–Oct. 16.
Y— Daily, May 8–Sept. 11.
Z— Daily, Sept. 12–Oct. 15.
AA—Daily, Sept. 12–Oct. 16.
BB—Daily, Oct. 3–30.
b— Daily except Mons., July 10–Aug. 21.
d— Rhine/Moselle excursion to/from Kobern (Moselle).
l— Fast ship, supplement payable (not applicable between and Koln Sept. 19–Oct. 2).
J— Fast ship, supplement payable applicable only from to Mainz.

(Connecting the Rhine and the Romantic Road gives you the most interesting route through Germany. For specifics, see later chapters.)

3
Transportation

Flying to Europe

Flying to Europe is a great travel bargain—for the well informed. The rules and regulations are confusing and always changing, but when you make the right choice, the price is right.

The key to budget flying is a good travel agent. You'll never beat the prices he can get. Save money and headaches by putting your energy into finding the right agent, not the cheapest flight. Rather than trying to keep up with the ever-changing world of airline tickets, I rely on the experience of my agent—who specializes in budget European travel—to come up with the best combination of economy, reliability, and convenience.

There is no great secret to getting to Europe for next to nothing. Basically, assuming you know your options, you get what you pay for. Remember this equation:

A dollar saved = more restrictions, less flexibility, or more risk.

There's no such thing as a free lunch (or a good one, for that matter) in the airline industry.

Your flight options include regular fare, advanced purchase excursion fare (APEX), standby, and charter flights. Regular fare is very expensive. You get the ultimate in flexibility, but I've never met anyone spending his own money who flew that way.

The popular **APEX** is the most flexible of the budget fares. You can pick your dates and ports but must prepurchase your ticket (usually 21 days in advance) and meet minimum and maximum stay requirements. (In England, it's a liberal 7 to 180 days.) APEX allows open-jaws plans (flying into one city and home from another) for no financial penalty. The major drawback of APEX is that you can't change your ticket once

you buy it. The only way to change your date is to refund your ticket (usually at a $50 loss) and buy a new one (if seats are still available) at the current fare, which is often higher. Return dates can sometimes be changed in Europe on the telephone with your airline, for a fee.

There's a new version of APEX—30 days in advance, 7- to 21-day stay, some open-jaws possibilities, absolutely no changes or refunds—that is normally the lowest regularly scheduled fare. Ask your agent for details.

Standby fares, while very rare these days, are the cheapest way to go. Your savings over the APEX fare is reflected in the risk you'll incur. During the busy season, there is a big risk that you won't get a seat, but the savings are substantial. During the off-season, the risk is low and so are the savings. If you have a very tight budget and don't mind the insecurity and possible delays, go standby. Ask your agent about the current situation. Many times when I fly, I meet someone spending $50 to $100 less for their ticket than I did. We're flying just as fast and eating the same food. The difference was that I went to bed the night before knowing I'd be on that flight. My friend went to the airport—and stood by. Obviously, in the case of a strike or something similar, those "cheapskates who scrounged up unsold seats at rock-bottom prices" (standby passengers) are rock-bottom on the airline's list of concerns.

The charter scene has its ups and downs. Some years offer exciting charter savings. Do some research. Remember, charter companies can cancel flights that don't fill. Anyone selling charters promotes an air of confidence, but at the last minute any flight can be "rescheduled" if it won't pay off. Those who "saved" by booking onto that charter are left all packed with nowhere to go. Get an explicit answer to what happens if the flight is canceled. "It won't be canceled" is not good enough. Some charter companies (such as Martinair) are very reliable. Ask about their track record. How many flights did they cancel last year?

Scheduled airlines are very reliable. If for some reason they can't fly you home, they find you a seat on another airline (unless you got a discounted ticket marked nonendorsable). You won't be stranded in Europe.

Thoughts on the Fear of Flying

Like many people, I'm afraid to fly. But, of course, I fly. It always scares me because I can't, for the life of me, imagine how a plane can take off and land safely. I always think of the little rubber wheels splashing down in a rainstorm and then hydroplaning. Or the spindly landing gear crumbling. Or if not that, then the plane tilting just a tad, catching a wing tip, and the whole thing flipping into a flaming trip finale.

I always remind myself that every day 60,000 planes take off and land safely in the United States alone. The pilot and crew fly daily and they don't seem to be terrified. They let an important guy like Ronald Reagan fly all over the place for eight years and nothing happened to him.

I guess it's a matter of aerodynamics. Somehow, air has mass and the plane maneuvers itself through that mass. I can understand a boat coming into a dock—maneuvering through the water. That doesn't scare me. So I tell myself that a plane's a boat with an extra dimension to navigate, and its water is a lot thinner.

Turbulence scares me, too. A United pilot once told me that he'd have bruises from his seat belt before any turbulence really bothered him. I never met anybody who came home complaining about turbulence bruises.

Still, every time the plane comes in for a landing I say a prayer, close my eyes, and take my pen out of my shirt pocket so it won't impale me if something goes wrong. And every time I stick my pen back in my shirt pocket, I feel thankful.

Flights within Europe

Europe is a small continent with big plane fares. There are a few economical flights available (London to Paris and to and from Athens), but unless you have a lot more money than time, you are generally better off on the ground. Special budget fares for inter-European flights can be purchased only in Europe—not in the United States. Remember, extending your flight from the United States deeper into the Continent (without stopovers) can be very cheap. Look into open-jaws possibilities before purchasing your ticket.

London and Athens have many "bucket shops"—agencies that clear out plane tickets at super-discounted prices. If your travel plans fit the tickets available and you're flexible enough to absorb delays, these can be a great deal. Any cheap flight from London must be bought in London. Your local library should have a London newspaper. Look in the classifieds under "Travel" to see what's available. Tickets from London to the Mediterranean can be incredibly—and reliably—cheap. There are normally special deals on round-trip flights from London to Paris or Frankfurt which are as inexpensive as surface travel. Paris to London is worth considering. Athens also has some great buys on tickets to London, Western Europe, and the Middle East. The German government subsidizes flights to and from Berlin, and the USSR's Aeroflot (and other Eastern European airlines) has some very cheap flights, often on a very roundabout route and, with some luck, a forced stopover in Moscow with a free hotel. Before buying any long train ticket, ask around for a cheap flight.

Train and Eurailpass Skills

The European train system makes life easy for the American visitor. The great trains of Europe shrink that already small continent, making the budget whirlwind or far-reaching tour an exciting possibility for anyone.

Generally, European trains are fast, frequent, and inexpensive (faster and more frequent in the north, less expensive but slower in the south). By using the train, you could easily have dinner in Paris, sleep on the train, and have breakfast in Rome, Madrid, Munich, or London.

The Eurailpass

The Eurailpass gives you unlimited first-class travel on all public railways in all the countries named on the map. It's open dated. Validate it at any train station ticket window just before you catch your first train.

The Eurailpass gives you Europe (except Britain) by the tail: you travel virtually anywhere, anytime without reservations. Just step on the proper train, sit in an unreserved seat, and when the uniformed conductor comes, flash your pass. For the average independent first-timer planning to see lots of Europe (from Norway to Portugal to Italy, for instance), the Eurailpass is probably the best way to go.

The Eurailpass is available in these forms (1991 prices):

Eurailpass, First Class: 15 days for $390; 21 days for $498; one month for $616; two months for $840; three months for $1,042; children under 12 go for half price; children under four go free.

Eurail Youthpass, Second Class (for those under 26): one month for $425, two months for $560. Youth flexipass: 15 days out of 3 months for $340, 30 days out of 3 months for $540.

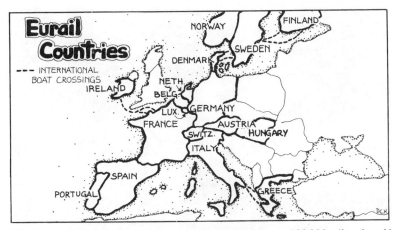

Eurail covers all countries on this map (except Britain)—over 100,000 miles of track!

Eurail Saver Passes (15 days): first-class travel for three people traveling together for $298 each rather than $390 (off-season, October 1-March 31, two traveling together qualify). With this pass all partners must travel together at all times.

Eurail Flexipass: gives you unlimited first-class travel for any 5 days out of 15 for $230; and 9 days out of 21 for $398; and any 14 days out of a month for $498. Night trains departing after 7:00 p.m. count as one flexipass day. (Most people find that the freedom to travel on those other 12 days is well worth the small extra price a normal 21-day pass costs.)

There is also a **Euraildrive pass** for people who'd like to mix, for instance, nine nonconsecutive rail days and three nonconsecutive rental car days out of a 21-day period. Your travel agent has details.

If you're traveling just barely enough to justify getting the pass, get one. There's more to it than economy. With the unlimited pass, you'll travel more, not worrying about the cost of spontaneous side trips. And the convenience of a train pass is worth a lot. You'll never have to worry about getting the best train ticket deal, no changing extra money to buy tickets, and you'll avoid the dreadful ticket lines that exasperate so many travelers. Train stations can be a mess. It's maddening to stand in line beating off all the Spaniards for half an hour and then learn you waited in the wrong line. Many trains are missed because of ticket line frustrations. (A surcharge is added to tickets bought on board.)

A few special trains (such as France's speedy TGV, and those with a boxed R in the schedules) require reservations as do all long runs in

Two Eurailers boarding a second-class no-smoking car for the overnight trip from Copenhagen to Paris.

Spain and Norway. Except for those trains that require reservations, worrying about reservations on Europe's trains makes as much sense as calling ahead for a Big Mac.

Know your extras. You get much more than just train travel with your Eurailpass. Your Eurail manual (included with purchase) lists all the free and discounted extras that come with a Eurailpass: international boats from Ireland to France, Italy to Greece, Sweden to Finland, and Germany to Denmark, cruises on the Rhine, Mosel, Danube, and all the Swiss lakes, local buses in some countries and more.

The Eurailpass must be purchased on this side of the Atlantic. If you're already in Europe, a friend at home can buy one for you (your legal name and money is all it takes) and mail or Federal Express it over. (That's as risky as mailing cash, but I do it routinely without problems.) The pass is irreplaceable and, after it's validated, nonrefundable. If you never use it, you can get a refund less 15 percent within one year.

Although Eurail promises nothing, you can probably, after much delay and hassle, get a replacement pass if you lose yours. The passes have a small receipt tab that is ripped off and given to you when you validate it in Europe. Save that tab. If you do lose your pass, take the tab and a good story to the nearest Eurail aid office where, after contacting your travel agent to verify your claim to Eurail ownership, they'll generally give you a second lease on Eurail life. If this gets out of hand, Eurail has every right to say "Sorry, Charlie." (My travel partner and I store each other's "proof tabs" in our own money belts.) Eurailpasses must be validated within six months of the issue date stamped on the back. They increase in price on January 1. If you're traveling early in the year, buy in December and save money. They cost the same everywhere. Buy your pass from an agent who can help you on your budget-independent Europe plans. Agents who do a lot of Eurail business can issue passes on the spot or within two days (see Back Door Catalog). Others take about one week to process your order.

Validate your pass thoughtfully. A 21-day pass can often cover a 30-day trip if you plan carefully. For example, many people start their pass at the French coast between London and Paris to cover the $20 ride into Paris. Then they spend four days in Paris, not using their pass. At the end of their trip, they wish they had four more days of train pass coverage. To get the most use out of your pass, start it when you're really ready to move (in this case, when you leave Paris). A train pass is not worthwhile in the Low Countries—distances are too short to justify a pass. So if your pass expires when you arrive in Amsterdam, that's no problem. Another trick to squeeze extra time out of your pass is to pay for the premidnight portion of a night train. For instance, for the 11:39 p.m. June 18 train from Frankfurt to Florence, have your pass validated for June 19 (before boarding), buy a ticket for the 30-minute ride to Heidelberg, and save an entire day of your pass.

A **Eurail Youthpass** is a second-class Eurailpass available only to those who will be under 26 on the day they validate their pass. Those 26 or over have no choice but a first-class pass—forced luxury. First-class passes are good on second class, and "second-class people" can pay extra to travel with stuffier first-class passengers. If you're under 26 and money matters, go second class. (The Inter-rail pass for European youths is explained in the Appendix.)

The Eurailpass isn't best for every tourist. In fact, I'd estimate that 20 percent of the people who buy a pass don't travel anywhere near enough to justify the purchase. That's an expensive mistake. Determine what it would cost if you simply bought second-class tickets for each of your expected journeys. Your travel agent can calculate this for you, or use the chart in the Appendix to calculate it yourself.

Second-class tickets from Amsterdam to Rome to Madrid and Amsterdam would cost a little more than a two-month Eurail Youthpass ($500). First-class tickets would cost the same as a two-month, first-class Eurailpass. Remember, only those under 26 can buy the second-class Eurailpass, but anyone can buy individual second-class rail tickets.

Trains

Virtually all trains have both first-class and second-class cars. Both go the same speed. First-class cars are filled with wealthy first-class Europeans (who paid 50 percent more than the second-class ticket cost to get away from the crowds) and other Eurailers. The people fun is down in the second-class cars—where the soldiers and nuns party and where picnics become potlucks.

Physically, first- and second-class compartments are fairly similar. The major advantage of first class is it's less crowded than second. This is most important for peak season night travel. Many people complain about overcrowded trains. I've felt like a sardine many times and spent more than my share of hours sitting on someone's suitcase in a crowded aisle. But more often than not, there's a nearly empty car on the same train, unnoticed by the complainers. Complainers are usually too busy being miserable to find answers to their problems. Look around. People get off and new cars are often added to ease the crowding.

Back in my youth, I always traveled second class. Now that I have no choice but to Eurail with a first-class pass, I have to admit that the roomy and less crowded first-class cars are great. I can pass pleasant hours reading, writing, eating, enjoying the view, and quietly daydreaming. Still, when I need to buy an individual ticket, it's second class.

You'll find two basic seating layouts on European trains: "bus-type," with all seats facing the same way, and "compartment seating," with six seats (three facing three) or, occasionally, eight in second class. Bus-type cars have comfortable reclining seats with a fold-out table on the seat in front of you. It's difficult to strike up a conversation with anyone other than the person next to you. You store your luggage on overhead racks or on shelves at each end of the car.

The three-facing-three seating configuration is a natural conversation starter. Window and aisle seats usually have fold-up tables. Baggage is stored on overhead racks or underneath your seat.

On all cars, rest rooms are located at each end. Vacancy is indicated by a light visible from your seat.

Other Rail Passes

Most countries have their own miniversion of a Eurailpass. The "Beyond Eurail" section in the Appendix explains the Britrail, Finrail, Francerail, Swissrail, Scandiarail, and Germrail. (I'm still waiting for the Israil.) The new 21-day Scandiarail (Nordturist) pass, given the high cost of train travel up there and the popularity of Scandinavian trips among Americans, is worth a good look.

Among these single-country train passes, only the **Britrail pass** is a big seller. England attracts more Americans than any other country, and Eurail doesn't cover the British Isles. Worthwhile if you're traveling from London to Edinburgh and back, the Britrail pass has just about the same rules and regulations as the Eurailpass.

The Britrail pass can be purchased in the United States or on the Continent—not in Britain—and is available for from 8 to 30 days. This pass differs from the Eurail in that seniors get a discount and people of any age can take advantage of a second-class economy pass. Britrail has some complexities, but everything is adequately explained in its brochure. The Sealink coupon, a discount ticket for the ride from London to the Continent across the Channel, confuses many. It's a bargain only for people over 26 who plan to cross the English Channel during the day (youth and night tickets bought at the Sealink office in Victoria Station are cheaper).

Travel without a Pass

Consider the alternatives to Eurail. If you know where you want to go, you can tailor your own "personalized train pass" at any European sta-

A typical European train station scene

tion. Just buy a second-class ticket connecting the cities you plan to visit. You'll get one ticket listing your route and up to two months to complete the journey, with unlimited stopovers. This can be very economical (see sample prices in the Appendix); for instance, if you plan to travel Amsterdam-Brussels-Paris-San Sebastian-Madrid-Lisbon, you can buy the second-class ticket with unlimited stopovers for $230, about half the cost of a 21-day Eurailpass.

You can buy tickets in train stations or at European travel agencies (same price, usually faster and easier). Buying tickets through your agent at home is unnecessary and probably more expensive. Always ask about special (night, family, senior, round-trip, weekend, etc.) prices.

To travel from London to the Continent, simply buy a train ticket (at the Sealink office in London's Victoria Station, not in the U.S.A.) from London to the European city of your choice. Many people agonize over which English Channel port to use and then worry about missing the boat if their train is late. Relax, don't worry, the boat is figured into the train ride. You'll get the most efficient boat, and it won't leave until the scheduled train butts up against it and all the people file on board. When you dock at the French or Belgian port, find the train with your destination label and you're home free. Eurail travelers generally buy tickets just to the coast of Europe, validate their pass at that station, and Eurail away.

Getting on the Right Track

Multistation Cities. Most large European cities and some small ones have more than one train station. For instance, there is "Brussels Nord," "Brussels Midi," and "Brussels Central." Be sure you know whether your train is leaving from Interlaken East or Interlaken West, even if that means asking what might seem like a stupid question. A city's stations are easily connected by train, subway, or bus.

Pay attention, get help. Managing on the trains is largely a matter of asking questions, letting people help you, assuming things are logical, and thinking. I always ask someone on the platform if the train is going where I think it is. (Point to the train and ask, "Roma?") Uniformed train personnel can answer any question you can communicate. Speak slowly, clearly, and with caveman simplicity. Be observant. If the loudspeaker comes on, gauge by the reaction of those around you if the announcement concerns you and if it's good or bad news. If, after the babble, everyone dashes across the station to track 15, you should assume your train is no longer arriving on track 2.

Train-splitting. Never assume the whole train is going where you are. Each car is labeled separately, because cars are usually added and dropped here and there all along the journey. Sometimes you'll be left sitting in your car on the track for 10 minutes, watching your train fade into the distance, until another train comes along and picks up your car. To survive all of this juggling easily, just check to be sure that the city on your car's nameplate is your destination. The nameplate lists the final stop and some (but not all) of the stops in between.

The configuration of most trains is charted in little display cases on the platform next to where your train will arrive. As you wait, study it to note where the first-class and sleeping cars are, whether there's a diner, and which cars are going where on your train. Also, some train schedules will list in the fine print, "Munich-bound cars in the front, Vienna-bound cars in the rear." Knowing which cars you're eligible for can be especially handy if you'll be competing with a mob for a seat. If I expect a real scramble, I'll stand on a bench at the far end of the track and study each car to know where the most empty places are. If there are several departures within an hour or so and the first train looks hopeless, I'll wait for the next.

Baggage. This has never been a problem for me on the trains. Every car has plenty of room for luggage, so the average tourist never checks baggage through. I've seen Turkish families moving all their worldly goods from Germany back to Turkey without checking a thing. They just packed everything into the compartment they reserved and were on their way.

People complain about the porters in the European train stations. I think they're great—I've never used one. Frankly, I don't feel sorry for anyone who travels with more luggage than he or she can carry.

Luggage is never completely safe. There is a thief on every train (union rules) planning to grab a bag (see the section "Theft and the Tourist" in chap. 5). Don't be careless. Before leaving my luggage in a compartment, I establish a relationship with everyone there. If they didn't know each other before the ride, I'm safe leaving it among mutual guards.

Using Train Time Wisely. Train travelers, especially Eurailers, spend a lot of time on the train. This time can be dull and unproductive, or you can make a point to use travel time wisely. This helps pass the time and frees up more leisure time away from the train. It makes no sense to sit on the train bored and then sit in the station for an hour reading your information and deciding where to go for hotels and what to do next.

Spend train time studying, reading, writing postcards or journal entries, eating, organizing, cleaning, writing a symphony, doing any-thing you can so you don't have to do it after you arrive. Talk to local people or other travelers. There is so much to be learned. Europeans are often less open and forward than Americans. You could sit across from a silent but fascinating and friendly European for an entire train ride, or you could break the ice by quietly offering him a cigarette or some candy, showing him your Hometown, U.S.A., postcards or by asking him a question. This may start the conversation flowing and the friendship growing.

Station Facilities. Europe's train stations can be one of the independent traveler's best and most helpful friends. Take advantage of the assistance they can offer. All stations have storage lockers or a luggage-checking service where, for about a dollar, you can leave your luggage. People traveling light can fit two rucksacks into one storage locker, cutting their storage costs in half.

Most stations have comfortable waiting rooms. The bigger stations are equipped with day hotels for those who want to shower, shave, rest, and so on. If you ever, for one reason or another, need a free, warm, and safe place to spend the night, a train station (or an airport) is my choice.

Every station has a train information office eager to help you with your scheduling. I usually consult the timetables myself first and write down my plan, then confirm this with the information desk. Written communication is easiest and safest.

This is a French train station. As you can see, arrivals and departures are clearly listed. Who says you can't read French?

Tourist information and room-booking service is usually either in the station (in the case of major tourist centers) or nearby. This is my first stop in a new city. I pick up a map with sightseeing information and, if I need it, advice on where to find budget accommodations. Often, the station's money-changing office is open long after others have closed for the night. Train stations are major bus stops, so connections from train to bus are generally no more difficult than crossing the street. Buses go from the stations to the nearby towns that lack train service. If you have a bus to catch, be quick, since many are scheduled to connect with the train and leave promptly.

Safety. Physically, I feel completely safe on trains. Women should use discretion, however, in choosing a compartment for an overnight ride. Sleeping in an empty compartment in southern Europe is an open invitation to your own private Casanova. Choose a room with a European granny or nun in it. That way you'll get a little peace, and he won't even try.

Train Schedules—Breaking the Code

A kind of schedule you'll need to understand are the listings of all trains that come to and go from a particular station each day. These are clearly posted in two separate listings: departures (the ones we're concerned with, usually in yellow) and arrivals (which you'll rarely use, normally in white).

You'll also find airport-type departure schedules that flip up and list the next 8 or 10 departures. These often befuddle travelers who don't realize that all over the world there are four easy-to-identify columns listed, and these are always: destination, type of train, track number, and departure time. I don't care what language they're in, you can accurately guess which column is what.

Train schedules are a great help to the traveler—if you can read them. Many Eurail travelers never take the time to figure them out. Here are a few pointers and a sample map and schedule to practice on. Understand it. You'll be glad you did.

You'll find these confusing-looking charts and maps in the Cook Timetable and in display cases in every station. Find the trip you want to take on the appropriate train map. Your route will be numbered, referring you to the proper timetable. That table is the schedule of the trains traveling along that line, in both directions (arr. = arrivals, dep. = departures).

As an example, let's go from Venice to Rome (the local spellings are always used, in this case, Venezia and Roma). This is #389 on the map. So refer to table 389. Locate your starting point, Venezia. Reading from

TABLE 389

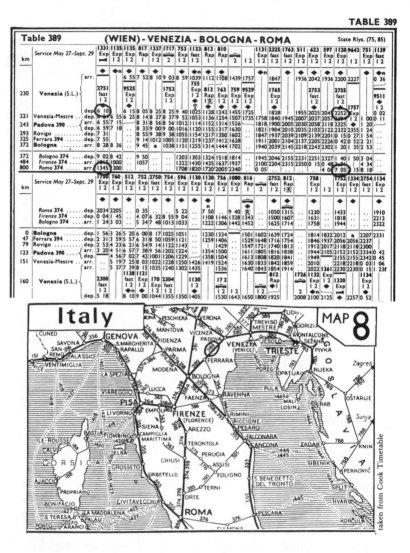

left to right, you will see that trains leave Venice for Rome at 6:10, 9:40, 10:25, 11:28, and so on. Those trains arrive in Rome at 13:45, 17:08, 18:20, and 17:20, respectively. (European schedules use the 24-hour clock.) As you can see, all departures don't go all the way to Rome. For example, the 8:25 train only goes to Bologna, arriving at 10:38. From there, the 11:51 train will get you to Rome by 17:08.

This schedule shows overnight trains in both directions. You could leave Venice at 22:52 (10:52 p.m.) and arrive in Rome by 7:05, just in time for breakfast. Traveling from Rome to Venice, your trip would start at 0:35 and end at 8:15.

Train schedules are helpful in planning your stopovers. For instance, this table shows a train leaving Venice at 8:05, arriving in Florence (Firenze) by 10:57. You could spend the middle of the day exploring that city and catch the 16:37 train to Rome (arr. 20:05). Remember: each table shows just some of the trains that travel along that track. Other tables feed onto the same line, and the only person who knows everything is the one at the train station information window. Let that person help you. He or she can fix mistakes and save you many hours. Each table has three parts: a schedule for each direction and a section explaining the many exceptions to the rules (not shown here). You never know when one of those confusing exceptions might affect your train. Schedule symbols also indicate problem-causing exceptions, such as which trains are first-class only, sleepers only, charge supplements, require reservations or leave only on certain days. Use the tables, but always confirm your plans with the person at the information window. Just show him or her your plan on a scrap of paper (i.e., Venezia-Firenze, 8:05-10:57; Firenze-Roma, 16:37-20:05) and ask, "OK?" If your plan is good, the information person will nod, direct you to your track, and you're on your way. If there's a problem, he or she will solve it. Uniformed train employees on the platforms or on board the trains can also confirm your plans.

The _Thomas Cook Continental Timetable_ is a handy tool that has become my itinerary-planning bible. Published several times a year, it has nearly every European train schedule in it, complete with maps. (To order the up-to-date Cook Timetable, about $20, and/or to get their fine travel guide catalog, call the Forsyth Travel Library, 1-800-FORSYTH.) I find that the schedules vary more with the season than with the year. I don't rely on them for the actual train I'll take, but I use an old one (which your travel agent might loan or give to you) at home before I leave to familiarize myself with how to read train schedules and to learn the frequency and duration of train trips I expect to take. Every station and most trains will be equipped with the same schedule, updated. Although I don't carry the bulky "Cook Book" with me, those who do find it very handy and enjoy tremendous popularity on the train.

How to Sleep on the Train

The economy of night travel is tremendous. You slaughter two birds with one stone. Sleeping while rolling down the tracks saves time and money, both of which, for most travelers, are limited resources. The first concern about night travel is usually, "Aren't you missing a lot of beautiful scenery? You just slept through half of Sweden!" Well, there are very few train rides that will have you leaning out the windows most of the time. (Across southern Switzerland and Oslo to Bergen in Norway are very scenic.) In other words, nearly every eight-hour train ride will be a bore unless you spend it sleeping. Obviously, you will miss a few beautiful sights, but that will be more than made up for by the entire extra day you gain in your itinerary.

The Economy of Night Travel

The typical traveler:

Friday	Finish sightseeing in Copenhagen.
Friday night	Sleep in Copenhagen. Room costs $30.
Saturday	Spend entire day on train traveling to Stockholm.
Saturday night	Arrive when most rooms are booked. Find acceptable but expensive room for $40.
Sunday	Free for sightseeing in Stockholm.

The clever traveler:

Friday	Finish sightseeing in Copenhagen.
Friday night	22:00-8:00: sleep on the train traveling to Stockholm.
Saturday	Arrive early when plenty of budget beds are available. Get set up in a hotel. Saturday is free for sightseeing in Stockholm!

The efficient traveler saved $70 and gained an entire day of sightseeing by sleeping on the train.

Some train seats make into a bed.

If you anticipate a very crowded train and must get some sleep, you can usually reserve a sleeping berth known as a couchette (pronounced "koo SHETT") a day in advance at the ticket counter or, if there are any available, from the conductor on the train. For about the cost of a

For $14, you can rent a couchette (bunk bed) on your overnight train.

cheap hotel bed ($14), you'll get sheets, pillow, blankets, a fold-out bunk bed in a compartment with three to five other people, and, hopefully, a good night's sleep. It's best (and easy) to book your couchette at the station the day you arrive in a city.

Without a bed, a major concern is, "How do you sleep?" Sleeping on an overnight train ride can be a waking nightmare. One night of endless bouncing of the head, with swollen toes and a screaming tailbone, sitting up straight in a dark eternity of steel wheels crashing along rails, trying doggedly—yet hopelessly—to get comfortable will teach you the importance of finding a spot to stretch out for the night. This is an art that night travelers cultivate. Those with the greatest skill at this game sleep. Those not so talented will spend the night gnashing their teeth and squirming for relief.

A traditional train car has about 10 compartments, each with six or eight seats (three or four facing three or four). Many of these compartments have seats that pull out and armrests that lift, allowing you to turn your compartment into a bed on wheels. This is only possible if you have more seats than people in your compartment. A compart-ment that seats six can sleep three. So, if between 30 and 60 people choose your car, some will sleep and some will sit. Your fate depends on how good you are at encouraging people to sit elsewhere. There are many ways to play this game (which has few rules and encourages creativity). Here are my two favorite techniques.

The Big Sleep. Arrive 30 minutes before your train leaves. Walk most of the length of the train but not to the last car. Choose a car that is going where you want to go, and find an empty compartment. Pull two seats out to make a bed, close the curtains, turn out the lights, and pre-tend you are sound asleep. It's amazing. At 9:00 p.m., everyone on that train is snoring away! The first 30 people to get on that car have room to sleep. No. 31 will go into any car with the lights on and people sitting up. The most convincing "sleepers" will be the last to be "woken up."

The Hare Krishna Approach. A more interesting way that works equally well and is more fun is to sit cross-legged on the floor and chant religious-sounding, exotically discordant harmonies, with a faraway look on your face. People will open the door, stare in for a few seconds—and leave, determined to sit in the aisle rather than share a compartment with the likes of you. You'll probably sleep alone, or with five other religious fanatics who want to chant the night away.

These tricks work not to take advantage of others but to equal out the train load. When all compartments are lightly loaded and people con-tinue to load in, the game is over. To minimize the misery on a full train, sit opposite your partner, pull out the seats, and share a single bed (and the smell of your feet).

Another trick is to use the reservation cards to your advantage. Each compartment will have a reservation board outside the door. Never sit in a seat that is reserved, because you'll be "bumped out" just before the train leaves. Few people realize that you can determine how far the people on a train will travel by reading their reservation tags. Each tag explains which segment of the journey that seat is reserved for. Find a compartment with three or four people traveling for just an hour or two, and then for the rest of the night you will probably have that com-partment all to yourself.

Remember that trains add and lose cars throughout the night. A train could be packed with tourists heading for Milan, and at 1:00 a.m. an empty Milan-bound car could be added. The difference between being packed like sardines and stretching out in your own fishbowl could be as little as one car away.

Many train travelers are ripped off while they sleep. A $14 couchette is safe because the car attendant monitors who comes and goes. Those

Losers in the "sleep-stakes"

sleeping for free should exercise extreme caution. Keep your valuables either in a money belt or at least securely attached to your body. For good measure, I clip and fasten my rucksack to the luggage rack. If one tug doesn't take the bag, a thief will usually leave it rather than ask you how your luggage is attached. You'll hear stories of entire train cars being gassed and robbed in Italy. It happens—but I wouldn't lose sleep over it.

For a more thorough and complete rundown on Eurail travel skills, see the Appendix.

Bus versus Train

Except in Ireland, Greece, Turkey, and Morocco, the trains are faster, more comfortable, and have more extensive schedules than buses. Bus trips are usually less expensive (especially in the British Isles) and are occasionally included on your Eurailpass (where operated by the train companies, as many are in Germany, Switzerland, and Belgium).

There are some cheap, long-haul buses (often hippie-type "magic buses") from the hub cities of London, Munich, Amsterdam, and Athens. These can save you plenty over train fares. For example, in 1991, Amsterdam to London costs $75 by train, $45 by bus; Amsterdam to Paris costs $57 by train, $35 by bus; and Amsterdam to Athens costs $247 by train and only $115 by bus.

Use buses mainly to pick up where Europe's great train system leaves off. Buses fan out from the smallest train stations to places too small for the train to cover.

Driving in Europe

Behind the wheel you are totally free. You go where you want to, when you want to. You're not limited by tracks and schedules. You can carry more luggage (if you didn't like the Pack Light chapter, you can even tow a trailer), and it's very economical for small groups.

Solo car travel is expensive, but three or four people sharing a car rental travel cheaper than three or four using train passes. The super-mobility of a car saves you time and money in locating budget

Car vs. Train—Rough Costs of Sample Trips per Person

Mode of Transportation	3 weeks 1,600 mi.	3 weeks 3,000 mi.	2 months 3,000 mi.	2 months 8,000 mi.
Eurailpass (first class)	$500	$500	$850	$850
Second-class individual train tickets	$270	$430	$430	$1,150
Subcompact car (two people)	$500	$600	$1,000	$1,400
Midsized car (four people)	$400	$450	$700	$800

Sample trips: Munich-Paris-Florence-Munich = 1,600 miles.
Amsterdam-Munich-Rome-Barcelona-Paris = 3,000 miles.
Amsterdam-Copenhagen-Stockholm-Oslo-Copenhagen- Berlin-Vienna-Athens-Rome-Nice-Madrid-Lisbon-Madrid-Paris-Amsterdam = 8,000 miles.

Train tickets cost about $.12 per mile in the south, $.22 per mile in the north. Car rates based on best rentals or leases including collision damage waiver (CDW) supplements, and figuring $4 per gallon and 30 mpg.

Ideal train travel: one or two traveling together, packing light, traveling mostly in big cities on a far-reaching trip.

Ideal car travel: three or more traveling together, packing heavy, focusing on one area and not primarily in big cities.

accommodations—a savings I use to help rationalize the "splurge" of a car rental. You can also play it riskier in peak season, arriving in a town late with no reservation. If it's full, you simply drive to the next town.

Gas in Europe is expensive—$2 to $4 a gallon—but their petite puddle-jumpers get great mileage. Europe's superhighways are wunderbar, but the smaller roads are slow and often congested. You'll make slower time in Europe than in the United States, but distances are short and you'll be impressed by how few miles you need to travel to enjoy the diversity of Europe.

Car travel is best for a group focusing on one area. Seven or eight people do wonderfully in a minibus (try to get a Ford Transit), dirt cheap per person. The British Isles are good for driving—reasonable rentals, no language barrier, exciting rural areas, fine roads, not covered on Eurail, and, after one near head-on collision scares the bloody heck out of you, you'll have no trouble remembering which side of the road to drive on.

Other good driving areas are Scandinavia (beware of long waits at ferry crossings), Belgium, Holland, and Luxembourg (yield for bikes —you're outnumbered), Germany, Switzerland, and Austria (driving down sunny Alpine valleys with yodeling on the tape deck is auto-ecstasy), and Spain and Portugal (with their exasperating public transportation system, I spell relief C-A-R). The whirlwind, see-Europe-from-top-to-bottom-type trip is best by train.

Renting a Car

There are two kinds of rental companies: international corporations (such as Hertz, Avis, Budget, and National/Europcar) and tour operators (such as Europe by Car—800/223-1516, Auto Europe—800/223-5555 for catalog, and Kemwel—800/678-0678). Tour operators are wheeler-dealers who can hook you up at a price you couldn't get on your own with one rental agency from a network of individual companies in Europe.

The big multinationals offer more flexibility (last-minute reservations, many pickup and drop-off options including open jaws, and various rental plans). The tour operators are usually cheaper.

The least-expensive rental cars are current model subcompact manual transmission Ford Fiestas, Toyota Starlets, and VW Polos or the equivalent. (Manuals are the norm. If you need a small automatic, try Hertz.) Standard midsized, manual transmission, 4-door or 5-door hatchback cars—such as current model Ford Sierras, Honda Accords, and VW Passats—cost from 50 percent to 100 percent more than the subcompacts. For four adults, however, it's worth the price.

The best rental rates are by the week, with unlimited mileage arranged in the United States before you depart. You can book directly or, for no extra charge, through your travel agent. Comparison shop at the various companies through your agent. The cheapest company for rental in one country might be the most expensive in the next. Rentals arranged from major companies in Europe are so expensive, you'd save money by having someone arrange your rental for you back in the United States.

You can usually return your car at any of the rental company's offices in the country in which you picked it up for no extra charge, and if you decide to turn it in or keep it longer, you'll be billed at a fair (1/7 of a week per day) daily rate. Ask about economy or "restricted" rates for people who pay long in advance and turn the car in where they picked it up. Ask also about international drop-off policies, which offer occasional pleasant surprises.

The rental rates vary substantially from country to country, depending on competition, taxes, and insurance costs. Spain, Germany, Luxembourg, and Belgium are usually the least expensive. Scandinavia, Switzerland, France, Italy, and Austria are more expensive than their neighbors. The only country where I could beat the advance-from-the-U.S.A. deals was in Greece. (Syngrou Street is Athens' auto row, and I found fierce competition and soft rental prices.)

A small Danish company, Rafco, rents nearly new Peugeots at a great price from offices in Copenhagen, Paris, Amsterdam, and Frankfurt. Contact them for a free brochure. (24 Energiveg, DK-2750 Ballerup DK, tel. 45-42-97-15-00. They offer my readers a 10% discount.)

Minimum legal insurance is included in the rental rates, but most companies have a very high (up to the value of the car) deductibles. A collision damage waiver (CDW) supplement is very expensive, as discussed in chapter 1, Planning.

Those traveling for more than three weeks should consider leasing, which is a scheme where you are technically buying the car and selling it back to avoid the steep local taxes. Leasing includes the CDW and is particularly good in Belgium and France.

Take full advantage of the multinationals' willingness to let you drop the car in a number of different locations, even in different countries. For instance, Hertz and Avis have more than 100 offices in France. To avoid driving in big cities such as London, pick up and drop off your car at the airport even if you're not flying in or out. It's best to take the subway or bus out of town and get used to driving in the easier-going countryside. In Paris, why not do without the headache and expense of a car in the big city, spend a day at Versailles and pick up your car there, avoiding altogether the crazy Parisian traffic.

Credit cards are always accepted for pre- and final payment. They are also required for collateral. If you are under 25 or over 68, ask about age restrictions.

Spontaneous car rental (with a major credit card) is easy, virtually at any date, anywhere in Europe. Even if you're doing Europe with a train pass, there are places—such as the hill town region of Tuscany and Umbria or France's Loire Valley—where train travel is frustrating and two days in a car can be $50 very well spent.

Although Americans rarely consider this budget option, Aussies and New Zealanders routinely buy used cars for their trip and sell them when they're done. The most popular places to buy one are London, Amsterdam, and U.S. military bases. Before your trip, or once in Europe, you can check the classified ads in the armed forces' _Stars and Stripes_ newspaper. In London, there's an informal van market at Provost Street (Old Street Tube Station). Budget-minded Aussies and New Zealanders find lots of related travel information (jobs, flats, cheap flights, travel partners, as well as used cars for sale) in London periodicals such as _TNT, Law,_ and _New Zealand-UK News._ Another good resource for buying and selling in London is the booklet, "Europe by Van," telephone 206/842-8469 in Seattle.

Savvy budget travelers offer rental companies their service to return cars to another office for them. You go now, direct, and pay the gas, but you can't beat the price—free.

When buying or renting a vehicle, consider the advantage of a van or station wagon, which gives you the flexibility to drive late and just pull over and camp for free.

Driving Miscellany

Horror stories about European traffic abound. They're fun to tell, but really, driving in Europe is a problem only to those who make it one. Any good American driver can cope with European traffic.

Europe is a continent of frustrated race-car drivers. You'll find highly skilled maniacal drivers in any country, but the most dangerous creature on the road is the timid American. Be aggressive, observe, fit in, minimize big-city driving, wear your seat belt, and pay extra for zero-deductible insurance.

Adapt, be observant, and try to drive European. After a few minutes on the autobahn (German freeway), you'll learn that you don't cruise in the passing lane. In Rome, my cabbie went through three red lights. White-knuckled, I asked, "Scusi, do you see red lights?" He said, "In Rome, red lights are discretionary. When I come to light, I look. If no cars come, red light stupido, I go through. If policeman sees no cars— no problem—red light is stupido." England's roundabouts work won- derfully if you take advantage of the yield system and don't stop. Stop- ping before a roundabout is as bothersome as stopping on our freeway on-ramps.

International driver's licenses are basically an official translation of your American driver's license. They make it easier for a European cop to write you a ticket. Exactly where international driver's licenses are required is unclear. They are sometimes required in Spain, Greece, Germany, Austria, Italy, and Eastern Europe. They are available, quick, cheap (around $5), and easy to get (bring in two little photos) in the United States from the AAA. For many, these licenses are a handy piece of legitimate but disposable photo-identity, whether needed for driv- ing or not.

The shortest distance between any two European points is found on the toll roads. Although tolls can be very high in Italy and France ($30 to get from Paris to the Italian border), I normally figure that the gas and time saved on European superfreeways justifies the expense.

Vanning through the windmills

Others prefer the more scenic and free national highway systems ("route national" in France). Small roads can be a breeze or they can be dreadfully jammed up.

Get the best maps possible. European maps are cheaper and better than those you get in the States, and they use the local spellings. The popular, yellow, 1:200,000 scale Michelin maps are very good. I buy maps in local bookstores and always ask the person who helps me to suggest the best local drive a visitor could take. That friend will be tickled to plan your itinerary—and no travel writer could do it better. "Back Doors" are best found from local sources, not in guidebooks.

For drivers in Europe, the language barrier is a road turtle. All of Europe uses the same simple set of road symbols. Just take a few minutes to learn them. Autobahn rest stops have free local driving almanacs explaining such signs, roadside facilities, and exits.

Americans are very timid about passing. In Europe, it's essential. On windy, narrow roads, you'll notice a kind of sign language from the slower car ahead of you: left-turn signal means OK to pass, right-turn signal means wait. This is used inconsistently and should not be relied on blindly.

I drive in and out of strange towns fairly smoothly by following a few basic signs. Most European towns will have signs directing you to the "old town" or the center (centrum, centro, centre ville, etc.). The tourist office, which is normally right downtown, will usually be clearly signposted ("i," "tourismo," "VVV," or various abbreviations that you'll learn in each country). To leave a city, I look for autobahn signs (usually green or blue) or "all directions" ("toutes directions") signs. Try to avoid heavy traffic times. Big cities are great fun and nearly traffic-free for Sunday drives.

Don't use your car for city sightseeing. Park it and use public transportation. City parking is a problem. Basically, find a spot as close to the center as possible (aim for the church spire, usually near the tourist office), grab it and keep it. For short stops, I park just about anywhere my car will fit without blocking traffic (I've been towed once—a memorable $30 experience). For overnight stops, it's crucial to choose a safe, well-traveled, and well-lit spot. Vandalism to a tourist's car parked overnight in a bad urban neighborhood is as certain as death and taxes. In big cities, it's often worth parking in a garage ($10 a day and up). Ask your hotel receptionist for advice.

Pumping gas in Europe is as easy as finding a gas station ("self-service" is universal), sticking the nozzle in, and pulling the big trigger. Gas prices are listed by the liter (about a quart). Don't get confused: gas is called "petrol" or "benzine," while diesel is known as "gasoil."

"Super" is super and "normal" or "essence" is normal and increasingly rare. In Eastern Europe, use the highest octane available. Unleaded gas is catching on fast and is easy to find in most of Europe. Freeway stations are more expensive than those in towns, but during siesta, only freeway stations are open.

Remember, on the Continent you'll be dealing with kilometers—to get miles, cut in half and add 10 percent (90 km/hr = 45 + 9 miles: 54 mph—not very fast in Europe).

Biking in Europe

While biking through Europe is about the cheapest way to go, most bikers choose to pedal for the sheer joy of it. Imagine low-gearing up a beautiful mountain road on a bike—scent of fresh-mown hay—then picture an air-conditioned Mercedes with the windows closed and the stereo on—scent of upholstery. Someone in the car might pass by and say, "Masochistic nut!" but he also might notice the biker's smiling face—that traveler who can see clear from mountain to village, smell the woods, hear birds singing, the trees breezing, and the bugs bouncing gaily off his teeth, while anticipating a well-earned and glorious downhill run on the other side. If this is for you, bike. Edwin McCain, who for years has gotten his travel thrills crisscrossing Europe by bike, helped me assemble these tips on biking in Europe.

Use good maps and biking guidebooks. Planning your trip is half the fun. The Michelin Europe map (#920) is fine for strategic planning. Once in Europe, pick up local maps that show the back roads and even some bike paths. Don't be obsessed with following a preplanned route. Delightful and spontaneous side trips are part of the spirit and joy of biking. And when you ride off a map, don't lug it; give it to someone going the other way or mail it home.

Some recommended guidebooks are *Europe by Bike* by Karen and Terry Whitehill (Mountaineers); *Cycle Touring Europe* by Nicholas Crane (Pan Books); *Bicycle Touring in Europe* by Karen and Gary Hawkins (Pantheon Books); and *CTC Cycle Touring Book of Great Britain and Ireland, Cyclist's Britain* (Pan/Ordnance Survey). Bike Nashbar in Ohio (1-800-345-2453) is a very cheap and reliable mail-order house.

Before setting out, get in shape. Don't rely on just an occasional ride to work or the store plus a two- or three-hour ride on Sunday. Try some 60-mile-a-day rides (five hours at 12 mph) around home and, if possible, for several days at a time with loaded panniers. Sixty miles (100 km) is a good daily target for a European tour.

You might want to join one of many good organized bike tours.

These usually average an easy 30 to 40 miles a day. For more information, check the American Youth Hostels Association, Box 37613, Washington, D.C. 20013-7613; Bikecentennial Inc., Box 8308, Missoula, MT 59807; and bicycling magazines available at bike shops or newsstands. Or you can go it alone, with occasional pickup pals on the way. As a loner, you'll go where, when, and as far and fast as you want. But going with one or a few good companions is more fun.

When to go depends somewhat on where you go. Ideal biking temperatures are between 50 and 68 degrees Fahrenheit, so May is a good time to bike in the Mediterranean countries. Edwin started in May in Greece before it got too hot and pedaled up through the Balkans to England, where, on his arrival five weeks later, it wasn't too cold. He had good temperatures all the way, but he also had head winds—the prevailing westerlies. The next year, he set out from Lyons, France, for Helsinki and had not only just-right temperatures but also tail winds, allowing him to cover as many as 130 miles in a day.

Expect rain, and bring good biker's rain gear. For necessary protection from the sun, take long pants as well as shorts, long sleeves, a hat or helmet (you see very few bikers in Europe wearing helmets), gloves (without holes in their backs), and a good sun block.

Taking your bike on an airplane is easy. Most airlines don't charge for this service, considering your bike as one of two checked pieces of luggage. Some require that the bike be boxed, and some provide these boxes. If not, get one at a bike store. Check with the individual airlines concerning their requirements. Many lines will take an unboxed bike if you sign a "fragile" waiver. Baggage handlers seem less liable to pile a lot of luggage on top of an unboxed bike. Prepare your bike by turning the lowered handlebars 90 degrees, lowering the seat, taking off the odometer and pedals, and unhooking the cantilever brakes. Leave on the panniers—good added protection. This way you can bike right into and out of the airports.

In Western Europe, you'll see touring bikers and racers as well as ladies biking in the rain with open umbrellas. Bike repair shops are hard to find in Eastern Europe, where most bikes are simple and heavy one-speeds. The bikes you see in Europe are quite different from those in the United States. A European touring bike has fenders, lights, and bells. Lights and a horn or bell are generally required on all but racers. Even if you never ride at night, have lights both fore and aft for those unavoidable long, dark tunnels. And bells are used to say a multilingual "Hi!" to other bikers as well as, "Look out, here I come!"

The small Penta valves are standard in Europe. If you take a bike over with the automotive-type Shraeder valves, take along an extra tube.

Because you're going to Europe to savor its differences, consider buying a bike there. France, England, and Italy have good selections at reasonable prices. Oddly, Holland does not. You can rent 10-speeds, but not the 15- or 18-speeds whose low gears are really appreciated on those long, steep grades and when bucking head winds.

Smart bikers travel very light. Although many go with full panniers, front and rear (in Sweden, Edwin met a couple on a tandem, towing a well-laden trailer), you'll enjoy your biking trip much more toting much less. Don't bring cooking and camping gear unless you'll be nearly always camping. Youth hosteling and biking are a wonderful budget mix.

Bike thieves abound in Europe, especially at a youth hostel after midnight. Precautions: use a good bike lock; never leave your pump, water bottle, or computer on your bike when you can't see it; take your bike inside whenever possible; at hostels, always ask if there is a locked bike room, and, if not, ask or even plead for a place inside to put your bike overnight; and remember that hotels don't really have rules against taking a bike up to your room. Just do it unobtrusively. You can even wheelie it into the elevator. You can also usually walk your bike right into banks, post offices, and telephone exchanges. Stores, rarely; restaurants, hardly ever.

Traffic rules in Europe apply to bikers. The closer one gets to Holland, the more bike signs one sees: a one-speed in a blue circle indicates a bike route; a bike in a red circle indicates bikes are not allowed. Be alert, follow the blue bike signs, and the required bike paths will get you through even some of the most complicated highway interchanges. Beware of the silent biker who might be right behind you, and use hand signals before stopping or turning. Stay off the freeways. Little roads are nicer for biking anyway. Not enjoyable but often unavoidable are the cobblestones and stone paving blocks found in older cities across Europe.

Those traveling by train or car can always rent a bike for a day (about $5) and enjoy a fun and practical change of pace. Wherever it's worth biking, there will be a bike rental shop. In many countries (especially France, Germany, Austria, Belgium, and the Netherlands), the train stations rent bikes (often with 50% discounts to those with train tickets or passes and easy "pick up here and drop off there" plans). For mixing train and bike travel, ask at stations for the "Fahrrad am Bahnhof" (German) or "Train et Velo" (French) booklet. You can generally ship your bike with you on the train for a reasonable price. If you decide to see less of Europe but want to be able to stop on the way and pick berries, go by bike. And may the wind always be at your back!

Hitchhiking—Rules of Thumb

Hitching, sometimes called "auto-stop," is a popular and acceptable means of getting around in Europe. Without a doubt, hitching is the cheapest means of transportation. It's also a great way to meet people. Most people who pick you up are genuinely interested in getting to know an American.

After picking up a Rhine riverboat captain in my rental car and running him back to his home port, I realized that hitchhiking doesn't wear the same hippie hat in Europe that it does in the United States. The farther you get from the militant self-sufficiency of our culture, the more volunteerism you'll encounter. Bumming a ride is a perfect example. In the Third World—rural Europe in the extreme—anything rolling with room will let you in. You don't hitch, you just flag the vehicle down.

Hitching has two drawbacks. First, it can be time-consuming. Some places have 20 or 30 people in a chorus line of thumbs, just waiting their turns. Once, I said what I thought was a good-bye forever to an Irishman after breakfast. He was heading north. We had dinner together that night, and I learned a lot about wasting a day on the side of a road. Second, although hitching in Europe is safer than hitching in the United States, there is the ever-present danger involved in hitchhiking.

Hitchhiking at the Bulgaria-Greece border or whenever the train and bus schedules leave you stranded

Discretion is important. Feel good about the situation before you commit yourself to it. Keep your luggage on your lap, or at least out of the trunk, so if things turn sour you can excuse yourself quickly and easily. Women should not sit in the back seat of a two-door car. A fake wedding ring and modest dress are indications that you're interested only in transportation.

Personally, I don't hitchhike at home, and I wouldn't rely solely on my thumb to get me through Europe. But I never sit frustrated in a station for two hours because there's no bus or train to take me 15 miles down the road. I thumb my way out of train and bus schedule problems, getting to my destination in a friendly snap. You'll find that Germany, Ireland, and Great Britain offer generally good hitchhiking, and southern countries are much slower for hitching.

Your success as a hitchhiker will be determined by how well you follow several rules. The hitchhiking gesture is not always the outstretched thumb. In some countries, you ring an imaginary bell. In others, you make a downward wave with your hand. Observe and learn. Consider what the driver will want to let into his car. Arrange your luggage so it looks as small and desirable as possible. Those hitching with very little or no luggage enjoy a tremendous advantage.

Look like the Cracker Jack boy or his sister—happy, wholesome, and a joy to have aboard. To get the long ride, take a local bus out of town to the open country on the road to your destination and make a cardboard sign with your destination printed big and bold in the local language, followed by the local "please."

Share-a-ride organizations (Mitfahrzentralen in Germany, Allostop in France) match rides and riders. You pay a small amount to join, and you help with gas expenses, but it works well and is much cheaper than train travel. Use student Tourist Information centers or big-city phone books. Informal ride services are on school and hostel bulletin boards all over Europe.

Speed and safety are a trade-off when it comes to hitching. A single woman maximizes speed and risk. Two women travel more safely and nearly as fast. A man and a woman together are the best combination. A single man with patience will do fine. Two guys go slow and three or more should split up and rendezvous later. Single men and women are better off traveling together; these alliances are easily made at hostels.

When I'm doing some serious hitchhiking, I work to create pity. I walk away from town and find a very lonely stretch of road. In a lot of cases, I feel that the sparser the traffic, the quicker I get a ride. On a busy road, people will assume that I'll manage without their ride. If only one car passes in five minutes, the driver senses that I might starve to death or die of exposure if he doesn't stop. Look clean, safe, respectable, and a little gaunt. Establish eye contact. Charm the driver. Stand up. Smile. Don't walk and hitch. Pick a good spot on the road, giving the driver both plenty of time to see you and a safe spot to pull over. When you're in a hurry, there are two surefire ways of getting a ride fast. Find a spot where cars stop, and you can encounter the driver face to thumb. A toll booth, border, gas station, or—best of all—a ferry ride each give you that chance to smile and convince him that he needs you in his car or truck. At borders, you might decide to choose only a ride entirely through that country. Use a car's home country decal and— as on German and Italian cars, which display initials representing the home city—the license plate as a destination label. Although it's easy to zoom past a hitchhiker at 60 mph and not feel guilty, it's much more difficult to turn down an in-person request for a ride. A man and a woman traveling together have it easy. If the woman hitches and the guy steps out of view around the corner or into a shop, you should both have a ride in a matter of minutes. (Dirty trick, but it works.)

With the "hitch when you can't get a bus or train" approach, you'll find yourself walking down lovely mountain or rural roads out of a village, getting rides from small-town folk—fanatically friendly and super safe. I can recall some "it's great to be alive and on the road" days riding my thumb from tiny town to waterfall to desolate Celtic graveyard to coastal village and remembering each ride as much as the destinations.

Sometimes hitching almost becomes an end in itself. In the British Isles, especially Ireland, I've found so much fun in the front seat that I've driven right by my planned destination to carry on with the conversation. In rural Ireland, I'd stand on the most desolate road in Connemara and hitch whichever way the car was coming. As I hopped in, the driver would ask, "Where you goin'?" I'd say, "Ireland."

Walking (and Dodging)

You'll walk a lot in Europe. It's a great way to see cities, towns, and the countryside. Walking tours are the most intimate look at a city or town. A walker complements the place she walks through by her interest and will be received warmly. Many areas, from the mountains to the beaches, are best seen on foot.

Be careful—walking is dangerous. Pedestrians are run down every day. More than 300 pedestrians are run down annually on the streets of Paris. The drivers are crazy, and politeness has no place on the roads of Europe. Cross carefully, but if you wait for a break in the traffic, you may never get a chance to cross the street. Look for a pedestrian underpass or, when all else fails, find a heavy-set local person and just follow him or her like a shadow—one busy lane at a time—across that seemingly impassable street.

Hiking

Hiking in Europe is a joy. Travelers explore entire regions on foot. The Jungfrau is an exciting sight from a hotel's terrace café. But those who hike the region enjoy nature's very own striptease as the mountain reveals herself in an endless string of powerful poses.

The Alps are especially suited to the walking tourist. The trails are well kept and carefully marked. Very precise maps (scale 1:25,000) are readily available. You're never more than a day's hike from a mountain village, where you can replenish your food supply or enjoy a hotel and a restaurant meal. By July, most trails are free of snow, and lifts take less-rugged visitors to the top in a sweat-free flash.

Hundreds of Alpine huts exist to provide food and shelter to hikers. I know a family that hiked from France to Yugoslavia, spending every night along the way in a mountain hut. The huts are generally spaced four to six hours apart. Most serve hot meals and provide bunk-style lodging. If you plan to use the huts extensively, join an Alpine club.

A firsthand look at fairy-tale Alpine culture is just a $10 gondola ride away.

Membership in one of these European or American clubs entitles you to discounts on the cost of lodging and priority over nonmembers. The club can provide information about the trails and huts at which reservations are likely to be necessary.

Do some research before you leave. Buy the most appropriate guidebook for your hiking plans. Ask for maps and information from the National Tourist Offices.

4
The Budget: Eating and Sleeping on $40 a Day

In the fifteen years I've been teaching travel, my notes on budgeting have had to be continuously revised. It looked for a while like "Europe on the Cheap" was on the road to extinction. We saw Mr. Frommer's book threaten to grow from *Europe on $5 a Day* to *Europe on $35 a Rest Stop* as the dollar dropped and dropped. Then, from 1980 to 1985, the dollar grew stronger. Life in Europe was very easy for the budget traveler. But since 1985, the value of our dollar has dropped back to a fair rate against most European currencies, and once again, surviving on a budget requires some artistry.

Overall, most of today's Europe is about as expensive as the United States, and the sloppy traveler can blow a small fortune in a hurry. Still, smart travelers can thrive on $40 a day in the South and $50 daily in the North plus transportation—less if necessary.

The big issue is knowing your options (budget alternatives to international-class hotels and restaurants) and consuming only what you want to consume. If you want real tablecloths and black-tie waiters, your tomato salad will cost 20 times what it costs in the market. If you want a private shower, toilet, room service, TV, a fax at your disposal, and chocolate on your pillow, you'll pay in a day what many travelers pay in a week for a good, quiet eight hours of sleep.

We consumers get what we order. They say it takes two incomes for the American family to make ends meet these days. And likewise, when we travel, we order and get lavish plumbing. The only thing that really changes is the material appetite of the rich and wishful. Trains are faster, cars are better, and thousands of showers and toilets clutter the corners of Europe's formerly square, spacious, and cheap hotel rooms. And "budget" travel, while more comfortable, has also become more expensive.

My idea of "cheap" is simple but not sleazy. My budget morality is to never sacrifice safety, reasonable cleanliness, sleep, or nutrition to save money. I go to safe, central, friendly, local-style hotels, shunning TVs, swimming pools, people in uniforms, private plumbing, and transplanted American niceties in favor of an opportunity to travel as a temporary European. Unfortunately, simple will be subversive in the 1990s, and the system will bully even the cozy Scottish bed and breakfast into more and more facilities, more and more debt, and higher and higher prices.

I'm very cautious about sending people to Europe without enough money, skills, and reservations. The ideas in this chapter are tried and tested in the worst circumstances every year. And the feedback I get from Back Door travelers bolsters my confidence. It can be done—by you.

In 1991, you can travel comfortably for eight weeks for around $4,700. That includes $1,600 for a round-trip plane ticket and a two-month Eurailpass or split car rental and $2,300 for room and board ($40 a day). Add $16 a day ($800) for souvenirs, personal incidentals, admissions, and sightseeing costs.

Your budget is basically transportation, room and board, sightseeing, and incidentals. Transportation expenses are fixed. Flying to Europe is a bargain. Get a good agent, understand all your options, and make the best choice. This cost cannot be cut. Transportation in Europe is reasonable if you take advantage of a Eurailpass or split a car rental between three or four people. This is also a fixed cost. Your budget should not dictate how freely you travel in Europe. If I want to go somewhere, I will, taking advantage of whatever money-saving options I can. I came to travel.

The area that will make or break your budget—where you have the most control—is in your eating and sleeping expenses. People who spend $8,000 for their vacation spend about the same on transportation as those whose trips cost half as much. Room and board is the beaver in your bankbook. If you have extra money, it's more fun to spend it in Europe, but if your trip will last only as long as your money does and you develop and deploy a good strong SDI (spending defense initiative), figure about $40 per day plus transportation.

Sightseeing costs have risen faster than anything else. Admissions to major attractions are now $5 to $8, $2 or $3 for smaller sights. Your incidentals will also add up: coffee, beer, ice cream, and soft drinks cost $1 to $2, bus and subway rides $1, postcards $.50.

I traveled every summer for years on a part-time piano teacher's income (and, boy, was she upset). I ate and slept great by learning and using the skills that follow. By following these same guidelines in 1991, you can travel when you like without reservations and sleep and eat well for an average of under $50 a day plus transportation.

Sleeping Cheap

Hotels

Hotels are the most expensive way to sleep and, of course, the most comfortable. With a reasonable budget, I spend most of my nights in hotels. Hotels, however, can rip through a tight budget like a grenade in a dollhouse.

I always hear people complaining about that "$160 double in Frankfurt" or the "$200-a-night room in London." They come back from their vacations with bruised and battered pocketbooks, telling stories that scare their friends out of international travel and back to Florida or Hawaii one more time. True, you can spend $200 for a double, but I never have. That's five days' accommodations budget for me.

As far as I'm concerned, spending more for your hotel just builds a bigger wall between you and what you came to see. If you spend enough, you won't know where you are. Think about it. "In·ter·con·ti·nen·tal"—that implies uniform sterility, a lobby full of stay-press Americans with wheels on their suitcases, English menus, lamps bolted to the tables, and all the warmth of a submarine.

In a Back Door-style hotel, you get more by spending less. Here, the shower's down the hall and the Alps are in your lap.

Europe is full of European hotels—dingy, old-fashioned, a bit run-down, central, friendly, safe, and government regulated, offering good-enough-for-the-European-good-enough-for-me beds for $15 to $25 a night ($30-$50 doubles). No matter what your favorite newspaper travel writer or travel agent says, these are hard-core Europe: fun, cheap, and easy to find.

What's a Cheap Room?

A typical cheap room in Europe (a one-star, $30 double in Paris, a $40 simple guest house-type hotel double in Germany, a $25 double for a pension in Madrid, or a $50 room in a mission-owned hotel in Oslo) is very basic. It has a simple bed (often old and saggy, so always check), a rickety, pre-World War II or plastic new chair and table, a freestanding closet, small window, old wallpaper, good sink under a neon light, mysterious bidet, view of another similar room across a tall, thin courtyard, peeling plaster, and a tiled or wood floor. Rooms often come with a continental breakfast (usually served from about 7:30 to 10:00 in the breakfast room near the front desk), which includes coffee, tea or hot chocolate, and a roll (that's firmer than your mattress and long enough). The light fixtures are very simple, often with a weak and sometimes even bare and dangling ceiling light bulb. Some travelers BYOB when they travel. A higher wattage kills a lot of dinginess. Naked neon is common in the south. You won't have a TV or telephone, and, while more and more European hotels are squeezing boat-type prefab showers and toilets into their rooms, the cheapest rooms give you only a W.C. and shower or tub down the hall, which you share with a half-dozen other rooms.

Although the rooms themselves lack en suite facilities, in the lobby there is nearly always a living room with a good TV, a couple of phone booths, and a man at the desk who is at your service and a good information source. You'll climb lots of stairs, as its lack of an elevator is often the only reason a cheap hotel can't raise its prices. You'll be given a front-door key because the desk is not staffed all night.

The bottom-of-the-line European hotel ($40 doubles in the north, $25 in the south) usually has clean enough but depressing shower rooms with hot water normally free and constant (but occasionally available only through a coin-op meter or at certain hours). The W.C., or toilet, is reliably clean and has toilet paper but is often missing its lid or has a cracked or broken plastic lid. In some hotels, you pay about $2 for a towel and a key to the shower room. The cheapest hotels are run by and filled with people from what we call the Third World.

I want to stress that there are places I find unacceptable. I don't mind dingy wallpaper, climbing stairs, and "going down the hall," but the place must be clean, central, friendly, safe, quiet enough for me to sleep well, and provide good beds. The hotel described above is appalling to many Americans; it's colorful, charming, or funky to others. It's good enough for Europeans, luxurious compared to the rest of the world, and fine for me. An extra $15 or $20 per night will buy you into a cheerier class of hotel.

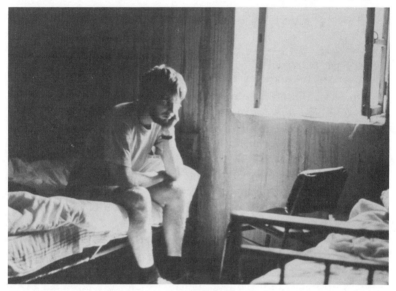

Cheap hotels aren't this bad—unless you're in eastern Turkey.

There is a real trend toward materialism throughout Europe. Land in big cities is so expensive that cheap hotels can't survive and are bought out, gutted, and turned into modern hotels. More and more Europeans are expecting what until now have been considered American standards of plumbing and comfort.

Reservations about Reservations

Reservations are a needless and expensive security blanket. They'll smother your spontaneity. Know how to manage without and make reservations only if you require a specific hotel or location or if you're hitting a crowded festival or event.

There are three problems with reservations. First, you can't see what you're getting before accepting. Second, booking ahead destroys your flexibility. Nobody knows how long they'll enjoy Paris or what the weather will be like in the Alps. Being shackled into a rigid calendar of hotel reservations all summer is a crushing blow to the spontaneity and independence that make travel such good living. And third, reservations are more expensive than playing it by ear. Through my agent, it was impossible to book a room in Madrid for less than $80. I'm sure it would have been a fine room, but I don't have $80 for a fine room. I went on my own and had no trouble finding a double for $30. Your agent is telling you the truth when she says there's nothing available, or "This is the cheapest room possible." But she's been taught to think all of Madrid is listed in her little book. Not so! Pedro's Pension never made it in any American travel agency's book of accommodations. You must have the courage and spirit to go there bedless and find it yourself.

Making Reservations

When you know where you want to stay and exactly which day, a reservation is a great idea. To make a long-distance reservation, call first ($1 a minute from the United States) to check on availability. If they have a room, send a signed traveler's check for $50 (most hotels require the first night to be paid in full; this is close enough). They can hold the check until you arrive and pay with local cash if you leave the "pay to" line blank. Include four international reply coupons (from your post office) and request a written confirmation. Allow a month for the round-trip correspondence. List clearly the number of beds, nights of arrival, and how many nights you'll stay. More and more, hotels are taking your credit card number for a deposit, which makes things quick and easy. (Still, request a written confirmation.)

If, after several calls, it seems that every hotel in town is full, don't panic. Hotels only take so many long-distance advance reservations. They never know how long guests will stay and like to keep a few beds for their regulars. The best time to make a telephone reservation is from 8:00 to 10:00 on the morning you plan to arrive. This is when the receptionist knows exactly who's leaving and which rooms he needs to fill and is eager to get a name on every available room. Those who are there in person are also more likely to land a room. Some very cheap hotels take no reservations at all. Just show up and sleep with your money belt on.

Remember, a hotel prefers a cash deposit with reservations unless there's not enough time to mail it in. In this case, most hotels will hold a room if you promise to arrive early. The earlier you promise, the better your chances of being trusted. If you'll be a little late, call again to assure them you're coming. Also, cancel if you won't make it. If someone cancels after 5:00 p.m. and the room-finding service is closed, the room will probably go unfilled that night. When that happens too often, hotel managers start to get really surly and insist on cash deposits.

Basic Bed-finding

In more than 1,500 unreserved nights in Europe, I've been shut out three times. That's a 99.8 percent bedding average earned in peak season and very often in crowded, touristy, or festive places. What's so traumatic about a night without a bed anyway? My survey shows those who have the opportunity to be a refugee for a night have their perspectives broadened and actually enjoy the experience—in retrospect.

The cost of a wonderfully reservation-free trip is the remote chance you'll end up spending the night on a bench in the train station waiting room. As in capitalism, the threat of losing gives an on-the-ball person the necessary incentive to win. Knowing the basic skills of bed-finding is much more valuable than having the best hotel list.

I'm concerned about making my readers overconfident. Every year, I travel peak season (lately with my wife and toddler), arrive in popular towns at 5:00 p.m., and manage fine by using the few tricks listed here.

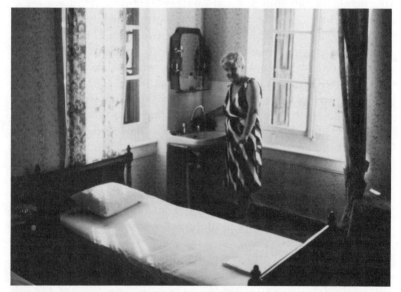

Budget hotels can be comfortable, cheery, and friendly.

1. Use hotel lists. Have a good guidebook's basic listing of hotels and budget alternatives. These lists, whose recommendations are often crowded with people using the same book, are reliable and work well. Never expect the prices to be the same. Few guidebooks have the guts to list the very least expensive options. Tourist information services usually have a better list of local hotels and alternative accommodations.

2. Use room-finding services. Popular tourist cities usually have a room-finding service at the train station or tourist information office. For a dollar or two, they'll get you a room in the price range and neighborhood of your choice. They have the complete listing of that town's available accommodations, and, especially in a big city, their service is usually well worth the price when you consider the time and money saved by avoiding the search on foot. Some are in the private service of a group of supporting hotels. Room-finding services are not above pushing you into their "favored" hotels, and kickbacks are powerful motivators. Room-finding services only give dormitory, hostel, and "sleep-in" (circus tents, gyms with mattresses on the floor, and other $3-a-night alternatives to the park or station) information if you insist. Remember, many popular towns open up hostels for the summer which are not listed in your guidebook. (If the line at the room-finding service is too long, ask someone who just got a room where they're going.)

3. Use the telephone. If you're looking on your own, telephone the places in your list that sound best. Not only will it save the time and money involved in chasing down these places with the risk of finding them full, but you're beating all the other tourists—with the same guidebook—who may be hoofing it as you dial. It's rewarding to arrive at a hotel when people are being turned away and see your name on the reservation list because you called first. If the room or price isn't what you were led to believe, you have every right to say, "No thank you." (See "Telephoning in Europe" in chap. 11.)

4. Consider hotel runners. Sometimes you'll be met by hotel runners as you step off the bus or train. My gut reaction is to steer clear, but these people are usually just hardworking entrepreneurs who lack the location or write-up in a popular guidebook that can make life easy for a small hotel owner. If you like the guy and what he promises, and the hotel isn't too far away, follow him to his hotel. You are obliged only to inspect the hotel. If it's good, take it. If it's not, leave. You're probably near other budget hotels anyway. Establish very clearly the location, as many of these people have good places stuck way out in the tules.

5. The early bird gets the room. If you anticipate crowds, go to great lengths to arrive in the morning when the most (and best) rooms are available. If the rooms aren't ready until noon, take one anyway; leave your luggage behind the desk; they'll move you in later and you're set up—free to relax and enjoy the city. I would leave Florence at 6:30 a.m. to arrive in Venice (a crowded city) early enough to get a decent choice of rooms. One of the beauties of overnight train rides is that you arrive, if not bright, at least early.

Your approach to room finding will be determined by the market situation—if it's a "buyer's market" or a "seller's market." Sometimes you'll grab anything with a pillow and a blanket. Other times you can arrive late, be selective, and even talk down the price.

When going door to door, rarely is the first place you check the best. It's worth 10 minutes of shopping around to find the going rate before you accept a room. You'll be surprised how prices vary as you walk far-ther from the station or down a street strewn with B&Bs. Never judge a hotel by its exterior or lobby. Lavish interiors with shabby exteriors are a cultural trait of Europe. (If there are two of you, let one watch the bags over a cup of coffee while the other runs around.)

6. Leave the trouble zone. If the room situation is impossible, don't struggle—just leave. An hour by car, train, or bus from the most miser-able hotel situation anywhere in Europe is a town—Dullsdorf or Nothingston—that has the Dullsdorf Inn or the Nothingston Gasthaus just across the street from the station or right on the main square. It's not full—never has been, never will be. There's a guy sleeping behind the reception desk. Drop in at 11:00 p.m., ask for 14 beds, and he'll say, "Take the second and third floors, the keys are in the doors." It always works. Oktoberfest, Cannes Film Festival, St. Tropez Running of the Girls, Easter at Lourdes—your bed awaits you in nearby Dullsdorf. If you anticipate trouble, stay at the last train stop before the crowded city.

7. Follow taxi tips. A great way to find a place in a tough situation is to let a cabbie take you to his favorite hotel. They are experts. Cabs are also handy when you're driving lost in a big city. Many times I've hired a cab, showed him that elusive address, and followed him in my car to my hotel.

8. Let hotel managers help. Have your current manager call ahead to make a reservation at your next destination. If you're in a town and having trouble finding a room, remember that nobody knows the hotel scene better than local hotel managers do. If one hotel is full, ask for help there. Often they have a list of neighborhood accommodations or will even telephone a friend who rarely fills up just around the corner. If the hotel is too expensive, there's nothing wrong with asking where you could find a "not so good place." I've always found hotel receptionists understanding and helpful.

The most expensive hotels have the best city maps (often with other hotels listed) and an English-speaking staff that can give advice to the polite traveler in search of a cheap room. You might get nowhere, but it doesn't hurt to try.

A person staying only one night is bad news to a hotel. If, before telling you whether there's a vacancy, they ask you how long you're staying, be ambiguous.

Remember, my experience is based on budget European-style situations. People who specialize in accommodating soft, rich Americans are more interested in your money than your happiness. The staffs of Europe's small hotels, guest houses, and bed and breakfast places may have no room service and offer only a shower down the hall, but they are more interested in seeing pictures of your children and helping you have a great time than in thinning out your wallet.

To Save Money, Remember . . .

Large hotels, international chains, big city hotels, and those in the north are more expensive. Prices usually rise with demand during festivals and in July and August. Off-season, try haggling. If the place is too expensive, tell them your limit; they might meet it. In Scandinavia, fancy "business hotels" are desperate in the summer and on weekends when their business customers stay away. They offer some amazing deals through the local tourist offices.

Many national governments regulate hotel prices according to class or rating. To overcome this price ceiling (especially in peak season when demand exceeds supply), hotels often require that you buy dinner and/or lunch there. Breakfast almost always comes with the room. One more meal (demi- or half-pension) or all three meals (full-pension) is usually uneconomical (although not always), since the hotel is skirting the governmental hotel price ceilings to maximize profit. I prefer the freedom to explore, experiment, and sample the atmosphere of restaurants in other neighborhoods.

Consume smart. Know the government ratings and don't stray above your needs. Hotel ratings, and therefore prices, are determined not by room quality but by hotel features—whether the reception desk stays open all night, whether there's an elevator, how classy the lobby is, the shower-to-room ratio, and age of facilities. If you can climb stairs, use the night key, manage without a TV in the room, and find a small old hotel without a modern shower in each room, you'll sleep well and save enough money to buy a memorable dinner.

Room prices vary tremendously within a hotel according to facilities provided. Most hotels have a room list clearly displayed, showing each room, its bed configuration, facilities, and price for one and for two. Also read the breakfast, tax, and extra bed policies. By studying this list, you'll see that, in many places, a shower is cheaper than a bath and a double bed is cheaper than twins. In other words, a sloppy couple who prefer a shower and a double bed can pay $20 more for a bath and twins. In some cases, if you want any room for two and you say "double," they'll think you'll only take a double bed. Be snoopy. Hotels downplay their cheap rooms.

Some hotels offer a special price for a long stay. It doesn't hurt to ask for this discount. If you came direct and point out that the Tourist Office didn't get their 10 percent, you have a better chance of talking the price down.

Avoid doing outside business through your hotel. It's much better style to go to the bullring and get the ticket yourself. You'll learn more and save money, and you won't sit with other tourists who drown your Spanish fire with Yankee-pankee. So often, tourists are herded together by a conspiracy of hotel managers and tour organizers and driven through touristy evenings—500 tourists in a gymnasium drinking cheap sangria and watching flamenco dancing on stage to the rhythm of their automatic rewinds—and leave disappointed. You can't relive your precious Madrid nights; do them right—on your own.

Check-in Procedure

Ask to see the room before accepting. Then the receptionist knows the room must pass your inspection. He'll have to earn your business. Notice the little boy is given two keys. You only asked for one room. He's instructed to show the hard-to-sell room first. If you insist on seeing both rooms, you'll get the best. Check out the rooms, and snarl at anything that deserves displeasure. The price will come down or they'll show you a better room. Think about heat and noise. I prefer climbing a few stairs to cheaper rooms higher off the noisy road. Some towns never quiet down. A room in back may lack a view, but it will also lack night noise. I accepted a bedroom without seeing it first and complained to the receptionist. He looked at me and shrugged, "Tough sheet."

When checking in, pick up the hotel's business card. In the most confusing cities, they come with a little map. Even the best pathfinders get lost in a big city, and not knowing where your hotel is can be scary. With the card, you can hop into a cab and be home in minutes.

Establish the complete and final price of a room before accepting. Know what's included and what taxes and services will be added on. More than once I've been given a bill that was double what I expected. Dinners were required and I was billed whether I ate them or not; so I was told—in very clear Italian.

When you pay is up to the hotel and you. Normally I pay upon departure. If they want prepayment, that's fine, but unless I'm absolutely certain I'll be staying on, I pay one night at a time. Don't assume your room is yours once you're in. Make it clear when you check in how long you intend to stay or you may get the boot.

If you didn't get the kind of room you wanted, ask to switch when possible. Although you don't want to be a pest, remember, hotels are in the business of accommodating people. If you need a different pillow, another blanket, mosquito netting, an electrical adapter, advice on a good restaurant or show, driving instructions for your departure, help telephoning your next hotel, and so on, be sure to ask.

Showers

Showers are a Yankee fetish. A morning without a shower is traumatic to many of us: it can ruin a day. Here are some tips on survival in a world that doesn't start and end with squeaky hair.

First of all, get used to the idea that you won't have a shower every night. The real winners are those who manage with three showers a week and a few sponge baths tossed in when needed.

Many times, you'll have a shower—but no pressure or hot water. When you check in, ask when the best time to take a hot shower is. Many have water pressure or hot water only during certain times. Heating water 24 hours a day is a luxury many of us take for granted. If a shower is important to you, take it while you can, whether you really need it or not.

Americans are notorious energy gluttons—wasting hot water and leaving lights on as if electricity is cheap. Who besides us sings in the shower or would even dream of using a special nozzle to take a hot water massage? European electric rates are shocking, and some hotels have had to put meters in their showers to survive. Fifty cents buys about five minutes of hot water. It's a good idea to have an extra token handy to avoid that lathered look. A "navy shower," using the water only to soap up and rinse off, is a wonderfully conservative method, and those who follow it will more likely enjoy some warm *wasser*. (Although starting and stopping the water doesn't start and stop the meter.) I think about half of all the cold showers Americans take in Europe were cold only because they didn't know how to turn the hot on. Study the particular system, and before you shiver, ask the receptionist for help. There are some very peculiar tricks. You'll find showers and baths of all kinds. Occasionally, the red knob is hot and the blue one is cold.

Nearly every hotel room in Europe comes with a sink and a bidet. Sponge baths are fast, easy, and European. A bidet is that mysterious porcelain (or rickety plastic) thing that looks like an oversized bedpan. Tourists use them as anything from a laundromat to a vomitorium to a watermelon rind receptacle to a urinal. They are used by locals to clean the parts of the body that rub together when they walk—in lieu of a shower. Give it the old four S's—straddle, squat, soap up, and swish off.

The cheapest hotels rarely provide a shower or toilet in your room. Each floor shares a toilet and a shower "down the hall." To such a batho-holic people, this sounds terrible. Imagine the congestion in the morning when the entire floor tries to pile into that bathtub! Remember, only Americans need a shower every morning. There are very few Americans in these "local" hotels; therefore, you've got a private bath—down the hall. I spend 100 nights a year in Europe—probably shower 80 times—and I have to wait four or five times. That's the price I pay to take advantage of Europe's simple hotels.

Many budget hotels and most dorm-style accommodations don't provide towels or soap. BYOS. Towels, like breakfast and people, get smaller as you go south. In simple places, you'll get no face towel and bath towels are not replaced every day. Hang them up to dry. In some Mediterranean countries, private baths are rare. People routinely use public baths.

I have a theory that after four days without a shower, you don't get any worse, but that's another book. If you are vagabonding or sleeping several nights in transit and would like a shower, you can buy one in train station "day hotels," at many freeway rest stops, in public baths or swimming pools, or even, if you don't mind asking, from hostels or small hotels. Most Mediterranean beaches have free, freshwater showers all the time. Otherwise, if you bunch the sheet around your neck, it's easier to get to sleep.

The Key to Keys

Tourists spend hours fumbling with old skeleton keys in rickety hotel doors. The haphazard, nothing-square construction of old hotels means the keys need babying. Don't push them in all the way. Pull the door in or up. Try a little in, quarter turn, and farther in for full turn. Always turn the top of the key away from the door to open it. Leave the key at the desk before leaving for the day. I've never had my room ripped off in Europe. Confirm closing time. Some hotels lock up after midnight.

Pensions, Zimmer, Bed and Breakfasts, and the Like

Between hotels and youth hostels or campgrounds in price and style are a special class of accommodations. These are small, warm, and family run and offer a personal touch at a budget price. They are the next best thing to staying with a local family, and even if hotels weren't more expensive, I'd choose this budget alternative.

Each country has these friendly accommodations in varying degrees of abundance. They have different names and offer slightly different facilities from country to country, but all have one thing in common: they satisfy the need for a place to stay that gives you the privacy of a hotel and the comforts of home at a price you can afford.

While information on some of the more established places is available in many budget travel guidebooks, I've always found that the best information is found locally, through tourist information offices, room-finding services, or even from the local man waiting for his bus or selling apples. Especially in the British Isles, each B&B host has a

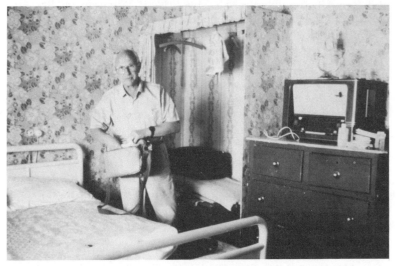

All over Europe people rent spare bedrooms to budget travelers. Bed and breakfasts give you double the cultural experience for half the price of a hotel.

network of favorites and can happily set you up in a good B&B in your next stop.

Many times, the information is brought to you. I'll never forget struggling off the bus on my arrival in Dubrovnik, Yugoslavia. Fifteen women were begging me to spend the night. Thrilled, I made a snap decision and followed the most attractive offer to a very nice, budget, Zimmer-type accommodation.

Don't confuse European bed and breakfasts with their rich cousins in America. B&Bs in the United States are doily, pretentious places, very cozy and colorful, but at least as expensive as hotels.

Britain's bed and breakfast places are the best of all. Very common throughout the British Isles, they are a boon to anyone touring England, Scotland, Wales, or Ireland. As the name indicates, a breakfast comes with the bed, and (except in London) this is no ordinary breakfast. Most women "doing B&B" take pride in their breakfasts. Their guests sit down to an elegant and very British table setting and feast on cereal, juice, bacon, sausages, eggs, broiled tomatoes, toast, marmalade, and coffee or tea, always an impressive meal. While you are finishing your coffee, the landlady (who by this time is probably on very friendly terms with you) will often present you with her guest book, pointing out the other guests from your state who have stayed in her house and inviting you to make an entry. Your hostess will sometimes cook you a simple dinner for a good price and, if you have time to chat, you'll undoubtedly get tea and biscuits. When you bid her farewell and thank her for the good sleep and full stomach, it is, more often than not, difficult to get away. Determined to fill you with as much information as food, she wants you to have the best day of sightseeing possible.

A list of recommended B&Bs is unnecessary and very likely out of date. The scene is constantly changing, with B&Bs coming and going as easily as they can put out or take in their signs. Except in big cities, the quality varies only in degrees of wonderful, and you really don't need a travel writer's particular recommendation. If you arrive by midafternoon, you won't need reservations (except in London and a few very touristy instances). I normally let the local tourist office find me a room or shop around and find it on my own near the train station or town center. I never take a B&B until I've checked out three. Styles and atmosphere vary from house to house, and besides, I enjoy looking through European homes.

Big city B&Bs are much less personal, and many have recently turned their breakfast room into another room or two and serve shrink-wrapped continental breakfasts in your room. Another sad

A special bonus when enjoying Britain's great bed and breakfasts; you get your own temporary local mother.

trend is the tourist board's new crown system, which rates, prices, and recommends places solely on their plumbing and appliances. Many small-time, easygoing proprietors have no choice but to go heavily into debt, gear up, and charge more. Mavericks don't play by the rules, don't get listed, and rely solely on their own followings.

Germany, Austria, and Switzerland call their B&B a _Zimmer Frei_ or _Privat Zimmer._ They are very common in areas popular with travelers (such as Austria's Salzkammergut Lakes District and Germany's Rhine, Romantic Road, and southern Bavaria). You'll see signs posted clearly indicating whether they have rooms (green) or not (orange). Some discourage one-night stays. Most charge from $10 to $15 per person with a hearty continental breakfast. _Pensionen_ and _Gasthäuser_ are similarly priced, small, family-run hotels.

France has a growing network of _Chambre d'Hote_ (CH) accommodations where locals, mainly in the countryside and in small towns, rent rooms for about the price of a cheap hotel ($25) but include breakfast. Some CHs post "Chambre" signs in their windows, but most are listed only through local tourist offices. While your hosts will rarely speak English, they will almost always be enthusiastic and a delight to share a home with. For longer stays in the countryside, look into France's popular network of _Gites._ Pick up regional listings at local tourist offices.

In Greece and Yugoslavia, you'll find many $8 per bed *dhomatia* and *sobe,* respectively. Especially in touristy coastal and island towns, hustlers will meet boats and buses as they come into town. In Yugoslavia, you'll often do better by avoiding the rule-laden tourist bureaus and just asking locals for sobe. Yugoslavians love to be paid in hard Western currency.

Spain and Portugal give budget travelers an intimate peak into their small-town, whitewashed worlds by renting out *quartos, camas,* and *casas particular.* In rural Iberia, where there's tourism, there are private B&B accommodations.

Italy has a number of important alternatives to its expensive hotels. *Albergo, locanda,* and *pensione* all mean simple budget beds. Private rooms, called *camere libere* or *camere affita,* are fairly common in the small towns and touristy countryside.

Scandinavia's normally luxurious B&Bs are called *rom,* or *hus rum.* At $15 per bed, these are incredibly cheap (well, not so incredibly, when you figure it's a common way for the most heavily taxed people in Europe to make a little money under the table). Unfortunately, local B&Bs are advertised only through the local tourist offices, which very often keep them a secret until all the hotels are full. Frommer's *Scandinavia on $60 a Day* and my *22 Days in Norway, Sweden, and Denmark* have some leads that can save you plenty. An evening with a Scandinavian family is a fascinating look at contemporary Nordic life. If they're serving breakfast, eat it.

Europe's 2,000 Hostels

Europe's cheapest beds are in hostels. Two thousand youth hostels provide beds throughout Europe for $3 to $10 per night.

Hostels are not hotels—not by a long shot. Many people hate hostels. Others love them and will be hostelers all their lives, regardless of their budgets. Hosteling is a philosophy. A hosteler trades service and privacy for a chance to live simply and communally with people from around the world.

A youth hostel is not limited to young people. You may be ready to jump to the next chapter because, by every other standard, you're older than young. Well, a few years ago, the Youth Hostel Association came out with a new card giving "youths" over the age of 55 a discount. People of any age can youth hostel if they have a membership card ($25 a year, less for people under 18 and over 54) available through Europe Through the Back Door, your local student travel office, or youth hostel office. (Bavaria is the only exception, with a strictly enforced 26-year-old age limit.)

One of Europe's 2,000 hostels—$3 a night, your own kitchen, a million dollar view of the Jungfrau, and lots of friends. Note the worldwide triangular hostel symbol.

A hostel provides "no frills" accommodations in clean dormitories. The average hosteler is 18 to 26, but every year there are more oldsters and families hosteling. The sexes are segregated, with 4 to 20 people packed in a room full of bunk beds. Pillows and blankets, but no sheets, are provided. You can bring a regular single bed sheet (sewn into a sack if you like), rent one each night ($2 each), or buy a regulation hostel sheet-sack at the first hostel you hit (lightweight, ideal design at a bargain price). Many hostels have a few doubles for couples and family rooms. The buildings are usually in a good, easily accessible location and come in all shapes and sizes. There are castles (Bacharach, Germany), cutter ships (Stockholm), Alpine chalets (Gimmelwald, Switzerland), huge modern buildings (Frankfurt), old tunnel-diggers' barracks (Chamonix), bomb shelters (Fribourg, Switzerland), and former royal residences (Holland Park, London).

The facilities vary, but most provide more than you would expect. Hearty, super-cheap meals are served, often in family-style settings. A typical dinner is meat and potatoes seasoned by conversation with new friends from Norway to New Zealand. The self-service kitchen, complete with utensils, pots, and pans, is a great budget aid that comes with most hostels. Larger hostels even have a small grocery store. Many international friendships rise with the bread in hostel kitchens. Very good hot showers (often with coin-op meters) are the norm, but simpler hostels have cold showers or even none at all. The hostel's recreation and living rooms are my favorite. People gather, play games, tell stories, share information, marvel at American foreign policy, read, write, and team up for future travels. Solo travelers find a family in every hostel. Hostels are ideal meeting places for those in search of a travel partner (or spouse). And those with partners do well to occasionally stay in a hostel to meet some new travelers.

And now the drawbacks. Hostels have strict rules. They lock up during the day (usually from 10:00-5:00), and they have a curfew at night (10:00, 11:00, or midnight) when the doors are locked and those outside stay there. These curfews are for the greater good—not to make you miserable. In the mountains, the curfew is early because most people are early-rising hikers. In London, the curfew is 11:45, giving you ample time to return from the theater. Amsterdam, where the sun shines at night, has a 1:45 a.m. curfew.

Many school groups (especially German) turn hostels into a teeming kindergarten. Try to be understanding (many groups are disadvantaged kids); we were all noisy kids at one time. Get to know the teacher and make a "cultural experience" out of it.

Hostel rooms can be large and packed. The first half-hour after "lights out" reminds me of Boy Scout camp—giggles, burps, jokes, and strange noises in many languages. Snoring is permitted and practiced openly.

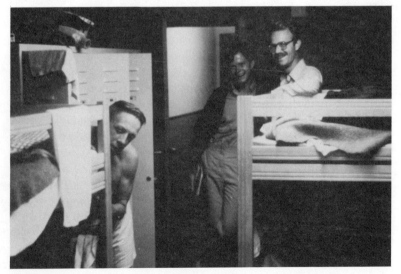

In a youth hostel, you'll have bunk beds and roommates.

Theft is a problem in hostels, but the answer is simple: don't leave valuables lying around (no one's going to steal your tennis shoes or journal). Use the storage lockers that are available in most hostels. Hostels were originally for hikers and bikers, but that isn't the case these days. Still, give your car a low profile; arriving by taxi is just plain bad taste. Traditionally, every hosteler does a chore before his card is returned to him. These duties are becoming very rare, and most remaining duties are token duties, never taking more than a few minutes.

The hostel is run by a "warden" or "house parent." They do their best to strictly enforce no-drinking rules, quiet hours, and other regulations. Some are loose and laid-back, others are like marine sergeants, but all are hostel wardens for the noble purpose of enabling travelers to better appreciate and enjoy that town or region. While they are often overworked and harried, most wardens are great people who enjoy a quiet cup of coffee with an American and are happy to give you some local travel tips or recommend a special nearby hostel. Be sensitive to the many demands on their time and never treat them like a hotel servant.

Selecting a Hostel
Hostel selectively; some hostels are ends in themselves. Survey other hostelers and hostel wardens for suggestions. I hostel much more in the north, where hostels are generally more comfortable and the savings over hotels more exciting. I rarely hostel in the south, where hostels are less common and two or three people can sleep just as cheaply in a budget hotel.

Big city hostels are the most crowded and institutional. Rural hostels, far from train lines and famous sights, are usually quiet and frequented by a more mature crowd. If you have a car, use that mobility to leave the Eurail zone and enjoy some of Europe's overlooked hostels.

Getting a hostel bed in peak season can be tricky. The most popular hostels fill up every day. Written reservations are possible, but I've never bothered. Telephone reservations work wonderfully where the warden will take them—about 50 percent of the time. I always call ahead to try to reserve and at least check on the availability of beds. Don't rely solely on the phone, because hostels are required to hold some beds for drop-ins. If you just show up, you have a much better chance of landing a bed or at least being sent to their recommended cheap alternative. Try to get there in the morning before the hostel closes. Otherwise, line up with the scruffy gang for the 5:00 opening of the office, when any remaining beds are doled out.

Thankfully, many hostels are putting out envelopes for each available bed, so you can drop by any time of day, pop your card into the reservation envelope and through the slot, and show up sometime that evening. Also, German hostels have a new telex reservation system where, for about $1, you can firmly reserve and pay for your next hostel bed before you leave the last one.

Hostel bed availability is very unpredictable. Some obscure hostels are booked out on certain days two months in advance. But I stumbled into Oberammergau one night during the jam-packed Passion Play festival and found beds for a group of eight.

The latest *International Youth Hostel Handbook*, Vol. I, is handy. That small directory, available where you get your card or at any European hostel, lists each of Europe's 2,000 hostels with which day the hostel is closed, what bus goes there, distance from the station, how many beds, its altitude, phone number with area code, and a great map locating all the hostels. Individual countries have an even more informative directory or handbook. England's is especially worthwhile.

There seem to be nearly as many unofficial or independent hostels as there are official (International Youth Hostel Federation [IYHF]) ones. Many wardens and student groups prefer to run their own show and avoid the occasionally heavy-handed bureaucracy of the IYHF. These hostels are looser and more casual but not as clean or organized.

Ireland's Independent Hostel Owners (IHO) Association is a less institutional (fewer rules, no membership required) network of these maverick independent hostels. Pick up their booklet at any IHO hostel or in Dublin (North Strand Hostel, 49 North Strand Road, tel. 01/364716).

Many large cities have wild and cheap student-run hostels that are popular with wild and cheap student travelers. If these sound right for you, *Let's Go: Europe* has great listings. In the Alps, look for the word *lager*, which means they have a loft full of $5-a-night mattresses. As in IYHF hostels, you'll usually save money if you provide your own sheets.

Camping European-style

Few Americans consider taking advantage of Europe's 10,000-plus campgrounds. Camping is the cheapest way to see Europe, the middle-class European family way to travel. And campers give it rave reviews.

"Camping" is the international word for campground. Every town has a camping with enough ground to pitch a tent or park a "caravan" (trailer), good showers and washing facilities, a grocery store and restaurant, and a handy bus connection into town, all for just a few dollars per person per night.

Unlike the picturesque, rustic American campground near a lake or forest, European camping is more functional, like spending the night in a Park-and-Ride. Campings forbid open fires, and you won't find a picturesque riverfront lot with a stove, table, and privacy. A camping is usually near or in the town—a place to sleep, eat, wash, and catch a bus downtown. They rarely fill up, and if they do, the "Full" sign usually refers to trailers (most Europeans are trailer campers). A small tent can almost always be squeezed in somewhere.

Campings are well signposted, and local tourist information offices have guides and maps listing nearby campgrounds. Every country has good and bad campgrounds. Campgrounds mirror their surroundings. If the region is overcrowded, dusty, dirty, unkempt, and generally chaotic, you're unlikely to find an oasis behind the campground's gates. A sleepy Austrian valley will most likely offer a sleepy Austrian campground.

Many campgrounds offer "bungalows" with four to six beds. These are very comfortable and much cheaper than hotels. Scandinavian bungalows are especially popular.

Camping with kids has many advantages. A family sleeps in a tent a lot cheaper than in a hotel. There's plenty to occupy children's attention, including playgrounds that come fully equipped with European kids. As your kids make European friends, your campground social circle will widen.

European campgrounds have great, if sometimes crowded, showers and washing facilities. Hot water, as in many hostels and hotels, is metered and you'll learn to carry coins and "douche" quickly.

European tenters appreciate the in-camp grocery store, café, and restaurant. The store, while high priced, stays open longer than most, offering latecomers a budget alternative to the restaurant. The restaurant or café is a likely camp "hangout," and Americans enjoy mixing in this easygoing European social scene. I've scuttled many nights on the town so I wouldn't miss the fun with new friends right in the camp. Camping, like hosteling, is a great way to meet Europeans. If the campground doesn't have a place to eat, you'll find one nearby.

Silence reigns in European campgrounds after the 10:00 or 11:00 p.m. curfew. Noisemakers are dealt with strictly. Many places close the gates to cars after 10:00. If you do arrive after the office closes, set up quietly and register in the morning.

Campgrounds, unlike youth hostels, are remarkably theft-free. "Campings" are full of basically honest middle-class European families, and someone's at the gate all day. Most people just leave their gear zipped inside their tents.

Prices vary from country to country and within countries according to facilities and style. Expect to spend $2 to $5 per night per person. You'll often pay by the tent, so four people in one tent sleep cheaper than four individual campers. (Beware: Italian campgrounds can be shockingly expensive.) Camp registration is easy. As with most hotels, you show your passport, fill out a short form, and learn the rules. Checkout time is usually noon. English is the second language of campings throughout Europe, and most managers will understand the monoglot American.

The International Camping carnet, a kind of international campground membership card, is required at some sites, handy at others. It is available for $25 through the National Campers and Hikers Association, Inc. (4804 Transit Road, Bldg. 2, Depew, NY 14043, tel. 716/668-6242; purchase includes membership in NCHA, a handy resource for campers) or at many European campgrounds. The Carnet will get you an occasional discount or preferential treatment in a very crowded situation. Sometimes you are required to leave either your passport or your camping carnet at the office.

European sites called weekend campings are rented out on a yearly basis to local urbanites. Too often, weekend sites are full or don't allow what they call "stop-and-go" campers (you). Camping guidebooks indicate which places are the "weekend" types.

Even if you don't have a car or trailer but are a camper at heart, camping may still be the way to go. Europe's campgrounds mix well with just about any mode of transportation. Tent and train is a winning combination for many. Nearly every train station has a tourist office nearby. Stop by and pick up a map with campgrounds marked, local camping leaflets, and bus directions. In most cases, buses shuttle campers from station to campground with ease. Every station has lockers, in which those with limited energy can leave unneeded baggage. (Very light modern camp gear makes camping without a car easier than ever.) Lenore Baken's *How to Camp Europe by Train* is a popular guide on this subject. The *Let's Go* guide gives good instructions on getting to and from the campgrounds.

Hitchhikers find camping just right for their tender budget. Many campgrounds are located near the major road out of town, where long rides are best snared. Any hitching camper with average social skills can find a friend driving his way with an empty seat. A note on the camp bulletin board can be very effective.

Tents and bikes also mix well. Bikers enjoy the same we-can-squeeze-one-more-in status as hikers and are rarely turned away.

Camping by car is my favorite combination. A car carries all your camp gear and gets you to any campground fast and easy. Good road maps always pinpoint "campings," and when you're within a few blocks, the road signs take over. In big cities, the money you save on parking alone will pay for your camping. I usually take the bus downtown, leaving the car next to my tent.

Commit yourself to a camping trip or to a no-camping trip and pack accordingly. Don't carry a sleeping bag and a tent just in case.

Your camping trip deserves first-class equipment. Spend some time and money outfitting yourself before your trip. There are plenty of stores with exciting new gear and expert salespeople to get you up to date in a hurry. European campers prefer a very lightweight "three-season" sleeping bag (consult a climate chart for your probable bedroom temperature) and an ensolite closed-cell pad to insulate and soften your bed. A camp stove is right for American-style camping but probably not your cup of tea in Europe. Start without a stove. If you figure you need one, buy one there. In Europe, it's much easier to find fuel for a European camp stove than for its Yankee counterpart. (If you take one from home, it should be the _gaz_ variety.) I kept it simple, picnicking and enjoying food and fun in the campground restaurant. (For a good catalog full of camping gear, call the REI cooperative at 1-800-426-4840.)

Informal camping, or "camping wild," is legal in most of Europe. Low-profile, pitch-the-tent-after-dark-and-move-on-first-thing-in-the-morning free camping is usually allowed even in countries where it is technically illegal. Use good judgment, and don't pitch your tent informally in carefully controlled areas such as cities, resorts, or Eastern European states.

It's a good idea to ask permission when possible. In the countryside, a landowner will rarely refuse a polite request to borrow a patch of land for the night.

Many cities, especially in France, allow camping in local stadiums. Formal camping is safer than camping wild. Never leave your gear and tent unattended without the gates of a formal campground to discourage thieves.

There are several good camping guidebooks out. The comprehensive _Europa Camping and Caravanning_ is available in many bookstores. _Gypsying After 40_ (Robert W. Harris, from John Muir Publications) is full of practical and ingenious ideas and guidance on self-discovery and adventure. Each country's national tourist office in the United States can send you information on camping in its country.

Sleeping Free

There are still people traveling in Europe on $5 a day. The one thing they have in common (apart from B.O.) is that they sleep free. If even cheap pensions and youth hostels are too expensive for your budget, you too can sleep free. I once went 29 out of 30 nights without paying for a bed. It's neither difficult nor dangerous, but it's not always comfortable, convenient, or legal, either. This is not a vagabonding guide, but any traveler may have an occasional free night. Faking it until the sun returns can become, at least in the long run, a good memory.

Europe has plenty of places to throw out your sleeping bag. Some large cities, such as Amsterdam and Athens, are flooded with tourists during peak season, and many of them spend their nights dangerously in a city park. Some cities enforce their "no sleeping in the parks" laws only selectively. Away from the cities, in forests or on beaches, you can pretty well sleep where you like. I have found that summer nights in the Mediterranean part of Europe are mild enough that I am comfortable with just my jeans, sweater, and hostel sheet. I no longer lug a sleeping bag around Europe, but if you'll be vagabonding a lot, bring a light bag.

Trains and stations are great for sleeping free. On the trains, success hinges on getting enough room to stretch out, and that can be quite a trick. See the section on sleeping on trains in the train transportation chapter.

When you have no place to go for the night in a city, you can always retreat to the station for a free, warm, safe, and uncomfortable place to spend the night (assuming the station stays open all night). Most popular tourist cities in Europe have stations whose concrete floors are painted nightly with a long rainbow of sleepy campers. This is allowed, but everyone is cleared out at dawn before the normal rush of travelers converges on the station. In some cases, you'll be asked to show a ticket. Any ticket or your Eurailpass entitles you to a free night in a station's waiting room: you are simply waiting for your early train. Whenever possible, avoid the second-class lounges; sleep with a better breed of hobo in first-class lounges.

It's tempting but quite risky to sleep in a train car that's just sitting there going nowhere. No awakening is ruder than having your bedroom jolt into motion and roll toward God-knows-where, although many would argue it's more pleasant to sleep on a train to God-knows-where than to be stuck in the station all night. If you do find a parked train car to sleep in, check to see when it's scheduled to leave. Some Eurailers get a free if disjointed night by riding a train out for four hours and catching one back in for another four hours.

An airport is a large, posh version of a train station, offering a great opportunity to sleep free. After a late landing, I crash on a comfortable sofa rather than waste sleeping time looking for a place that will sell me a bed for the remainder of the night. I usually spend the night before a very early flight in the airport as well. Many cut-rate inter-European flights leave or arrive at ungodly hours. The Frankfurt airport is served conveniently by the train and is great for sleeping free—even if you aren't flying anywhere.

Imaginative vagabonds see Europe as one big free hotel (barns, churches, buildings under construction, ruins, college dorms, etc.). Just carry your passport with you, attach your belongings to you so they don't get stolen, and use good judgment in your choice of a free bed.

Friends and Relatives

There is no better way to really enjoy a strange country than as the guest of a local family. And, of course, a night with a friend or relative is very easy on the budget. I've had nothing but good experiences (and good sleep) at my "addresses" in Europe. There are two kinds of addresses: European addresses brought from home and those you pick up while traveling.

Before you leave, do some research. Dig up some European relatives. No matter how far out on the family tree they are, unless you are a real

The Europeans you visit don't need to be next of kin. This Tirolean is the father of my sister's ski teacher. That's close enough.

jerk, they're tickled to have an American visitor. I send mine a card announcing my visit to their town and telling them when I'll arrive. They answer with "Please come visit us" or "Have a good trip." It is obvious from their letter (or lack of one) if I'm invited to stop by.

Follow the same procedure with indirect contacts. I have dear "parents away from home" in Austria and London. My Austrian "parents" are really the parents of my sister's ski teacher. In London, they are the parents of a friend of my uncle. Neither relationship was terribly close—until I visited. Now we are friends for life.

This is not cultural freeloading. Both parties benefit from such a visit. Never forget that a Greek family is just as curious and interested in you as you are in them (and the same old nightly family meals are probably pretty boring). Equipped with hometown postcards and pictures of my family, I make a point to give as much from my culture as I am taking from the culture of my host. In this sort of cultural intercourse there are only winners. I insist on no special treatment, telling my host that I am most comfortable when no fuss is made over me. I try to help with the chores, I don't wear out my welcome, and I follow up each visit with postcards to share the rest of my trip with my friends. I pay or reimburse my hosts for their hospitality only with a thank-you letter from home, possibly with color prints of me with their family.

The other kind of address is one you pick up during your travels. Exchanging addresses is almost as common as a handshake in Europe. If you have a business or personal card, bring a pile. When people meet, they invite each other to visit. I warn my friend that I may very well show up some day at his house, whether it's in Osaka, New Zealand, New Mexico, or Dublin. When I have, it's been a good experience.

Servas

Servas is a worldwide organization that sets up travelers with host families in hopes of building world peace through international understanding. Participants pay $45 to join, open their homes up to travelers, and can stay for two nights (more only if invited; arrangements are made after an exchange of letters—no money changes hands) in homes of other members around the world. This is not a crash-pad exchange. It's cultural sightseeing through a real live-in experience, a cultural exchange—so plan to hang around to talk and share and learn. Many travelers swear by Servas as the only way to really travel and build a truly global list of friends. For more information, write to Servas at 11 John St., #706, New York, NY 10037, tel. 212/267-0252.

House Swapping

Many families enjoy a great budget option year after year. They trade houses (sometimes cars, too, but draw the line at pets) with someone at the destination of their choice. Ask your travel agent for information or read Arthur Frommer's _Swap and Go_ guide to house swapping.

Eating Cheap

Many vacations revolve around great restaurant meals and for good reason. Europe serves some of the world's top cuisine—at some of the world's top prices.

I'm no gourmet, so most of my experience lies in eating well cheaply. Galloping gluttons thrive on $10 a day—by picnicking. Those with a more refined palate and a little more money can mix picnics with satisfying, atmospheric, and enjoyable restaurant meals and eat just fine for $15 a day.

This $15-a-day budget includes a $3 continental breakfast (usually figured into your hotel bill), a $3 to $5 picnic midday feast, and an $8 to $10 good and filling restaurant dinner (with no wine or dessert).

European restaurant meals are about as expensive as those in the United States. The cost of eating is determined not by the local standard but by your personal standard. Many Americans can't find an edible meal for less than $20 in their hometown. Their neighbors enjoy eating out for half that. If you can enjoy a $10 meal in Boston, Detroit, or Seattle, you'll eat well in London, Rome, or Helsinki for the same price.

Forget the scare stories. People who spend $50 for a dinner in Dublin and complain either enjoy complaining or are fools. Let me fill you in on filling up in Europe.

Restaurants

Restaurants are the most expensive way to eat. They can rape, pillage, and plunder a tight budget, but it would be criminal to pass through Europe without sampling the local specialties served in good restaurants. Experience every country's high cuisine; it's just as important culturally as its museums.

When I splurge on a restaurant meal (about once a day—less in the expensive north and more in the cheaper Mediterranean countries), I want good value. Average tourists are attracted—like flies to cow pies—to the biggest neon sign that boasts, "We speak English and accept credit cards." Wrong! The key to finding a good meal is to find a restaurant filled with loyal, local customers enjoying themselves. After a few days in Europe, you'll have no trouble telling a local hang-out from a tourist trap. Take advantage of local favorites.

Restaurants listed in your guidebook are usually fine, but too often when a place becomes famous this way it goes downhill. You don't need those listings to find your own good restaurant. Leave the tourist center and stroll around until you find a happy crowd of locals eating. Ask your hotel receptionist, or even someone on the street, for a good place—not a good place for tourists but a place they'd take a local guest.

European restaurants post their menus outside. Check the price and selection before entering. If the menu's not posted, ask to see one.

A fun neighborhood restaurant; no English menus, no credit cards, but good food, good prices, and a friendly chef.

Deciphering the Menu

Finding the right restaurant is half the battle. Then you need to order a good meal. Ordering in a foreign language can be fun, or it can be an ordeal. Ask for an English menu—if nothing else, you might get the waiter who speaks the goodest English. Most waiters can give at least a very basic translation—pork, chicken, zuppa, green salat, and so on. A pocket phrase book or menu reader (especially the handy little

Marling Menu Masters) is very helpful for those who want to avoid ordering sheep stomach when all they want is a lamb chop.

If you don't know what to order, go with the waiter's recommendation or look for your dream meal on another table and order by pointing. You can't go wrong. People are usually helpful and understanding to the poor monoglot tourist. If they aren't, you probably picked a place that sees too many of them. Europeans with the most patience with tourists are the ones who rarely deal with them. People who agonize over each word on the menu season the whole experience with stress. Get a basic idea of what's cooking, have some fun with the waiter, be loose and adventurous, and just order something.

To max out culturally, I never order the same meal as my partner. We share, sampling twice as many dishes. My groups cut every dish into bits and our table becomes a lazy susan. If anything, the waiters are impressed by our interest in their food, and very often they'll run over with a special treat for all of us to sample—like squid eggs.

I like to order a high-risk and a low-risk meal with my partner. At worst, we learn what we don't like and split the veal and fries. Meals don't always come simultaneously, and in Europe, it's fine to eat when served. If you're eating alone, fight the loneliness by bringing something to read.

The menu turistico (tourist menu), prix fixe menu, or menu du jour is very popular and normally a good value. For a set price, you get the "special of the day" multicourse meal complete with bread, service, and sometimes wine. Often you can choose from several appetizers and entrées. When I'm lazy and the price is right, I go for it, and it usually turns out OK. But you'll notice people in the know (locals) order à la carte.

The best values in European entrées are fish, veal, and chicken. Drinks (besides wine in France and Italy, which is very reasonable) and desserts are the worst value. Skipping those, I can enjoy some surprisingly classy meals for $10.

Although fast food has gained a foothold in Europe, a real Continental meal is a leisurely experience, the focus of the evening. In a good restaurant, service will be slower, and you won't get your bill until you ask for it. A European meal is an end in itself. Europeans will spend at least two hours enjoying a good dinner and, for the full experience, so should you.

To get the bill, you'll have to ask for it (catch the waiter's eye and, with raised hands, scribble with an imaginary pencil on your palm). Before it comes, make a mental tally of roughly how much your meal should cost. The bill should vaguely resemble the figure you expected. It should have the same number of digits. If the total is a surprise, ask to have it itemized and explained. All too often, waiters make the same "innocent" mistakes repeatedly, knowing most tourists are so befuddled by the money and menu that they'll pay whatever number lies at the bottom of the bill.

Fast-food places are everywhere. Yes, the Hamburgerization of the world is a shame, but face it—the busiest McDonald's in the world is in Tokyo, the biggest is in Rome, and the burger is becoming a global thing. You'll find Big Macs in every language—not exciting (and double the American price), but at least at McDonald's you know exactly what you're getting—and it's fast. A hamburger, fries, and shake are fun halfway through your trip. Each country has its equivalent of the hamburger or hot dog stand. Whatever their origin, they're a hit with the young locals and a handy place for a quick, cheap bite.

Self-service is an international word. You'll find self-service restaurants in big cities everywhere offering low-price, low-risk, low-stress, what-you-see-is-what-you-get meals. A sure value for your dollar, franc, or shilling is a department store cafeteria. These places are designed for the shopping housewife who has a sharp eye for a good value, and that's what you'll get—good values and housewives with sharp eyes.

Tipping

I'm not known for flashy tipping (in fact, I think it's an archaic way of paying people), and tipping is a minuscule concern of mine during a European trip. Front-door travel agents advise going to Europe armed with dollar bills for tipping. They'll advise putting five bucks under your pillow to get extra towels from the maids. Traveling through the Back Door, the only tipping you'll do is in the rare restaurant where service isn't included, rounding the taxi bill up, or when someone assists me in seeing some sight and is paid no other way (such as the man who shows people an Etruscan tomb that just happens to be in his backyard).

In restaurants, a service charge of about 15 percent is usually included in the menu price or added automatically to your bill. If that's the case, a tip is not expected. (It should say so on the menu or bill; e.g., *service compris* for included, or *service non compris*.) Rounding up the bill (less than 5%) is a nice touch for good service. Overtipping is Ugly-American. Americans in the days of the big buck shaped an image that Yankees in the days of the smaller dollar are having a hard time living down. If your bucks talk at home, muzzle them in Europe. As a matter of principle, if not economy, the local price should prevail. Don't overtip.

Local Specialties, One Country at a Time

Greece

The menus are all Greek to me. It is common and accepted for you to go into the kitchen and physically point to the dish you want. This is a good way to make some friends, sample from each kettle, get what you want (or at least know what you're getting), and have a very memorable meal. (The same is true in Turkey.) Be brave; try the local food. My favorite Greek snack is a tasty shish kebab in a muffin—called a souvlaki pita. Souvlaki stands are all over Athens. On the islands, eat fresh seafood and the creamy yogurt with honey. The feta (goat) cheese salads and the flaky nut 'n honey dessert called baklava are two other taste treats.

If possible, go to a wine festival. The Dafni Wine Festival (nightly mid-July through August, $2 entry, buses from downtown Athens, fine campground right there) just outside of Athens is best. Retsina is a pine resin-flavored wine that is a dangerous taste to acquire. Eat when the locals do—late. For American-style coffee, order "Nescafe."

Italy

Italy is no longer so cheap. In fact, it's caught up with and passed much of Europe in price. Florence, Venice, and Rome are most expensive.

Italians eat huge meals consisting of a first course of pasta, a second plate of meat plus a salad, fruit and wine. The pasta course alone is enough to fill the average tourist. While some restaurants won't serve just pasta, for a cheap meal I find one that will and enjoy reasonably priced lasagna or minestrone and a salad. Anytime you sit down, you'll be charged a cover (*coperto*) charge of a dollar or two. That, plus service, makes even a cheap, one-course restaurant meal close to $10.

For inexpensive Italian eateries, look for the term *osteria, tavola calda, rosticceria, trattoria, pizzeria,* or, recently, "self-service." A big pizza (everywhere for $4) and a cold beer is my idea of a good, fast, cheap Italian meal. Look for a "Pizza Rustica" (which serves pizza by the slice sold by weight) for a stand-up super bargain meal. Just point to the best-looking pizza and tell them how much you want; they heat it up and it's yours.

Piatti del giorno (plate of the day), *pane e coperto* (charge for bread and cover), and *servizio compreso* (service included) are three important phrases to know. But the most important word in your Italian vocabulary is *gelato*—probably the best ice cream you'll ever taste. A big cone or cup with a variety of flavors costs about $2.

Gelati! Delizioso! Say "lick a little Italy" three times to get your tongue in shape.

Cappuccino—rich coffee with a frothy head of steamed milk—is everywhere, and it should be. Tiny coffee shops are tucked away on just about every street. All have a price list, and most have a system where you pay the cashier first and take the receipt to the man with the drinks. Experiment; try coffee- or tea-*freddo* (cold) or a *frappe*. Discover a new specialty each day. Bars sell large bottles of cold mineral water, with or without gas, for about $1. *Panini* (sandwiches) are widely available and cheap.

Bar-hopping is fun. A bottle of wine serves four or five people for four dollars, and most bars have delicious *cicheti* (pronounced cheh-KAY-tee), local toothpick munchies. A *cicheteria* is a great place for an entire meal of these pint-sized taste treats.

Spain

The greatest pleasure in Spanish eating is the price tag. Take advantage of the house wine. Fit the local schedule—lunch late (noon-3:00) and dinner later (8:30-11:30). Restaurants are generally closed except at mealtimes. At other times, bars and coffee spots serve snacks of *bocadillos* (sandwiches) and *tortillas* (omelets) along with *tapas* (hors d'oeuvres). On my last trip, I found myself eating at least one easy, quick, and very cheap tapa meal a day. Restaurants associated with bars are often excellent and inexpensive.

Portugal
Portugal has some of the best and cheapest food I've found in Europe. Find a local sailors' hangout and fill up on fresh seafood, especially clams and cockles. While Portuguese restaurants are not expensive, food stands in the fairs and amusement parks are even cheaper. _Vinho verde_ (green wine) is an addictive local specialty and a favorite of visiting wine buffoons.

Switzerland
A fondue is a must. Order a steak-and-potatoes dish and a cheese fondue for two people. _Rösti_ (a sort of hash browns with onions dish) is a good budget standby. Swiss chocolates are deservedly famous. The Migros and Co-op grocery stores sell groceries for about the same price as you'd find in American stores—cheap by European standards. Youth hostels usually serve large family-style dinners at a low, low price. Expensive Swiss restaurant prices make these budget food alternatives especially attractive. The remote mountain huts offer more than shelter. Eat there. Many have provisions helicoptered in, are reasonably priced, and bubble with Alpine atmosphere. Swiss wine (Fendant) is expensive and worth every franc. Local beer is cheap and good.

The Netherlands
My favorite Dutch food is Indonesian. Indonesia, a former colony of the Netherlands, fled the nest, leaving behind plenty of great Indonesian restaurants. The cheapest meals, as well as some of the best splurges, are found in Holland's many Indonesian (or "Chinese-Indish") restaurants. The famous _rijstafel_ (rice table) is the ultimate Indonesian meal, with as many as 36 delightfully exotic courses, all eaten with rice. One meal is plenty for two, so order carefully.

In a small town restaurant a rijstafel can be a great bargain—12 exotic courses with rice for $8. _Bami_ or _nasi goring_ are smaller, cheaper, but still filling versions of rijstafel.

Scandinavia
Most Scandinavians avoid their highly taxed and very expensive restaurants. The key to budget eating in Nordic Europe is to take advantage of the smorgasbord. For about $8 (cheap in Scandinavia), the breakfast smorgasbords of Denmark, Norway, and Sweden will fill you with plenty of hearty food. Smorgasbords do not provide doggie bags, but I have noticed many empty rucksacks (or zip-lock baggies) filling out as fast as their owners. Since my stomach is the same size all day

long and both meals are, by definition, all-you-can-eat, I opt for the budget breakfast meal over the fancier and more expensive ($20) *middag*, or midday, smorgasbord.

Many train stations and boats serve smorgasbords. The boat from Stockholm to Helsinki, Bergen's Hotel Norge, and, best of all, the lovely Centralens restaurant right in the Stockholm train station each serve up especially good smorgasms. No seasoned traveler leaves the Stockholm station after his overnight train ride from Oslo or Copenhagen without enjoying a smorgasbord breakfast in its restaurant.

For a smaller budget meal in Denmark, find a Smorrebrod (open-face sandwich) shop. A delightful alternative to a fast-food joint, these places make artistic and delicious picnics to go.

Kro restaurants in Denmark and Bundeheimen (literally, "farmer's house") found all over Norway serve, as their name suggests, good, hearty, "meat-and-potatoes" meals that a peasant would like and could almost afford. Keep your eyes peeled for daily lunch specials called *dagens ratt*. Alcohol-free restaurants enjoy a special tax status and can serve cheaper meals. And you can normally have all the vegetables (normally potatoes) you want when you order a restaurant's entrée. Just ask for seconds. The cheapest cafeterias often close at 5:00 or 6:00 p.m. Fresh produce, colorful markets, and efficient supermarkets abound in Europe's most expensive corner. Picnic.

Germany
Germany is ideal for the "meat-and-potatoes" person. With straightforward, no-nonsense food at budget prices, I eat very well in Deutschland. Small-town restaurants serve up wonderful plates of hearty local specialties for around $7. The wurst is the best anywhere, and kraut is entirely different from the sour stuff you hate at home. Eat ugly things whenever possible. So many tasty European specialties come in gross packages.

Drink beer in Bavaria and wine on the Rhine, choosing the most atmospheric brauhaus or weinstube possible.

Browse through supermarkets and see what Germany eats when there's no more beer and pretzels. Try Gummi Bears, a bear-shaped jelly bean with a cult following, and Nutella, a choco-nut spread that can turn anything into a first-class dessert. Fast-food stands are called Schnell-imbiss. For budget relief in big city Germany, find a Greek, Turkish, or Italian restaurant.

France
France is famous for its cuisine—and rightly so. Dining in France can be surprisingly easy on a budget, especially in the countryside. Small

restaurants throughout the country love their local specialties and take great pride in serving them. Wine is the cheapest drink, and every region has its own wine and cheese. Order the house wine in a carafe. Bars serve reasonable omelettes, salads, and the *croque monsieur*—your standard grilled cheese and ham sandwich. The *Plat du jour* is a good value, and to afford a classy restaurant, remember lunch is the same food at substantially reduced prices.

Degustation gratuite is not a laxative but an invitation to sample the wine. You'll find "D.G." signs throughout France's wine-growing regions. When buying cheese, be sure to ask for samples of the local specialties. Croissants are served warm with breakfast, and baguettes (long, skinny loaves of French bread) are great for budget munching.

Regardless of your budget, picnic for a royal tour of French delicacies. Make a point to visit the small specialty shops and pick up the finest (most expensive) pâtés, cheeses, and hors d'oeuvres. As you spread out your tablecloth, every passerby will wish you a cheery "Bon appetit!"

French food deserves the coverage normally reserved for Europe's inedible attractions, so I've included a Back Door later in the book on French cuisine.

Mensas

When you're in a European university town, with a wallet as empty as your stomach, find a "mensa." Mensa is the universal word for a government-subsidized institutional (university, fire station, union of gondoliers, etc.) cafeteria. If the place welcomes tourists, you can fill yourself with a plate of dull but nourishing food in the company of local students or workers for an unbeatable price.

University cafeterias (often closed during summer holidays) offer a surefire way to meet educated English-speaking young locals with open and stimulating minds. They're often anxious to practice their politics and economics as well as their English on a foreign friend. This is especially handy as you travel beyond Europe.

The Continental Breakfast

In Europe (except for Britain, Holland, and Scandinavia), breakfast is a roll with marmalade or jam, occasionally a slice of ham or cheese, and coffee and tea. Even the finest hotels serve the same thing—on better plates. It's the European way to start the day. (Sorry, no Mueslix.) I supplement my CBs with a piece of fruit and a separately wrapped chunk of cheese from my rucksack stash. If you're a coffee drinker, remember this is the only cheap time to caffeinate yourself. Most hotels will serve you a bottomless cup of a rich brew only with breakfast. After that, the cups acquire bottoms. Juice is often available for free, but you have to ask, and you might be charged.

I'm a big-breakfast person at home. When I feel the urge for a typical American breakfast in Europe, I beat it to death with a hard roll. You can find bacon, eggs, and orange juice in the morning, but it's nearly always overpriced and a disappointment. Breakfast, normally "included" in your hotel bill, can sometimes be skipped and deducted from the price of your room. Ask what it includes and costs. You can usually save money and gain atmosphere by buying a coffee and roll or croissant at the café down the street or by brunching picnic-style in the park. Never buy breakfast in a restaurant. You'll get the same meal with a better price and more atmosphere in a bar or café.

Drinks

As I'll discuss in chapter 7, Health, European water has a different bacterial content than what our systems are accustomed to. Many people will have some problem adjusting—not because European water is dirty but because our systems are weak.

For me, the trouble involved in avoiding European water outweighs the benefits. As long as my sources are obviously for drinking, I drink the water—even in Italy, Sicily, Greece, Spain, and Portugal. Generally, avoid water in North Africa and east of Bulgaria.

In restaurants, however, even the Europeans drink bottled water (for taste, not health). Tap water is not normally served (except in France). You can get free tap water, but you'll need to be polite, patient, and inventive and know the correct phrase. There's nothing wrong with ordering tap water (I often do), and waiters are accustomed to this American request. But it is a special favor, and while your glass or carafe of tap water is often served politely, occasionally it just isn't worth the trouble and it's best to just put up with the bottle of Perrier or order a drink from the menu.

Tap water in five languages
Italian—*l'agua di rubinetto*
French—*l'eau du robinet*
German—*Leitungswasser*
Spanish—*agua del grifo*
Portuguese—*agua a torneira*

Bottled water is usually quite cheap, served crisp and cold, either with or without carbonation and usually with happier waiters. Most tourists don't like the bubbly stuff. Learn the phrase (*con/avec/mit/*with gas or _senza/sans/ohne/_without gas in Italian/Spanish, French, German, and English, respectively, will get the message across). Acquire a taste for acqua con gas. It's a lot more fun (and read on the label what it'll do for your rheumatism).

In all other languages, just do the international charade: hold imaginary glass in left hand; turn on tap with right; make sound of faucet. Stop it with a click and drink it with a smile.

If your budget is tight and you want to save $5 a day, never buy a restaurant drink. Scoff if you have the money, but remember—the drink is, along with the dessert, the worst value on any menu. Water is jokingly called "the American champagne" by the waiters of Europe.

Drink like a European. Cold milk, coffee with rather than after your meal, orange juice, and ice cubes are American habits, either overpriced or nonexistent in European restaurants. Insisting on cold milk, tap water, or ice cubes will get you nothing but strange looks and a reputation as the ugly—if not downright crazy—American. Order local drinks, not just to save money but to experience that part of the culture and to get the best quality and service. The "American waters" (Coke, Fanta, and 7-Up) are sold everywhere. Orange juice fans pick up the liter ($1) boxes in the grocery store and start the day with a glass in their hotel room.

Buying local alcohol is much cheaper than insisting on your favorite import. A shot of the local hard drink in Portugal should cost 50 cents, while an American drink would cost several dollars. Drink the local stuff with the local people in the local bars; a better experience altogether than a gin and tonic in your hotel with a guy from Los Angeles. Drink wine in wine countries and beer in beer countries. Sample the local specialties. Let a local person order you her favorite. You may hate it, but you'll never forget it.

Seek out and eat, at least once, the notorious "gross" specialties— lutefisk, ouzo, horse meat, snails, and so on. All your life you'll hear references to them, and you'll have actually experienced what everyone's talking about.

Picnic—Spend Like a Pauper, Eat Like a Prince

There is only one way left to feast for $3 or $4 anywhere in Europe— picnic. I am a picnic connoisseur. (After four months in Europe, the first thing I do when I get home is put some cheese on a hard roll.) I think I eat better while spending $10 to $15 a day less than those who eat exclusively in restaurants.

While I am the first to admit that restaurant meals are an important aspect of any culture, I picnic almost daily. This is not solely for budgetary reasons. I love to dive into a marketplace and actually get a chance to do business. I can't get enough of Europe's varied cheeses, meats, fresh fruits, vegetables, and still-warm-out-of-the-bakery-oven bread. Many of my favorite foods made their debut in a European picnic. I pride myself in my ability to create unbeatable atmosphere for a meal by choosing just the right picnic spot.

I don't like to spend a lot of time looking for a decent restaurant, then waiting around to get served. And nothing frustrates me more than to tangle with a budget-threatening menu, finally order a meal, then walk away feeling unsatisfied, knowing my money could have done much more for my stomach if I had invested it in a marketplace. So, let me talk a bit about picnicking.

Every town, large or small, has at least one very colorful outdoor marketplace. Assemble your picnic here. The unit of measure throughout the Continent is a kilo, which is 2.2 pounds. A kilo has 1,000 grams. One hundred grams (a common unit of sale, in Italy called *un etto*) of cheese or meat tucked into a chunk of French bread gives you about a quarter-pounder. Make an effort to communicate with the merchants in the markets. Know what you are buying and what you are spending.

Most markets are not self-service. Point to what you want, and let the merchant bag it up and weigh it for you. But you may want only one or two pieces of fruit and many merchants refuse to deal in such small quantities. The way to get what you want and no more is to estimate about what it would cost if he were to weigh it and then just hold out a coin worth about that much in one hand and the apple, or whatever, in the other. Rarely will he refuse the deal. Timidity will get you nowhere.

If no prices are posted, be wary. I've seen terrible cases of tourists getting ripped off by market merchants in tourist centers. Find places that print the prices. I suspect that any market with no printed prices has a double price standard—one for locals and a more expensive one for tourists. Watch the scale when your food is being weighed (it'll show grams, which are thousandths of a kilo). The produce is priced per kilo. So if it's "32," that means 32 francs per kilo (about $5, or $2.25 per pound), and the scale says 400, that means 4/10 of 32 francs (or $5), which is about $2. Whether you understand the numbers or not, act as though you do.

I'll never forget a friend of mine who bought two bananas for our London picnic. He grabbed the fruit, held out a handful of change, and said, "How much?" The merchant took two 50 pence coins. My friend turned to me and said, "Wow, London really is expensive." People like this go home and spread wild, misleading rumors: "Bananas sell for a

Youth hostelers picnicking on a Swiss mountaintop

buck apiece in London!" Anytime you hold out a handful of money to a banana salesman, you're just asking for trouble.

Picnic Drinks
There are plenty of cheap ways to wash down a picnic. Milk is always cheap, available in quarter, half, or whole liters. Be sure it's normal drinking milk. More than once I've been stuck with buttermilk or something I didn't want. Look for local words for whole or light, such as *voll* or *lett*. Nutritionally, half a liter provides about 25 percent of your daily protein needs. Cold milk is rare in most countries. You will often find a "long-life" kind of milk that needs no refrigeration. This milk will never go bad—or taste good.

Liter bottles of Coke are cheap, as is wine in most countries. The local wine gives your picnic a very nice touch. Fruit juice (look for 100 percent no sugar to avoid stuff that's closer to Fanta without the fizz) comes in handy boxes costing about $1 per quart. Any place that serves coffee has free boiling water. Those who have more nerve than pride get their plastic water bottle (a sturdy plastic bottle will not melt) filled with free boiling water at a café, then add their own instant coffee or tea bag later.

Picnic Atmosphere

There is nothing second class about a picnic. A few special touches will even make your budget meal a first-class affair.

Proper site selection can make the difference between just another meal and *le picnic extraordinaire.* Since you've decided to skip the restaurant, it's up to you to create the atmosphere. I try to incorporate a picnic brunch, lunch, or dinner into the day's sightseeing plans. For example, I'll start the day by scouring the thriving market with my senses and my camera. Then I fill up my shopping bag and have brunch on a riverbank. I combine lunch and a siesta in a cool park to fill my stomach, rest my body, and escape the early afternoon heat. It's fun to eat dinner on a castle wall enjoying a commanding view and the setting sun.

Picnic on the train—cheap, hearty, scenic.

To pleasantly pass time normally wasted in transit, plan a picnic meal to coincide with a train or boat ride. When you arrive, you are nourished, fat, happy, rested, and ready to go, rather than weak and in search of food. Mountain hikes are punctuated nicely by picnics. Food tastes even better on top of a mountain. Europeans are great picnickers, and I've had many a picnic become a potluck, resulting in a new friend as well as a full stomach.

Nutritionally, a picnic is unbeatable. Consider this example: 100 grams of cheese, 100 grams of thin-sliced salami, fresh bread, peaches, carrots, a cucumber, a half liter of milk, and fruit yogurt for dessert. When sandwiches get old, there are plenty of variations, such as cooked fish or roasted chicken and quiche. A pizza to go is fun. Cold cereal is a fun switch. Cornflakes can be found in any small grocery store. European yogurt is delicious and can be drunk right out of its container.

A quick dashboard picnic halfway through a busy day of sightseeing.

"Table Scraps" and Miscellaneous Tips
Bring zip-lock baggies (large and small), a little can opener, and a good knife; a dish towel serves as a small tablecloth and comes in handy. In addition to being a handy plate, fan, and a lousy frisbee, a plastic coffee can lid makes an easy-to-clean cutting board with a juice-containing lip. And a fancy hotel shower cap contains messy food nicely on your picnic cloth. Bread has always been cheap in Europe. (Leaders have learned from history that when stomachs rumble, so do the mobs in the streets.) Cheese is a specialty nearly everywhere and is, along with milk, one of Europe's cheapest sources of protein. Super-

markets hide out in the basements of big city department stores. In many countries outside of Europe, eating can be hazardous to your health. In these cases, eat only peelable fruit and vegetables. A travelers' guidebook to health or your doctor can tell you where you'll have to be careful. I don't worry in Europe. Tourists who have been in a country for a while usually know how to stay healthy and are excellent information sources.

Know where certain foods are good and reasonably priced by doing quick market surveys. For instance, tomatoes, cucumbers, and watermelons are good deals in Italy. Citrus fruits are terribly expensive (and not very good) in Eastern Europe, while the Eastern countries have some of the best and cheapest ice cream anywhere. Ice cream is costly in Scandinavia (what isn't?), and wine is a best buy in France. Anything American is usually expensive and rarely satisfying. Europeans have not yet mastered the fine art of the American hamburger, although each has its own variation on McDonald's: I saw a "MacCheap" in Switzerland.

My big meal of the day is often a picnic lunch or dinner. Only a glutton can spend more than $5 for a picnic feast. In a park in Paris, on a Norwegian ferry, high in the Alps, on your dashboard at an autobahn rest stop, on your convent rooftop, or in your hotel room, picnicking is the budget traveler's key to cheap and good eating.

Serious snackers artfully equip their hotel rooms with local drinks, munchies, even immersion heaters for hot drinks to go with the fancy pastry they picked up to eat before calling it a day.

Vegetarians

Vegetarians find life a little frustrating in Europe. Very often, Europeans think "vegetarian" means "no red meat" or "not much meat." If you are a strict vegetarian, you'll have to make things very clear. Write the appropriate phrase below on the back of a business card and show it to each waiter before ordering:

German: *Wir sind Vegetarier. Wir essen kein Fleisch, Fisch oder Geflügel. Eier und Käse OK.*

French: *Nous sommes vegetarian. Nous ne mangons pas des viandes, des poissons or des poullets. Oeuf et fromage OK.*

Italian: *Noi siamo vegetarian. Non mangiare carne, pesce o polli. Uovo e formaggio OK.*

Dutch: We are vegetarian. We do not eat meat, fish, or chicken. Eggs and cheese are OK. (Most Dutch speak English.)

Vegetarians have no problem with continental breakfasts, which are meatless anyway. Meat-free picnic lunches are delicious: bread, cheese, and yogurt are wonderful throughout Europe. It's in restaurants that your patience may be minced. Big city tourist offices list restaurants by category. Look under "V." Italy seems to sprinkle a little meat in just about everything. German cooking normally keeps the meat separate from the vegetables. Hearty German salads, with beets, cheese, and eggs, are a vegetarian's delight. Vegetarians enjoy Third World cuisine and ethnic restaurants throughout Europe.

Eating and Sleeping on a Budget—The Five Commandments

You could get eight good hours of sleep and three square meals in Europe for $20 a day if your budget required it. If your budget is tight, keep the following rules of thumb in your wallet.

1. **Minimize the use of hotels and restaurants.** Enjoying the sights and culture of Europe has nothing to do with how much you're spending to eat and sleep. Learn about and take advantage of each country's many alternatives to hotels and restaurants.

If your budget dictated, you could feel the fjords and caress the castles without hotels and restaurants—and probably learn, experience, and enjoy more than the tourist who spends in a day what you spend in a week.

2. **Budget for price variances.** Prices as much as triple from south to north. Budget more for the north and get by on less than your daily allowance in Spain, Portugal, and Greece. Exercise those budget alternatives where they'll save you the most money. A hostel saves $3 in Crete and $30 in Finland. I walk, sleep on trains, and picnic in Sweden and live like a king in the south, where my splurge dollars go the farthest. And if your trip will last only as long as your money does, travel fast in the north and hang out in the south.

3. **Adapt to European tastes.** Most unhappy people I meet in my travels could find the source of their problems in their own stubborn desire to find the United States in Europe. If you accept and at least try doing things the European way, besides saving money, you'll be happier and learn more on your trip. You cannot expect the local people to be warm and accepting of you if you don't accept them. Things are different in Europe—that's why you go. European travel is a package deal, and you have no choice but to accept the good with the "bad." If you require the comforts of home, that's where you'll be happiest.

4. Avoid the tourist centers. The best values are not in the places that boast, in neon signs, "We Speak English." Find local restaurants and hotels. You'll get more for your money. If you do follow the tourists, follow the savvy Germans, not the Japanese.

5. Swallow pride and save money. This is a personal matter, depending largely on how important pride is to you and how much money you have. Many people cringe every time I use the word "cheap"—others appreciate the directness. I'm not talking about begging and groveling around Europe. I'm talking about insisting on the room with no shower ($15 saved), drinking tap water ($3 saved), finding out the complete price before ordering anything, and saying "no thanks" if the price isn't right. Expect equal and fair treatment as a tourist; when appropriate, fight the price, set a limit, and search on. Remember, even if the same thing would cost much more at home, the local rate should prevail.

5
Finances and Money

Traveler's Checks

Smart travelers use traveler's checks. These checks function almost like cash but are replaceable if lost or stolen. Before you buy your checks, choose the best company, currency, and mix of denominations.

What company? Choose a big, well-known company—American Express, Cooks, Barclays, or Visa. Traveler's checks only cost 1 to 2 percent of their face value, and it's not worth getting obscure checks to save. Ask around; there are plenty of ways to avoid that extra charge. Any legitimate check is good at banks, but it's nice to have a well-known check that private parties and small shops will recognize and honor. (In many cases, traveler's checks get a 2% to 3% better exchange rate than cash, so they even save you money.)

Understand the refund policies and compare services provided. AmExCo is popular for its centrally located "landmark" offices, travel service, and clients' mail service—and they're free through AAA. The American Express Company has two services very helpful to people planning long-term trips or carrying lots of money. You can keep your money belt thin by using their $500 checks, which can be broken at no charge into smaller checks (in dollars) at their foreign offices. And those with AmExCo cards can travel anywhere, buying, as they go, up to $1,000 a week of traveler's checks with checks from their personal bank account from AmExCo offices abroad.

You'll hear many stories about slow or fast refunds. None of them matters. Extenuating circumstances—not the company—dictate the refund speed. If you keep your money belt tied around your waist and your brain tied to your head, you won't lose your checks, anyway. I'd choose whichever well-known company's checks I can get without the 1 to 2 percent charge through my savings bank or automobile club.

If you're only traveling in England, go with Barclays—a British bank with a branch in every town. They waive the service charge if you have their checks, saving you $2 per transaction. AmExCo does not give preferential rates or lower fees to clients exchanging their checks at their banks.

What kind of currency? Traveler's checks come in U.S. dollars, Swiss francs, British pounds, deutsche marks, and even Japanese yen. When the dollar is shaky and unpredictable, many travelers consider bailing out early and buying traveler's checks in another, more stable, currency. The problem with that, since banks always buy low and sell high, is you lose a couple of percent with this transaction, and then you lose 2 or 3 percent more when you change your strong currency into the local currency you need. The dollar does not drop drastically or predictably enough to merit this move. I get my traveler's checks in U.S. dollars for

Banks that change money normally display their buy and sell rates in the window. You always lose. Notice U.S. dollars—4% loss.

this reason and because merchants around the world generally know what their currency is worth in dollars. Besides, it's simpler for me— I think in dollars.

If my trip is mostly in one country, however, and the dollar is on a downward trend, I buy my checks in the currency of that country.

Which denominations? Large bills and small bills each have advantages and disadvantages. Large checks ($100, $500) save on signing and bulk. Small checks ($20, $50) are more exact and, in some cases, easier to cash. If you're only passing through a country, you may want just $20. If you have only $100 checks, you'll have to change back $80. (You'll be changing a total of $180 at that uniform 2 or 3% loss plus two bank fees for the privilege of spending 20 expensive dollars.) If you're out of cash and the banks are closed, it's easy to find a merchant or even another traveler who will change a $20 traveler's check. Changing a large check in such a situation would be tough.

For $1,000 in checks, I would choose three $100, ten $50, and ten $20 checks.

Remember, traveler's checks are replaceable if lost or stolen, but you must keep track of the serial numbers and know exactly which checks you've cashed. Leave a copy of all your check numbers (along with photocopies of your passport, plane ticket, and any other vital statistics) with someone at home, and carry another photocopy in your luggage and in your wallet. I update one list regularly as I cash checks. If I lose them, I'll know exactly which checks to claim.

Changing Money in Europe

Remember, it's expensive and time-consuming to change money. Estimate carefully what you'll need and get it all at once at a bank when you enter a new country.

Rather than risk having to endure another round of bank hassles and expenses on my last day in a country, I usually change a little more than I think I'll need. If I leave the country with some extra local money, I can always change that over later.

The cost of changing can be measured by the percent split between a bank's buying and selling rates, usually about 4 percent. The true value of your money lies halfway between these rates. You'll normally lose 2 percent plus their fee. If both rates aren't shown, be wary. Rather than shop for different rates, analyze the profit margin; if it's within 5 percent and the service charge is reasonable, it's fine with me.

Most banks, especially in touristy places, levy an extra service charge for each transaction. This added charge is usually higher for checks than cash, but many banks give a slightly better exchange rate for checks than cash. (They prefer traveler's checks to cash for the same reason we do.) In Norway and a few other places, they charge (up to $2) per check rather than per transaction. Have the extra charge policy explained before you start signing checks. Remember, an added cost is the time you'll spend looking for a bank and waiting in the exchange line—up to an hour in peak season madhouses like Venice.

You normally need your passport to change a check. Whenever possible, avoid the lousy exchange rates at hotels, shops, and nightclubs. Many Americans exclaim with glee, "Gee, they accept bank cards and dollars! There's no need ever to change money." Without knowing it, they're changing money every time they buy something—at a loss. Use the local money and get it at banks.

Paper money of any Western country is good at banks anywhere. If you leave Italy with paper money, that 10,000 lire note is just as convertible as dollars in any European bank or exchange office. Many people change excess local money back to dollars before they leave a country. Then they change those dollars into the next country's money. This double changing makes no sense and is expensive. It can be handy, however, to change your remaining local currency into the next country's currency before leaving a country.

Coins are generally worthless outside their country. Since $2 coins are common in Europe, exporting a pocketful of change can be an expensive mistake. Spend them (postcards, newspaper, food or drink for the train ride) or change them into paper before you cross the border. Otherwise, you've just bought a bunch of souvenirs.

Most border towns use both currencies interchangeably. For instance, waiters in Salzburg keep German money in one side of their coin bags, Austrian in the other and give a fair rate for both.

Credit cards are widely accepted throughout Europe. Plastic fans gloat that you get a better exchange rate by using your card. While this may be true, credit card users are buying from businesses that have enough slack in their prices to absorb the bank's charge for the credit card service. They're getting a better rate on a worse price. (As more and more consumers believe they are getting "free use of the bank's money," we're all absorbing the 4% the banks are making in higher purchase prices.) Credit cards work fine in Europe. But Pedro's Pension and the merchants in the market accept no plastic. You need local cash to get through the Back Door.

Be careful when you use your plastic money. Many people have been terribly ripped off. Take one. MasterCard is most widely accepted. Visa is best for cash advances (write for their free *International Travel Guide*, to Chase Visa, Box 5111, 1400 Union Turnpike, New Hyde Park, NY

11042). AmExCo is less widely accepted but popular for its extra services (for specifics, write for the _AmExCo Traveler's Companion_, 65 Broadway, New York, NY 10006, tel. 800/528-4800). You'll need a credit card
for cash advances (much easier and cheaper than wiring money), making hotel reservations over the telephone, major purchases (such as car
rentals and plane tickets), and for car rental security. But budget
travelers should rely basically on cash.

While paper money from any Western country is good at banks in
every other country, the money of Eastern Europe is "soft"—kept at
unrealistically high rates by its government. You can't avoid buying this
money when you're in Bulgaria, Romania, Hungary, Czechoslovakia,
East Germany, or Poland. It's a government-sponsored rip-off
designed to get "hard" Western currency—desperately needed to purchase Western goods on the international market. This money is worthless in Western Europe, so exchange it, spend it, buy candles in
churches, ice cream cones for strangers—give it away if you have to—
but don't take it out of its country.

Cash

Carry plenty of cash. In some places, it's getting expensive or difficult
to change a traveler's check, but hard cash is cash. You don't need a
bank: people always know roughly what a dollar, mark, or pound is
worth and, for a price, you can sell it. Several hundred dollars cash in
your money belt (safe enough, see chapter 11) comes in handy for
emergencies, such as when banks go on strike. I've been in Greece and
Ireland when every bank went on strike—shutting down without
warning.

Bring one day's budget in each country's currency with you from
home. Your bank can sell you one bill worth $30 to $50 from each country for a fair price. With six bills—for six countries—hidden safely in
your money belt, you'll have enough money to get settled in each new
country without worrying about banking. This is a wonderful
convenience—especially if you arrive at night or when the banks are
closed. Most stations have a bank with long hours, long lines, and bad
exchange rates.

Many Americans refuse to understand the "funny money" of
Europe. You won't find George Washington or Abe Lincoln, but it's all
logical. Each system is decimalized just like ours. There are a hundred
"little ones" (cents, pence, centimes, pfennig, stotinki, etc.) in every "big
one" (dollar, pound, franc, mark, leva, etc.). Only the names have been
changed—to confuse the tourist. Get a good sampling of coins after

you arrive and in two minutes you'll be comfortable with the "nickels, dimes, and quarters" of each new currency. A currency converting calculator isn't worth the trouble. Upon arrival, make a point to figure out the money.

Very roughly figure out what the unit of currency (franc, mark, krona, or whatever) is worth in American cents. (For example, if there are one and a half deutsche marks in a dollar, each DM is a 70-cent piece.) If a hot dog costs 5 marks, then it costs five 70-cent pieces or $3.50. Fifty little ones (pfennig) is half a mark (35 cents). If mustard costs 10 pfennig (a tenth of a 70-cent piece), it costs the equivalent of 7 cents. Ten marks is $7. 250 DM = $175 (250 x .7 or 250 less ⅓). Quiz yourself. Soon it will be second nature. You can't survive on a budget until you are comfortable with the local currency.

The Black Market — Soft Currency and Hard Facts

Sooner or later in your travels—in Eastern Europe and the Third World—you'll be approached by a local person wanting to buy or sell money or goods from you in a way that skirts his government's regulations or taxes. This is the "black market."

While most of the world's currencies have their true value determined by the international exchange market, some countries artificially overvalue their money. At a bank, you'll be charged the "official" rate of exchange—more than that money is really worth. When this happens, the currency becomes "soft"—difficult or impossible to change outside of that country.

In these countries, "hard," realistically valued currency—such as U.S. dollars and all Western European currencies—are in high demand for purchasing imported goods. A second economy or "black market" is created, and with it a major new sport—the search for "real money" and the special items only it can buy. Tourists are known to have plenty of hard money and will commonly be approached by people trying to gather enough hard cash to buy a car or stereo or camera that cannot be purchased with their country's soft money.

Most Eastern European countries tie their currencies to the Russian ruble. The ruble is as soft as a month-old banana, and as a result, these countries have a thriving black market. Even though factory workers make just a few hundred dollars a month, many have a difficult time spending their money. What they want can only be purchased with hard foreign currency (usually through government-run hard currency-only shops), so they will pay up to triple the official rate to acquire hard dollars. That means a Polish or Bulgarian worker will eagerly trade one month's pay for US$40 to save for his imported dream. Governments continue to artificially control the value and flow of money and goods. And they allow their black markets to thrive, knowing this brings in a substantial amount of much-needed currency into their economy.

Dealing in the black market is illegal and risky. Nevertheless, in many countries, the underground economy is the one that keeps things going. You will be tempted by the black market. When traveling in the USSR, Eastern Europe, or elsewhere, the black market is the forbidden fruit. Don't mess with it. You can end up in jail. You should, however, know something about it.

Many people finance their travels by playing the black market. They know what to buy, what to sell—and where. I'm not talking about drugs and Uzi machine guns. I'm talking pettiness: a bottle of gin, a Bon Jovi record, a pair of Levis, $20 bills. Here are some examples of black market activity. Names won't be used, to protect the guilty.

In a Warsaw nightclub, a man wearing a large money pouch— complete with "change maker"—sits down with a couple of Americans and loudly announces that he will pay them triple the official exchange rate for their dollars. Poland is Eastern Europe's bargain basement, even at the government's inflated exchange rate.

In Moscow, a traveler sells a _Playboy_ magazine for $50 (that's $50 worth of Russian currency at the official rate), a Beatles "White Album" for $80, and a Bible (in Russian) for $100. The total paid was nearly one month's local wages.

In East Berlin's most popular disco, a young American pays the five mark ($3) cover charge in West German marks rather than East German soft marks. For his hard currency, he is given hard drinks—free, all night long.

On a Bulgarian train, the conductor checks the tickets. Then, with eyes darting and the excitement of a little boy, he asks, "Black market? Change dollars?" The tourist follows him to the train's W.C., where the conductor gives him triple the going rate. He is undoubtedly a middleman who makes more money buying and selling hard currency than he does punching tickets. He'll have no trouble selling those dollars at a profit to Bulgarians in need of hard cash.

A stewardess on an Eastern European airline makes the equivalent of 40 cents (U.S.) an hour but gets $20 for lunch expenses during a half-day stopover in Amsterdam. She skips lunch, knowing that the black market value of her lunch money is equal to three weeks wages for her husband in a factory back home.

The governments of countries that refuse to acknowledge the magic of the marketplace often require tourists to spend a minimum amount of hard currency per day. In Romania, as you enter by train, you are issued a seven-day visa only after changing seven times their minimum daily expenditure requirement. To extend your visa, you must show a bank slip proving that you changed enough money—legally. In the USSR and several other countries, there are special shops, gas stations, tours, and hotels that are especially for foreign visitors and accept only hard currency. In some cases, these are the only hotels, tours, or gas stations the guests are allowed to use. To change soft money back into hard currency, you must have exchanged more than your daily minimum and have bank receipts to prove it. In actuality, this is often a wild goose chase. In some cases, they'll hold your leftover money for you "until you return."

Countries with soft currencies generally require proof that you changed your money through official channels before you're allowed to make any major purchase. This includes hotel bills, plane tickets, and car rentals. Because of this tight control, many tourists who "make a killing" on the black market have a very difficult time spending all their local wealth. That money can't be exchanged again for hard currency, and it becomes "funny money" once it crosses the border. It's a strange feeling, not knowing how to blow your money. You can only eat so many ice cream cones (fancy restaurant meals, long taxi rides, and buying rounds of drinks in large bars are about the only substantial ways to consume black market windfalls).

Certain items that are very popular but can't be purchased with local currency make wonderful gifts for East European locals, if you can get them across the border. If the customs official sees your gifts and determines that they aren't for your personal use, he'll probably confiscate them—and take them home. I once brought a Romanian friend well-chosen gifts costing $70 in America: a blank Sony recording tape, a pair of jeans, a rock and roll album (the "harder," the better), and a pocket calculator. That Romanian glowed with pride as he wore his "real American jeans." Within two days his record was taped a dozen times—all over the village. He figured the value of those gifts at over a month's wages.

Black market dealings are illegal, and a tourist is expected to understand and obey the laws of the country he is visiting. Note: While the "black market" survives in Eastern Europe, recent changes are leading thankfully to a day when this chapter will be unnecessary.

Keys to Successful Bargaining

In much of the world, the price tag is only an excuse to argue. Bargaining is the accepted and expected method of finding a compromise between the wishful thinking of the merchant and the tourist. Prices are "soft" in much of the Mediterranean world. In Europe, bargaining is common only in the south. You should fight the price in flea markets and with people selling handicrafts and tourist items on the streets in all but the most developed countries.

While bargaining is important from a budgetary standpoint (if you're traveling beyond Europe), it can also become an enjoyable game. Many travelers are addicted hagglers who would gladly skip a tour of a Portuguese palace to get the price down on the black-clad lady's handmade sweater.

Here are the 10 commandments of the successful haggler:

1. Determine whether bargaining is appropriate. It's bad shopping etiquette to "make an offer" for a tweed hat in a London department store. It's foolish not to at a Greek outdoor market. To learn if the price is fixed, fall in love with that item right in front of the merchant. Look longingly into the eyes of that porcelain Buddha, then decide that "it's just too much money." You've put him in a position to make the first offer. If he comes down even 2 percent, there's nothing sacred about the price tag. Haggle away.

2. Determine the merchant's cost. Many merchants will settle for a nickel profit rather than lose the sale entirely. Promise yourself that, no matter how exciting the price becomes, you won't buy. Then work the cost down to rock bottom. When it seems to have fallen to a record low, walk away. That last price he hollers out as you turn the corner is usually about a nickel above cost. Armed with this knowledge, you can confidently demand a fair price for the same item at the next souvenir stand—and probably get it. (Bid carefully, though. If a merchant accepts your price, the rules are you must buy it.)

3. Find out what the locals pay. If the price is not posted, assume there's a double price standard—one for locals and one for you. If only tourists buy the item you're pricing, see what an Arab, Spanish, or Italian tourist would be charged. I remember thinking I did well in Istanbul's Grand Bazaar until I learned my Spanish friend bought the same shirt for 30 percent less. Merchants assume American tourists are rich.

4. Preprice each item. What's it really worth to you? Remember that price tags are meaningless and serve to distort your idea of an item's true worth. The merchant is playing a psychological game. Many think that if they can cut the price by 50 percent, they are doing great. So the merchant quadruples his prices and the tourist happily pays double the fair value. The best way to deal with crazy price tags is to ignore them. Before you even see the price tag, determine what it's worth to you, considering the hassles involved in packing it or shipping it home.

5. Don't hurry. Get to know the shopkeeper. Accept his offer for tea, talk with him. Leave him to shop around and get a feel for the market. Then return. He'll know you are serious. Dealing with the owner (no salesman's commission) lowers your best possible price.

6. Be indifferent; never look impressed. As soon as the merchant perceives the "I gotta have that!" in you, you'll never get the best price. He knows you have the money to buy what you really want. He knows about U.S. prices. (Sorry, commandments 1 and 6 are contradictory.)

7. Impress him with your knowledge—real or otherwise. This way he respects you, and you are more likely to get good quality. Istanbul has very good leather coats for a fraction of the U.S. cost. I wanted one. Before my trip, I talked to some leather coat salesmen and was much better prepared to confidently pick out a good coat in Istanbul for $70.

8. Employ a third person. Use your friend who is worried about the ever-dwindling budget or who doesn't like the price or who is bored and wants to return to the hotel. This trick may work to bring the price down faster.

9. Show the merchant your money. Physically hold out your money and offer him "all you have" to pay for whatever you are bickering over. The temptation will be greater for him just to grab your money and say, "Oh, all right."

10. If the price is too much, leave. Never worry about having taken too much of the merchant's time and tea. They are experts at making the tourist feel guilty for not buying. It's all part of the game. Most merchants, by local standards, are financially well off.

A final point for the no-nonsense budget shopper: you can generally find the same souvenirs in large department stores at fair and firm, often government-regulated prices. Department store shopping is quicker, easier, often cheaper—but not nearly as much fun.

6
Hurdling the Language Barrier

Communicating in a Language You Don't Speak

That notorious language barrier is about two feet tall. While it keeps many people out of Europe, with a few communication tricks and a polite approach, you can step right over it.

While it's nothing to brag about, I speak only English. Of course, if I spoke more languages, I could enjoy a much deeper understanding of the people and cultures I visit, but with English only I have no problems getting transportation, rooms, eating, and seeing the sights. While we can manage fine with the blunt weapon of English only, only Ugly Americans don't learn and use a few basic phrases and polite words.

Having an interest in the local language wins the respect of those you'll meet. Get an English-German (or whatever) dictionary and start your practical vocabulary growing right off the bat. You're surrounded by expert, native-speaking tutors in every country. Let them teach you. Spend bus and train rides learning. Start learning the language when you arrive. Psychologically, it's hard to start later because you'll be leaving so soon. I try to learn five new words a day. You'd be surprised how handy a working vocabulary of fifty words is. The practical phrase lists following this chapter are a good place to start. A two-language dictionary is cheap and easy to buy locally and more helpful than a phrase book.

We English speakers are the one linguistic group that can afford to be lazy. English is the world's linguistic common denominator. When a Greek meets a Norwegian, they speak English. What Greek speaks Norwegian?

While Americans are terrible monoglots, Europeans are very good with languages. Most young North Europeans speak several languages.

Scandinavian students of our language actually decide between English and "American." My Norwegian cousin speaks with a touch of Texas and knows more slang than I do! Most Swiss grow up trilingual like their country. People speaking minor languages (Dutch, Belgians, Scandinavians) have more reason to learn German, French, or English, since their linguistic world is so small.

Imagine if each of our states spoke its own language. That's the European situation. They've done a great job of minimizing the communication problems you'd expect to find in a small continent with such a Babel of tongues. Not only are most educated people multilingual but most signs that the traveler must understand (such as road signs, menus, telephone instructions, and safety warnings) are printed either in several languages or in universal symbols. Europe's uniform road sign system enables drivers to roll right over the language barrier.

Europe is multilingual where necessary. At Yugoslavian truck stops, the packet says sugar *in five languages.*

English may be Europe's lingua franca, and we don't need to be afraid of the language barrier, but communicating does require some skill. How well you communicate with the Europeans you meet depends on your ability to get a basic idea across, not on how many words you know in that language.

When communicating with people who don't speak your language, be polite, patient, and undemanding. Any European who speaks Eng-

lish is doing you a favor. She'd be more comfortable in her own language. Never assume anyone can speak English. Ease in with the local
phrase for "Do you speak English?" Learn the niceties and use them
generously with your simple English.

Speak slowly, clearly, and with carefully chosen words. The "Voice
of America" is in business to communicate, and they use what they call
"simple English." You're dealing with someone who learned English
out of a book, reading British words, not hearing American ones. Your
lips are being read. They're wishing you would write it down so they
can actually see the spelling. Choose easy words and clearly pronounce
each letter. (Cris·py po·ta·to chips.) Use no contractions. When they
aren't understood, most Americans speak louder and toss in a few extra
words. Listen to other tourists and you'll hear your own shortcomings.

Can the slang. Our American dialect has become a super·deluxe
slang pizza not found on any European menu. The sentence, "Cut out
all slang," for example, would baffle the average European. "Speak no
idioms" would be better understood. If you learned English in school
for two years, how would you respond to the American who exclaims,
"What a day!" or "Hang in there." Listen to yourself. If you want to be
understood, talk like a Dick and Jane primer. For several months out
of every year, I speak with simple words, pronouncing every letter.
When I get home my friends say (very deliberately), "Rick, you can
relax now, we speak English."

Keep your messages and sentences grunt simple. Make single nouns
work as entire sentences. When asking for something, a one·word question ("Photo?") is more effective than an attempt at something more
grammatically correct. ("May I take your picture, sir?") Be a caveman.
Strip your message naked and drag it by the hair into the other person's mind.

Use internationally understood words. Some spend an entire trip
telling people they're on vacation, draw only blank stares, and slowly
find themselves in a soundproof, culture·resistant cell. The sensitive
communicator notices that Europeans understand the word "holiday"
(probably because that's what the English say), plugs that word into her
simple English vocabulary, is understood, and enjoys a much closer
contact with Europe. If my car is broken in Portugal, I don't say "Excuse
me, my car is broken." I point to the vehicle and say clearly, "Auto
kaput."

Risk looking like a fool. Even with no common language, rudimentary communication is easy. Butcher the language if you must, but communicate. I'll never forget the lady in the French post office who
flapped her arms and asked, "Tweet, tweet, tweet?" I understood

immediately, answered with a nod, and she gave me the airmail stamps
I needed. At the risk of getting bird seed, I communicated successfully.
If you're hungry, clutch your stomach and growl. If you want milk,
"moo" and pull two imaginary udders. If the liquor was too strong,
simulate an atomic explosion starting from your stomach and
mushrooming to your head. If you're attracted to someone, pant.

Pick up gestures. Every culture has peculiar—and fun—hand and
face gestures. In Turkey, you signal "no" by jerking your eyebrows and
head upward. In Bulgaria, "yes" is indicated by happily bouncing your
head back and forth as if you were one of those oriental dolls with a
spring neck and someone slapped you. "Expensive" is often shaking
your hand and sucking in like you just burned yourself. To praise something, act like you've just tasted something exquisite.

Figure things out. Most major European languages are related, coming from Latin. With that awareness and an effort to make some sense
of the puzzle, lots of words become meaningful. The French word for
Monday (our day of the moon) is *Lundi* (lunar day). The Germans say
the same thing—*Montag. Sonn* is sun so *Sonntag* is Sunday. If *buon giorno*
means good day, *zuppa del giorno* must mean soup of the day. If *tiergar-
ten* is zoo (literally "animal garden") in German, then *stinktier* is "skunk"
and kindergarten is children's garden. Think of *vater, mutter, trink, gross,*

Step over the language barrier. This says "Sentralsyke house" and that's just what it is.

gut, nacht, rapide, grand, economico, delicioso, and you can _muy comprendo._ Many letters travel predictable courses (determined by the physical way a sound is made) as one language melts into the next over the centuries. For instance, "p" often becomes "v" or "b" in the next language. Italian menus always have a charge for _coperto_—a "cover" charge. Practice your understanding. Read time schedules, concert posters, multilingual signs in bathrooms, and newspaper headlines. Develop your ear for foreign languages by tuning into the other languages on a multilingual tour. It's a puzzle. The more you play, the better you get. **Be melodramatic.** Exaggerate the local accent. In France, communicate more effectively (and have more fun) by sounding like Maurice Chevalier or Inspector Clousseau. The locals won't be insulted; they'll be impressed. Use whatever French you know. But even English, spoken with a sexy French accent, makes more sense to the French ear. In Italy, be melodic, exuberant, and wave those hands. Go ahead, try it: Mama Mia! You've got to be uninhibited. Self-consciousness kills communication.

Make your communicating job easier by choosing a multilingual person to begin communicating with. Business people, urbanites, young well-dressed people, and anyone in the tourist trade is most likely to speak English.

A small notepad works wonders in a tough spot. The written word or number is understood much easier than when it's spoken—and mispronounced. (My back-pocket notepad is my constant travel buddy.) To repeatedly communicate something difficult and important (such as medical instructions, "I'm vegetarian," "boiled water," "well-done meat," or "your finest ice cream"), have it written in the local language on your notepad.

Confessions of a Monoglot

When asked, "Do you speak English?" many Europeans will say no. In this case, I begin the communication struggle in their tongue. Very often a few butchered sentences in my German or French refreshes that European's memory, and he'll say, "OK, let's speak English." One thing we Americans can do expertly with our linguistic skills is put our self-conscious European friends at ease with their less-than-perfect English.

Even if you have no real language in common, you can have some fun communicating. Consider this profound conversation I had with a cobbler in Sicily:

"Spaghetti," I said, with a very saucy Italian accent.

"Ronald Reagan," was the old man's reply.

"Mama mia!" I said, tossing my hands and head into the air.

"Yes, no, one, two, tree," he returned, slowly and proudly.

By now we'd grown fond of each other and I whispered, secretively, "Molto buono, ravioli."

He spit, "Be sexy, drink Pepsi!"

And I waved good-bye saying, "Arrivederci."

"Ciao," he smiled.

While phrase books can be helpful in your efforts to communicate, I find them more fun than practical. I can't imagine anyone ever hauling out their phrase book to say, "I've broken my leg. Can you please show me to the nearest hospital?" In that case, a point and a scream works in any language. A phrase book is useful, for instance, when you are sitting, bored, in a restaurant waiting for your meal. Call the waitress over, and, with a pained look, ask for a shampoo. The Berlitz *14 European Languages Phrase Book* is ideal for the average traveler.

Assume you understand and go with your educated guess. My master key to communication is to see most communication problems as multiple choice questions, make an educated guess at the meaning of a message—verbal or written—and proceed confidently as if I understood it correctly. This applies to rudimentary things like instructions on customs forms, museum hours, menus, questions the hotel maid asks you, and so on. With this approach, I find that 80 percent of the time I'm correct. Half the time I'm wrong I never know it, so it doesn't really matter. So 10 percent of the time I really blow it. My trip becomes easier—and occasionally much more interesting.

Let's take a border crossing as an example. I speak no Bulgarian. At the border, a uniformed guard struts up to my car and asks a question. Not understanding a word he said, but guessing what the average border guard would ask the average tourist, I look at him and answer with a solid "Nyet." He steps back, swings his arm open like a gate and says, "OK." I'm on my way, quick and easy. I could have gotten out of the car, struggled with the phrase book, and made a big deal out of it, but I'd rather fake it, assuming he was asking if I'm smuggling anything in and keep things simple. It works.

International Words

As our world shrinks, more and more words leap their linguistic boundaries and become international. Sensitive travelers develop a knack for choosing words most likely to be universally understood ("auto" instead of "car," "kaput" rather than "broken," "photo," not "picture"). They also internationalize their pronunciation. "University," if you play around with its sound (Oo-nee-vehr-see-tay) will be understood anywhere. The average American is a real flunky in this area. Be creative.

Analogy communication is effective. Anywhere in Europe, "Attila" means "the crude bully." When a bulky Italian crowds in front of you, say, "Scuzi, Ah-tee-la" and retake your place. If you like your haircut and want to compliment your Venetian barber, put your hand sensually on your hair and say "Casanova." Nickname the hairstylist "Michelangelo," or "Rambo."

Here are a few internationally understood words. Remember, cut out the Yankee accent and give each word a pan-European sound.

Stop	Kaput	Vino
Restaurant	Ciao	Bank
Hotel	Bye-bye	Rock 'n roll
Post	Camping	OK
Auto	Picnic	Amigo
Autobus (booos)	Nuclear	English (Engleesh)
Yankee, Americano	Tourist	Mama mia
Michelangelo (artistic)	Beer	Oo la la
Casanova (romantic)	Coffee	Moment
Disneyland (wonderland)	Tea	Hercules (strong)
Coke, Coca-Cola	No problem	Attila (mean, crude)
Sexy	Europa	Self-service
Toilet	Police	Super
Taxi	Telephone	Photo
Photocopy	Central	Information
Mañana	University	Passport
Chocolate	Pardon	Fascist
Rambo		

America's favorite four-letter words
Elephante (a big clod)

A Yankee-English Phrase Book

Oscar Wilde said, "The English have everything in common with the Americans—except, of course, language."

On your first trip to England, you'll find plenty of linguistic surprises. I'll never forget checking into a small-town bed-and-breakfast, a teenager on my first solo European adventure. The landlady cheerily asked me, "And what time would you like to be knocked up in the

This is German for "tour bus." These days most come with air-conditioning.

morning?" I looked over at her husband, who winked, "Would a fry at eight be suitable?" The next morning, I got a rap on the door at 7:30 and a huge British breakfast a half-hour later.

Traveling through England is an adventure in accents and idioms. Every day you'll see babies in "prams," sucking "dummies" as mothers change wet "nappies." Soon the kids can trade in their "nappies" for "smalls" and "spend a penny" on their own. "Spend a penny" is British for a visit to the "loo" (bathroom). Older British kids enjoy "candy floss" (cotton candy), "naughts and crosses" (tic-tac-toe), "big dippers" (roller coasters), and "iced lollies" (popsicles) and are constantly in need of an "elastoplast" (Band-Aid).

If you're just "muckin' about," it's fun to browse through an "ironmonger's" (hardware store), "chemist's shop" (pharmacy), or Woolworths and notice the many familiar items with unfamiliar names. The school supplies section includes "sticking plaster" (adhesive tape), "rubbers" (erasers), and "scribbling blocks" (scratch pads). Those with "green fingers" (a green thumb) might pick up some "courgette" (zucchini), "swede" (rutabaga), or "aubergine" (eggplant) seeds.

In England, "chips" are fries and "crisps" are potato chips. A hamburger is best on a toasted "bap." You wipe your fingers with a serviette—never a napkin.

The English have a great way with names. You'll find towns with names like Upper and Lower Piddle, Once Brewed, and Itching Field. I saw a hair salon called "Curl Up and Dye." This cute coziness comes through in their language as well. Your car is built with a "bonnet" and a "boot" rather than a hood and trunk. You drive it on "motorways," and when the freeway divides, it becomes a "dual carriageway." Gas is "petrol," a truck is a "lorry," and when you hit a traffic jam, don't "get your knickers in a twist" (make a fuss), just "queue up" (line up) and study your American-English phrase book.

A two-week vacation in England is unheard of, but many locals "holiday for a fortnight" in a "homely" (pleasant) rural cottage, possibly on the "Continent" (continental Europe). They'll pack a "face flannel" (washcloth), "torch" (flashlight), "hoover" (vacuum cleaner), and "hair grips" (bobby pins) before leaving their "flat" (apartment). You can "post" letters in the "pillar box" and give your "bird" (girlfriend) a "trunk" (long distance) call, "reversing the charges" (collect), of course. On a cold evening it's best to pick up a "pimp" (bundle of kindling) and make a fire or take a walk wearing the warmest "mackintosh" (raincoat) you can find or an "anorak" (parka) with "press studs" (snaps).

After "washing up" (doing the dishes), you can go up to the first floor (second floor) with a "neat" (straight) Scotch and a plate of "biscuits" (sweet cookies) and just enjoy the view. It's a "smashing" view, guaranteed to give you "goose pimples" (goose bumps) every time.

All across the British Isles, you'll find new words, crazy local humor, and countless accents. Pubs are colloquial treasure chests. Church services, sporting events, the House of Parliament, live plays featuring local comedy, the streets of Liverpool, the docks of London, and children in parks are playgrounds for the American ear. One of the beauties of touring the British Isles is the illusion of hearing a foreign language and actually understanding it—most of the time.

Practical Foreign Phrases

FRENCH

1. hello	bonjour	bohn-ZHOOR
2. good-bye	au revoir	oh reh-VWAH
3. see you later	à bientôt	ah byuhn-TOH
4. goodnight	bonne nuit	bohn NWEE
5. please	s'il vous plaît	seel voo PLAY
6. thank you	merci	mehr-SEE
7. yes/no	oui/non	wee/noh
8. one/two/three	un/deux/trois	uh/DOO/twah
9. cheap/expensive	bon marché/cher	bohn mar-shay/shehr
10. good/bad	bon/mauvais	bohn/mo-VAY
11. beautiful/ugly	joli/laid	zho-LEE/lay
12. big/small	grand/petit	grahn/pehTEE
13. fast/slow	rapide/lent	rah-PEED/lah
14. very	très	tray
15. where is. . .?	ou est. . .?	oo ay
16. how much. . .?	combien	kohm-bee-ah
17. I don't understand	je ne comprends pas	zhuh neh KOHM-prahn PAH
18. What do you call this?	qu'est-ce que c'est?	KESS koo SAY
19. I'm lost	je me suis perdu	zhuh meh swee perh-DOO
20. complete price (every thing included)	tout est compris	toot-ay cohm-PREE
21. I'm tired	je suis fatigué	zhuh swee fah-tee-GAY
22. I'm hungry	j'ai faim	zhay fah
23. cheers!	santé!	sahn-TAY
24. food	nourriture	new-ree-TOOR
25. grocery store	epicerie	eh-PEES-REE
26. picnic	pique-nique	peek-neek
27. delicious	délicieux	de-lee-syoh
28. market	marché	mar-SHAY
29. drunk	saoul	soo
30. money	argent	ar-ZHA
31. station	gare	gar
32. private accommodations	chambre	shambr
33. toilet	w.c.	VAY say
34. I	je	zhuh
35. you	vous	voo
36. love	amour	ah-MOOR
37. sleep	sommeil	so-MAY
38. train	train	tran
39. The bill, please	L'addition, s'il vous plait	lah-dee-see-OHN, see voo play
49. friend	ami	ah-MEE
41. water/tap water	eau/eau douce	OH/OL dooss
42. castle	château	shat-TOH
43. How are you?/I'm fine	ça va?/ça va	sah VAH
44. Tourist Information	syndicat d'initiative	san-dee-KAH dee nee-see-ah-TEEV

GERMAN

1. hello	Guten Tag	goo·ten tock
2. good·bye	Auf Wiedersehn	awf VEE·der·sayn
3. see you later	bis bald	beess bald
4. goodnight	Gute Nacht	gooteh nahkt
5. please	bitte	BIT·teh
6. thank you	danke schön	DONG·kuh shurn
7. yes/no	ja/nein	yah/nine
8. one/two/three	eins/zwei/drei	aintz/tzvy/dry
9. cheap/expensive	billig/teuer	BIL·ikh/TOY·err
10. good/bad	gut/schlecht	goot/schlehkht
11. beautiful/ugly	schön/hässlich	shurn/HESS·leek
12. big/small	gross/klein	groass/kline
13. fast/slow	schnell/langsam	shnel/LONG·zahm
14. very	sehr	zair
15. Where is...?	wo ist...?	voh ist
16. How much...?	wieviel...?	vee·FEEL
17. I don't understand	ich verstehe nicht	ikh vehr·SHTAY·eh nicht
18. What do you call this?	wie heisst das?	vee HEIST dahss
19. I'm lost	ich habe mich verirrt	ikh hah·beh mikh fehr·IRT
20. complete price	alles ist inbegriffen	alles ist IN·ber·grif—ern
(everything included)		
21. I'm tired	ich bin müde	ikh bin MEW·duh
22. I'm hungry	ich habe hunger	ikh hah·beh HOONG·guh
23. cheers!	prosit!	proast
24. food	Speise	SHPY·zuh
25. grocery store	Supermarkt	supermarket
26. picnic	Picknick	pik·nik
27. delicious	lecker	LECK·uh
28. market	Markt	markt
29. drunk	betrunken	bay TROON kin
30. money	Geld	geld
31. station	Bahnhof	BAHN·hof
32. private accommodations	Zimmer	TSIMM·er
33. toilet	Klo/W.C.	kloh
34. I	ich	eekh
35. you	Du	doo
36. love	Liebe	LEE·beh
37. sleep	schlaf	shloff
38. train	Zug	tsoog
39. The bill, please	die Rechnung, bitte	dee RECK·nung, BIT·teh
40. friend	Freund	froint
41. water	Wasser	VOSS·ehr
42. castle	Schloss	shlohss
43. How are you?/	wie geht es?/Es geht	vee GATES/ess GATE
I'm fine, thanks	mir gut, danke	mehrGOOT, DONG·kah
44. Tourist Information	Reisebüro	RIE·suh·BYOO·ro

GREEK

1.	hello	YAHSS-ahss
2.	good-bye	YAHSS-ahss
3.	see you later	EESS to ehpahnee DHEEN
4.	goodnight	kahleeNEEK tah
5.	please	pahrahkahLO
6.	thank you	ehvkhahreeSTO
7.	yes/no	neh/O-khee
8.	one/two/three	EHnah/DHEEo/TREEah
9.	cheap/expensive	ftee-NOHSS/ah-kree-VOHSS
10.	good/bad	kah-LOHSS/kah-KOHSS
11.	beautiful/ugly	or-AY-ohss/AHSS-kee-mahss
12.	big/small	meh-GAH-lohss/mahss
13.	fast/slow	GREE-gor-ohss/ahr-GOHSS
14.	very	poLEE
15.	Where is. . .?	poo IN-neh
16.	How much. . .?	POH-so
17.	I don't understand	DEN kah-tah-lah-VENN-o
18.	What do you call this?	poss LEHyehteh ahvto
19.	I'm lost	KAHtheekah
20.	complete price	Olah pehreelahm VAH-nondheh
	(everything included)	
21.	I'm tired	EEmeh koorahSMEHnoss
22.	I'm hungry	peeNo
23.	cheers!	YAH-sahss
24.	food	tro-FEE
25.	grocery store	mah-gah-ZEE
26.	delicious	thaumasios
27.	market	aGORa
28.	money	lep-TAH
29.	station	stathmos
30.	private accommodations	doeMAHteeo
31.	toilet	meros
32.	I	AY-go
33.	you	eh-SAYSS
34.	love	ah-GAH-pay
35.	sleep	kim-MOM-may
36.	train	TREN-no
37.	The bill, please	Toh log-a-ree-ahz MO, pah-rah-kah-LOH
38.	friend	FEE-lohss
39.	water	neh-RO
40.	Tourist Information	toor-is-MOHSS

ITALIAN

1. hello	buongiorno	bohn·JOOR·no
2. good·bye	ciao	chow
3. see you later	ci vediamo	chee vey·dee·OMM·o
4. goodnight	buona notte	BWONN·ah NOT·tay
5. please	per favore	pair fah·VOR·ay
6. thank you	grazie	GRAH·tsee·ay
7. yes/no	si/no	see/no
8. one/two/three	uno/due/tre	oo·noh/doo·ay/tray
9. cheap/expensive	e tropo caro/caro	ay tropo CARR·o/CARR·o
10. good/bad	buone/cattivo	BWON·o/kaht·TEE·vo
11. beautiful/ugly	bellow/brutto	BEHL·lo/BROOT·to
12. big/small	grande/piccolo	GRAHN·day/PEEKkoh·lo
13. fast/slow	rapido/lento	RAHH·pee·do/LEHN·to
14. very	molto	MOHL·to
15. Where is...?	Dov'e...?	do·VAY
16. How much...?	Quanto?	KWAHN·to
17. I don't understand	non capisco	nohn kay·PEESS·ko
18. What do you call this?	Che cosi questo?	kay KO·zay KWAY·sto
19. I'm lost	mi sono perso	mee SOH·no PEHR·so
20. I'm tired	sono stanco	SOH·no STAHNG·ko
21. I'm hungry	ho fame	oh FAH·may
22. food	cibo	CHEE·bo
23. grocery store	alimentari	al·ee·men·TAR·ee
24. picnic	picnic	pičnic
25. delicious	delizioso	day·leet·see·OH·so
26. market	mercato	mayr·COT·to
27. drunk	ubriacarsi	oo·bree·ah·KAR·see
28. money	denaro	day·NAHR·ro
29. station	stazione	STAHT·see·OH·nay
30. private accommodations	camera affittata	CAH·may·rah ah·fee·tah·tah
31. toilet	toilet	toy·LET
32. I	io	ee·OH
33. you	lei	lay
34. love	amore	AH·MOH·ray
35. sleep	dormire	dor·MEER·ay
36. train	treno	TRAY·no
37. The bill, please	Il contro, prego	ell KON·to, pray·go
38. friend	amico	ah·mee·ko
39. water/mineral water	acqua/acqua naturale	AH·kwa nah·toor·ALL·ay
40. castle	castello	kah·STELL·o
41. church	chiesa	kee·ay·za
42. How are you?	Come va?	KO·may VAH
43. Tourist Information	ufficio informazioni	oo·FEE·cho EEn·for·MATZ·ee·OH·nee
44. You're welcome	Prego	PRAY·go
45. doing sweet nothing	dolce far niente	DOL·chay far nee·YEN·tay

PORTUGUESE

1. hello	bom dia	bohm DEE·ah
2. good·bye	adeus	eh·DAY·oosh
3. see you later	até logo	eh·TAY LO·go
4. goodnight	boa noite	BOH·eh NOY·teh
5. please	por favor	poor feh·VOR
6. thank you	obrigado	obree GAHdhoo
7. yes/no	sim/não	see/NAH·oh
8. one/two/three	um/dois/tres	uh/dovsh/travsh
9. cheap/expensive	barato/caro	beh·RAW·to/CARR·o
10. good/bad	bom/mau	BOHM/MAH·oh
11. beautiful/ugly	belo/feio	BEHloo/FAYoo
12. big/small	grande/pequeno	GRAHN·day/peh·KAYN·yo
13. fast/slow	rápido/lento	RAHpeedo/LENN·to
14. very	muito	MOO·to
15. Where is...?	Donde está...?	OHN·deh eesh·TAH
16. How much...?	Quanto?	KWAHN·to
17. I don't understand	não compreendo	NAH·oh kohm·pree·AYN·do
18. What do you call this?	Como se chama isto?	KO·moo sehr SHAR·ma EESH·to
19. I'm lost	estou perdido	esh·TOH·ah perr·DEE·do
20. complete price (everything included)	tudo incluido	TOO·do ANN·kloo·EE·do
21. I'm tired	estou cansado	esh·TOH·ah cahn·SAH·do
22. I'm hungry	tenho fome	TEN·no FO·meh
23. cheers!	saude!	sah·OO·duh
24. food	alimento	ah·lee·MEN·tu
25. grocery store	mercearia	mehr·say·ah·REE·ah
26. picnic	piquenique	PEEK·ah·NEEK
27. delicious	delicioso	deh·LEE·see·OH·zuh
28. market	mercado	mehr·KA·du
29. drunk	bebado	be·BA·du
30. money	dinheiro	dee·NEER·u
31. station	estacão	eh·stah·SAH·oh
32. private accommodations	case particular	casa parr·teek·u·LARR
33. toilet	retrete	ray·TRAY·tay
34. I	eu	yo
35. you	tu	tu
36. love	amor	a·MOHR
37. sleep	dormir	DOR·MEE
38. train	trem	trehm
39. The bill, please	A conta, por favor	AH KOHN·tah, poor feh·VOR
40. friend	amigo	eh·MEE·go
41. water	agua	AH·guah
42. castle	castelo	coss·TELL·o
43. Tourist Information	informação turistico	ann·for·mah·SAH·o
44. How are you?	Coma vi?	CO·MO VIE

SERBO-CROATIAN

1.	hello	dobar	DO-bar DUN
2.	good-bye	dan	DUN
3.	see you later	dovidjenja	do-vee-TEN-ya
4.	goodnight	laku noc	LAH-koo NOACH
5.	please	molim	MO-lem
6.	thank you	hvala	HVAH-lah
7.	yes/no	da/ne	dah/neh
8.	one/two/three	jedan/dva/tri	YEH-dahn/dvah/tree
9.	cheap/expensive	jeftino/skupo	YEHF-tee-no/SKOO/po
10.	good/bad	dobro/lose	DObro/LOsheh
11.	beautiful/ugly	lepo/ruzno	LEHpo/ROOzhno
12.	big/small	veliko/malo	VEHleeko/MAHlo
13.	fast/slow	brzo/sporo	BERzo/SPOro
14.	very	vrio	VERlo
15.	Where is...?	Gde je...?	g'DAY-yeh
16.	How much...?	Koliko?	koLEEko
17.	I don't understand	ne rezumem	neh rah-ZOO-mem
18.	What is that?	Sto je to?	SHTAH yeh-toh
19.	I'm lost	zalutao sam	zah-LOOT-ow sahm
20.	complete price	sve je uracunato	sveh yeh OOrachoonahto
	(everything included)		
21.	I'm tired	umoran sam	OOmorahn sahm
22.	I'm hungry	gladan sam	GLAHdahn sahm
23.	cheers!	ziveli	ZHEE-vehlee
24.	food	hrana	HRA-ra
25.	grocery store	bakalnica	bah-KAHL-nee-kah
26.	picnic	izlet	EEZH-let
27.	delicious	ukusan	OO-koo-shawn
28.	market	trg	turg
29.	drunk	pijan	PEE-yahn
30.	money	novac	NOH-vak
31.	station	stanica	STAHN-eetz-ah
32.	private accommodations	podesavenje	poh-deh-sah-VAHN-yeh
33.	toilet	toaleta	toh-LET-tah
34.	I	ja	yah
35.	you	vi	vee
36.	love	ljubav	LYOO-bahv
37.	sleep	spavati	SPAH-va-tee
38.	train	voz	voze
39.	The bill, please	Racun, molim	RAW-choon, MO-leem
40.	friend	prijatelj	PREE-yah-tell
41.	water	vode	VO-day
42.	Tourist Information	turisticki ured	TOO-rist-eech-kee-OO-red
43.	How are you?	Kako ste?	KOCK-O stay

SPANISH

1. hello	hola	OH·lah
2. good·bye	adiós	AH·dee·OHSS
3. see you later	hasta luego	AHSS·tah LWAY·go
4. goodnight	buenas noches	BWAY·nahss NOH·chayss
5. please	por favor	por fav·VOHR
6. thank you	gracias	GRAH·SEE·ahss
7. yes/no	si/no	see/no
8. one/two/three	uno/dos/tres	OO·no/dohs/trayss
9. cheap/expensive	barato/caro	bah·RAH·to/KAH·ro
10. good/bad	bueno/malo	BWAY·no/MAH·lo
11. beautiful/ugly	bonito/feo	bo·NEE·to/FAY·o
12. big/small	grande/pequeño	GRAHN·day/pay·KAYN·yo
13. fast/slow	rápido/lento	RAH·pee·do/LAYN·to
14. very	muy	mwee
15. Where is. . .?	Donde está. . .?	DOHN·day ayss·TAH
16. How much. . .?	Cuanto?	KWAHN·to
17. I don't understand	No comprendo	no kom·PRAYN·do
18. What do you call this?	Como se llama esto?	KO·mo say YAH·ma AYSS·to
19. I'm lost	me ha perdido	may ay pehr·DEE·do
20. complete price	todo esta incluido	TOH·doh ayssTAH eenklooEED
(everything included)		
22. I'm hungry	tengo hambre	TAYNG·go AHM·bray
23. cheers!	a su salud!	ah soo sah·LOOD
24. food	alimento	ah·lee·MAYN·to
25. grocery store	abaceria	ah·bah·say·REE·ah
27. delicious	delicioso	day·lee·see·OH·so
28. market	mercado	mayr·KAH·do
29. drunk	borracho	boh·RAH·choh
30. money	dinero	dee·NAY·ro
31. station	estación	ay·STAH·see·OHN
32. private accommodations	casa particular	KAH·ssah pahr·tee·koo·LAHR
33. toilet	retrete	ray·TRAY·tay
34. I	yo	yo
35. you	usted	usted
36. love	amor	AH·MOHR
37. sleep	sueño	SWAYN·yo
38. train	tren	train
39. The bill, please	la cuenta, por favor	lah KWAYN·tah, por fah·VOHR
40. friend	amigo	ah·MEE·go
41. water	agua	AH·gwah
42. castle	castillo	coss·TEE·yoh
43. How are you/	Como está?/	co·mo STAH/
I'm fine, thanks	Estoy bien, gracias	Estoy bee·AYN
44. Tourist Information	Informacion turistica	EEN·for·MAH·SEE·OHN

SWEDISH

1. hello	god dag	goo dagh
2. good-bye	adjo	ah JUR
3. see you later	vi ses	vee SAYSS
4. goodnight	god natt	goo NACHT
5. please	varsagod	VAHR-sah-gude
6. thank you	tack	tock
7. yes/no	ja/nej	yah/nay
8. one/two/three	ett/tva/tre	eht/tvoh/tray
9. cheap/expensive	bollog/dyr	BIL-lig/deer
10. good/bad	god/dalig	goat/DAW-lig
11. beautiful/ugly	vacker/ful	VAHkeer/fewl
12. big/small	stor/	store/LEE-tern
13. fast/slow	snabb/langsam	snob/LONG-sahm
14. very	mycket	MEWkert
15. Where is. . .?	var ar. . .?	VARRahr
16. How much. . .?	hur mycket?	hewr MEWkert
17. I don't understand	jag forstar inte	yawg furr-SHTOAR IN-ter
18. What do you call this?	vad heter det har?	vod HET-ter det HARE
19. I'm lost	jag har gatt vilse	yawg harr got VIL-ser
20. complete price	allt ingar	ahlt in-GOAR
(everything included)		
21. I'm tired	jar ar trott	yog ayr TRUTT
22. I'm hungry	jag ar hungrig	jog ayr HEWN-rig
23. cheers!	skal!	skoal
24. food	naring	NAYR-ing
25. grocery store	specerihandel	SPEES-er-ee-HAN-del
26. picnic	utflykt	OOT-flekt
27. delicious	harlig	HAR-lig
28. market	torg	torg
29. drunk	drunken	DROO-ken
30. money	pengar	PENG-yar
31. station	station	stah-SHONE
32. private accommodations	husrom	HOOSS-rum
33. toilet	toalett	to-ah-LET
34. I	jag	yog
35. you	du	doo
36. love	karlet	SHAR-lik
37. sleep	sova	SO-vah
38. train	tag	towg
39. The bill, please	var vanlig ge mig notan	var VAYN-lig yay mee NO
40. friend	van	venn
41. water	vatten	vott-en
42. castle	borg	borg
43. How are you?	Hur star det till?	hoor STOAR der till
44. I am rich and single.	Jag ar rik och ogift.	

DUTCH/FLEMISH

	English	Dutch	Pronunciation
1.	hello	Goedendag	goo den dahch
2.	good-bye	Tot ziens	tot zeenz
3.	see you later	Tot straks	tot straks
4.	sleep well	slaaftwel	slaapt wel
5.	please	Alsdubleift (A.U.B.)	als doo bleeft
6.	thank you	Dank U	dank oo
7.	yes, no	ja, neen	yah, nayn
8.	one, two, three	een, twee, drie	ayn, tvay, dree
9.	cheap	goedkop	goot kope
10.	expensive	durr	duer
11.	good, bad	goed, slecht	goot, slekt
12.	beautiful	mooi	mow ee
13.	ugly	lelijk	lay lick
14.	big, small	groot, klein	groat, kline
15.	fast, slow	snel, langzaam	snell, langzaam
16.	very	zeer	zehr
17.	Where is. . .?	waar is	wehr is
18.	How much. . .?	hoe veel	who veel
19.	I don't understand	Ik versta u niet	ik verSTA oo neet
20.	What do you call this?	Hoe noemt u dat	who noomt oo dat
21.	I'm lost	Ik ben verloren gelopen	Ik ben vehrloren geloopen
22.	complete price	de totale prijs	Deh totaleh prize
23.	I'm tired	Ik ben moe	ik ben moo
24.	I'm hungry	Ik hep hoonger	ik hep hoonger
25.	cheers!	Gezondheid	geh zond heit
26.	food	Eten	ay ten
27.	grocery store	Voedingswinkel	Vod ings venkle
28.	delicious	heerlijk	hair lick
29.	market	markt	markt
30.	drunk	zat	zat
31.	money	geld	geld
32.	station	station	stah sheon
33.	private accommodations	kamer	kam er
34.	toilet	WC	vay say
35.	I/you	ik/jij	ik-yay
36.	love	liefde	leef da
37.	sleep	slapen	sla pen
38.	train	trein	train
39.	the bill, please	De Rekening	dah Ray kaning
40.	friend	vriend	vreend
41.	tap water	Kraatjewater	krantges water
42.	castle	Kasteel	ka steel
43.	tourist info	toeristische informatie	toor is tische in for mat see
44.	how are you?	Hoe gaat het	who gaat het
45.	the sweetness of doing nothing	Het is fijn niets tedoen	het is fayn neetz teh doon

The insults that follow are taken from *The Insult Dictionary—How to Snarl Back in Five Languages,* which can be ordered through James H. Heineman, Inc., 475 Park Ave., New York, NY 10022. (To be used in jest.)

English	German	French	Italian	Spanish
Hairy creep	Oller Leisetreter (*oller lysetrayter*)	Troglodyte (*Troglodeet*)	Stupido scrimmione (*Stoo-peedoh scheemee-ohneh*)	Espantapajaros (*Spantahpahharos*)
Moron	Nackter Wilder (*Naackter veelder*)	Cretin (*Craytan*)	Deficiente (*Deh-fee-chenteh*)	Carcamal (*Carcamahl*)
Ass	Narr (*Naarr*)	Ane bate (*Ann battay*)	Somaro (*Soh-mah-roh*)	Asno (*Assnoh*)
Donkey	Esel (*Ayzel*)	Bourricot (*Booreeko*)	Asino (*Ah-zeenoh*)	Burro (*Booroh*)
Crazy in the head	Schwach Kopf (*Shvaach kopf*)	Dingue (*Dang*)	Pazzoide (*Pah-tzo-ee-deh*)	Majareta (*Mahharetah*)
Ugly	Hasslick (*Haesslich*)	Laideron (*Laidron*)	Brutto (*Broot-toh*)	Asqueroso (*Askehrosoh*)
Useless vampire	Blutsaugendes Gespenst (*Blootsaogendes geshpenst*)	Vampire a la gomme (*Vampeer a la gom*)	vampiro innutile (*Vam-peeroh in-ootee-leh*)	Vampiro caduco (*Bahm-peeroh cadookoh*)
Blood-sucking leech	Schmarotzer (*Schmaarotser*)	Sangsue (*Sansi*)	Sanguisuga (*Sangoo-ee-songa*)	Tacaño (*Tahkanyoh*)
Repulsive, evil-smelling dog	Widerlicher Lump (*Veederlicher loomp*)	Repugnant voyou (*Raipvnan rvwahyoo*)	Repulsivo vagabondo puzzolent (*Ree-pul-see-vo vagabond-oh poot-zolehnteh*)	Roñoso (*Ronyoso*)
Dribbling, senile fool	Bloder Sabberer (*Bloeder zaabberer*)	Vieux baveux (*Vyer bavehr*)	Stupido vecchio rincitrullito (*Stoopeedoh veh-keeoh reen-chee-trool-leeto*)	Viejo baboso (*Beeyehho babbosoh*)

TRAIN PHRASES

English	French	German
English	**French**	**German**
1. National Railway	SNCF	DB/DBB
2. station	gare	Bahnof
3. information	resignements	Auskunft
4. Tourist Office	Syndicat D'Initiative	Auskunft
5. currency exchange	change	Wechsel
6. lockers	consigne-automatique	Spinde
7. check room	consignee	Garderobe
8. toilets	toilettes	Toiletten
9. men	messieurs	Herren
10. women	dames	Damen
11. waiting room	salle d'attente	Wartesaal
12. entrance	entre	Eingang
13. exit	sortie	Ausgang
14. timetable	horaire	Fahrplan
15. arrival	arrivee	Ankunft
16. departure	depart	Abfahrt
17. train	train	Zug
18. tickets	billet	Fahrkarten
19. reservation	reservation	Platzkarte
20. one way/round-trip	aller/retour	Einfach/Zurück
21. 1st/2nd	premiere/deuxieme	erster/zweiter
22. change	change	Umsteigen
23. ferry	bateau	Schiff
24. track	quai	Gleis
25. car	wagon	Wagen
26. seat	place	Platz
27. smoking	fumeurs	Raucher
28. couchette	couchette	Liegewagen
29. sleeping	wagon-lit	Schlafwagen
30. restaurant	wagon-restaurant	Speisewagen

Train Phrases, continued

Italian	Spanish	Danish
1. FS	RENFE	DSB
2. stazione ferroviario	estación	bandgarden
3. informazioni	información	oplysning
4. (EPT)	información turistica	turistbureau
5. cambio	cambio	veksling/valuth
6. armadietto	casilleros	autobousene
7. deposito	la consigna	oppbevaring-boks
8. gabinetto	servicios	toilet
9. uomini	caballeros	herrer
10. donne	señoras	damer
11. sala d'espetto	sala de espera	ventesalen
12. entrata	entrada	indgang
13. uscita	salida	udgang
14. orario	horarios	timeplan
15. arrivi	llegada	ankomst
16. partenze	partida	afgang
17. treno	tren	tog
18. biglietto	billetes	billet
19. prenotazione	reserva	pladsbestillingen
20. andata/andata e ritorno	ida/ida y vuelta	enkelt/retur
21. prima/seconda	primera/segunda	forte/anden
22. cambio	cambio	skifte
23. traghetto	balsadero	faerge
24. binario	andennes	perron/spor
25. carrozza	vagon	vogn
26. posto	place/asiento	sete
27. fumatori	coche-fumador	roker
28. cuccetta	coche-litera	liggevogn
29. vagone letto	coche-cama	sovevogn
30. ristorante	coche-restaurante	spisvogn

7
Health

Before Your Trip

Checkup

Just as you'd give your car a good checkup before a long journey, it's smart to meet with your doctor before your trip. Get a general checkup. Tell the doctor about every place you plan to visit and any place you may go. Then you can have the flexibility to take that impulsive swing through Turkey or Morocco knowing that you're prepared medically and have the required shots. At the time of this printing, no shots are required for basic European travel, although some shots are recommended. It's always best to check (keeping in mind that a government "requires" shots to protect its people and "recommends" shots to protect those who visit). Get advice on maintaining your health and about drinking the water. Obtain recommended immunizations and discuss proper care on the road of any preexisting medical conditions. Bring along a letter from your doctor describing any special health problems. If you plan to travel beyond Europe, ask your doctor about gamma globulin, antidiarrheal medicines, and any special precautions necessary.

Investigate the weather conditions you'll encounter and pack proper clothing. Will you need an umbrella or a sunscreen ointment?

Remember, only travel medicine specialists keep entirely up to date on health conditions for travelers around the world. While I consider Europe as safe as the United States, those traveling to more exotic destinations should consult one of these specialists. Many travelers join the International Association for Medical Assistance to Travelers (free, but donation requested, 417 Center St., Lewiston, NY 14092, tel. 716/754-4883) for a list of English- or American-trained doctors in member countries that you'll have access to at special rates and from whom you can get travel medicine advice and updates.

Have a dental checkup. Emergency dental care during your trip is time- and money-consuming, and it can be hazardous and painful. Give yourself a psychological prep talk. Europe can do to certain travelers what south France did to van Gogh. Romantics can get the sensory bends, patriots can get their flags burned, and anyone can suffer from culture shock. Europe is intense, and travel is a spin cycle for dainties that have always hung in the sun. Europe is crowded, smoky, and not particularly impressed by Americans or America. It will challenge givens that you always assumed were above the test of reason, and most of Europe on the street doesn't really care that much about what you, the historical and cultural pilgrim, have waited so long to see. If you need a break, a long, dark, air-conditioned trip back to California in a movie theater, a pleasant sit in an American embassy reading room surrounded by eagles, photos of presidents, _Time_ magazines, and other Yankees, or a break in the lobby of a world-class hotel, where any hint of the local culture has been lost under a big business bucket of intercontinental whitewash, can do wonders for the struggling traveler's spirit.

A Traveler's First-Aid Kit

My kit contains soap, supplemental vitamins, aspirin, cold capsules, bandages, and medications—antibiotic and antidiarrheal and motion sickness medicine. Tweezers and a thermometer in a hard case are also recommended.

Soap prevents and controls infections. Young travelers concerned about acne (which can be especially troublesome when traveling) should wash with soap five times a day, six if you're touring the Swiss chocolate factories. Supplemental vitamins (with iron, for women) are most effective when taken with the day's largest meal. Aspirin is a great general pain reliever for headaches, sore feet, sprains, bruises, Italian traffic, hangovers, and many other minor problems.

A high fever merits medical help. (To convert from Celsius to Fahrenheit, use the formula $F = [(C \times 9/5) + 32]$.) 101 degrees Fahrenheit equals 38.8 degrees Celsius. To be effective, medication for motion sickness (Dramamine) should be taken several hours before the upsetting motion is expected to begin. This medication can also serve as a mild sleeping pill. Ask your doctor to recommend an antidiarrheal medication.

If you have any serious dietary restrictions (like no wheat products), have a multilingual friend write it in the local language on the back of a business card and use it to order in restaurants.

Bandages help keep wounds clean but are not a substitute for thorough cleaning. A piece of clean cloth can be sterilized by boiling for ten minutes or by scorching with a match. Bandages, tape, moleskin, or two pairs of socks can prevent or retard problems with the feet. Cover any irritated area before it blisters.

Those with corrected vision should bring extra glasses in a solid pro-tective case as well as the lens prescription. Contact lenses are used all over Europe, and the required solutions for their care are easy to find. Soft lenses can be boiled like eggs. (Be sure to remind your helpful landlady to leave them in their case.) If you have the money, you can avoid all the cleaning headaches and enjoy the comfort of home wear with a trip's worth of disposable-once-a-week contacts. Do not assume that you can wear your contacts as comfortably in Europe as you can at home. I find that the hot, dusty cities and my style of travel make con-tacts impossible, and every summer I end up wearing my glasses and carrying my contacts.

Jet Lag and the First Day of Your Trip

Flying halfway around the world is stressful. If you leave frazzled after a hectic last night and a wild bon voyage party, there's a good chance you won't be healthy for the first part of your trip. Just a hint of a cold coupled with the stress of a long flight will mean a sniffly first week. Once you're on the road, it's pretty hard to slow down enough to fight that cold properly.

Leave home well rested. An early trip cold used to be a regular part of my vacation until I learned a very important trick. Plan from the start as if you're leaving two days before you really are. Keep that last 48-hour period sacred, even if it means being hectic before your false departure date. Then you have two orderly, peaceful days after you've packed so that you are physically ready to fly. Mentally, you'll be com-fortable about leaving home and starting this adventure. You'll fly away well rested and 100 percent capable of enjoying the bombardment of your senses that will follow.

Anyone who flies through time zones has to grapple with the biorhythmic confusion known as jet lag. When you switch your wrist-watch eight hours forward, your body says, "Hey, what's going on?" Body clocks don't reset so easily. All your life, you've done things on a 24-hour cycle. Now, after crossing the Atlantic, your body wants to eat when you tell it to sleep and sleep when you tell it to enjoy a museum. You can't avoid jet lag, but with a few tips, you can minimize the symptoms.

You dehydrate during a long flight, so drink plenty of liquids. I ask for "two orange juices with no ice" every chance I get. Eat light and have no coffee and only minimal sugar until the flight's almost over. Alcohol is stressful to your body and will aggravate jet lag. The in-flight movie is good for one thing—nap time. With three hours of sleep during the transoceanic flight, you will be functional the day you land.

Reset your wristwatch to local time as soon as the pilot announces it. And don't prolong jet lag by reminding yourself what time it is back home.

On arrival, make yourself stay awake until an early local bedtime. Plan a good walk until early evening. Jet lag hates fresh air, strong daylight, and exercise. Your body may beg for sleep but refuse. You must force your body's transition to the local time. Then, after a solid eight hours of sleep, you should wake up feeling like super-tourist.

Asleep at his spaghetti, a traveling two-year-old learns that jet lag hits even the very young.

Too many people assume their first day will be made worthless by jet lag. Don't prematurely condemn yourself to zombiedom. Most people of all ages who I've traveled with have enjoyed very productive—even hyper—first days. Many people wake very early on their first morning. Trying to sleep late is normally futile. Jet lag is a joke to some and a major problem to others. It's hard to predict just how serious your jet lag will be. Those who keep strict twenty-four-hour schedules will probably feel more jet lag than those who work the swing shift or keep crazy hours.

You'll read about many jet lag "cures." Most are worse than the disease. Just leave unfrazzled, minimize jet lag's symptoms, and give yourself a chance to enjoy your trip from the moment you step off the plane. Remember, this is the first day of the rest of your trip.

Health in Europe

Europe is generally safe. All the talk of gamma globulin, doxycycline, and treating water with purification tablets is applicable only south and east of Europe.

Many people might disagree with me, but, with discretion and common sense, I eat and drink whatever I like in Europe. If any area deserves a little extra caution, it is rural areas in the southern countries of Spain, Portugal, Italy, and Greece. As our world becomes more chemical, reasons for concern and caution will increase on both sides of the Atlantic.

I was able to stay healthy while traveling from Europe to India. By following these basic guidelines, I never once suffered from Tehran Tummy, Delhi Belly, or the Tegucigallop.

Outside of Europe, use good judgment when eating. Avoid unhealthy-looking restaurants. Peel all fruit. When in serious doubt, eat only thick-skinned fruit (peeled). Even in the worst places, anything well cooked and still hot is safe. Meat should be well cooked and in some places avoided altogether. Have "well done" written on a piece of paper in the local language and use it when ordering. Avoid possibly spoiled foods, and remember, preprepared foods gather germs. The train station restaurants are India's safest because they have the fastest turnover. Germs just don't have time to congregate.

Honor your diet. An adequate diet is very important for a traveler. The longer your trip, the more you'll be affected by an inadequate diet. Budget travelers often eat more carbohydrates and less protein to stretch their travel dollar. This is the root of many nutritional problems encountered by travelers. Protein is necessary for resistance to infection and to rebuild muscles. Get the most nutritional mileage from your protein by eating it with the day's largest meal (in the presence of all those "essential" amino acids). Supplemental super-vitamins, taken regularly, help me to at least feel healthy.

A basic hygiene hint is to wash your hands often, keep your nails clean, and never touch your fingers to your mouth.

Venereal disease is widespread. Obviously, the best way to prevent VD is to avoid exposure. Condoms (readily available in rest room vending machines) are fairly effective in preventing transmission for those unable to avoid exposure. Cleaning with soap and water before and after exposure is also helpful if not downright pleasurable. AIDS has been reported in Europe's heterosexual population.

Physically, travel is great living—healthy food, lots of activity, fresh air, and all those stairs! Still, you may want to work out during your trip. Jogging, while not as widespread in Europe, is nothing weird. Traveling joggers enjoy Europe from a special perspective—at dawn. Europe has plenty of good, inexpensive public swimming pools. Whatever your racket, if you want to badly enough, you'll find ways to keep in practice as you travel. Most big-city private tennis and swim clubs welcome foreign guests for a small fee. This is a good way to make friends as well as exercise.

Drink the Water

I drink the water in Europe. Read signs carefully, however, because some taps, like those on the trains, are not for drinking. If there's any hint of nonpotability—a decal showing a glass with a red "X" over it or a skull and crossbones—don't drink it. I drink any water served in restaurants.

East of Bulgaria and south of the Mediterranean, do not drink untreated water. Water can be treated by boiling it for 10 minutes or by using tablets or a porcelain filter.

Bottled water, beer, wine, boiled coffee and tea, and bottled soft drinks are safe. Coca-Cola products (if the top is on and the carbonation is still there) are as safe in the Sudan as they are at home.

You Will Get Sick—Loosen Up

Travel is a package deal. You will probably get sick in Europe. Get used to the fact that you'll have diarrhea for a day. (Practice that thought in front of the mirror tonight.) When you get the runs, take it in stride. If you stay healthy, you'll feel lucky.

It's simply not worth taking eight Pepto Bismol tablets a day or brushing your teeth in Coca-Cola all summer long to avoid a day of the runs. I take my health seriously, and for me, traveling in India or Mexico is a major health concern. But I find Europe very mild.

The water (or, just as likely, the general stress of travel on your immune system) may, sooner or later, make you sick. The water is not necessarily dirty. The bacteria in European water is different from that in American water. Our bodily systems—raised proudly on bread that rips in a straight line—are the most pampered on earth. We are capable of handling American bacteria with no problem at all, but some people can go to London and get sick. Some French people visit Boston and get sick. Some Americans travel around the world, eating and drinking everything in sight, and don't get sick, while others spend weeks on the toilet. It all depends on the person.

"Traveling makes a man wiser, but less happy." (Thomas Jefferson)

If (or when) you get diarrhea, it will run its course. Revise your diet, don't panic, and take it easy for a day. When I get diarrhea, I make my diet as bland and boring as possible for a day or so (bread, rice, baked potatoes, clear soup, weak tea). Keep telling yourself that tomorrow you'll feel much better. You will. Most conditions are self-limiting. For me, the bland diet is the best remedy. If your loose stools persist, replenish lost liquids and minerals. (Bananas are effective in replacing potassium, which is lost during a bout with diarrhea.) If you have a prolonged case of diarrhea (especially dangerous for an infant), a temperature greater than 101 degrees F (38.8 degrees C) or if you notice blood in your stools, get a doctor's help. Europeans use a pill called Enterovioform to get you solid. American doctors warn that it can harm your eyesight. Don't use it.

I visited the Red Cross in Athens after a miserable three-week tour of the toilets of Syria and Jordan. My intestinal commotion was finally stilled by a strict diet of boiled rice and plain tea. As a matter of fact, after five days on that dull diet, I was constipated.

With all the bread you'll be eating, constipation, the other side of the intestinal pendulum, is (according to my surveys) as prevalent as diarrhea. Know what roughage is—raw fruits, leafy vegetables, prunes, or bran tablets from home—and everything will come out all right in the end.

If You Get Really Sick

Throughout Europe, people with a health problem go first to the local pharmacy, not to their doctor. European pharmacists diagnose and prescribe remedies for most simple problems. They are usually friendly and English-speaking.

Swelling, which often accompanies a physical injury, is painful and retards healing. Ice and elevate any sprain or bruise for 48 hours. An "ace" bandage is useful to immobilize and to stop swelling and, later, provides support. It is not helpful to "work out" a sprain.

Serious medical treatment in Europe is generally of high quality. To facilitate smooth communication, it's best to find an English-speaking doctor. Information leading you to these doctors can be obtained through agencies that deal with Americans, such as embassies, consulates, American Express companies, and large hotels.

8
The Woman Traveling Alone

Every year, more and more single women travel alone around Europe. Women outnumber the men in the travel classes I teach. And many are asking, "Is it safe for me to travel alone in Europe?" This is a topic that is best understood and discussed by a woman. Pam Kasardi, who has traveled more than any woman I know, agreed to share her thoughts on the subject in this chapter if I promised not to entitle it "Tips from Abroad."

A woman traveling alone faces two special problems. First, the usual danger associated with solo travel—crime—might be greater because a woman is seen as more vulnerable than a man. And second, a woman traveler will endure more sexual harassment while on the road than she would find acceptable at home. Aside from these problems, however, the lone woman traveler does enjoy some advantages.

If you have the desire to travel alone in Europe, do it. While I don't recommend traveling alone in North Africa or the Middle East, I have never regretted traveling alone in Europe. My feeling (and most of the solo woman travelers I've met on the road agree with me) is that you will be safe as long as you are careful and exercise the same common sense you would in any big American city. The woman traveler has a tremendous social advantage over men. I'd say, flirt but don't act like a bimbo. Be wary of the people you meet. Withhold your trust longer than you would at home. To put it bluntly, Europe has more than its share of horny men roaming about with no other purpose in mind than to hustle women tourists.

As far as crime and your safety are concerned, I would say Europe is on par with the United States. If you don't feel safe traveling alone in America, think twice before embarking on a solo European adventure. The Mediterranean world is most troublesome. The Moslem countries, while not necessarily a criminal threat, are the leaders of the pack in hassling women travelers. In these countries you are safest in the more touristed areas, where the Western traveler is a relatively common sight.

Fit in. Women's Liberation has yet to reach southern Europe, and you're not going to bring it there. When you enter a new country, observe. See how the women are treated and how they are expected to act. Don't forget that you are in a different culture with different morals and mores. Just as you must learn to fit in as a guest, you must learn to adapt to the local expectations of proper relations between the sexes. Learn to see your actions as the local people see them. Don't flaunt your relative liberation. If you wear skimpy cutoffs and a T-shirt amid women shrouded from head to toe in black, you will certainly be calling attention to yourself, offending people, and asking for trouble. In a situation such as this, a skirt or long pants would be more appropriate—even if less comfortable.

Don't be a temptation. The flashy female tourist is often equated with the dreamy women the southern European man sees in American movies. You may be considered "loose" just because you're from the same country as Marilyn Monroe. Work hard to fit in so you don't encourage that sort of appraisal of your character. Be especially careful with your clothing and physical movements (eye contact, smiles, winks, etc.). I'll never forget the day I left my Naples hotel wearing a cool tank top. Within a few minutes I realized that, heat or no heat, I would have to wear something much less interesting.

Many foreign men will look at you for anything they can interpret as a sexual invitation. I have found that the most harmless gesture, like a warm smile or eye contact, can be misinterpreted. Sadly, you will sometimes have to act colder than you really are to remain unharassed.

No matter how you dress or act, you will probably be the object of much admiration, some advances, and plenty of less-than-discreet stares. Try not to let crude gestures of appreciation (whistles and so forth) bother you. I have found them to be generally harmless (if annoying) compliments as well as invitations. The best policy is to ignore them and keep on walking. If things get out of hand, a harsh scolding, in any language, especially in the presence of onlookers, will usually work wonders. "Basta!" means "enough" in Italian.

Stares are a fact of traveling. The farther off the beaten path you get, the more you'll be stared at. In the countryside of Spain, foreigners of any sex are stared at constantly. Admittedly, stares, wolf whistles, pinches, and macho come-ons are not to your or my liking, but they are as much a part of Italian and Spanish culture as spaghetti and bullfights. Even if you don't like it, accept it as inevitable.

Southern European women have a habit of strolling arm in arm to let men they pass know that they are in no need of "companionship." When traveling in the south with another woman, I do the same thing. This and avoiding eye contact work very well in reducing harassment.

If you find yourself in a conversation that is leading in the wrong direction, you may want to tell the man or men involved about your husband or children—even if they are imaginary. One summer, I wore a fake wedding band whenever I wanted to be considered unavailable and uninterested. When I want to sit unpestered in a café, I write in my journal. If you are doing something, you don't look like you're just waiting to be picked up.

In Europe, it's macho to try. Train conductors may lie down next to you on the train, hotel managers may try to escort you farther than your room, shoeshine boys may polish your thighs. These are not rape attempts. These are men asking for a date the only way they know how with a very impressive woman from a skyscraper land that speaks and thinks a strange language. Don't overreact—just firmly refuse and mace their eyes out (just kidding).

Be very careful who you trust. Believe me, European men, especially the ones who get a lot of practice, can be incredibly smooth and impressive. I've heard several stories about women travelers who joined up with some "classy" European only to wake up abandoned and left without any of their belongings. Avoid this mess by withholding your trust.

Women traveling with partners are less likely to find themselves in difficult situations than those traveling alone. Many people start their trips alone, intending to pick up partners as they go along. This is easy since there are many solo travelers of both sexes all over Europe traveling with the same intention—befriending and teaming up with a compatible travel partner. I find this particularly easy in youth hostels. European hotels don't care if roommates are married or not.

You will enjoy rewarding experiences and wonderful hospitality because you are a woman—dinner invitations, escorted tours, rides, cups of tea, and so on. American women are often looked on with awe by foreign men. While there may be hassles, I think these hassles are more than compensated for by the generous offers of hospitality. You will have many advantages over your male counterpart. Most men would have to travel months to receive the same amount of tangible hospitality that a woman receives in a few days. Needless to say, this sort of friendliness can make a visit to any country special. As you travel beyond Europe, you will notice even greater hospitality and attention.

I'll never forget the Egyptian man who let me ride his donkey. As I rode sleepily along a bank of the Nile, he begged me to stay with him in Egypt. He promised to build me "a castle on the hilltop."

The problem, of course, is that all too often those things come with strings attached. (My Egyptian friend fondled my leg while he promised me the world.) I find that these amount to little more than minor irritations. Before you curse the attention you are getting, remember that you may actually miss it a little after you get home.

A woman who finds herself in any sort of serious trouble should know that a few well-placed tears will often do wonders to clear things up. While a man could conceivably starve on the street corner, a "damsel in distress" is never far from help.

I think the most common negative result from this kind of harassment is that the woman escapes to more comfortable terrain, such as England or Germany, and takes with her a disdain for "those rude men in the south."

There's only one thing I don't like about being a woman traveler — my period. Having your period on the road can be a mess but no more than at home. Remember, it's a global phenomenon. Tampons are widely available and Europeans are understanding. Plan ahead. If you expect a serious problem (e.g., long bus ride), wear both a napkin and a tampon. If you really anticipate a bad day, treat yourself to a good hotel, with a bidet. Europeans use nonapplicator types (OB). These are handy since there's less to throw away. Consider the easy and more environmentally correct natural sea sponge, available at health food places and large drugstores. You just need privacy and a sink. Rinse it out and reinsert.

Now that you've read this chapter, keep in mind that, if anything, I have made traveling as a woman sound worse than it really is. Proceed with a cautious but positive attitude and you'll have a great trip.

9
Travel Photography

If my hotel were burning down and I could just grab one thing, it would be my exposed film—my most prized souvenirs. Every year I ask myself whether it's worth the worry and expense of mixing photography with my travels. After my film is developed and I relive my trip through those pictures, the answer is always, "Yes!" Here are some tips and lessons that I've learned from the photographic school of hard knocks.

The Camera

Good shots are made by the photographer, not the camera. For most people, a very expensive camera is a bad idea. Your camera is more likely to be lost, broken, or stolen than anything else you'll travel with. A very expensive model may not be worth the risks and headaches that accompany it.

A good basic 35mm single-lens reflex camera (such as my Pentax ME) provides everything I need. When buying a camera, think about size, weight, and durability. Name brands are easier to repair or outfit with a new body or lenses when you're traveling. Those who want an extremely simple lightweight camera that takes good pictures enjoy the popular 35mm miniautomatics. These are far better than instamatic snapshot cameras, have handy built-in flash attachments, fit comfortably in your coat pocket, and cost around $150. But the point-and-shoot automatics limit your creative control since the focus, exposure, depth of field, and shutter speed is given to you—automatically. With one of these very simple cameras much of this chapter is needless. But even a point-and-shoot photographer should understand the basics.

Research before you buy. Shutter bugs love to talk photography. Learn from them. Visit some camera shops and ask questions. Most people are limited by their skills, not by their camera. A common and serious mistake is to buy a new camera and not really know how to use it for your trip. Understand your camera. Shoot a sample roll taking notes on each shot to learn from as you review your developed photos.

You may put a lot of expense and energy into your travel photography. If you don't understand ASA numbers, "f-stops," or "depth of field," find a photography class or book and learn. Camera stores offer many good books on photography and even on travel photography. I shutter to think how many people are underexposed or at least lacking depth in this field.

Lenses

Most cameras come with a "normal" 50 to 55mm lens that goes "down" to about "f-2." To start with, this is all you need. The f-stop numbers indicate how wide you can open the aperture (how much light can be let in at once). A better and more expensive lens can be opened wider (set at a lower f-stop), enabling you to take a picture when less light is available. Your lens should go at least as low as f-2. Since I use no flash, I really appreciate my f-1.7 stop.

The length of the lens (such as 55mm) determines the size of the image it takes. A wide-angle lens is shorter (28 or 35mm), letting you fit more into your picture. This is especially useful when photographing interiors, where it's impossible to back up enough to get much in. A lens with a very wide angle distorts the picture. A 28mm lens—which is as wide as you can go before the distortion becomes very noticeable—is best.

A good eye is more important than an extra lens.

A longer telephoto lens (such as 150mm) allows you to get a closer shot of your subject. A telephoto lens is especially handy for taking portraits inconspicuously. And they have a short depth of field, allowing you to isolate a subject by arranging the shot so only he or she is in focus. The longer or more powerful the lens, the more it magnifies any vibrations, thus requiring a faster shutter speed for a good, crisp shot.

A zoom lens has an adjustable length. A common size zoom lens has a range from 70 to 205mm. You could fit your subject's entire body in the picture (at 70mm), then zoom right in to get just the face (at 205mm). This is a lot of fun, but, like the telephoto, it's bulkier and heavier than either the regular or the wide-angle lenses.

For travel photography, unless you are particularly interested in candid portraiture, the wide-angle is a more valuable second lens than the telephoto or zoom.

Many travel with only the popular 28mm to 85mm midrange zoom lens, happily trading away two f-stops for the convenience of three lenses in one. Remember, the capacity to zoom adds weight and limits your f-stop range. There is also a device called a doubler that is attached between the body of the camera and the lens. This doubles the power of that lens's magnification but also doubles the loss of light and requires a faster shutter speed because the magnification also magnifies any shaking.

Filters

There is a wide variety of filters to play with. Every lens should have a clear, ultraviolet, or haze filter to protect the lens. The only other filter I use is a polarizer, which can eliminate reflection and glare and intensify colors. A polarizer (perpendicular to the sun) will sharpen the contrast between the white and blue of a cloudy sky, giving you more dramatic skyscapes and landscapes.

Film

Travel photographers around the world debate the merits of different film. There's no real right or wrong choice—just trade-offs and personal preferences.

Each brand has its own personality when it comes to color and sharpness. (Kodachrome is known for reds, Fuji for greens and blues, Agfa for yellows and orange.) Rather than trying to evaluate the various films, I'll explain what I buy and why.

Slides are cheaper than prints and offer the best color and sharpness. I get prints made only of the shots I really like. I save time, bulk, and expense by buying rolls of 36 rather than 20 exposures.

Films come with different ASA numbers or "speeds." The average traveler carries film with ASA numbers ranging from 64 to 400. The ASA number indicates the film's light sensitivity. Greater light sensitivity (higher number ASA) allows you to take pictures with less light, but the cost is a grainier quality. In choosing your film, you must decide how "fast" you need it and how important it is for you to minimize graininess and get the best color. In a small print or on a slide projected on a screen, I see no difference in graininess between ASA 400 and ASA 64; in fact, with the faster film, I get a faster shutter speed, and this contributes to the sharpness more than the graininess hurts it. Graininess does become a factor in large prints.

It's a confusing field. You will make the best choice if you understand the trade-offs between speed, color, and graininess. Kodachrome 64 is the best-selling slide film and is the best general-purpose film on the market. I get Kodak film in ASA 64 for color and 400 for speed.

Film prices vary, and if you find a good price, you can stock up. (Keep what film you don't use fresh by freezing it.) Film is much more expensive in Europe. Before buying film or any photographic equipment, it's wise to pick up a photography magazine and read the advertisements. Wholesale warehouses all over the country sell cameras, accessories, and film at prices no retail outlet can match.

A Galaxy of Gadgets

Like many hobbies, photography is one that allows you to spend endless amounts of money on a galaxy of gadgets. I have some favorites that are particularly useful to the traveling photographer.

First of all, you need a gadget bag. The most functional and economical one is simply a small nylon stuff bag made for hikers. When I'm in a market or somewhere taking a lot of pictures, I like to wear a nylon belt pouch (designed to carry a canteen). This is a handy way to have your different lenses and filters accessible, allowing you to make necessary changes quickly and easily. A formal camera bag is unnecessary and attracts thieves.

A mini C-clamp/tripod is a great gadget. About 5 inches high, this tool screws into most any camera, sprouts three legs, and holds the camera perfectly still for slow shutter speeds and time exposure shots. (It looks like a small lunar landing module.) The C-clamp works where the tripod won't, such as on a fence or a handrail. A conventional tripod is too large to lug around Europe. Those without a mini tripod get good at balancing their camera on anything solid, adjusting the tilt with the lens cap or strap and still getting good timed exposures and automatic shutter release shots.

A cable release (especially helpful for cameras with no built-in automatic shutter release) is a gadget that allows you to snap a shot or hold the shutter open without moving the camera. Proper use of this and a C-clamp/tripod will let you take some exciting time exposures and night shots.

If you are traveling with a friend and want to share lenses, it's possible to buy an adapter ring that will make lenses of different mounts compatible. A dust blower, lens cleaning tissue, and a small bag of cleaning solution are wise additions to any gadget bag. I take my camera without its protective case and protect my lens with a cap that dangles on its string when I'm shooting. For most people, a camera case is unnecessary.

Tricks for a Good Shot

A sharp eye and a wild imagination will be your most valuable piece of equipment. Develop an eye for what will look good and be interesting after the trip. The skilled photographer's eye sees interesting light, shade, form, lines, patterns, and colors. Weed out dull shots before you take them, not after you get them home. It's cheaper.

Postcard-type shots are boring. Everyone knows what the Eiffel Tower looks like. Find a unique or different approach to sights that everyone has seen. Shoot the bell tower through the horse's legs or lay your camera on the floor to shoot the Gothic ceiling.

Buildings, in general, are not interesting. It doesn't matter if Karl Marx or Beethoven was born there, a house is as dead as they are. As travel photographers gain experience, they take more people shots and fewer buildings or general landscapes. Show the personal and intimate details of your trip: how you lived, who you met, what made each day an adventure (a close-up of the remains of a picnic, your leech bite, a local schoolboy playing games with his nose, or a shot of how you washed your clothes).

Vary the perspective of your camera—close, far, low, high, day, night, and so on. Don't fall into the rut of always centering a shot. Use foregrounds to add color, depth, and interest to landscapes.

Break rules and be gamey. For instance, we are told never to shoot into the sun. Some into-the-sun shots bring surprising results. Try to use bad weather to your advantage. Experiment with strange or difficult light situations. Buy a handbook on photographing in existing light.

Real photographers get one-minded at the magic hours—early morning and late afternoon when the sun is very low and the colors glow. Plan for these times.

Get close; notice details. Get closer, real close. Eliminate distractions. Get so close, you only show one thing. Don't try to show it all in one shot. Take several.

People are the most interesting subjects. It takes nerve to walk up to people and take their picture. It can be difficult, but if you want some great shots, be nervy. Ask for permission. The way to do this in any language is to point at your camera and ask, "Photo?" Your subject will probably be delighted. You most likely just made his day, as well as a good picture. Try to show action. A candid is better than a posed shot. Even a posed candid is better than a posed shot. Many photographers take a second shot immediately after the first portrait to capture a looser, warmer subject. If the portrait isn't good, you probably weren't close enough. My best portraits are so close that the entire head can't fit into the frame. You know the old saying: "Don't fire until you can see the whites of his pimples."

I traveled through Spain and Morocco with a professional photographer. One of the lessons I learned from him was not to intimidate your subject. If you walk right up, shake his hand, and act like a bloody fool, he will consider you just that and ignore you while you feast on some great material.

It's very important to be able to take a quick shot. Know your camera, practice setting it, understand depth of field and metering. In a marketplace situation, where speed is crucial, I preset my camera. I set the meter on the sunlit ground and focus at, let's say, 12 feet. Now I know that, with my depth of field, anything from about 10 to 15 feet will be in focus and, if it's in the sunshine, properly exposed. I can take a perfect picture in an instant, provided my subject meets these preset requirements. It's possible to get some good shots by presetting the camera and shooting from the waist. Ideally, I get eye contact while I shoot from the hip.

Be sure you expose for your subject. Even if your camera is automatic, your subject can turn out a silhouette. Meter without the sky. Get those faces in the sun, ideally lit from the side. For slides, you'll get richer tones if you underexpose just a bit. Expose for the highlights.

You'll hear that the focal length of your lens dictates the slowest safe handheld shutter speed you can use. For instance, a 50mm lens should shoot no slower than a 50th of a second. That rule is too conservative. I get decent shots out of my 50mm lens at a 30th of a second, even a 15th. Don't be afraid to handhold a slow shot, but do what you can to make it steady. If you can lean against a wall, for instance, you become a tripod instead of a bipod. If you have a self-timer, it can click the shutter smoother than your finger. Using these tricks, I can get good-looking pictures inside a museum at a 15th of a second. With ASA 400 film, I manage indoors without a flash.

A lot of time-exposure photography is guesswork. The best way to get good shots of difficult lighting situations is to "bracket" your shots by trying several different exposures of the same scene. You'll have to throw out a few slides that way, but one good shot is worth several in the garbage can. Automatic cameras usually meter properly up to eight or ten seconds, making night shots easy and bracketing unnecessary. A "no-frills" camera will not have a timed shutter release, but the accessory self-timer attachment is cheap and worthwhile.

Contrary to what you may think, you won't be able to remember the name of every monastery, fellow hosteler, or mountain that you take a picture of. A running list of shots is unnecessary, but I record the name of anything I want to be sure to remember.

When you put your slide show together, remember to limit the length of your show. Nothing is worse than to sit through an endless parade of lackluster and look-alike shots. Set a limit (maximum two carousels of 140 slides each) and prune your show down until it bleeds. Keep it tight. Keep it moving. Leave the audience crying for more.

10
Museums

Culture Beyond the Petri Dish

Europe is a treasure chest of great art. Many of the world's greatest museums will be a part of your trip. Here are a few hints on how to get the most out of these museums.

I've found that some studying before the trip makes the art I see in Europe more exciting. It's criminal to visit Rome or Greece with no background in those civilizations' art. I remember touring the National Museum of Archaeology in Athens as an obligation. It was boring. I was convinced that those who looked like they were enjoying it were actually just faking it—trying to look sophisticated. Two years later, after a class in ancient art history, that same museum was a fascinating trip into the world of Pericles and Socrates, all because of some background knowledge.

A common misconception is that a great museum has only great art. A museum like the Louvre in Paris is so big (the building itself was, at one time, the largest in Europe), you can't possibly cover everything—so don't try. Be selective. Only a fraction of a museum's pieces are really "greats" anyway. It's generally best, with the help of a guide or guidebook, to focus on just the museum's best two hours. Some of Europe's great museums provide brief guide pamphlets recommending the best basic visit. With this selective strategy, you'll appreciate the highlights when you're fresh. If you still have any energy left, you can explore other areas of specific interest to you. For me, museum-going is the hardest work I do in Europe, and I'm rarely good for more than two or three hours at a time. If you're determined to cover a large museum thoroughly, try to tackle one section a day for several days.

If you are especially interested in one piece of art, spend half an hour studying it and listening to each passing tour guide tell his or her story about *David* or the *Mona Lisa* or whatever. They each do their own research and come up with different information to share. There's nothing wrong with this sort of tour freeloading. Just don't stand in the front and ask a lot of questions.

On arrival, I always thumb through a museum guidebook index or look through the postcards to make sure I won't miss anything of importance to me. For instance, I love Dali. One time I thought I was finished with a museum, but as I browsed through the postcards— Hello, Dali. A museum guide was happy to show me where this Dali painting was hiding. I saved myself the agony of discovering after my trip was over that I was there but didn't see it.

Readable English guidebooks are rare. To get the most out of your trip, consider getting *Mona Winks: Self-Guided Tours of Europe's Top Museums* (Santa Fe, N.M.: John Muir Publications). This book (by Gene Openshaw and me) is a collection of fun and easy-to-follow take-you-by-the-hand two-hour tours of Europe's twenty most important (and difficult) museums and sights. It's just me and you together in the greatest art of our civilization. (See the back of this book for ordering instructions.)

Remember, most museums are closed one day during the week. Your local guidebook or tourist information has that information. Many also stop selling tickets 30 to 60 minutes before closing. Free admission days are usually the most crowded. In many cases, it's worth the entrance fee to avoid the crowds.

A victim of the Louvre

Try to get a tour. If it's French or German only, let the guide know politely, persistently, and early on that there are several English-speaking people in the group who'd love some information. Occasionally, if you call ahead, you can meet a scheduled English group and tag along.

Open-Air Folk Museums

Many travel in search of the old life and traditional culture in action. While we book a round-trip ticket into the romantic past, those we photograph with the Old World balanced on their heads are struggling to dump that load and climb into our world. In Europe, most are succeeding.

The easiest way and, more than ever, the only way to see the "real culture" is by exploring that country's open-air folk museum. True, it's culture on a "lazy Susan," but the future is becoming the past faster than ever, and, in many places, it's the only "Old World" you're going to find.

An open-air folk museum is a collection of traditional buildings from every corner of the country or region carefully reassembled in a park, usually near the capital or major city. These sprawling museums are the best bet for the hurried (or tired) tourist craving a magic carpet ride through that country's past. Log cabins, thatched cottages, mills, old schoolhouses, shops, and farms come complete with original furnishings and usually a local person dressed in the traditional costume who's happy to answer any of your questions about life then and there.

In the summer, folk museums buzz with colorful folk dances, live music performances, and young craftsmen specializing in old crafts. Many traditional arts and crafts are dying, and these artisans do what they can to keep the cuckoo clock from going the way of the dodo bird. Some of my favorite souvenirs are those I watched being dyed, woven, or carved by folk museum craftsmen.

To get the most out of your visit, start by picking up a list of special exhibits, events, and activities at the information center and take advantage of any walking tours.

Popularized in Scandinavia, these sightseeing centers of the future are now found all over the world. The best folk museums are still in the Nordic capitals. Oslo's, with 150 historic buildings and a twelfth-century stave church, is just a boat ride across the harbor from the city hall. Skansen in Stockholm gets my first-place ribbon for its guided tours, feisty folk entertainment, and Lapp camp complete with reindeer.

Switzerland's Ballenberg Open-Air Museum near Interlaken is a good alternative when the Alps hide behind clouds.

The British Isles have no shortage of folk museums. For an unrivaled look at the Industrial Revolution, spend a day at the Blists Hill Open-Air Museum in the Iron Bridge Gorge, north of Stratford. You can cross the world's first iron bridge to see the factories that lit the fuse of our modern age.

The "Knotts Berry Farm" of Bulgaria is in Gabrovo and offers a refreshing splash of free enterprise-type crafts in a rather drab socialist world.

Every year, new folk museums open. Travel with a current guide and use tourist information centers abroad. Before your trip, send a card to each country's National Tourist Office (addresses are listed in chapter 1, Planning) requesting, among other things, lists of open-air folk museums.

Folk museums teach traditional life-styles better than any other kind of museum. As the world plunges toward 100 billion McDonald's hamburgers served, these museums will become even more important. Of course, they're as realistic as Santa's Village. but how else will you see the elves?

Here is a list of some of Europe's best open-air folk museums:

Norway
Norwegian Folk Museum, at Bygdoy near Oslo. *150 old buildings from all over Norway and a twelfth-century stave church.*

Maihaugen Folk Museum, at Lillehammer. *Folk culture of the Gudbrandsdalen. Even better than Oslo's.*

Trondheim and Trondelag Folk Museum at Sverresborg fortress near Trondheim. *60 buildings showing old Trondheim, Lapp village, and farm life.*

Sweden
Skansen, Stockholm. *One of the best museums, with over 100 buildings from all over Sweden, craftspeople at work, live entertainment, and a Lapp camp complete with reindeer.*

Kulteren, Lund. *Features Southern Sweden and Viking exhibits.*

Finland
Seurasaari Island, near Helsinki. *Buildings reconstructed from all over Finland.*

Handicraft Museum, Turku. *The life and work of nineteenth-century craftspeople.*

Denmark
Funen Village (Den Fynske Landsby), just south of Odense.

Old Town, Arhus. *60 houses and shops show Danish life from 1580-1850.*

Lyngby Park, north of Copenhagen.

Hjerl Hode Iron Age Village, 10 miles south of Skive in northern Jutland. *Life-styles in prehistoric times.*

Oldtidsbyen Iron Age Village, near Roskilde.

Germany
Cloppenburg Open-Air Museum, southwest of Bremen. _Traditional life in Lower Saxony, seventeenth and eighteenth centuries._

Switzerland
Ballenberg Swiss Open-Air Museum, just northeast of Lake Brienz. _A fine collection of old Swiss buildings with furnished interiors._

Benelux
Zaandijk, 30 miles north of Amsterdam. _Windmills, wooden shoes, etc._

De Zeven Marken Open-Air Museum, in Schoonoord.

Netherlands Open-Air Museum at Arnhem. _70 old Dutch buildings, the Netherlands' first, biggest, and best museum of its kind._

Bokrijk Open-Air Museum, between Hasselt and Genk, in Belgium. _Old Flemish buildings and culture in a native reserve._

Great Britain
Blists Hill Open-Air Museum, near Coalport. _Shows life from the early days of the Industrial Revolution._

Beamish Open-Air Museum, northwest of Durham. _Life in northeast England in 1900._

Welsh Folk Museum, at St. Fagan's near Cardiff. _Old buildings and craftspeople illustrate traditional Welsh ways._

Ireland
Bunratty Folk Park, near Limerick. _Buildings from the Shannon area and artisans at work._

Irish Open-Air Folk Museum, at Cultra near Belfast. _Traditional Irish lifestyles. Buildings from all over Ireland._

Glencolumbkille Folk Museum, Donegal. _Thatched cottages show life from 1700-1900. A Gaelic-speaking cooperative runs the folk village and a traditional crafts industry._

Bulgaria
Gabrovo Folk Museum, Gabrovo. _Old buildings and skilled craftspeople._

Spain
Pueblo Español, Barcelona. _Buildings from all over Spain depict regional architecture, costumes, and folk craft._

This is not a complete listing, and new ones are opening every year. Ask for more information at European tourist offices.

11
Coping Abroad — Everyday Survival Skills

City Survival

Many Americans are overwhelmed by European big city shock. Struggling with the L.A.'s, Chicagos, and New Yorks of Europe is easier if you follow three rules: (1) get and use information; (2) orient yourself; (3) take advantage of the public transportation systems.

Getting Information Out of Local Tourist Offices

You can't Magoo Europe's large cities. Get information and plan. Have a directory-type guidebook for wherever you're traveling. Spend the last hour as you approach by train or bus reading and planning. Know what you want to see. Your sightseeing strategy should cover the city systematically, arranged efficiently, one neighborhood at a time. Check for closed days and free days.

No matter how well I know a town, my first stop is the tourist office. Any place with a tourist industry has an information service for visitors located on the central square, in the city hall building, at the train station, or at the freeway entrance. You don't need the address—just follow the signs. An often hectic but normally friendly and multilingual staff will equip you with a map and general sightseeing and tour information, reserve a room for you, sell you concert or play tickets, and answer your questions. I always prepare a list of needs and questions so I'm well organized and get the most out of my visit.

A checklist of concerns includes a written-out proposed sightseeing schedule for the information person to check (is it workable, efficient, anything missing, or changes recommended); what's going on in the way of special events (pick up any local periodical entertainment guide); a map of the town with public transit information; list of sights with current hours; ideas on eating and sleeping if necessary (remember, they don't volunteer information on cheap alternatives to hotels); walking tours available or self-guided walking tour brochures; and any miscellaneous needs (such as laundry, bike rental, transportation tips for your departure, map of the next town you'll be visiting, book-a-room-ahead help, and safety). If you're arriving late, this information is worth a long distance phone call (guidebooks list numbers). If the TI is closed, youth hostel wardens, big hotel information desks, and other travelers are alternative information sources.

All big cities have English bookstores. Large bookstores and university bookstores have English sections. Most kiosks and newsstands sell local guides in English.

Find a good map. The best and cheapest map is often the public transit map. Try to get one that shows bus lines, subway stops, and major sights. Many hotels can give you a free city map.

If you find yourself in a town with no information and the tourist office is closed, a glance through a postcard rack will quickly show you what the town's most proud of.

Big European cities bubble with entertainment, festivities, and nightlife. But it won't come to you. Without the right information and not speaking the local language, it's easy to be completely oblivious to a once-in-a-lifetime event erupting just across the bridge. In this case, a periodical entertainment guide is the ticket. Every big city has one, either in English (such as London's _What's On_ or _This Week in Oslo_), or in the local language but easy to decipher (such as the _Pariscope_ guide).

Ask at your hotel and at the tourist office about entertainment. Read posters. Events are posted on city walls everywhere. They are in a foreign language but that really doesn't matter when it reads: Weinfest, Musica Folklorico, 9 Juni, 21:00, Piazza Major, Entre Libre, and so on. Figure out the signs—or miss the party.

Orientation

Get the feel of the city. Once oriented, you're more at home there. It warms up and sightseeing is more enjoyable. Study the map to understand the city's layout. Relate the location of landmarks—your hotel, major sights, the river, main streets, and station—to each other. Use any viewpoint—such as a church spire, tower, top story of a skyscraper, or hilltop—to look over the city. Retrace where you've been, see where you're going. Back on the ground, you won't be in such constant need of your map.

Many cities have fast-orientation bus tours like London's famous "Round London" tour. If you're feeling overwhelmed, these show you the major sights and give you a feel for the urban lay of the land. Some cities have inexpensive public transit buses designed to orient visitors and move them conveniently from one major sight to the next, often with printed or recorded narrations.

Public Transportation

When you master a city's subway or bus system, you've got it by the tail. Europe's public transit systems are so good that many Europeans choose not to own a car. Their wheels are trains, buses, and subways.

The buses and subways all work logically and are run by people who are happy to help the lost tourist locate himself. Anyone can decipher the code to cheap and easy urban transportation. Too many timid tourists never venture into the subways or onto the buses and end up wasting money on taxis or time walking.

Paris and London have the most extensive—and the most needed—subway systems. Both cities are covered with subway maps and expert subway tutors. Paris even has maps that plan your route for you. Just push your destination's button and the proper route lights up! Subways are speedy and comfortable, never slowed by traffic jams. While they actually feel safe, be constantly on guard.

Make a point to get adequate transit information. Pick up a map. Find out about any specials—like packets of tickets sold at a discount (Paris) or tourist tickets allowing unlimited travel for a day or several days (London). These "go as you please" passes may seem expensive, but if you do any amount of running around, they can be a convenient money-saver. And remember, they are more than economical. With a transit pass, you'll avoid the often-long ticket lines.

Have a local person explain your ticket to you. A dollar and a half may seem expensive for the bus ride until you learn that your ticket is good for round-trip, two hours, or several transfers. And if you tell them where you're going, bus drivers and local people sitting around you will gladly tell you where to get off.

Taxis are often a reasonable option. In southern countries, they are cheap, and, while expensive for the lone budget traveler, a group of three or four people can often travel cheaper by taxi than by buying three or four bus tickets. Don't be bullied by cabbie con men (common only in the south). Insist on the meter, agree on a rate, or know the going rate. Taxi drivers intimidate too many tourists. If I'm charged a ridiculous price for a ride, I put a reasonable sum on the seat and say good-bye. Be careful, though. Many tourists are sure their cabbie is taking the long way around or adding unfair extras, even though cabbies are generally honest. There are lots of legitimate supplements (nights, weekends, baggage, extra person, ride out of town, etc.) and winding through medieval street plans is rarely even close to direct.

You can always call for a cab, but the meter will be well under way by the time you get in. It's cheaper and easy to just flag one down or walk to the nearest taxi stand. If it seems unusually frustrating to hail a cab, ask a shop keeper to direct you to the nearest taxi stand.

Bus Tour Self-Defense

The average American tourist sees Europe on an organized bus tour and doesn't even consider using a guidebook. They pay a guide to show them around.

The independent-minded traveler can do very well on a big bus tour if he knows how to get the most out of it and doesn't allow himself to be taken advantage of. Keep in mind that many savvy travelers take escorted coach tours year after year only for the hotels, meals, and transportation provided. Every day they do their own sightseeing, simply applying the skills of independent travel to the efficient, economical base an organized coach tour provides. You can take a tour and still go "on your own."

Most bus tours come with a ready-made circle of friends.

A typical big bus tour has a professional multilingual European guide and 40 to 50 people on board. The tour company is probably very big, booking rooms by the thousand and often even owning the hotels it uses.

Typically, the bus is a luxurious, fairly new 48-seater with a high, quiet ride, comfy seats, air-conditioning, and a toilet on board. The hotels will be fit for American standards—large, not too personal, and offering mass-produced comfort, good plumbing, and all double rooms. Most meals are included, generally in unmemorable hotel restaurants that can serve large groups.

As long as people on board don't think too much or try to deviate from the plan, things go smoothly and reliably and you really do see a lot of Europe. Note I said "see" rather than "experience." If you like the itinerary, weather, guide, and the people on your bus, it's a good, easy, and inexpensive way to go.

Having escorted several European coach tours and now owning and operating a tour company of my own, I've learned that you must understand the guide and his position. Leading a tour is a demanding job with lots of responsibility, paperwork, baby-sitting, and miserable hours. Very often, your guide is tired. He's away from his home and family often for months on end and is surrounded by foreigners having an extended party that he's probably not in the mood for. Most guides treasure their time alone and, socially, keep their distance from the group. Each tourist has personal demands, and a group of 50 can often amount to one big pain in the bus for the tour guide.

To the guide, the best group is one that lets him do the thinking, is happy to be herded around, and enjoys being spoon-fed Europe. The guide's base salary is normally low (about $10 a day from most companies), but an experienced guide can do very well when that is supplemented by his percentage of the optional excursions, kickbacks from merchants that he patronizes, and the trip-end tips from his busload.

The best guide is a happy one. It's very important to be independent without alienating him. Independent-type tourists tend to threaten guides. Don't insist on individual attention when he's hounded by 49 others. Wait for the quiet moment to ask for advice. If the guide wants to, he can give the entire group a lot of unrequired extras that will add greatly to your tour—but only if he wants to. Your objective, which requires some artistry, is to keep the guide on your side without letting him take advantage of you.

Most tours don't include the daily sightseeing programs. Each day, one or two special excursions or evening activities, called "options," are offered for $20 to $25 apiece. Each person decides which options to take and pay for. Since budget tours are so competitive, the profit margin on their base price is very thin. The tour company and guide sell these options aggressively (discouraging people from going off on their own and even withholding information from them). The profit is theirs when 40 people pay $20 each for an evening bus tour of Rome.

Discriminate among options. Some are great, others are not worth the time or money. In general, the half-day city sightseeing tours are a good value. A local guide will usually show you his or her city much more thoroughly than you could do on your own given your time limitations. Illuminated night tours of Rome and Paris can be marvelous. I'd skip most other illuminated tours and "nights on the town." On a typical big bus tour evening, several bus tours come together for the "evening of local color." Two hundred tourists having a glass of sangria watching flamenco dancing onstage in a huge room, with buses lined up outside, isn't exactly local.

Many who take an organized bus tour could have managed fine on their own.

I'd rather save the money and take a cab or a bus downtown to just poke around. A major problem with tours is that the groups only see a thin slice of people—not real locals but hardened business people who know how to make money off tour groups. Make a point to break away and meet locals who never deal with tourist groups. One summer night in Regensburg, I skipped out. While the tour waited to get off the bus, the great-great-great-grandson of Johannes Kepler bought me a beer and we drank it under the stars, overlooking the Danube.

Your guide may pressure you into taking the "options." Stand firm. In spite of what you may be told, you are capable of doing plenty on your own. Maintain your independence. Get maps and tourist information from your hotel desk (or another hotel desk) or a tourist information office. Tour hotels are often located outside the city, where they cost the tour company less and where they figure you are more likely to book the options just to get into town. Some tours promise to take you downtown if the hotel is outside the city limits. Ask the man or woman behind the desk how to get downtown using public transportation. Taxis are always a possibility, and with three or four people sharing, they're not expensive.

Team up with others on your tour to explore on your own. No city is dead after the shops are closed. Go downtown and stroll.

Do your own research. Know what you want to see. Don't just sit back and count on your guide to give you the Europe you're looking for. The guide will be happy to spoon-feed you Europe, but it will be from his menu. This often distorts the importance of sights in order to fit the tour. For instance, many tours seem to make a big deal out of a statue in Lucerne called the Dying Lion. Most tourists are impressed on command. The guide declares that this mediocre-at-best sight is great, and that's how it's perceived. What makes it "great" for the guide is that Lucerne (which doesn't have a lot of interesting sights) was given too much time in the itinerary and it's easy for the bus to park and wait. The *Last Supper* by Leonardo da Vinci, however, is often passed over as bus tours skirt Milan. It's an inconvenient sight.

Remember, you can't take 40 people into a cozy pub and enjoy a cozy pub. A good stop for a guide is one with great freeway accessibility where he can easily park his bus, where guides and drivers are buttered up with free coffee and cakes, where they serve bottomless cups of American-style coffee, speak English, accept bank cards, and will mail it home, and where 30 people can go to the bathroom at the same time. Arrivederci Roma.

Many people make their European holiday one long shopping spree. This suits your guide and the local tourist industry just fine. In Venice and Florence, guides bringing in a busload of tourists get a standard 15 percent commission. Every tour guide in Europe knows just where to park his bus in Lucerne for Swiss clocks. You get $40 and a bottle of champagne as soon as you park, and 45 minutes later, when all the tourists are back on the bus, the guide steps into the back room and gets 15 percent of whatever went into the till. That's good business. And any tour guide in Europe knows that if he's got Americans on board, he's carting around a busload of stark raving shoppers.

Don't necessarily reject your guide's shopping tips; just keep in mind that the prices you see often include that 15 percent kickback. Shop around and never swallow the line, "This is a special price available only to your tour, but you must buy now." The salesmen who prey on tour buses are smooth. They zero right in on the timid and gullible group member who has no idea what a good buy is. If you buy, buy carefully.

When you're traveling with a group, it's fun, as well as economical, to create a kitty for communal "niceties." If each person contributes $10, the "kitty-keeper" can augment dry continental breakfasts with fresh fruit, provide snacks and drinks at rest stops for a fraction of the exorbitant prices you'll find in the freeway restaurants, get stamps for postcards so each person doesn't have to find the post office himself, and so on.

Remember that the best-selling tours are the ones that promise you the most in the time you have available. No tour can give you more than 24 hours in a day or seven days in a week. What the "blitz" tour can do is give you more hours on the bus. Choose carefully among the itineraries available, and don't assume more is better.

The groups I have escorted on typical European big bus tours have been almost universally happy and satisfied with their vacations. They got the most out of their tour—and their tour didn't get the most out of them—because they exercised a measure of independence.

Organized Half-Day City Bus Tours

Throughout your trip—whether on a group tour or on your own—you'll encounter hour-long, half-day, and all-day sightseeing excursions or tours. There are several kinds. Orientation bus tours are fast, inexpensive, and superficial. Rarely do you even get out of the bus. They cost around $25, and, if you've got the money and not much time, they provide a good orientation. If you only had a day in a big city, I'd spend half of it on one of these bus tours.

There are also cases when a bus tour is worthwhile for the transportation it provides. For instance, the chateaus of the Loire, the sights of southern Bavaria (Ludwig's castles), and the stave church and Greig's home outside Bergen are all awkward to get to on your own; an organized tour not only whisks you effortlessly from one hard-to-reach-without-a-car sight to the next but gives you lots of information as you go.

Walking tours are my favorite. They are thorough, since they focus on just a small part of a city. They are usually conducted by a well-trained local person who is sharing his town for the noble purpose of giving you an appreciation of his city's history, people, and culture—not to make a lot of money. Walking tours are personal, inexpensive, and a valuable education. I can't recall a bad one. Many local tourist offices organize the tours or provide a do-it-yourself walking tour leaflet. The avid walking tourist should consider purchasing the guidebook called *Turn Right at the Fountain.*

Fancy coach tours—the kinds that leave from the big international hotels—are expensive. Some are great. Others are boring and so depersonalized, sometimes to the point of multilingual taped messages, that you may find the Chinese sound track more interesting than the English. These tours can, however, be of value to the budget-minded do-it-yourselfer. Pick up the brochure for a well-thought-out tour itinerary and do it on your own. Take local buses at your leisure and tour every sight for a fraction of the cost. A popular trend in Europe these days is a bus or boat route that connects all the major sightseeing attractions. Tourists buy the one-day pass and make the circuit at their leisure.

The best guides are often those whose tours you can pick up at the specific sight. These guides usually really know their museum or castle or whatever.

Telephoning in Europe

The more I travel, the more I use the telephone. I call hotels and hostels to make or confirm reservations, tourist information offices to check my sightseeing plans, restaurants, train stations, and local friends. In every country, the phone can save you lots of time and money. Each country's phone system is different, but each one works—logically.

The key to figuring out a foreign phone is to approach it without comparing it to yours back home. It works for the locals, and it can work for you. Many people flee in terror when a British phone starts its famous "rapid pips." They go home telling tales of the impossibility of using England's phones.

Each country has phone booths with multilingual instructions. If you follow these step by step, the phone will work—usually. Operators generally speak English and are helpful. International codes, instructions, and international assistance numbers are usually on the wall or in the front of the phone book. If I can't manage in a strange phone booth, I let a nearby local person help me out.

The first step is to find the right phone. The increasingly rare coin-op phones are being replaced by more convenient and vandal-resistant phones that accept only credit cards or strip cards that you buy at post offices or tobacco shops. For coin-op phones, have enough small coins to complete your call. The instructions may say the local minimum, your credit total is generally shown, and only entirely unused coins will be returned. Many phones allow run-on calls, so you won't lose your big-coin credit (if you have one and need to make another call). Look for this (usually black) button. In some countries, your voice won't be heard until you push a button to engage the call.

Phone cards, already popular and widespread in Germany, France, Britain, and Italy, and soon to be everywhere, are much easier to use than you'd think. You usually just slide your card into a slot and dial. The phone's digital readout ticks off the money remaining on your card. The only drawback is that the cheapest cards can cost $5, more phone time than you may need in that country. Still, you can't travel smart without using the phone. So use these cards.

Prefixes are a common source of phone booth frustration. They are usually listed by city on the wall or in the book. There are three prefixes: the international access number, the country code (1 for U.S.A.), and the city or area code. "Areas" are much smaller in Europe than in the United States, and nearly any call out of town will require one. When calling long distance in Europe, you must dial the area code first. Area codes start with a zero, which is only used when calling within the country. Calling internationally, drop the zero and replace it with the country code. Local numbers vary in length from three to eight digits.

Next you'll hear strange noises. Every country has its own version of rings and busy signals. Assume that the beep/click/buzz you hear is the phone ringing or trying to ring and wait. If no one answers, hang up and try again or get help.

Once you've made the connection, the real challenge begins—communication. With no visual aids, getting the message across in a language you don't speak requires some artistry.

Some key rules are speak slowly and clearly, pronouncing every consonant; keep it very simple—don't clutter your message with anything less than essential; don't overcommunicate—many things are already understood and don't need to be said (those last six words didn't need to be written); use international or carefully chosen English words. When all else fails, let a local person on your end (such as a hotel receptionist) do the talking after you explain to him, with visual help, the message.

Let me illustrate with a hypothetical telephone conversation. I'm calling a hotel in Barcelona from a phone booth in the train station. I just arrived, read my guidebook's list of budget hotels, and I like Pedro's Hotel. Here's what happens:

Pedro answers, "Hotel Pedro, grabdaboodogalaysk."

I ask, "Hotel Pedro?" (Question marks are created melodically.)

He affirms, already a bit impatient, "Si, Hotel Pedro."

I ask, "Habla Eng-leesh?"

He says, "No, dees ees Spain." (Actually, he probably would speak a little English or would say "moment" and get someone who did. But we'll make this particularly challenging. Not only does he not speak English—he doesn't want to.)

Remembering not to overcommunicate, you don't need to tell him you're a tourist looking for a bed. Who else calls a hotel speaking in a foreign language? Also, you can assume he's got a room available. If he's full, he's very busy and he'd say "complete" or "no hotel" and hang up. If he's still talking to you, he wants your business. Now you must communicate just a few things, like how many beds you need and who you are.

I say, "OK, hotel." (OK is international for, "Roger, prepare for the next transmission.") "Two people"—he doesn't understand. I get fancy, "Dos people"—he still doesn't get it. Internationalize, "Dos pehr-son"—no comprende. "Dos hombre"—nope. Digging deep into my bag of international linguistic tricks, I say, "Dos Yankees." "OK!" he understands, you want beds for two Americans. He says, "Si," and I say, "Very good" or "Muy bueno."

Now I need to tell him who I am. If I say, "My name is Mr. Steves and I'll be over promptly," I'll lose him. I say, "My name Ricardo (Ree-KAR-do)." In Italy, I say, "My name Luigi." Your name really doesn't matter; you're communicating just a password so you can identify yourself when you walk through the door. Say anything to be understood.

He says, "OK."

You repeat slowly, "Hotel, dos Yankees, Ricardo, coming pronto, OK?"

He says, "OK."

You say, "Gracias, ciao!"

Twenty minutes later you walk up to the reception desk, and Pedro greets you with a robust, "Eh, Ricardo!"

Calling Home

Most European countries have direct connections to the United States now, and you can get through for as little as 50 cents—the cost of a postcard stamp. Rather than write postcards, I just call in my "scenery's here, wish you were beautiful" messages.

You can call home in three ways—from your hotel's phone, the post office phone, or a public phone booth. Telephoning through your hotel's phone system is fine for local calls but an almost criminal rip-off for long distance. I only do this when I'm feeling flush and lazy for a quick "Call me in Stockholm at this number" message. Post offices are much cheaper, with metered international phone booths. The person who sells stamps will plug you in, assign you a booth, and help you with your long distance prefixes. You sit in your private sweat-box, make the call, and pay the bill when you're done. I normally just get a local phone credit card or a pile of coins, find a public phone booth, dial direct, and keep it short and sweet. Beware: a popular new rip-off is small businesses on main tourist streets which look like telephone company long distance services but actually charge like hotels. Ask the price per minute before you take a metered phone booth.

While less common in the south, nearly all European countries have "dial direct to anywhere" phone booths. Calls to the United States cost $2 to $4 per minute. There is no minimum. First get a pile of coins. Then find an international phone booth (if it lists country codes on the wall, you're in business). These often have instructions in English in the first few pages of the phone book or on the wall. Put in a coin and dial: (1) international access code, wait for tone; (2) country code; (3) area code; and (4) the seven-digit number. Try calling me from France: put in two francs (30 cents), dial 19-1-206-771-8303, and talk fast. Every country has its quirks—try pausing between codes if you're having trouble or dial the English-speaking international operator for help. Off-hours are cheaper per minute.

I start with a small coin worth 25 to 50 cents to be sure I get the person I need or can say, "I'm calling back in five minutes, so wake him up." (Remember, it's about six hours earlier in New York and nine hours earlier in California.) Then I plug in the larger coins. I keep one last sign-off coin ready. When my time is done, I pop it in and say good-bye. The digital meter warns you when you're about to be cut off.

Calling collect is sometimes more complicated and always more expensive. It's cheaper (about $1 a minute—and he pays) and easier (coin-free) if you have your friend call you back, dialing direct from the states. Tell them to dial 011 (the U.S. international access code), your country code (see below), your area code without the zero, and your number.

Country	International access code	Country code	Emergency for much of country
Austria	900	43	144
Belgium	00	32	900
Denmark	009	45	100
Finland	990	358	002

Country	International access code	Country code	Emergency for much of country
France	19	33	17
Germany	00	49	110
Great Britain	010	44	999
Ireland	16	353	999
Italy	00	39	113
Netherlands	09	31	222222
Norway	095	47	000
Spain	07	34	091
Sweden	009	46	90000
Switzerland	00	41	117

Theft and the Tourist

While violent crime is very rare in Europe, petty theft is a pain in the pocket for tourists from Bergen to Barcelona. As the notion of trickle-down goes global, pickpockets and purse-snatchers get hungrier, and the tourist becomes a richer and very tempting target.

If you're not constantly on guard, you'll have something stolen. One summer, four out of five friends I traveled with lost cameras in one way or another. (Don't look at me.) I've heard countless stories of tourists getting ripped off: pickpocketed in a bad neighborhood in London; shoulder bag snatched by a motorcycle bandit in Rome; suitcase taken from the train during a long, dark French tunnel; camera slipped right off the neck of a guy napping in Barcelona, and so on.

You can't be too careful. A tourist is an easy target. Loaded down with all his valuables in a strange new environment, he sticks out like a jeweled thumb and is a favorite victim of thieves—many of whom specialize solely in "the tourist trade." I read of people whose trips are ruined by thieves who snatch their purse or wallet. There is no excuse for this kind of vulnerability. Nearly all crimes suffered by tourists are nonviolent and are avoidable by thinking. Many of the most successful scams require a very naive and trusting tourist. If you exercise the proper caution and aren't overly trusting, you should have no problem. Here are some tips given to me by a gypsy who won the lotto.

First of all, don't bring things that will ruin your trip if they are lost, broken, or stolen. Everything that is crucial should fit into your money belt. Purses and wallets are fine for odds and ends and one day's spending money but not for irreplaceables. Luxurious luggage lures thieves like a well-polished flasher lures fish. Why brag to the thief that your luggage is the most expensive? The thief chooses the most impressive suitcase in the pile—never mine.

Those with nothing worth stealing (cars, video cameras, jewelry, and so on, which don't fit into their money belt) are virtually invulnerable. My money belt is my key to peace of mind. I'll never again travel without one. The money belt is a small, nylon-zippered bag that ties around the waist under your pants or skirt. It costs only a few dollars (see Back Door Catalog). In it, I keep my passport, cash, traveler's checks, train pass, airline ticket, and any very important documents, vouchers, or identity cards. Bring only one credit card and keep it in your money belt. I keep bulky or replaceable documents in a second money belt or small zipper bag (a three-ring notebook pencil bag) that I tie or sew to the inside of my rucksack or suitcase. It's important to keep the money belt slim so it's comfortable and hidden. I wear it all summer, even sleeping with it when necessary. It's only uncomfortable when I'm not wearing it.

With a money belt, all your essential documents are on you as securely and thoughtlessly as your underpants. Have you ever thought about that? Every morning you put your underpants on, and you don't even think about them all day long. And every night when you undress, sure enough, there they are, exactly where you put them. When I travel, I enjoy the luxury of having my valuables just as securely out of sight and out of mind, around my waist in a money belt.

My camera is, to a potential thief, the most tempting item in my luggage. I never leave it lying around where hotel workers and others can see it and be tempted. It's either around my neck or zipped safely out of sight.

If I ever sleep in public (on a train or at an airport or wherever), I clip or fasten my pack (or suitcase) to the chair or the luggage rack or to me. Even the slight inconvenience of undoing a clip foils most thieves. Don't sleep in an empty train compartment (especially women). Women are safest sharing a compartment with a family or a couple of nuns.

Be on guard for the modern-day artful dodgers. Imaginative thief teams often create a fight or commotion to distract their curious victims. Groups of gypsy kids with big eyes and colorful dresses play a game where they politely mob the unsuspecting tourist, beggar-style. As their pleading eyes grab yours and they hold up their sad message scrawled on cardboard, your purse, fanny-bag, or rucksack is being delicately rifled. (This is particularly common in Paris and Rome.) Thieves know that anyone leaving a bank with their bags just changed money. Keep things zipped, buttoned, and secure. Be alert and aware! Somewhere, sometime, when you least expect it most, you'll meet the thieves.

Your hotel is a relative haven from thieves. My bags are much safer in my room than with me on the streets. Hotels are a good resource for advice on personal and parking safety.

Cars are a favorite target of thieves. Be very careful never to leave anything even hinting of value in view in your parked car. Put anything worth stealing in the trunk. Leave your glove compartment open so the thief can look in without breaking in. Choose your parking place carefully. (Get advice on safe parking from your hotel.) Foreign/tourist's/rental cars get ripped off anywhere at night. Over half of the work that European automobile glass shops get is repairing wings broken by thieves. Before I leave my car, I notice how many crumbled wing windows glitter on the parking lot's asphalt. In Paris, I was warned to take absolutely everything inside my hotel. I did. They stole my mirror! In Spain these days, crude thieves are smashing the windows of occupied cars at stop lights to grab a purse or camera. In Rome, my favorite pension is next to a large police station—a safe place to park, if you're legal.

Invest in an extra key. Most rental cars come with only one, and that is needlessly risky. Besides, it's more convenient for two people to have access to the locked car.

Photocopy your valuable documents and tickets. It's a lot easier to replace a lost or stolen plane ticket, passport, Eurailpass, or rental voucher if you have a picture proving that you really owned what you are claiming is lost. This is especially helpful if you lose your Eurailpass.

American embassies or consulates are located in nearly every major European city. They are there to help American citizens in trouble but don't fancy themselves as travelers' aid offices. Things they'll do happily are help find medical or legal assistance, inform those at home that you need help, assist in replacing lost or stolen passports, arrange for emergency funds to be sent from home or, in rare cases, loan it to you directly, give travel advisories, supply tax forms, and help with absentee voting.

Be aware of the pitfalls of traveling, but relax and have fun. Limit your vulnerability rather than your travels. Most people in every country are on your side. If you exercise adequate discretion, aren't overly trusting, and don't put yourself into risky situations, your travels will be about as dangerous as hometown grocery shopping. Don't travel afraid—travel carefully.

Traveler's Toilet Trauma

Every traveler has one or two great toilet stories. Foreign toilets can be traumatic. And they can be hard to find. But, when all is said and done, they are one of those little things that make travel so much more interesting than staying home. Before you dive into that world of memorable porcelain experiences, let me prepare you for toilet-shock, and pass on a few tips on finding a W.C. quickly when you need one.

First, about toilet trauma. While most European toilets are reasonably similar to our own, be prepared for some toilets that are dirtier than and different from what you're used to. Only Americans need disposable bibs to sit on and a paper strip draped over their toilet, assuring them that no one has sat there yet. In fact, those of us who need a throne to sit on are in the minority. Most humans sit on their haunches and nothing more. When many Asian refugees are de-Oriented in the United States, they have to be taught not to stand on our rims.

So, if you plan to venture away from the international-style hotels in your Mediterranean travels and become a temporary local person, "going local" will take on a very real meaning. Experienced travelers enjoy recalling the shock they got the first time they opened the door and found only porcelain footprints and a squat-and-aim hole in the

One of Europe's many unforgettable experiences, the squat-and-aim toilet

ground—complete with flies in a holding pattern. When confronted by the "nontoilet," remind yourself that if a Western-style toilet were there, it would be so filthy you wouldn't want to get near it.

Toilet paper (like a spoon or a fork) is another Western "essential" that most people on our planet do not use. What they use varies. I won't get too graphic here, but remember that a billion people in south Asia never eat with their left hand. Some countries have very frail plumbing, and toilet paper will jam up the W.C.s. If wastebaskets are full of dirty paper, leave yours there, too.

Don't leave home without a week's supply of toilet paper. When you run out, tour a first-class hotel or restaurant and borrow 10 or 12 more yards of good, soft stuff. Local grade TP can be closer to wax or crepe paper—good for a laugh but not much more. The TP scene has improved markedly in the last few years, but you'll still find some strange stuff worth taking home to show your friends.

Finding a Toilet

Finding a decent public toilet can be frustrating. I dropped a group off in a town for a potty stop, and when I picked them up 20 minutes later, none had found relief. Most countries have few public rest rooms. You'll need to develop a knack for finding a private W.C.

I can sniff out a biffy in a jiffy. Any place that serves food or drinks has a rest room. No restaurateur would label his W.C. so those on the street can see, but you can walk into nearly any café or restaurant, politely and confidently, and find a bathroom. Assume it's somewhere in the back. It's easiest in large places that have outdoor seating, because waiters will think you're a customer just making a quick trip inside. Some call it rude—I call it survival. If you feel like it, ask permission. Just smile, "Toilet?" I'm rarely turned down. Timid people buy a drink they don't want in order to leave one. That's unnecessary. American-type fast-food places are very common these days and always have a decent and fairly "public" rest room. When nature beckons and there's no restaurant or bar handy, look in parks, train stations, on trains, in museums, hotel lobbies, government buildings, and on upper floors of department stores.

Large, classy old hotels are as impressive as many palaces you'll pay to see. You can always find a royal retreat here and plenty of very soft TP. These are an oasis in Third World countries, where a pleasant Western sit-down toilet experience is a rare treat.

Many cities (Paris, London, Amsterdam) are dotted with coin-op telephone booth-type W.C.'s on street corners. You insert a coin, the door opens, and you have 15 minutes of toilet accompanied by Sinatra Muzak. When you leave, it disinfects itself.

After you've found and used a toilet, you're down to your last challenge—flushing it. Rarely will you find the basic handle you grew up with. Find some protuberance and push, pull, twist, squeeze, step on, or pray to it until the waterfall starts. Electric-eye sinks and urinals are increasingly popular.

In many countries, you'll need to be selective to avoid the gag-a-maggot variety of toilets. Public toilets like those in parks are often repulsive. I never leave a museum without taking advantage of its rest rooms—free, clean, and full of artistic graffiti. Use the toilets on the train rather than in the station to save time and money. Toilets on first-class cars are a cut above second-class toilets. I go first class even with a second-class ticket. Train toilets are located on the ends of cars, where it's most jiggly. A trip to the train's john always reminds me of the rodeo. Never use a train W.C. while stopped in a station.

Tipping or paying to use a public W.C. is a European custom that irks many Americans. But isn't it really worth a quarter, considering the cost of water, maintenance, and cleanliness? And you're probably in no state to argue, anyway. Many times, the toilet is free but the woman in the corner sells sheets of toilet paper. Most common is the tip dish by the entry. The local equivalent of about 25 cents is plenty. Caution:

many ladies leave only bills and too-big coins in the tray to bewilder the full-bladdered tourist. The keepers of Europe's public toilets have earned a reputation of crabbiness. You would be, too, if you lived under the street in a room full of public toilets. Humor them, understand them, and leave them a coin.

Men: The women who seem to inhabit Europe's W.C.'s are a popular topic of conversation among Yankee travelers. Sooner or later, you'll be minding your own business at the urinal and the lady will bring you your change or sweep under your feet. Yes, it is distracting, but you'll just have to get used to it—she has.

And finally, there are countries where the people don't use rest rooms at all. I've been on buses that have just stopped, and 50 people scatter. Three minutes later they reload, relieved. It takes a little adjusting, but that's travel. When in Rome, do as the Romans do—and before you know it . . . Euro-peein'.

Counting and Other Bugaboos

Europeans do many things different from the way we do. Simple as these things are, they can be frustrating and cause needless, occasionally serious problems.

Their numbers 7 and 1 are slightly different from ours. European "ones" have an upswing 1. To make the seven more distinctive, add a cross 7. Fours often look like short lightning bolts.

Europeans reverse the day and month in numbered dates. Therefore, Christmas is 25-12-91 instead of 12-25-91, as we would write it. Commas are decimal points and decimals commas, so a dollar and a half is 1,50 and there are 5.280 feet in a mile.

Floors are numbered differently. The bottom floor is called the ground floor. What we would call the second floor is a European's first floor. So if your room is on the second floor (European), bad news— you're on the third floor (American). On the elevator, push whatever's below "1" to get to the ground floor.

Just like when they're driving, Europeans keep the left lane on moving sidewalks and escalators open for passing. Stand to the right.

When counting with your fingers, start with your thumb. If you hold up your first finger, you'll probably get two, and making a "peace" sign to indicate the number 2 may get you a punch in the nose in countries where that is an obscene gesture.

The 24-hour clock is used in any official timetable. This includes bus, train, and tour schedules. Learn to use it quickly and easily. Everything is the same until 12:00 noon. Then, instead of starting over again at 1:00 p.m., the Europeans keep on going—13:00, 14:00, and so on. 18:00 is 6:00 p.m. (subtract 12 and add p.m.).

Europeans measure temperatures in degrees Celsius. Zero degrees C = 32 degrees F (C x 9/5 + 32 = F); or, easier and nearly as accurate, double the Celsius temperature and add 30. A memory aid: 28° C = 82° F—darn hot.

European countries (except Great Britain) use kilometers instead of miles. A kilometer is six-tenths of a mile. To translate kilometers to miles quickly, I cut the kilometer figure in half and add 10 percent of the original figure (e.g., 420 km = 210 + 42 = 252 miles). Quick, what's 360 km? (180 + 36 = 216 miles.) "36 26 36" means nothing to a European (or metric) girl-watcher. But a "90 60 90" is a real pistachio.

Italian lire, with 1,350 to the dollar, drive visiting Yankees crazy. To translate, just cover the last three digits with your finger and cut what's left by about a quarter (e.g., 18,000 lire for dinner equals about $14; 45,000 lire for a hotel is about $35; 620,000 lire for a taxi ride is about . . .oh oh . . .).

House numbers often have no correlation to what's across the street. While odd is normally on one side and even is on the other, #27 may be directly across from #2.

Drugs, no matter how casual, are illegal in Europe. Dogs with incredible noses can turn up just about anywhere. Borders are high risk. Even in Holland, travelers are arrested, some jailed, and when the United States Embassy is asked for help, they "just say no."

Geriatric Globe-trotting

More people than ever are hocking their rockers and buying plane tickets. To many senior adventurers, travel is the fountain of youth. I spent 22 days last summer in Europe with a group of people who made my parents look young. They taught me many things, including the fact that it's never too late to have a happy childhood. Special discounts in much of the world encourage many older travelers, but the trend I see is for energetic elders to leave their seniority at home and expect to get the same respect as budget travelers a third their age.

I spend a lot of time meeting with retired couples who fly off to Europe with Eurailpasses, carryon suitcases (9 x 22 x 14 inches) that convert into rucksacks, and $40 a day. Most of them are on their second or third retirement trip, and each time as they walk out my door, I think, "Wow, I've got a good 40 years of travel ahead of me."

Gertrude and Vernon Johnson, both 68, are in Europe now. Nobody knows where. Before they left, I quizzed them on geriatric globe-trotting.

Was this your first major trip abroad? "Last year's trip was our first trip anywhere! We spent six weeks with a train pass and $70 a day for the both of us. Out of that $70, we spent $50 on room and board, going the B&B way, and $20 a day covered everything else, including miscellaneous transportation, admissions, little souvenirs, and even a weekly phone call home to the kids."

Were you hesitant at first? "Yes, indeed. I remember climbing into that airplane thinking I might be making a big mistake. But when we got over there and tackled problem after problem successfully, our confidence soared. Friendly people were always coming out of the woodwork to help us when we needed it."

What about theft and physical safety for a couple of retired people like yourselves running around Europe independently? "As far as retired people go, we never felt like we were 'retired.' I never felt any different from anyone else and people accepted us as just two more travelers."

Gertrude added, "Later on, as we remembered our trip, we thought maybe people treated us 'gray-haired rucksackers' a little kinder because of our age. We never had a bit of a problem with theft or safety. Of course, we'd wear our money belts every day and choose our neighborhoods carefully. It's pretty obvious when you're getting into a bad neighborhood. We never felt that Ugly American problem. People treated us very well. If anything, there was more help for seniors in public in Europe than we find at home."

Were the Europeans impressed by a retired couple with such an independent travel style? "I'd say they were. In fact, at one place, Rick, we were sitting down and—"

Then the table jolted as Gertrude grabbed Vernon's knee, saying, "Nothin' doing! That's too good an anecdote." She plans, at 68, on becoming a travel writer some day—so we'll just have to wait for the rest of that story.

Do you speak any languages? "No, but we worked on a Berlitz French record for three weeks and that was helpful. We found that the best way to get along with the locals was to try to speak their language. They'd laugh a lot, but they appreciated our effort and would bend over backward to help us. They could usually speak enough English to help us out."

Did you have trouble finding rooms? "No. We traveled from May 1 to June 15 without reservations. Arthur Frommer's guide was handy, and, of course, we got help from the tourist offices and people in the towns. We had no problems. Decent budget hotels are close to the station, and that made setting up a snap.

"We always planned to arrive early. The overnight trains were ideal because they arrived first thing in the morning. We took our From-mer's guide into the tourist office, which was always in or near the station, and they'd call the hotel for us. A few times they charged extra for their service, but it was always very convenient. For older people, I would insist on arriving early in the day, using Frommer's, and having local money with you when you arrive."

How much did you pack? "Our luggage weighed a total of 25 pounds. Gertrude carried 11 and I packed 14. We just packed a few easy-wash and fast-dry clothes. Before our first trip you told us to bring nothing electrical. We didn't listen, and we almost burned down our hotel in Paris." (The table jolted again.) "So this time we're bringing nothing electrical."

What was the most important lesson you learned on your first trip? "Pack even less. When you pack light you're younger—footloose and fancy-free. And that's the way we like to be."

Organizations that arrange discounts and provide information and special help to the growing legions of senior globe-trotters include AARP (tel. 800/227-7737) for those over 50, Elderhostel (tel. 617/426-7788) with Boston-based study programs around the world for those over 60, and the National Council of Senior Citizens (tel. 202/347-8800) in Washington, D.C. There are also more guidebooks on the subject, including a guide to Elderhostel programs, _Elderhostels: The Students' Choice_ (Santa Fe, N.M.: John Muir Publications).

His fountain of youth is in Europe.

Travels with Baby Andy— Leashes and Valium?

My wife (Anne), 3-year-old (Andy), and VW van (Vinnie) have spent five months on three trips with me traveling from Norway to Naples and Dublin to Dubrovnik. It's not hell, but it's not terrific travel, either. Still, we'd rather change diapers in Paris than in Seattle.

Young European families, like their Yuppie American counterparts, are traveling, babies and all. You'll find more and more kid's menus, hotel playrooms, and kid-go-crazy zones at freeway rest stops all over Europe. And people, especially southern Europeans, love babies. Babies are a great ice breaker—socially and in the Arctic.

An international adventure is a great foundation for a mountain of family memories. Here are some of the lessons we've learned whining and giggling through Europe with baby, and now toddler, Andy.

Baby Gear

Since a happy baby on the road requires a lot of gear, a key to survival with a baby in Europe is to have a rental car or stay in one place. Of course, you'll pack as light as you can, but if Mom figures you'll need it, trust her.

Bring a car seat, buy one in Europe, or see if your car rental company can provide one. If you're visiting friends, with enough notice, they can often borrow a car seat and a stroller for you. Since you'll be driving long hours while the baby sleeps, try to get one that reclines.

A stroller is essential. Umbrella models are lightest, but we found a heavy-duty Aprica model with reclining back worth bringing for the baby. Andy could nap in it, and it served as a luggage cart for the Bataan Death March parts of our trip when we had to use public transportation. Carry the stroller onto the plane—you'll need it in the airport. Big wheels handle cobblestones best.

A small travel crib was a godsend. No matter what kind of hotel, pension, or hostel we ended up in, as long as we could clear a 4 x 4-foot space on the floor, we'd have a safe, clean, and familiar home for Andy to sleep and play in. During the day, we'd salvage a little room by flipping it up on its side and shoving it against the wall.

We got a lot of use out of our baby backpack (when he was age 1). Rucksacks in general are great for parents who wish they had the hands of an octopus. Prepare to tote more than a tot. A combo purse/diaper bag with shoulder straps is ideal. Be on guard: purse-snatchers target mothers (especially while busy and off guard, as when changing diapers).

There's lots more to pack. Encourage bonding to a blanket or stuffed critter and take it along. We used a lot of Heinz dehydrated food dumped into zip-lock baggies. Tiny Tupperware containers with lids were great for crackers, raisins, and snacks. You'll find plenty of disposable diapers, wipes, baby food, and so on, in Europe, so don't take the whole works from home. Before you fly away, be sure you've packed fluoride, ipecac, a decongestant, Acetaminophen, and a thermometer. For a toddler, bring a few favorite books and a soft (easy on hotel rooms) ball, and buy little European toys as you go.

Common sense and lessons learned from day trips at home are your best sources of information. The best book we found on traveling with infants was Maureen Wheeler's _Travel with Children_ (Lonely Planet Publications). Though designed for Asian travel, it's good advice for Europe-bound parents. (For a catalog full of family travel guides. write to Carousel Press, Box 6061, Albany, CA 94706. John Muir publishes a new series of children's guides called "Kidding Around"; see back pages for titles.)

Parenting at 32,000 Feet

Gurgling junior might become an airborne Antichrist as soon as the seat belt light goes off. If possible, take a domestic practice flight with your baby before attempting a marathon ocean crossing. You'll pay 10 percent of the ticket cost to take your under-2-year-old on an international flight. The child doesn't get a seat, but many airlines have flying baby perks for moms and dads who ask for them in advance—roomier bulkhead seats, hang-from-the-ceiling bassinets, and baby meals. After age 2, a toddler's ticket costs 67 percent of the adult fare—a major financial owie.

Ask your pediatrician about sedating your baby for a 10-hour intercontinental flight. We think it's the only merciful (for the entire family) thing to do. (Dimetapp, Tylenol, and Pediacare worked well for us.) Bring special toys. Those colored links are handy to attach toys to the seat, crib, high chairs, jail cells, and so on. The in-flight headphones are great entertainment for flying toddlers.

Landings and takeoffs can be painful for ears of all ages. A bottle, a pacifier, or anything to suck helps equalize the baby's inner ear pressure. For this reason, nursing moms will be glad they do when it comes to flying. If your kid cries, remember: crying, too, is a great equalizer.

Once on foreign soil, remember that your footloose and see-it-all days of travel are over for a while. Go easy. Traveling with a tyke is tiring, wet, sticky, and smelly. Your mobility is way down.

Be warned—jet lag is nursery purgatory. On his first night in Europe, baby Andy was furious that darkness had bullied daylight out of his up-till-then reliable 24-hour body clock cycle. Luckily, we were settled in a good hotel with thick walls, and most of the guests were able to find accommodations elsewhere.

Whizzing through Europe with your child

Shelter

We slept in rooms of all kinds, from youth hostels (many have family rooms) to hotels. We've never been charged for the child, and, while we always use our own bedding, many doubles have a sofa or extra bed we can barricade with chairs and use rather than the crib.

Childproof immediately on arrival. A roll of masking tape makes quick work of electrical outlets. Anything breakable goes on top of the free-standing closet. Proprietors are generally helpful to considerate and undemanding parents. We'd often store our bottles and milk cartons in their fridge, ask for baby-sitting, and so on.

Every room had a sink where baby Andy could pose for cute pictures, have a little fun, and get clean. With a toddler, budget extra for private baths—a practical need and a fun diversion. Toddlers and campgrounds—with swings, slides, and plenty of friends—mix wonderfully.

Food

We found European restaurants and their customers cool to noisy babies. High chairs are rare. We learned to eat at places with outdoor seating, at the many McDonald's-type, baby-friendly fast-food places, or picnic.

Nursing babies are easiest to feed and travel with. Remember, some cultures are uncomfortable with public breast feeding. Be sensitive.

With a toddler, we stocked up on munchies (fruit, pretzels, tiny boxes of juice). A 7:00 a.m. banana worked wonders, and a 7:00 p.m. snack made late European dinners workable. In restaurants, we ordered an extra plate for Andy, who just nibbled off of our meals. We'd order "fizzy" (but not sticky) mineral water, call it "pop," and the many spills were no problem. With all the candy and sweet temptations at toddler eye level in Europe, you can forget a low-sugar diet. While gelati and pastries are expensive, Andy's favorite suckers and Popsicles were very cheap and available everywhere.

Plan to spend more money. You'll travel in taxis rather than buses and subways. Hotels can get baby-sitters, usually from professional agencies. The service is expensive but well worth the splurge when you crave a leisurely, peaceful evening sans bibs and cribs.

With a baby, we arranged our schedule around naps and sleep time. A well-rested baby is worth the limitation. Driving while Andy siestaed worked well. As a toddler, however, Andy was up very late, playing soccer with his new Italian friends on the piazza or eating huge ice creams in the hotel kitchen with the manager's kids. We gave up keeping any rigid naptime or bedtime, and we enjoyed Europe's evening ambience as a family.

OK, you're there, watered, fed, and only a little bleary. Europe is your cultural playpen, a living fairy tale, a sandbox of family fun and adventure. Grab your kid and dive in.

Travel Laundry

I met a woman in Italy who wore her T-shirt frontward, backward, inside-out frontward, and inside-out backward to delay the laundry day. A guy in Germany showed me his take-it-into-the-tub-with-you-and-make-waves method of washing his troublesome jeans. Some travelers just ignore their laundry needs and stink.

Anybody traveling anywhere has to wash clothes. My washer and dryer won't fit under the airplane seat, so I've learned to do without. Here are some tips.

Choose a quick-dry and no-wrinkle travel wardrobe. Your self-service laundry kit should include a stretchable "travel clothesline." Stretch it over your bathtub or across the back of your car, and you're on the road to dry clothes. Pack a concentrated liquid detergent in a sturdy small plastic squeeze bottle wrapped for safety in a zip-lock baggie. A large plastic bag with a drawstring is handy for dirty laundry.

Every real hotel room in Europe has a sink. And many have multilingual "no washing clothes in the room" signs. This may be the most ignored rule on earth after "eat your peas." Interpret this as an "I-have-lots-of-good-furniture-and-a-fine-carpet-in-this-room-and-I-don't-want-your-drippy-laundry-ruining-things" order. In other words, you can wash clothes very carefully, wring them nearly dry, and hang them in an undestructive way. Occasionally, a hotel will keep the stoppers in an attempt to discourage in-room washing. A plastic bag stuffed into the hole stops the sink nicely.

Your laundry should keep a low profile. Don't hang it out the window. The maid hardly notices my laundry. It's hanging quietly in the bathroom or shuffled among my dry clothes in the closet.

Some hotels will let your laundry join theirs on the lines out back or on the rooftop. Many youth hostels have coin-op washer and dryers or heated drying rooms to ease your laundry hassles.

Wring your wet laundry as dry as possible. Rolling it in a towel (putting it on the floor and stomping on it) can be helpful. Always separate the back and front of clothes to speed drying. Some travelers pack an inflatable hanger. Smooth out your wet clothes, button shirts, and set collars and "hand iron" to encourage wrinkle-free drying. If your shirt or dress dries wrinkled, hang it in a steamy bathroom. A piece of tape is a good ad-lib lint brush. In very hot climates, I wash my shirt several times a day, wring it and put it on wet. It's clean and refreshing, and in fifteen minutes it's dry.

For a thorough washing, ask your hotel to direct you to the nearest laundromat. Nearly every neighborhood has one. It takes about an hour and $6 if there's no line. Better laundromats have coin-op soap dispensers, change machines, and a helpful attendant. Others can be very frustrating. Use the time to catch up on postcards and your journal or chat with the local crowd that's causing the delay. Laundromats throughout the world seem to give people the gift of gab. Full-service places are quicker—just drop it off and come back in the afternoon—but much more expensive. Still, every time I slip into a fresh pair of jeans, I figure it was worth the hassle and expense.

Whistler's Laundry

Souvenir Strategy

Gift shopping is getting very expensive. I remember buying a cuckoo clock 10 years ago for $4. Now a hamburger, shake, and fries at the Munich McDonald's will cost that much.

I try to do my souvenir and gift shopping in countries like Turkey, Morocco, Spain, Portugal, Greece and Italy—in that order. By gift shopping in the cheaper countries, my dollar goes two or three times as far.

In the interest of packing light, try to put off shopping until the end of the trip. Ideally, you should end your trip in a cheap country, do all of your shopping, then fly home. One summer, I had a 16-pound rucksack and nothing more until the last week of my trip when, in Spain and Morocco, I managed to accumulate two medieval chairs, two sets of bongos, a camel-hair coat, swords, a mace, and a lace tablecloth.

Large department stores often have a souvenir section with prices much less than what you would pay in the cute little tourist shops nearby. Shop around and remember that, in the southern countries, most things sold on the streets or in markets have soft prices. When appropriate, bargain like mad.

Shopping is an important part of the average person's trip, but be careful not to lose control. All too often, slick marketing and cutesy, romantic window displays can succeed in shifting the entire focus of your trip toward things in the tourist shops. (It's a lucrative business. Many souvenir merchants in Italy work through the tourist season, then retire for the rest of the year.) This sort of tourist brainwashing can turn you into one of the hundreds of people who set out to see and experience Europe but find themselves wandering in a trancelike search for signs announcing Duty Free Shopping. I've seen half the members of a British Halls of Parliament guided tour skip out to survey an enticing display of plastic "bobbie" hats and Union Jack panties. Even if the sign says, "Keep Italy green, spend dollars," don't let your trip degenerate into a glorified shopping spree.

I think it's wise to restrict your shopping to stipulated time during the trip. Most people have an idea of what they want to buy in each country. Set aside a time to shop in each of these areas and stick to it. This way you avoid drifting through a day thinking only of souvenirs.

Some of the most colorful shopping in Europe is at its flea markets. Among the best are Amsterdam (Waterlooplein, Saturdays), London (Bermondsey early Fridays, bus 1 from Trafalgar and Portobello Market on Saturdays, and many others), Madrid (El Rastro, Sundays), and Paris (Porte de Clignancourt, best on Sundays, also on Saturdays and Mondays, go by taxi).

When you are shopping, ask yourself if your enthusiasm is merited. More often than not, you can pick up a very similar item of better quality and for a cheaper price at home. Unless you're a real romantic, the thrill of where you bought something fades long before the item's usefulness. My life has more room for a functional souvenir than for a useless symbol of a place I visited. Even thoughtful shoppers go overboard.

I have several large boxes in my attic labeled "great souvenirs."

My favorite souvenirs are books (a great value all over Europe, and many impossible-to-find-in-the-U.S. editions), local crafts (well explained in guidebooks, such as hand-knit sweaters in Portugal or Ireland, glass in Sweden, lace in Belgium), strange stuffed animals (at flea markets), cassettes of music I experienced live, posters (one sturdy tube stores eight or 10 posters safely), clothing, photographs I've taken, and memories whittled carefully into my journal.

Value Added Tax (VAT) Refunds

Local European sales taxes vary from 8 to 33 percent. Tourists who buy something new and don't use it until it's out of the country can often get this tax refunded.

Typically, VAT refunds are not worth the trouble. But if you're buying something worth over $100 in a country with high taxes (Britain and most of northern Europe), ask about the possibility of a refund. Normally, you buy the item, collect and save the receipt, process this at the border as you leave the country, go home, and wait for your refund check, which usually comes in the foreign currency. Considering all the hoops you went through to get it, and the bank charges to change the foreign check into dollars, your final refund is often a joke. Ideally, you'll talk your merchant into deducting the VAT from your purchase price and let her process the refund. In Scandinavia, you normally get a cash refund at the border.

Customs and Postage for American Shoppers

You are allowed to take $400 of souvenirs home duty-free. The next $1,000 is dutied at a flat 10 percent. After that, you pay the individual items duty rate. You can also bring in a liter of alcohol and more cigarettes than you'd ever want to bring home duty-free.

You can mail one package per person per day worth up to $50 duty-free from Europe to the U.S.A. Mark it "Unsolicited Gift." You can mail home all the "American Goods Returned" you like with no customs concerns.

If you do some shopping, it's easy to lighten your load by sending packages home by surface mail. Postage is getting expensive. A box the size of a fruit crate costs about $30 slow boat, a small price to pay to substantially lighten your load. Books are much cheaper if they are sent separately. Customs regulations amount to 10 or 15 frustrating minutes filling out forms with the normally unhelpful postal clerk's semi-assistance. Remember, the postal clerks you'll deal with in Europe are every bit as friendly, speedy, and multilingual as those back home.

I've never had to pay any duty. Keep it simple (contents: clothing, carving, gifts, a poster, value $50). Post offices usually provide boxes and string or tape for about $1. Service is best from the Alps north and in France. Small-town post offices can be less crowded and more user-friendly. Every box I've ever mailed has arrived—bruised and battered, but all there—within six weeks.

12
Attitude Adjustment for a Better Trip

The Ugly American

Europe sees two kinds of travelers: those who view Europe through air-conditioned bus windows, socializing with their noisy American friends, and those who are taking a vacation from America, immersing themselves in different cultures, experiencing different people and life-styles, broadening their perspective.

Europeans judge you as an individual, not by your government. A Greek fisherman once told me, "For me, Reagan is big problem—but I like you." I have never been treated like the Ugly American. I've been proud to wear our flag on my lapel. My Americanness in Europe, if anything, has been an asset.

You'll see plenty of Ugly Americans. Europeans recognize them and treat them accordingly, often souring their vacation. Ugly American-ism is a disease cured by a change in attitude. The best over-the-counter medicine is a mirror.

Here are the symptoms and the cure. The Ugly American:

—does not try to understand or respect strange customs and cultural differences. Only a Hindu can understand the value of India's sacred cows. Only a devout Spanish Catholic can appreciate the true worth of his town's patron saint. No American has the right, as a visitor, to show disrespect for these customs.

—demands the niceties of American life in Europe—orange juice and eggs (sunny-side up) for breakfast, long beds, English menus, punctuality in Italy, or cold beer in England. He should remember that he invited himself to a land that enjoys its continental breakfasts, that doesn't grow six-foot four-inch men, that speaks its own language, that lacks the "fast-food efficiency" of the United States and drinks beer at room temperature. Live as a European for a few weeks; it's cheaper, you'll make more friends, you'll have a better trip, and you'll enjoy a great chance to learn something about good living.

—is ethnocentric, traveling in packs, more or less invading each country while making no effort to communicate with "the natives." He talks at Europeans and about them in a condescending manner. He finds satisfaction in flaunting his relative affluence and measures well-being by material consumption. He sees the world as a pyramid with the United States on top and everyone else trying to get there. It's important to remember the average European does not envy and is not impressed by the average but richer American.

You can be a "Beautiful American." Your fate as a tourist lies in your own hands. A graduate of the Back Door School of Touristic Beauty:

—maintains a moderate sense of humility, not flashing signs of affluence, such as overtipping or joking about the local money. His money does not talk.

—not only accepts but also seeks out European styles of living. He forgets his discomfort if he's the only one in a group who feels it. The customer is not "always right" in Europe.

—is genuinely interested in the people and cultures he visits. He wants to learn by trying things.

—accepts that there's more than one way to skin cats. Paying for your Italian coffee at one counter, then picking it up at another may seem inefficient, until you realize it's more sanitary: the person handling the food handles no money.

—makes an effort to bridge that flimsy language barrier. Rudimentary communication in any language is fun and simple with a few basic words. While a debate over the economics of Marx on the train to Budapest (with a common vocabulary of 20 words) is frustrating, he surprises himself at how well he communicates—by just breaking the ice and trying. Don't worry about making mistakes—communicate! (See chapter 6, Hurdling the Language Barrier.)

—is positive and optimistic in the extreme. Discipline yourself to focus on the good points of each country. Don't dwell on problems or compare things to "back home." With a positive attitude, things go great.

Thank You			
Arabic	_shukran_	French	_merçi_
Bulgarian	_blagodarya_	German	_danke_
Danish	_tak_	Greek	_efharisto_
Dutch	_dank u wel_	Russian	_spasibo_
English	_thank you_	Serbo-Croatian	_hvala_
Italian	_grazie_	Spanish	_gracias_
Portuguese	_obrigado_	Turkish	_tesekkur_
Finnish	_kiitos_		

I've been accepted as an American friend throughout Europe, Russia, the Middle East, and North Africa. Coming as an American visitor, I've been hugged by Bulgarian workers on a Balkan mountaintop; discussed Contragate and the Olympics over dinner in the home of a Greek family; explained to a young frustrated Irishman that California girls aren't really two-legged fantasies; and hiked through the Alps with a Swiss school teacher, learning German and teaching English.

There is no excuse for being an Ugly American. Go as a guest; act like one and you'll be treated like one. In travel, too, you reap what you sow.

Responsible Tourism

As we learn more about the problems that confront the earth and humankind, more and more people are recognizing the need for the world's industries, such as tourism, to function as tools for peace. Tourism is a two-trillion-dollar industry that employs more than 60 million people. As travelers become more sophisticated and gain a global perspective, the demand for socially, environmentally, and economically responsible means of traveling will grow. Peace is much more than the absence of war, and if we are to enjoy the good things of life—such as travel—into the next century, the serious issues that confront humankind must be addressed now.

Late last year, more than 500 leaders from the tourist industry and academia (including executives from airlines and hotel chains, tour organizers, professors, futurists, and scholars), travel writers, journalists, environmental leaders, and politicians representing 65 countries met in Vancouver, Canada, at a conference called "Tourism—A Vital Force for Peace." At the end of the conference, they concluded that a healthy tourist industry requires peace.

The delegates drafted the Columbia Charter, which, among other things, cautions that the world has reached the critical crossroads that demand responsive strategies that address the political, economic, and environmental problems facing humankind. The charter renounces tourism developments that cause turmoil or conflict as well as the exploitation of the world's natural and cultural resources. It challenges all governmental bodies, organizations, and individuals to eliminate war and injustice and stop the arms race. It calls for the tourist industry to help build a world in which tourism promotes mutual understanding, trust, and goodwill; reduces economic inequities; develops in an integrated manner with the full participation of local host communities; improves the quality of life; protects and preserves the environment; and contributes to the world conservation strategy of sustainable development.

Well, these are high-and-mighty-sounding ideals. But the concrete news is (1) that mainstream supercorporate industry big shots said these things and acknowledge the need for change, and (2) that there are now more and more ways for travelers to make travel a constructive rather than a destructive activity in a cultural, environmental, and economic sense.

Although the most obvious problems relate specifically to travel in the Third World, European travel also offers some exciting socially responsible opportunities. Below are a few sources of information for the budding "green" traveler.

Co-op America is a great source of general information on responsible tourism, and its Travel-Links service can book you into the best-value socially responsible travel options (Co-op America, 2100 M Street, NW #310, Washington, D.C. 20063, tel. 1-800-424-2667). The North America Coordinating Center for Responsible Tourism (2 Kensington Road, San Anselmo, CA 94960-2905, tel. 415/258-6594) is busy with similar projects. The Lost Valley Center (Box 111, 81868 Lost Valley Lane, Dexter, OR 97431, tel. 503/937-3351) publishes the "Directory of Alternative Travel Resources" and the "Directory of Environmentally Responsible Travel and Volunteer Opportunities" (both by Diane Brause and available for $8 each, post-paid). Each of these resources are very creative at connecting concerned travelers with good information and resource people.

Arthur Frommer's newest book, *The New Age of Travel*, is an understandably popular listing of exciting and sensitive alternative travel ideas. "The Directory of Low-Cost Vacations with a Difference" (by J. Crawford, 103 Cooper Street, Babylon, NY 11702, $5.95) lists hundreds of ideas, from farm vacations to home exchanges and people-to-people programs to volunteer work opportunities. If you'd like to help the homeless, watch whales, or dig up old bones, send $11.95 to *Chicago Review* (814 N. Franklin, Chicago, IL 60610) for "Volunteer Vacations," which lists 500 options for one- to six-week domestic and foreign volunteer programs. Or get in touch with SERVAS (see chapter 4, The Budget), which puts travelers in touch with host families.

Be Open-minded

Among the palaces, quaint folk dancers, and museums, you'll find a living civilization—grasping for the future while we romantic tourists grope for its past. This presents us with a sometimes painful dose of truth.

Today's Europe is a complex, mixed bag of tricks. It can rudely slap you in the face if you aren't prepared to accept it with open eyes and an open mind. Europe is getting crowded, tense, seedy, polluted, industrialized, hamburgerized, and far from the everything-in-its-place fairytale land I'm sure it used to be.

If you're not mentally braced for some shocks, local trends can tinge your travels. Hans Christian Andersen's statue has internationally understood four-letter words scrawled across its base. Whites are now the minority in London; Amsterdam's sex shops and McDonald's share the same street lamp. In Paris, a Sudanese salesman accosts tourists at Notre-Dame with ivory bracelets and crocodile purses. Many a Mediterranean hotel keeper would consider himself a disgrace to his sex if he didn't follow a single woman to her room. Drunk punk rockers do their best to repulse you as you climb to St. Patrick's grave in Ireland, and Greek ferryboats dump mountains of trash into their dying Aegean Sea. An 8-year-old boy in Denmark smokes a cigarette like he was born with it in his mouth, and in a Munich beer hall, an old drunk spits "sieg heils" all over you. The Barcelona shoeshine man will triple-charge you, and people everywhere eat strange and wondrous things.

They eat next to nothing for breakfast, mud for coffee, mussels in Brussels, and snails in Paris, and dinner's at 10 p.m. in Spain. Beer is warm here, flat there, coffee isn't served with dinner, and ice cubes can only be dreamed of. Roman cars stay in their lanes like rocks in an avalanche, and beermaids with huge pretzels pull mustard packets from their cleavage.

Contemporary Europe is alive and groping. Today's problems will fill tomorrow's museums. Feel privileged to walk the vibrant streets of Europe as a sponge—not a judge. Be open-minded. Absorb, accept, and learn.

Don't Be a Creative Worrier

Travelers tend to be creative worriers. Many sit at home before their trip, all alone, just thinking of things to be stressed by. Travel problems are always there; you just notice them when they're yours. (Like people only notice the continual newspaper ads for tire sales when they're shopping for tires.) Every year, there are air controller strikes, train strikes, terrorist attacks, new problems, and deciduous problems sprouting new leaves.

Travel is ad-libbing, incurring and conquering surprise problems. Make an art out of taking the unexpected in stride. Relax; you're on the other side of the world, playing games in a continental backyard. Be a good sport, enjoy the uncertainty, frolic in the pits.

Many of my readers' richest travel experiences were the result of seemingly terrible mishaps: the lost passport in Yugoslavia, falling and having to find a doctor in Ireland, the blowout in Portugal, and the moped accident on Corfu.

Expect problems, tackle them creatively. You'll miss a museum or two and maybe blow your budget for the week. But you'll make some local friends and stack up some memories. And this is the essence of travel which you'll enjoy long after the journal is shelved and your trip is stored neatly in the slide carousel of your mind.

The KISS Rule — "Keep it Simple, Stupid!"

Don't complicate your trip. Simplify! Travelers get stressed and cluttered over the silliest things. Here are some common complexities that in their nibbly way can suffocate a happy holiday.

Registering your camera with customs before leaving home, spending several hours trying to phone home on a sunny day in the Alps, worrying about the correct answers to meaningless bureaucratic forms, making a long distance hotel reservation in a strange language and then trying to settle on what's served for breakfast, having a picnic in pants that worry about grass stains, sending away for Swedish hotel vouchers.

People can complicate their trips with video cameras, lead-lined film bags, special tickets for free entry to all the sights they won't see in England, immersion heaters, instant coffee, 65 Handi-wipes, and a special calculator that figures the value of the franc out to the third decimal. They ask for a toilet in 17 words or more, steal Sweet-n-Low and plastic silverware off the plane, and take notes on facts that don't matter.

Travel more like Gandhi — with simple clothes, open eyes, and an uncluttered mind.

Be Militantly Humble — Attila Had a Lousy Trip

As one of the world's elite who are rich and free enough to travel, you are leaving home to experience a different culture. If things aren't to your liking, don't change the things, change your liking.

Legions of tourists tramp through Europe like they're at the zoo — throwing a crust to the monkey, asking the guy in lederhosen to yodel, begging the peacock to spread his tail again, and bellowing Italian arias out Florentine hotel windows. If a culture misperforms or doesn't perform, they feel gypped. Easygoing travelers leave the Attila-type tourists mired in a swamp of complaints.

All summer long I'm pushing a bargain, often for groups. It's the hottest, toughest time of year. Tourists and locals clash. Many tourists leave soured.

When I catch a Spanish merchant shortchanging me, I correct the bill and smile, "Adios." A French hotel owner can blow up at me for no legitimate reason. Rather than return the fire, I wait, smile, and sheepishly ask again. Asking for action, innocently assertive, but never demanding "justice," I usually see the irate ranter come to his senses, forget the problem, and work things out.

"Turn the other cheek" applies perfectly to those riding Europe's magic carousel. If you fight the slaps, the ride is over. The militantly humble can spin forever.

Swallow Pride, Ask Questions, Be Crazy

If you're too proud to ask questions and be crazy, your trip will certainly be dignified—but dull. Make yourself an extrovert, even if you aren't one. Be a catalyst for adventure and excitement. Make things happen, or often they won't.

Extroverts have more fun. If you see four cute men on a bench, ask them to scoot over. Or, start a conversation . . . "Hey, where'd you get those jackets?"

I'm not naturally a wild-and-crazy kind of guy. But when I'm shy and quiet, things don't happen, and that's a bad rut to travel in. It's not easy, but this special awareness can really pay off. Let me describe the same evening twice—first, with the mild and lazy me, and then, with the wild and crazy me.

The traffic held me up, so by the time I got to that great historical building that I've always wanted to see, it was six minutes before closing. No one was allowed to enter. Disappointed, I walked over to a restaurant and couldn't make heads or tails out of the menu. I recognized "steak-frites" and settled for the typical meat patty and french fries. On the way home, I looked into a very colorful local tavern, but tourists didn't seem welcome, so I walked on. In a park, I was making some noise, and a couple came out on their balcony and told me to be quiet. I went back to the room and did some washing.

That's not a night to be proud of. A better traveler's journal entry would read like this:

I was late and got to the museum only six minutes before closing. The guard said no one could go in now, but I begged, joked, and pleaded with him. I had traveled all the way to see this place and I would be leaving early in the morning. I assured him that I'd be out by six o'clock, and he gave me a glorious six minutes in that building. You can do a lot in six minutes when that's all you've got. Across the street at a restaurant that the same guard recommended, I couldn't make heads or tails out of the menu. Inviting myself into the kitchen, I met the cooks and got a firsthand look at "what's cookin'." Now I could order an exciting local dish and know just what I was getting. It was delicious! On the way home, I passed a classic local bar, and while it was dark and sort of uninviting to a foreigner, I stepped in and was met by the only guy in the place who spoke any English. He proudly befriended me and told me, in very broken English, of his salty past and his six kids, while treating me to his favorite local drink. I'll never forget that guy or that evening. Later, I was making noise in a park, and a middle-aged couple told me to shut up. I continued the conversation, and they eventually invited me up to their apartment. We joked around—not understanding a lot of what we were saying to each other—and they invited me to their summer cottage tomorrow. What a lucky break! There's no better way to learn about this country than to spend an afternoon with a local family. And to think that I could be back in my room doing the laundry.

Many tourists are actually afraid or too timid to ask a local person a question. The meek may inherit the earth, but they make lousy travelers. Local sources are a wealth of information. People are happy to help a traveler. Hurdle the language barrier. Use a paper and pencil, charades, or whatever it takes to be understood. Don't be afraid to butcher the language.

Ask questions—or be lost. If you're lost, get out a map and look lost. You'll get help. If lonely or in need of contact with a local person, get out a map and look lost again. Pledge every morning to do something entirely different today. Perceive friendliness and you'll find it. Create adventure—or bring home a boring journal.

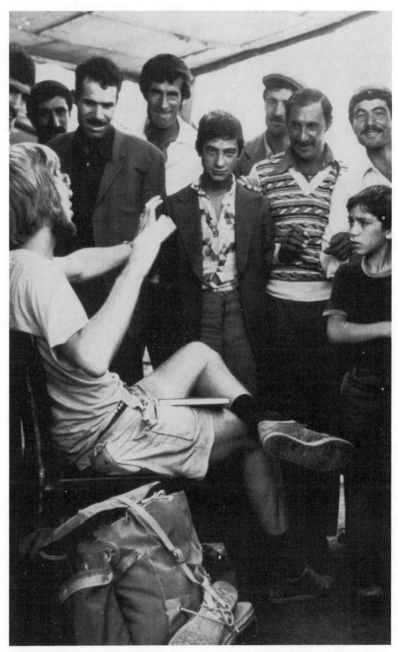

Put yourself where you become the oddity. If people stare, sing to them.

Polite Paris

Let's explore this "mean Parisian" problem. The French, as a culture, are pouting. They used to be the "crème de la crème," the definition of high class. Their language was the lingua franca—everyone wanted to speak French. There was a time when the czar of Russia and his family actually spoke better French than Russian. Your passport even has French on it—leftovers from those French glory days.

Modern French culture is reeling—humiliated by Nazis, lashed by Levis, and crushed by the Big Mac of American culture. And our two cultures aren't natural buddies. The French enjoy subtleties and sophistication. American culture sneers at these fine points. We're proud, brash, and in love with rugged individualism. We are a smiley face culture whose bank tellers are fined if they forget to say, "Have a nice day." The French don't find slap-on-the-back niceness terribly sincere. And too often, we judge a people on their "niceness."

Typically, Americans judge the French by the Parisians they meet. That's as fair as judging American friendliness by a three-day visit to New York City. And remember, most of us see Paris at the height of hot, busy summer when those Parisians who can't escape for the summer see their hometown flooded with insensitive foreigners who butcher their language and put ketchup on their meat. That's tough to take smiling, and, if you're looking for coldness, this is a good place to start.

To make the Parisians suddenly 40 percent friendlier, learn and use liberally these four phrases: *bonjour, s'il vous plaît, merçi,* and *pardon.* And to really revel in French friendliness, visit an untouristy part of the countryside and use those four phrases.

Political Unrest and Tourism

An awareness of current social and political problems is as vital to smart travel as a listing of top sights. Many popular tourist destinations are entertaining tourists with "sound and light" shows in the old town while quelling terrorist and separatist movements in the new. Countries from England to Italy are dealing with serious or potentially serious internal threats.

Newspaper headlines shape many trips. Many people skip Rome because of the Red Brigade, avoid Spain in fear of the militant Basques, and refuse to fly out of Athens or Frankfurt because of a recent bomb attack. This is like avoiding a particular stretch of highway at home because there was an accident there. Don't let these problems dictate your itinerary. They are no threat to you. I stay up on the news and exercise good common sense (don't sing Catholic songs in Ulster pubs) and travel safely, enjoying a firsthand look at the demographic chaos that explains much of what fills the front pages of our newspapers.

Travel broadens your perspective, enabling you to rise above the 6 o'clock news and see things as a citizen of our world. While monuments from the past are worthy of your sightseeing energy, travel plugs you directly into the present.

There are many peoples fighting the same thrilling battles we Americans won 200 years ago, and while your globe may paint Turkey orange and Iran green, no political boundaries can divide racial, linguistic, or religious groups that simply.

Look beyond the beaches and hotels in your tourist brochures for background on how your vacation target's cultural, racial, and religious makeup is causing problems today or may bring grief tomorrow. With this foundation and awareness you can enjoy the nearly unavoidable opportunities to talk with involved locals about complex current situations. If you're looking to talk politics you must be approachable— free from the American mob on the air-conditioned coach.

Like it or not, people around the world look at "capitalist Americans" as the kingpins of a global game of Monopoly. Young, well-dressed people are most likely to speak (and want to speak) English. Universities are the perfect place to solve the world's problems in English with a liberal, open-minded foreigner over a government-subsidized budget cafeteria lunch.

In Ireland, "the troubles" are on everyone's mind. Hitchhiking through the Emerald Isle, I always get an earful of someone's very passionate feelings. In the USSR and throughout Eastern Europe, whenever I want some political or economic gossip, I sit alone in a café. After a few minutes and some James Bond eye contact, I have company and a thrilling chat with a resident dissident.

After your smashingly successful European adventure, you'll graduate to more distant cultural nooks and geographic crannies. If you mistakenly refer to a Persian or Iranian as Arabic, you'll get a stern education on the distinction, and in eastern Turkey, you'll learn there is a fiercely nationalistic group of people called Kurds who won't rest until that orange and green on the globe is divided by a hunk of land called Kurdistan.

Understand a country's linguistic divisions. It's next to impossible to keep everyone in a multilingual country happy. Switzerland has four languages—Deutsche ist über alles. In Belgium, there's tension between the Dutch- and French-speaking halves. Like many French

Canadians, Europe's linguistic underdogs will tell you their language receives equal treatment only on Corn Flakes boxes, and many are scheming up ways to correct the situation.

Terrorism and Tourism

It's refreshing to be so out of touch while traveling that you forget what day it is. But even in areas that aren't "hot spots," it's wise to be up on the news. American and English newspapers are available in most of the world, as are English radio broadcasts. Other tourists can be valuable links with the outside world as well. Most important, the nearest American or British consulate can advise you on problems that merit concern. Take their advice seriously even if it means scrubbing your mission.

Talking to people about local problems is fine. Dodging bullets isn't. I can't remember ever hearing a gun or a bomb in my Mediterranean travels. Many times, however, I've had the thrill of a firsthand experience merely by talking with people who were personally involved.

Your tour memories can include lunch with a group of Palestinian college students, an evening walk through Moscow with a Russian dissident, listening to the Voice of America with curious Bulgarians in a Black Sea coast campground, and learning why the French aren't promoting the reunification of Germany. Or your travel memories can be built on the blare of your tour guide's bullhorn in empty Gothic cathedrals and polished palaces learning who did the stucco.

Terrorism in Europe has been a hot topic in recent years. Since things are relatively quiet now, I hesitate to even bring up the subject. But I'm concerned that people are planning their trips assuming terrorism is over. That's a dangerous approach. There's always been terrorism, and I'm afraid there will always be terrorism. It's in your best interest to plan your trip assuming there will be a terrorist event sometime between now and your departure date—most likely in the city you're flying into. Understand the risk of terrorism. And travel in a way that minimizes that tiny threat. Let me explain.

First of all, terrorism is nothing new. There have always been terrorists—Basque separatists, the Red Brigade in Italy, and so on. What's new is that Americans are being targeted and our media and government reward the terrorists royally by bringing its horrors into our homes in living color and by treating it as a matter of foreign policy rather than as a common crime.

The news media profit from terrorism. Terror sells ads. TV has a sliding pay scale for its advertising time, determined by how many of us tune in. There's a terrible temptation for the media to sensationalize terrorism. It's tailor-made for TV—quick, emotional, and gruesome 90-second spots. Consider the emotional style in which terrorism is covered and how expertly terrorists are milking that—even providing TV news broadcasts with video footage.

Understand that loved ones often take TV news to heart, lack a broad understanding of the world, and may stand between us and our travel dreams—begging and even bribing us not to go. If I'm in Europe and there's a boat hijacked or a train wreck in Italy, my mother assumes I'm involved (as a victim). I always call to let her know I survived. Assure those who'll worry about you that you'll call home every few days. If you're a teenager with worrying parents, hit them up for a $1-per-30-second "I'm doing fine" call, and call home regularly.

Certainly we need to consider the real risk of terrorism, evaluate the risk, and if we decide to travel, travel in a way that minimizes that risk. It's either accept the risk or settle for a lifetime of National Geographic specials.

Travel is accelerated living. It's riskier than staying home. Terrorism is just another risk, much smaller than the ones tourists have always taken without a second thought. Let's look at it in cold unemotional statistics. In all of 1985, the year we let terrorism change our way of looking at the world, 28 Americans, out of 25 million who traveled, were killed by terrorists. Sure, that's a risk, but in the same year, 8,000 Americans were killed by handguns on our own Streets. Europeans

laugh out loud when they read of Americans choosing to stay home so they won't be murdered. Statistically, even in the worst times of terrorism, you're much safer in Europe.

Flying is also risky. I know people die in planes, but I also know that, in the United States alone, over 60,000 planes take off and land safely every day. I take the risk. I remind myself that there's about one plane crash or hijacking for every million flying hours and travel. Every year, several hundred pedestrians are run down on the streets of Paris—not glamorous enough for headlines, but dead is dead. By the way, according to our State Department, more Americans were killed by terrorists in 1974 than in 1985, but the media didn't pick up on it and we tourists didn't notice.

OK, the risks are small. But it's smart to travel in ways that make the risks even more minuscule. Terrorist targets are predictable. They lash out at the high-profile symbols of our powerful and wealthy society—airplanes, luxury cruise ships, elegant high-rise hotels, posh restaurants, military and diplomatic locations. These have been the targets of nearly every terrorist incident to date. Traveling through the back door, you'll stay in simple, local-style places. . . Pedro's Pension. Terrorists don't bomb Pedro's Pension. That's where they sleep.

The answer to the violence isn't to strike back, to kill Khadafy and sit back thinking everything will be fine. And the answer isn't to stay home in Fortress America, either. Terrorism is caused by a lack of understanding. Travel teaches understanding. And since we're all trapped here on this ever-smaller planet in a high-tech drama that will sooner or later force us to choose between living together or dying together, what could be better than to continue to travel and, by doing so, help our world take a much-needed step toward global harmony?

Anti-Americanism

Apart from the actual terrorist problem, many are concerned about anti-American sentiment in Europe. Anti-Americanism is nothing new. It rises and falls with the headlines. But thankfully, people around the world understand the distance between citizens and their governments, and the vast majority of Europeans, regardless of how their banners insult Uncle Sam, want to like you. These days, many foreigners strongly oppose what they see as American militarism or "imperialism," especially in Central America. "Ugly Americans" will see an awful lot of "peace-niks" and naive wimps who lack a good healthy fear and hatred of communism. But those traveling to better understand the world will be welcomed warmly in Europe.

Travel is a blunt teacher. It's taught me that there are values other than the Judeo-Christian, democratic, and materialistic ones that America finds "God-given" and "self-evident" and that there are always local Nathan Hales willing to die for "strange notions." It's also taught me that some nationalities, like whales, are endangered species. For example, five languages die out every year.

When I think of terrorism, 1914 keeps coming to mind. History teaches us loud and clear the power of nationalism and the tragic consequences of superpower ignorance. In 1914, a Serbian terrorist killed the Hapsburg archduke because his people wanted a homeland for the South Slavs. To teach the Serbs a lesson, the superpower of the day, Austria, declared war. Four years and many million deaths later, the Serbs got exactly what they wanted—the creation of "the union of the South Slavs," Yugoslavia. Problems that involve entire national groups don't just go away. One way or another, they must be faced.

It's difficult for us Americans, whose revolution was so long ago and whose incredible prosperity gives us a redcoat perspective on "radical fringe groups," to tune in to the patriotic struggles going on in Europe today. But if we can develop an empathy for the Ethan Allens and Nathan Hales of today's Europe, our travels gain a whole new dimension.

The graffiti you see is usually not anti-us or anti-them, it's pro-peace.

13
The Whirlwind Tour — Europe's Best Two-Month Trip

Let's assume that you have ten weeks, plenty of energy, and a desire to see as much of Europe as is reasonable. It's most economical to fly to London and travel around Europe with a two-month Eurailpass. You'll spend two months on the Continent and use any remaining time in England, before or after you start your train pass. Budgeting for a $700 round-trip ticket to London, a $840 two-month first-class Eurailpass, and $50 a day, the entire trip will cost about $4,500. It can be done. Green, but thinking, budget travelers of all ages do it all the time — often for less.

If I could relive my first two months in Europe, this is the trip I'd take. I'll have to admit, I itch just thinking about this itinerary. Fasten your seat belts, raise your travel dreams to their upright and locked position, and prepare to take off.

London is Europe's great entertainer, wonderfully historic and mild compared to anything but the United States. It's the best starting point for a European adventure. The English speak English, but their accents will give you the sensation of understanding a foreign language. Every day will be busy and each night filled with a play and a pub. But the Continent beckons.

Paris is a quick overnight train ride away. Ascend the Eiffel Tower to survey a Paris studded with architectural gems and historical one-of-a-kinds. You'll recognize Notre-Dame, Sacré-Coeur, the Louvre, and much more. A busy four days awaits you back on the ground — especially with a visit to Europe's greatest palace, Louis XIV's Versailles.

On the way to Spain, explore the dreamy chateaus of the Loire Valley. Take the train to Madrid, where bullfights, shopping, the Prado museum, and nearby Toledo fill your sunny days. Then sleep on the train to Lisbon, Portugal's friendly capital.

Lisbon can keep a visitor busy for days. Its highlight is the Alfama. This salty old sailor's quarter is a photographer's delight. You'll feel rich here in Europe's bargain basement, where a taxi ride is cheaper than a London bus ticket.

Break the long train ride to the French Riviera with a day or two in
Madrid and Barcelona. A rest on a south France beach is in order
before diving into intense Italy.

Italy, steeped in history and art, is a bright spot in any itinerary. An
entire trip could be spent climbing through the classical monuments
of Rome, absorbing the art treasures of Florence, and cruising the
canals of colorful Venice. These cities, Pompeii, the leaning tower of
Pisa, the hill towns of Tuscany, and so much more just might kidnap
your heart.

Your favorite place in Italy may be the Cinque Terre. Cinque Terre?
Your friends will believe it only after they see your pictures. Unknown
to most tourists and the ultimate Italian coastal paradise, you'll find
pure Italy in these five sleepy traffic-free villages near Genoa.

Savor the Old World elegance of Hapsburg Vienna for a few days
and then enjoy Salzburg's unrivaled music festival. Classical music
sounds so right in its birthplace.

Tour Mad King Ludwig's fairy tale castle at Neuschwanstein before visiting the Tirolean town of Reutte and its two forgotten—yet unforgettable—hill-crowning, ruined castles. These are the Ehrenburg Ruins. Running along the overgrown ramparts, your imagination works itself loose and suddenly you're under attack a thousand years ago.

Europe's most scenic train ride is across southern Switzerland from Chur to Martigny. Be careful: mixing sunshine and a full dose of Alpine beauty can be intoxicating.

For the best of the Swiss Alps, establish a home base in the rugged Berner Oberland, south of Interlaken. The traffic-free village of Gimmelwald in Lauterbrunnen Valley is everything an Alp-lover could possibly want.

Munich, the capital of Bavaria, has the world's greatest street singers. But they probably won't be good enough to keep you out of the beer halls. Huge mugs of beer, bigger pretzels, and even bigger beermaids! If you're smart, you'll skip the touristy Hofbrau House and patronize Mathäuser's Beer Hall for the best local crowd, a rowdy oom-pah band, and thick German atmosphere.

The Romantic Road bus tour (included on the Eurailpass) is the best way to get from Munich to Frankfurt. The bus rolls through the heart of medieval Germany, stopping at Dinkelsbühl and the always popular queen of quaint German towns, Rothenburg.

After the bus tour, take the Rhine cruise (also covered by Eurail) from Bingen to Koblenz to enjoy a parade of old castles. Sleep in Bacharach's classic castle youth hostel with a panoramic view of the Rhine for $4.

Finish your Continental experience with a blitz tour of the capitals of Scandinavia: Copenhagen, Stockholm, and Oslo. Smorgasbords, Viking ships, and healthy, smiling blondes are the memories you'll pack on the train south to Amsterdam.

After a few days in crazy Amsterdam and a bike ride through the countryside, sail for England. Any remaining time is happily spent in the English countryside.

This trip is just a sampler. There's plenty more to see, but I can't imagine a better first two months in Europe. See Part Two: Forty Back Doors for details.

The Itinerary—
Some Specifics

If I was planning my first European trip and wanted to see as much as I could comfortably in two months (and I had the experience I now have to help me plan), this is the trip I'd take.

Days	Place	
?	**London**	Cheapest place in Europe to fly to, easiest place to adjust. From airport (easy RR or subway access from Gatwick or Heathrow), go to Victoria Station. Get ticket to Continent (Paris, overnight, or youth under 26 is cheapest) at Sealink Office. Great tourist information office in Victoria. Round London orientation bus tour from park in front of station departs every half-hour. Lay groundwork for your return to London (if ending trip there)—reserve good B&B, get tickets to a hot play. Hotel Holland Park (hotelesque, tel. 727-8166), Hotel Ravna Gora (funky, tel. 727-7725), Abbey House Bed and Breakfast (charming, tel. 727-2594). Consider the insanity of traveling to Paris on jet lag night since you'll sleep fitfully anyway. Night train (NT) and boat to Paris. 20:40-6:25.
4	**Paris**	Arrive in morning—easy to find budget one- or two-star hotel room. Near Eiffel Tower on Rue Cler: Hotel Leveque (tel. 47-05-49-15), Hotel du Centre (tel. 47-05-52-33), or Hotel du Champs de Mars (tel. 45-51-52-30). Use Paris subway. It's fast, easy, and cheap. Walk—Latin Quarter, Notre-Dame, monument to victims of the Nazis (open 10:00), St. Chapelle, Pont-Neuf, self-serve lunch in Samaritaine department store, Louvre, Tuillieries Gardens, Champs-Elysées to the Arc de Triomphe. Ask hotel to recommend small family-owned restaurant for dinner. Evening on Montmartre,

soak in the spiritual waters of the Sacré-Coeur, browse among the shops and artists of the Place du Tertre. Later, be sure to enjoy Napoleon's Tomb, Les Invalides (Europe's best military museum), the Rodin Museum (*The Thinker* and *Kiss*), the great new Orsay Museum (Impressionism), Pompidou Modern Art Gallery, a jazz club, and Latin Quarter nightlife. Pick up the "Pariscope" entertainment guide. Most museums are closed on Tuesdays. ST (side trip) #1—Versailles, a must. Europe's grandest palace (take the RER train to end of line, Versailles R.G.). ST #2—Chartres, great gothic cathedral, lectures by Malcom Miller at 12:00 and 2:45.

2	**Loire Valley**	Make Amboise or Tours your headquarters. Good all day bus tours of chateaus. If not really into chateaus, skip Loire. Consider 30-minute ST from Paris to epitome of a French chateau, Chantilly. NT direct Paris to Madrid, 20:00-8:55.
2	**Madrid**	On arrival, reserve train out. Reservations on long trains are required in Spain (and Norway) even with Eurail. Taxi to Puerto del Sol for central budget room. Try Plaza Santa Anna (#15, Hostel Fila, tel. 522-4056). Prado museum (Bosch, Goya, El Greco, Velázquez), *Guernica*, and Royal Palace (Europe's most lavish interior) are musts. Bullfights on Sundays through the summer, ask at hotel, buy tickets at arena. El Rastro (flea market), for great shopping on Sundays.
1	**Toledo**	Whole city perfectly preserved, best at night, El Greco's home and masterpieces. NT, Madrid-Lisbon, 23:30-9:45.
3	**Lisbon**	Europe's bargain basement capital, see "Back Door." ST—Sintra (ruined Moorish

		castle), Estoril (casino nightlife). NT—Madrid, 21:00-8:16.
1	**Madrid**	On arrival, reserve NT to Barcy (22:30-7:49). Spend the day here. Night travel is best in Iberia—long distances, boring, hot, crowded, slow day trains. Beds (couchettes) are cheap on these trains.
2	**Barcelona**	Picasso's house (excellent), relax, shop, Gothic Quarter, watch out for thieves. NT—19:49-7:00.
3	**Rhone Valley or French Riviera**	Avignon—(Papal Palace), Nimes, and Arles (Roman ruins). Nice (where the jet set lies on rocks, great Chagall Museum), Riviera (crowded, expensive, stressful, good modern art). Best overnights in Arles (Hotel Regence, tel. 90-96-39-85) and Nice (Hotel Star, tel. 93-85-19-03).
2	**Cinque Terre**	Great villages, coastal Italy at its best, see "Back Door."
2	**Florence**	Europe's art capital, packed in the summer, worth the headaches. Sleep in Sorelli Bandini (Old World elegant ramshackle, tel. 215308), Hotel La Scaletta (warm, friendly, tel. 283028) or Cassa Cristina (quiet, traditional, elegant, tel. 496730).
2	**Hill Towns of Tuscany and Umbria**	See "Back Door." Most neglected and underrated side of Italy. Accommodations easy, leave Florence late, arrive Rome early.
4	**Rome**	Day #1—Classical: Colosseum, Forum, Capitol Hill (both museums), Pantheon. Evening—Piazza Navona (buy Tartufo ice cream). Day #2—Vatican, St. Peter's, climb the dome, Sistine (see *Mona Winks* or rent headphone guide) and Vatican Museum (great market 100 yards in front of museum

entry, picnic). Take advantage of the Vatican's Post, much better than Italy's. Day #3—Ostia Antica, Ancient Rome's seaport (like Pompeii, but just a subway ride away from Rome). Piazza Barberini, Bernini fountain, Cappuccin crypt, thousands of bones in first church on Via Veneto, do the Dolce Vita stroll from Piazza del Popolo to Spanish Steps at 6 p.m., dinner on Campo di Fiori. Bus from station to Tivoli, garden of fountains outside of Rome. Explore Trastevere, old Rome alive today, good place for dinner. Sleep near Vatican Museum at Pension Alimandi, tel. 318404, or near the station at Pension Nardizzi, tel. 460368. NT—Venice, 0:20-7:10.

2	**Venice**	Best introduction—slow boat (#1) down Canale Grande. Sit in front and soak it in. Sleep at Locanda Sturion (near Rialto, tel. 523-6243). Academy Gallery—best Venetian art. Doges Palace, St. Mark's, and view from Campanile are musts, then wander, leave the tourists, get as lost as possible. Don't worry, you're on an island and you can't get off. NT—Vienna, 20:32-6:53.
2	**Vienna**	Paris' eastern rival. Grand capital of the mighty Hapsburg Empire. Lots of art history and more Old World charm and elegance than anywhere. Great tourist information behind Opera. Good half-day tours from Opera. Tour Opera. Sleep at Pension Columbia (tel. 426757). Consider ST to Budapest or Prague (visas required but relatively easy in Vienna). NT—Switzerland.
6	**Switzerland**	Pray for sun. Most scenic train—Chur-Martigny (two non-Eurail segments). Best region—Berner Oberland, south of Interlaken, see "Back Door." Best big city: Bern,

lovely towns along Lake Geneva and in West (Murten and Fribourg). Bodensee (Meersburg castle town, tropical isle of Mainau, Lindau—Venice of North, Eurail covers boats on Swiss lakes).

2	**Tirol**	Reutte ("Back Door" castle ruins), Innsbruck, with its great Tirolean folk museum. Sleep in tiny medieval town of Hall, 3 miles from Innsbruck (Gasthof Badl, tel. 05223/6784).
2	**Bavaria**	Füssen, Mad Ludwig's castles, Wies Church (scaffolded through 1990), villages. See "Back Door."
3	**Munich**	Cultural capital, great palace, museums, Mathäuser's Beer Hall (best, halfway between station and old town on right). Tourist information and room-finding service in station (open late, tel. 089/239-1256). Lay groundwork for departure on Romantic Road bus tour on arrival (make reservation, if necessary, confirm place and time of departure). ST—Salzburg, only 90-minute train ride away.
1	**Romantic Road**	Bus tour, free with Eurailpass (see "Back Door"). Munich-Frankfurt 9:00-20:00 with stops in Dinkelsbühl and Rothenburg. Eve on the Rhine (Hotel Kranenturm in Bacharach, tel. 06743/1308). Consider overnight in Rothenburg (Hotel Goldener Rose, tel. 09861/4638).
3	**Rhine/Mosel River Valleys**	Cruise from Bacharach to St. Goar, best castles, free with train pass, hike from St. Goar to Rheinfels castle, great castle youth hostel in Bacharach (tel. 06743/1266). Mosel Valley, including cruises, Cochem town and castle, Trier-Roman town, Burg Eltz—long walk, great castle. NT—Köln or Frankfurt to Copenhagen, 22:39-9:09.

1	**Copenhagen**	Leave bags at station, evening at Tivoli just across the street. If you spend the night, sleep in the Kongstad home (tel. 01/572466). NT—23:21-7:46.
3	**Stockholm**	See "Back Door." Sleep on trains in Scandinavia—long, boring rides, capitals ten hours apart, hotels expensive. NT—23:10-7:55.
2	**Oslo**	See "Back Door." Consider ST to Bergen, very scenic train ride, 8 hours over, evening in Bergen, NT back, or "Norway in a Nutshell" program.
1	**Copenhagen**	NT—22:35-8:54. Another day in Copenhagen. NT—22:10-9:54. Train goes right on to Puttgarten ferry.
4	**Amsterdam**	Many great side trips. Consider headquarters in small town nearby (Haarlem, Hotel Carillon, tel. 023/310591) as Amsterdam is getting awfully sleazy and seedy for many visiting Americans' tastes. Consider open-jaws flight into London, out of Amsterdam, to avoid surface return to London ($50 and 12 hours). NT—20:31-9:00.
?	**London**	Spend remaining time in English countryside, Bath, Cotswolds, Cambridge. Call to reconfirm flight home.

Sixty days scheduled on the Continent. Train times are outdated; use only as a rough guide. Eurailpass is good for two calendar months (e.g., the 15th through midnight on the 14th). If you validate when you leave Paris and expire (the Eurailpass, not you) on arrival in Amsterdam, you spend 52 days, leaving 8 days of train pass time to slow down or add options.

Books recommended for this tour: *Let's Go: Europe, Mona Winks,* and *22 Days in Europe* (all published by John Muir Publications).

Excursions You May Want to Add

England—Oxford, Stratford, the Cotswold villages, Bath
Geneva, Chamonix, Aiguille du Midi, Aosta (Italy)
Berlin
Morocco and South Spain
South Italy or Greece
Finland or the Arctic
Eastern Europe or the USSR
A day for showers and laundry
Visiting and resting
Travel days to avoid sleeping on the train
A free day here and there. Every itinerary needs some slack.

The Whirlwind Tour includes fourteen nights on the train, saving about $200 in hotel costs, and fourteen days for doing more interesting things than sitting on a train.

People of all ages are letting their hair down in Europe.

Part Two:
Forty Back Doors

Contents

Front Door Cities, Back Door Angles

Beyond Europe: Maximum Thrills per Mile, Minute, and Dollar

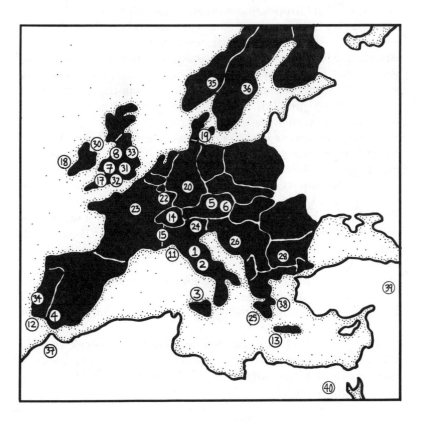

What Is a Back Door, and How Can I Find One of My Own?

The travel skills covered so far in this book enable you to open doors most travelers don't even know exist. The rest of the book is a chance for you and the travel bug to get intimate. It takes you by the hand through my favorite European experiences. I hope you'll not only be able to enjoy these special places but that you'll use your travel skills to go farther than Europe's museums and bus tours to find your own.

Europe is a bubbling stew of many cultures. A back door is a steaming ladle—just one taste—of that stew. It could be an Alpine hike, an Andalusian hill town, a French pastry, a ruined castle, a little Warsaw Pact country that everyone ignores, a new angle on a famous city, or a way to splice some beyond-Europe thrills into your trip. Each element of this delicious jumble of travel adventures is a cultural truth; taken together, they create Europe.

I've organized these Back Doors into five groups. If you can travel with me as you read, you'll gain enough experience in each of these groupings to make your own similar travel adventures.

The first clump is **undiscovered towns**. The big cities lead Europe's tourist parade. Discovered small towns actively promoting themselves follow right behind. But many of Europe's towns have, for various reasons, missed the modern parade. With no promotional budgets to attract us travelers, they are ignored as they quietly make their traditional way through just another century.

Then we'll explore the **natural nooks and undeveloped crannies**. These are rare opportunities to enjoy Europe's sun, beaches, mountains, and natural wonders without the glitz. Europeans are the original romantics. While they love nature, they have an impressive knack for enjoying themselves in hellish crowds. There are quiet alternatives. It's possible to find forgotten stone circles, desolate castles, peaceful bike rides, and snippets of the Riviera that are not geared up to make money from visitors.

Next, we'll travel through a series of **misunderstood regions and countries.** Some areas lie in the shadow of a touristic superstar, like the rarely visited sights near Venice. War and other international problems have left a legacy of fascinating sights, such as the remains of Nazi Europe. Because of politics and history, Eastern Europe is busy with travelers from Angola, China, Cuba, and the socialist world, while relatively few Westerners venture in. And some "countries" are forgotten entirely, like most of the dozen or so that combined to make Yugoslavia after World War I.

There are plenty of well-discovered **Front Door cities that need Back Door angles** so you can get far enough away from the tourist commotion and staged culture to feel the city's real pulse. Even London has a warm underbelly where you'll actually hear a heart that has been beating for 2,000 years.

And finally, for maximum thrills per mile, minute, and dollar, it's important to look **beyond Europe.** Europe is exciting, but a dip into Morocco, Egypt, or Turkey is rewarding beyond your wildest travel dreams—and well worth the diarrhea.

These Back Doors combine to give you a Whitman's sampler of travel thrills. While it's very important for you to use the listings of my favorite accommodations and some of the nitty-gritty I've listed in the Appendix, these chapters are written to give you the flavor of the place, not to navigate by. An appropriate directory-type guidebook (like my 22 Days series or the Let's Go series) will give you the details necessary to splice your chosen highlights into a smooth trip.

Many of these places are subtle and won't hit you with their cultural razzle-dazzle. The sensitive traveler will make his own fun, learning from the experiences described in each chapter.

Europe is so popular and crowded—and its tourist industry is so developed with ever-more-sophisticated travelers and good guidebooks pointing them in the right direction—that places I "discovered" eight or ten years ago are generally undeveloped and uncommercial only in a relative sense. And I should warn you that certain places that I really rave about will suffer from Back Door congestion. At least, from my experience, Back Door readers are pleasant people to share Europe with.

By the way, I am impressed and pleased by reports from people recommended in this book that Back Door readers are travelers who do much to undo the "ugly" image created by many demanding and ethnocentric American tourists. It's clear to me that by traveling sensitively, you're doing yourself a favor as well as those you'll deal with, travelers who'll follow. . .and me. Thanks.

The promotion of a tender place that has so far avoided the tourist industry is a strange problem. It reminds me of the whaler who screams, "Quick, harpoon it before it's extinct!" I love travel. These places are what make it special. Publicizing them gnaws at what makes them so great. But what kind of a travel writer can keep his favorite discoveries secret? I keep no secrets. These days, great finds are too hard to come by not to share. In fact, I enjoy bumping into readers in my special hideaways.

The style of travel that's developed by internalizing the countless little travel moments that I've enjoyed and compiled here lets you experience Europe with the same eternal enthusiasm that has kept me on this wonderful path for so long. And I can hardly stop dreaming about all the travel fun that awaits me in my next European adventure. I hope you'll love Europe, as I do—through the Back Door.

Undiscovered Towns

1. The Hill Towns of Tuscany and Umbria

Too many people connect Rome and Florence with a straight line. If you break out of the Venice-Florence-Rome syndrome, you'll lick a little Italy that the splash of Venice, the finesse of Florence, and the grandeur of Rome were built on.

The hill towns of Tuscany and Umbria hold their crumbling heads proudly above the noisy flood of the twentieth century and offer a peaceful taste of what eludes so many tourists. Sitting on a timeless rampart high above the traffic and trains, hearing only children in the market and the rustling of the wind aging the already aged red-tile patchwork that surrounds me, I find the essence of Italy in this small-town package.

Hill towns, like Greek islands, come in two basic varieties—touristy and untouristy. There are a dozen great touristed towns and countless ignored communities casually doing time and drinking their wine. Make a point to see some of each.

Historic San Gimignano bristles with towers and bustles with tourists. Tuscany's best-preserved medieval skyline is a thrilling silhouette from a distance, and it gets better as you approach. Nighttime's the right time to conquer the castle. Sit on its summit and imagine the battles these old cobbles and floodlit towers have endured. Even with crowds, San Gimignano is a must.

Siena, unlike its rival, Florence, is a city to be seen as a whole rather than as a collection of sights. Climb to the dizzy top of the bell tower and reign over urban harmony at its best. As you tour Siena, compare and contrast it with Florence, which was the big gun but didn't call all the shots.

Assisi, a worthy hometown of St. Francis, is battling a commercial cancer of tourist clutter. A quiet hour in the awesome Basilica of St.

Francis, some appropriate reading (there's a great bookstore next door), and a meditative stroll through the back streets can still put you in a properly Franciscan frame of mind to dissolve the tour buses and melt into the magic of Assisi.

Orvieto, the typical tourist's token hill town, sits majestically on its tufa throne, offering those on the train or autostrada to Rome its impressive hill-capping profile. Its cathedral, with some fascinating Signorelli frescoes, is surrounded by an excellent tourist information office, a fine Etruscan museum, a world-class gelati shop, and the most pleasant public toilet you'll find in Italy.

Any guidebook lists these popular hill towns. But if you want to dance at noon with a toothless lady while the pizza cooks, press a good

luck coin into the moldy ceiling of an Etruscan wine cellar, be introduced to a less than mediocre altarpiece as proudly as if it were a Michelangelo, or have the local cop unlock the last remaining city tower and escort you to the top for a bird's-eye view of the town and the gawkers who just emptied out of the barber shop below, stow your guidebook, buy the best local map you can find, and explore.

Perfect Back Door villages, like hidden pharaohs' tombs, await discovery. Photographers delight in Italian hill towns. Their pictorial collections are the best information source (I used _Italian Hill Towns_ by Norman Carver). Study these, circling the most intriguing towns on your map. Debrief those who have studied or lived in Italy. Ask locals for their favorites. Most important, follow your wanderlust blindly. Find a frog and kiss it.

Gubbio, Volterra, Cortona, and Arezzo are discovered but rarely visited. Città di Bagnoregio (next Back Door), Sorano, Pitigliano, Trevi, Poppi, Orte (just north of Rome off the freeway), and Bagnaia (near Viterbo) are virgin hill towns. The difference between "discovered" and "virgin," touristically speaking, is that "discovered" knows what tourism is and how to use it economically. "Virgin" is simply pleased that you dropped in. "Virgin" doesn't want to, or know how to, take advantage of you. It wants only to enjoy, and to be enjoyed.

San Marino, just another magic Italian hill town

Hill towns are a vital slice of the Italian pizza—thin crust with a thick gooey culture. Leave the train lines. Take the bus, hitch, or rent a car for a few days. (Many towns have a train station nearby. Your ticket includes a bus shuttle that begins its windy climb shortly after your train arrives.) Don't just chase down my favorites or your guidebook's recommendations. Find your own treasure—the social slumber of Umbria and the human texture of Tuscany.

2. Città di Bagnoregio

People who've been there just say "Città" (pronounced: CHIV·ee·tah) with a special warmth and love. I hesitate to promote this precious chip of Italy, a traffic-free community with a grow·it·in·the·valley economy which until now has escaped the ravages of modernity. But it's so perfect—I have to share it. Please approach it with the same respect and sensitivity you would a dying relative, because—in a sense—that's Città.

Twenty people still live here. There's no car traffic, only a man with a donkey who works all day ferrying the town's goods across the long umbilical bridge that connects the town with a small distant parking lot and the rest of Italy. Rome is just 60 miles to the south but might as well be on the other side of the moon.

Cività's sights are subtle, and many tourists wouldn't know what to do in a town without arcade tourism. No English menus, lists of attractions, orientation tours, or museum hours. Just Italy.

Sit in the piazza. Smile and nod at each local who passes by. It's a social jigsaw puzzle and each person fits. Look up at the old woman hanging out the window. She's in charge of gossip and knows all. A tiny hunchback lady is everyone's daughter, and 2,500-year-old pillars from an ancient buried Etruscan temple stick up like bar stools on the square.

Cività's population is revised downward with each edition of this book. As old people get frail, they move into apartments in Bagnoregio. Most of the young people are gone, lured away by the dazzle of today to grab their place in Italy's cosmopolitan parade.

Today, Cività's social pie has three slices: the aging, full-time resident community (winter population: three), the rich Italians from Rome and Milan who are slowly buying up the place for their country escape (I had dinner in the town restaurant next to the Ferrari family, who own the house next to the town gate—and Cività's only Jacuzzi), and a small University of Washington architecture program headed by Professor Astra Zarina, who owns a villa in Cività. When in session, 10 to 20 UW students live and study here. Over the years, alumni and their families have made Cività their Italian retreat, and you'll often find a Seattleite or two enjoying *la dolce far niente* (the sweetness of doing nothing) here.

Explore Cività. Anna introduces you to a baby donkey as if it were her child. Anna is the keeper of the keys to the church. Cività's church is the heartbeat and pride of the village. Festivals and processions start here, visitors are taken here, and the town's past is honored here. Enjoy paintings by students of famous artists, relics of the hometown boy-made-saint Bonaventura, a dried floral decoration spread across the floor, and a cool, quiet sit in a pew.

Cività is a man-gripped pinnacle in a vast canyon. Erosion and the wind rule the valley. Victoria, ignoring her eye-boggling view, took me into an ancient Etruscan cave to see her olive press. Just around the corner from the church is Domenica's cantina. Sit on a stump, enjoy a glass of her family wine. The white has a taste reminiscent of dirty socks, the red tastes cleaner. But it's made right here. That donkey brought up the grapes. Climb down into her ancient cellar. Tap the kegs to measure their fullness. Even on a blistering day, those caves are always cool, and an endless supply of local Cività wine is kept chilled, awaiting future fun.

The perfect hill town, Cività di Bagnoregio

Cività has one restaurant. You can see its green door and handmade sign from the piazza. At Al Forno (the oven), you eat what's cooking. Mom and Pop slice and quarter happily through the day. Spaghetti, salad and wine, cuddled by Cività on the Al Forno patio—I wouldn't trade it for all-you-can-eat at Maxims.

Spend the evening. Sit on the church steps with people who've done exactly that together for 60 years. Al Forno serves late, and children play on the piazza until midnight. As you walk back to your car—that scourge of the modern world that enabled you to get here—stop under a lamp on the donkey path, listen to the canyon. . .distant voices. . . cranked-up crickets.

Cività is an artist's dream, a town in the nude. Each lane and foot-path holds a surprise. Horses pose, the warm stone walls glow, each stairway is dessert to a sketch pad or camera, and the grand moat does its best to keep things that way. It's changing, however, as the aggressive present eats at the last strongholds of the past. With recent exposure in German and French travel magazines, summer weekends see up to 200 tourists a day. Cività will be great for years but never as great as today.

You won't find Cività on your map. Take the train to Orvieto and catch a bus to Bagnoregio. From Bagnoregio you walk to Cività.

Città has no hotel. Bagnoregio has two. The most colorful is a 20-minute walk out of town. Ask for Boschetto di Angelino Catarcia. Angelino is a character who runs through life like a hyper child in a wading pool. He doesn't speak English; he doesn't need to. Have an English-speaking Italian call him for you—tel. 0761/792369; address: Strada Monterado, Bagnoregio, Viterbo, Italy. His family is wonderful, and if you so desire, he'll get his sons, Dominico and Franco, together and take you deep into the gooey, fragrant bowels of "La Cantina." Music and vino kill the language barrier in Angelino's wine cellar, where he will teach you his theme song, "Trinka, Trinka, Trinka."

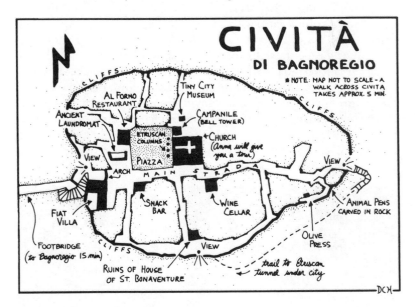

Warning: Angelino is Bacchus squared. Descend into his cantina at your own risk. There are no rules unless female participants set them. If you are lucky enough to eat dinner at Angelino's (bunny is the house specialty), ask to try the sweet dessert wine. Everything at Angelino's is deliciously homegrown—figs, fruit, wine, rabbit, pasta. This is the Italy you always dreamed of finding.

3. Palermo, Sicily's Urban Carnival

The European tourist boom is just a distant hum in Sicily. It took me seven trips to get down past Italy's "boot," but I finally made it. The Sicilians (along with the Irish) are the warmest and friendliest Europeans I've met.

Palermo is intense—Italy in the extreme—with lots of purse snatchers, lousy showers, and grueling heat. It is generally run down and chaotic, but if you want exotic, untouristic urban Italian thrills, there's no better place.

The overnight train ride south from Rome or Naples drops you right into this rich culture living peacefully oblivious to the touristic bustle that takes such a toll on Venice, Florence, and Rome.

Eating and sleeping in high style at low prices is easy. From the Palermo train station, walk straight down Via Roma for your choice of many hotels. A reservation is unnecessary. My favorite hotel is the Hotel Moderno, Via Roma 276. My double (room 23) was large and airy and included a rooftop patio with a view. The bathroom was bigger than some entire hotel bedrooms I've stayed in. The management was friendly and eager to share lots of tourist information.

Eating in Palermo is a treat. Colorful street markets make shopping for picnics a joy. Pizzeria Bellini on Piazza Bellini, near the central "four corners" of Palermo, was my dinnertime hangout. Over the course of several meals, I ate my way through their menu, discovering for myself why Italians like to eat. Their fanciest pizza, "Quatro Gusti con Fungi," cost $3 and is permanently etched on my palate.

One reason Palermo lacks tourist crowds is that it has very few tourist

Travelers in search of back-street treats

A balcony of friends, Palermo, Sicily

sights as such. It does have a way of life that, in its own way, offers the tourist more than any monument or museum ever could. Don't tour Palermo, live in it.

Thriving marketplaces abound. If you've ever wondered what it would be like to be a celebrity, go on a photo-safari through the urban jungles of Palermo. The warmth and excitement will give you smile wrinkles. Scores of merchants, housewives, and children compete for your attention. Cries of "Photo?" come from all corners as you venture down busy alleys. Morning markets and eternal hawkers can be found in nearly any neighborhood.

Visit a vertical neighborhood. Small apartments stack high above the side streets. If you stop to chat, six floors of balconies will fill up, each with its own waving family. I found a wobbly stack of tenements facing one another, a faded rainbow with lots of laundry and people hanging out. One wave worked wonders. Walking around, craning my neck upward, I felt like a victorious politician among hordes of sup-porters. They called out for pictures and wouldn't let me go until I had filmed each window and balcony full of people: mothers held up babies, sisters posed arm in arm, a wild pregnant woman stood on a fruit crate, holding her bulging stomach, and an old, wrinkled woman, cheery in a paint-starved window frame. I was showered with scraps of paper, each with an address on it. A contagious energy filled the air, and saying good-bye hurt.

For a strange journey through an eerie cellar of the dead, visit the Catacombs of the Cappuccin Monks (Convento di Cappuccini). This dark and dreary basement has 8,000 clothed and very dead ex-monks hanging on its walls. A strange but meaningful habit. While you're there, notice how much the monks look like that wonderful cup of cappuccino you start your Italian day with. Their rich brown cowls with the frothy white tops look just like the cup of coffee, hence the name. . .of the coffee.

For a more typical tourist attraction and a respite from the skelter and heat of Palermo, bus inland to the soothing mountain town of Monreale. Inside Monreale's Benedictine church, you'll find a collection of mosaics that rival Ravenna's. Dozens of Bible scenes, in mosaic, cover the walls of this church. Since I was wearing shorts, I was given a blanket to wear as a skirt. With my hairy, unholy legs covered, I worked my way, scene by scene, through the Bible.

Palermo has no must-see museum and nothing to compete with the tipsy Pisa Tower or Big Ben. Palermo lets you become a temporary Sicilian, and that's a great reason to visit.

4. South Spain's Pueblos Blancos: Andalusia's Route of the White Villages

When tourists head south from Madrid, it's generally with Granada, Córdoba, Seville, or the Costa del Sol in mind. These places have lots to offer—as big cities. The Costa del Sol, in my mind, is a concrete nightmare, worthwhile only as a bad example. The most Spanish thing about the south coast is the sunshine—but that's everywhere. For something different and a bit more authentic, try exploring the interior of Andalusia on the "route of the white villages."

Make this an exercise in going where no tourist has gone before. If you don't know where you are, you've arrived. I spent several days driving rather aimlessly from town to village on the back roads of southern Spain, enjoying a wonderfully untouched Spanish culture. All you need is time, a car, and a willingness to follow your nose, winning some and losing some. I found some great towns and learned some valuable lessons.

Ronda is a good starting point. Straddling an impressive gorge and with lots of history spicing its cobbled streets, it's a joy. The Pileta Caves (open 9:00-2:00 and 4:00-7:00, a rocky drive or a 2-hour uphill hike from the nearest train station) are nearby. Follow the signs past groves

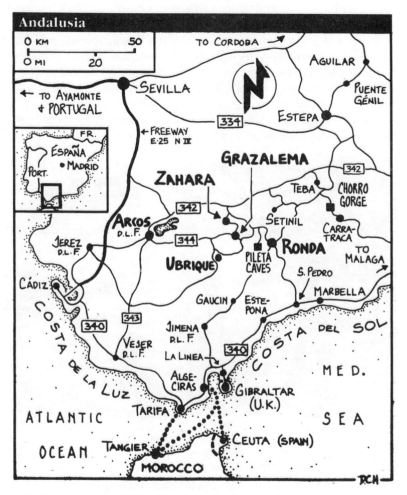

Andalusia

0 KM   50
0 MI   20

TO CORDOBA →

TO AYAMONTE
& PORTUGAL

SEVILLA

AGUILAR

PUENTE
GÉNIL

FREEWAY
E-25 N II

334

ESTEPA

342

FR.

ESPAÑA · MADRID
PORT.

GRAZALEMA

ZAHARA

TEBA   CHORRO
GORGE

342

ARCOS
D.L.F.

344

SETINIL

CARRA-
TRACA

JEREZ
D.L.F.

UBRIQUE

PILETA
CAVES

RONDA

TO
MALAGA

S. PEDRO

MARBELLA

CÁDIZ

GAUCIN   ESTE-
PONA

340   343

JIMENA
D.L.F.

VEJER
D.L.F.

LA LINEA

340

COSTA DEL SOL

MED.

COSTA DE LA LUZ

ATLANTIC

OCEAN

ALGE-
CIRAS

TARIFA

TANGIER

GIBRALTAR
(U.K.)

CEUTA (SPAIN)

MOROCCO

SEA

DCH

of cork trees to the desolate parking lot. If no one's there, a sign says (in
four languages) to "call." That means scream down into the valley, and
the old man will mosey up, unlock the caves, light the lanterns, and take
you on a memorable, hour-long, half-mile journey through the caves.
He is a master at hurdling the language barrier, and you'll get a good
look at countless natural formations as well as paintings done by prehistoric "hombres" 25,000 years ago. (That's five times as old as the
oldest Egyptian pyramid.) The famous caves at Altamira are closed, so
these are the best Neolithic paintings you'll see in Spain.

From Ronda, the road to Arcos de la Frontera is a charm bracelet of
whitewashed villages. You'll see Zahara (climb to its ruined castle for a
view that would knock Sancho Panza off his ass) and Grazalema (ideal

for a picnic on its grand canyon balcony). Other memorable towns within easy striking distance are Puente-Genil and Aguilar de la Frontera with a pleasant square, outdoor dancing, and people who are fascinated by tourists with hairy legs. My other favorites were Manzanares, Caratraca, hill-capping Tepa (where people burst into hysterics when you take their picture), and the inviting village of Setenil, northwest of Ronda.

Arcos de la Frontera is a more substantial town with a labyrinthine old quarter overlooking a vast plain. (Driving here is about as easy as

Estepa, southern Spain

threading a needle while you're giggling.) This is a great overnight stop. Be sure to climb the bell towers of both churches (possibly with a picnic for the summit). You'll walk right through the keeper of the tower's living room, get the key, leave a tip, and climb to the top. Cover your ears when the giant old clappers whip into action.

Estepa was my Spanish treasure chest. Below a hill crowned with a castle and a convent spreads a freshly washed and very happy town that fit my dreams of southern Spain.

Except for the busy truck route that skirts the town, peace abounds here. Situated halfway between Córdoba and Málaga (a seven-mile hitch from the La Roda train station), but light years away from either, Estepa hugs a small hill. The hill is crowned by the convent of Santa Clara, worth five stars in any guidebook but found in none. Enjoy the territorial view from the summit, then step into the quiet, spiritual perfection of the church. (If it's locked, find someone with a key.) Just sit in the chapel all alone and feel the beauty soak through your body. The evening is prime time in Estepa. The promenade begins as everyone gravitates to the central square. Estepa's spotless streets are shined nightly by the feet of ice cream-licking strollers. The whole town strolls—it's like "cruising" without cars. Buy an "ice cream bocadillo" and follow suit. There's a great barber—a real artist—located right on the square. Estepa's drawback is its lack of decent accommodations. I found only one place, and its location on the truck route made sleeping impossible. I ended up sleeping under the stars on the porch of Santa Clara's convent. It was a beautiful night, and the police agreed with my taste in impromptu campgrounds.

Good information on small-town Andalusia is rare. There's almost nothing written on the "Pueblos Blancos." This area is unvisited, so there aren't a lot of facilities for tourists. The Michelin Guide, which is usually invaluable, skips the Andalusian countryside. Get the best map you can find, ask the people you meet for touring suggestions, and pick up the excellent "Route of the White Towns" booklet in Seville or at any major Spanish tourist office. The farther from the tourist trade you get, the more difficult finding a hotel becomes (See the Appendix for hotel listings).

This Andalusian adventure is best by car. The roads are fine, traffic is light. Car rental is inexpensive, hitching is dreary, and public transportation is pretty bad. Gas, while expensive, is easy to get and the people are friendly. Hit the back roads and find that perfect village.

5. Hallstatt, in Austria's Commune-with-Nature Lakes District

With the longest life span and the shortest workweek in Europe, Austrians are experts at good living. They focus their free time on the fine points of life: music, a stroll, a pastry, and a good cup of coffee. The uniquely Austrian Gemütlichkeit (as difficult a word to translate as it is to pronounce, meaning something like a warm, cozy, friendly, focus-on-the-moment feeling) is especially evident in the Salzkammergut Lakes District, where big-city Austrians go to relax.

Far from the urban rat race, though just 60 minutes from Salzburg, this is the perfect place for a weekend cottage, to commune with nature, Austrian-style. The Salzkammergut is a lushly forested playground. Trains, buses, or boats lead the traveler through gentle mountains and shy lakes, winding from relaxed village to relaxed village.

Hallstatt in Austria's Salzkammergut lakes district

The Salzkammergut's pride and joy is the town of Hallstatt. The minute it came into view, I knew Hallstatt was my Alpine Oz. It's just the right size (1,200 people), wonderfully remote—and almost traffic-free. A tiny ferry takes you from the nearest train station across the fjordlike lake to Hallstatt, dropping you off on the storybook town square.

Hallstatt is tiny—bullied onto a ledge by a selfish mountain and a lovely lake. Its pint-sized square is surrounded by ivy-covered guest houses and cobbled lanes. The town can be toured on foot in about 10 minutes.

While there was no shortage of pleasant $15 per person Zimmer (which don't look like one-night stands), I splurged, spending $40 for a double with breakfast in the Gasthof Simony (tel. 06134/231). This hotel separates the square from the lake, with balconies overlooking each. My room was rustic with a hardwood floor, rag rugs, an antique wooden bed with a free-standing closet to match, grandmother lamps, and a lakeside, flower-decked balcony. The view almost changed my itinerary. Note: August tourist crowds trample most of Hallstatt's charm.

Just 3,000 years ago, this town was the salt-mining capital of Europe. An economic and cultural boom put this area on the map way back in Flintstone times. In fact, an entire 1,000-year era is called "The Hallstatt Period."

Today, you can tour the world's first salt mine, located a thrilling funicular ride above downtown Hallstatt. A humble museum next to the helpful tourist office shows off Hallstatt's ancient past.

The town outgrew its little ledge, and many of its buildings climb the mountainside, with street level on one side being three floors above street level on the other. The church cemetery in town is so old that the bones of the long dead have had to make way for those of the newly dead. The result is a fascinating chapel of decorated bones.

Passing time in and around Hallstatt is easy. The little tourist office will recommend a hike—the 9,000-foot Mt. Dachstein looms overhead. Or maybe a peaceful cruise in a rented canoe is more your style. Most people go to Hallstatt simply to relax, eat, shop and stroll. To best cloak yourself in the cobblestones, flowers, and the rich blues and greens of Austria's gemütlich Salzkammergut Lakes District, visit Hallstatt.

6. Hall, in the Shadow of Innsbruck

It's a brisk mountain morning in the Tirolean town of Hall. Merchants in aprons hustle and roses, peppers, and piles of pears fill their street side stalls, competing for my photograph. There's not a tourist in sight. They're all five miles up the river, in Innsbruck.

Hall was a rich salt-mining center when Innsbruck was just a humble bridge (bruck) town on the Inn River. Sprawling Innsbruck's tourist industry crowds into its tiny old town center. Hall, a tiny village in comparison, actually has a bigger old center.

The town, a rich bundle of old pastel buildings and cobbled streets, feels refreshingly real. Too real if you're trying to accomplish anything more than a leisurely lunch from 12:00 to 2:00 when everything closes. The tourist office organizes daily walking tours—in English when necessary. The church—a luxurious example of Tiroler baroque—the elegant architecture lining the streets and the fun-to-tour and still plugging-along 500-year-old mint combine to make it clear that in its day, this town was a local powerhouse.

Back when salt was money, Hall was loaded. You can tour salt mines in nearby places like Hallein and Hallstaat ("Hall" means salt). You'll dress up in an old miner's outfit, ride trains into the mountain where the salt was mined, cruise subterranean lakes, slide down long and slick wooden banisters, and read brief and dry English explanations while very entertaining guides tell the fascinating story in German. These tours are fun but often very crowded with long lines and cost about $8. I find them only marginally worth the money, time, and trouble.

Hall has a great alternative—its Bergbaumuseum; a cheaper ($2), faster (30-minute tours in English), and easier reconstruction of one of its original salt mines which was working until 1967, complete with pits, shafts, drills, tools, and—the climax of any salt mine tour—the slippery wooden slide. It feels like a real mine.

Give your trip a special splash by spending a sunny afternoon at Hall's magnificent Freischwimmbad. This huge outdoor swimming pool has four diving boards, a giant lap pool, and a kiddies pool bigger than anything in my hometown, all surrounded by a lush garden, a sauna, minigolf, and lounging locals.

The same mountains that put Innsbruck on the vacation map surround Hall. For a lazy man's look at life in the high Alps, drive up to 5,000-foot-high Hinterhornalm and walk from there to a remote working farm.

The village of Hall near Innsbruck

In Gnadenwald, sandwiched between Hall and its Alps, pay $3 and pick up a brochure at the toll hut. Then wind your way upward, marveling at the crazy amount of energy put into such a remote road project, to a parking lot at the rustic Hinterhornalm Berg restaurant. The hardworking, blond-braided, and English-speaking Mayr family runs this place very traditionally, serving hearty food and offering three simple double rooms ($12 per person) and a precarious dorm hut or "lager" with $8 beds and a cliff-hanger of a view (tel. 05223/2170, crowded on summer weekends, closed by avalanches from November to April).

It's a level 20-minute walk from the restaurant to the Walderalm farm, where you can wander around a working dairy farm that shares its meadow with the clouds. Its cows ramble along ridge-top lanes surrounded by cut-glass peaks. The lady of the farm serves snacks and drinks (very fresh milk in the afternoon) on rough plank tables. Below you spreads the Inn River Valley and, in the distance, Innsbruck.

7. The Cotswold Villages: Inventors of Quaint

Travel writers try not to overuse the word "quaint." I save my use of that word for England's Cotswold villages. These sleepy towns are the epitome of quaint. They're almost edible!

Cuddled by woodlands, pastures, and grazing sheep ("Cotswold" is Saxon for "the hills of the sheep's coats") and cradled by the rolling Cotswold Hills, these villages are just two hours by train west of London. The 50-by-25 mile region is officially called an "area of outstanding natural beauty." An understatement. This is an area of outstanding natural beauty, historic importance, touristic interest, and people whose warm smiles will take the bite out of the Gloucestershire wind.

Stow-on-the-Wold is my favorite home base town. Located in the heart of the region, any Cotswold site is within easy striking distance of Stow. Eight roads converge on Stow, but none interrupts the peacefulness of its main square. The town has no real sights other than itself. There are several good pubs, plenty of B&Bs (see Appendix), some pleasant shops, and a handy little walking tour brochure called "Town Trail."

To the south, just 20 miles along what the Romans called "Foss Way" (and we call A-429), is Cirencester. Two thousand years ago, five Roman roads met here, and the town, then called Corinium, was the second biggest city in Roman Britain (after Londinium). As you wander through the town's Roman museum and perhaps explore the nearby Chadworth Roman Villa with its impressive ancient mosaics, you'll know why they say, "If you scratch Gloucestershire, you'll find Rome."

Meanwhile, in the crafts center just down the street, traditional craftspeople are weaving, baking, and potting creative odds and old-fashioned ends. If possible, be in Cirencester on Friday for its bustling market.

While Cirencester may be old, it's just a baby compared with the over 70 ancient sites from the Stonehenge era—4,000 years old—which litter the surrounding hills. I guess they could say, "If you scratch a

Roman, you'll find a Druid." *Mysterious Britain* by Janet and Colin Bord explains these fascinating glimpses of England's distant past.

To the north of Stow is Broadway, a pleasant but overcrowded town. Climb its hill for a great Cotswold panorama. Just a bit farther down the road is Chipping Campden, a rich, old town that refuses to forget that, once upon a time, it was the center of this region's wool trade. In late May and early June, Chipping Campden hosts the rowdy Dover Games, which include fun—if painful—events like "shin-kicking."

Bourton-on-the-Water is very popular. I can't figure out if they call this the "Venice of the Cotswolds" because of its quaint canals, its miserable crowds, or just to make more money. It's too cute—worth a drive through but no more.

Like many fairy-tale regions of Europe, the present-day beauty of the Cotswolds is explained by economic ups and downs. The area grew rich on the wool trade and built lovely towns and houses. Then foreign markets stole their trade and they slumped—too poor even to be knocked down. The forgotten, time-passed villages have now been discovered by us twentieth-century romantics, and the Cotswold villages are enjoying a new prosperity.

The charm of the Cotswolds is best savored in the tiniest towns, like Stanton, Snowshill, Upper Slaughter, and its cuddly sister, Lower Slaughter near Stow. Winson, Coln St. Dennis, and Coln Rogers, near the entertaining but money-grubbing town of Bibury, are my finalists for the most thatch-happy and cobble-cute towns in England.

A typical Cotswold village

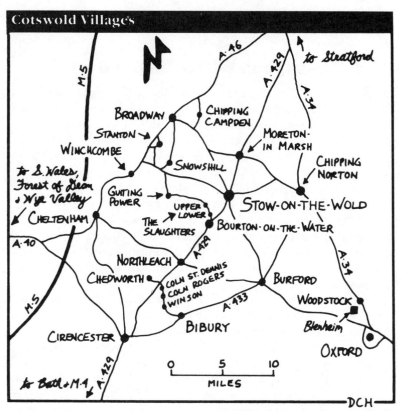

Cotswold Villages

For an English dreamscape in real life, be sure to leave London for a few days in this region. There are no trains but plenty of intervillage buses. Driving is as easy as tea and crumpets, and cars rent for $140 a week with unlimited mileage. Pick up and drop off your car at London's Heathrow Airport in the countryside, an easy Airbus or subway ride from downtown. If you can rub your stomach and pat your head, you can drive British.

Biking is a fun way to tour the villages, and the British love to walk the peaceful footpaths that shepherds walked long before polyester sheep. Hikers know that in England, just when your weary body needs it most, a village complete with a thirst-quenching and spirit-lifting pub seems to appear.

The Cotswolds have plenty of inns, guest houses, youth hostels, and bed and breakfasts. You can drop into any town before dinner and make yourself at home in a B&B for $18 a night (including a hearty breakfast). Local tourist information offices and gift shops have plenty of helpful booklets, maps, and tips on enjoying this most English of English regions.

8. Blackpool, Where England Parties

England's tacky glittering fun city, complete with bells and blinkers, is Blackpool. This mid-sized city with a six-mile beach promenade is ignored by guidebooks (*Let's Go: Britain* in 570 pages of small print never even mentions Blackpool). Even the most thorough bus tour shows you castles until your brain blisters but never takes an American visitor to Blackpool. Blackpool, located on the coast north of Liverpool, is the private playground of North England's working class. When I told Brits I was Blackpool-bound, their expression soured and they asked, "Oh God, why?" Because it's the place local widows and workers go year after year to escape. Tacky, yes. Lowbrow, OK. But it's as English as can be, and that's what I'm after. Give yourself a vacation from your sightseeing vacation. Spend a day just "muckin' about" in Blackpool. If you're bored here, you're tired of life.

Upon arrival, plan your stay with a visit to Blackpool's helpful tourist information office. Get the city map, pick up brochures from all the amusement centers, and go over your plans. Ask for advice on rooms and about special shows and evening events. Remember, Blackpool is second only to London as a center for live theater.

Blackpool is dominated by the Blackpool Tower—much more than a tower, it's a giant fun center. Entry is $5. After that, the fun is free. Working your way up from the bottom, check out the fascinating aquarium, the bad house of silly horrors, the very elegant ballroom with live music and dancing all day, and the dance of discovery (funny mirrors and lots of hands-on curiosities—don't miss the "Meet Your Friends" chamber and the robot that will actually verbalize whatever you type). The finale is the tower. This symbol of Blackpool is a stubby version of its more famous Parisian cousin. Still, the view from the top is smashing. Consider a coffee break before leaving to watch the golden oldies dance to the grand pipe organ in the ballroom.

Survey Blackpool's six-mile beach promenade from a vintage trolley car. They go constantly up and down the waterfront and make much more sense than driving. The gypsy-type spiritualists are another fixture at Blackpool. I was told I mustn't leave without having my fortune told, but at $4 per palm, I'll read them myself.

Don't miss an evening at an old-time music hall show. There are many shows at Blackpool, but its specialty is the old-fashioned variety that went out with vaudeville. These are a great hit with "Twirlies" (the senior citizens who are infamous for using their senior bus passes, good only outside of rush hour, "too early"). It's definitely a corny show—neither hip nor polished—but it's fascinating to be surrounded by hundreds of partying British seniors, swooning again, waving their hankies to the predictable beat, and giggling at jokes I'd never tell my grandma. Busloads of merry widows come from all corners of England to enjoy an old-time music hall show. Buy your ticket in the afternoon (around $5). Ask a local for the best show, probably on a pier.

Blackpool's "Illuminations" are the talk of England every late September and October. Blackpool stretches its season by illuminating its six-mile waterfront with countless lights, all blinking and twinkling to the delight of those who visit this electronic festival. The American inside me kept saying, "I've seen bigger and I've seen better," but I stuffed him with cotton candy and just had some simple fun like everyone on my specially decorated tram.

For a fun forest of amusements, Pleasure Beach is tops. These 42 acres of rides (over 80, including "the best selection of big thrill rides in Europe"), ice-skating shows, cabarets, and amusements attract 6 million people a year, making it England's most popular single attraction.

For me, Blackpool's top sight is its people. You'll see England here like nowhere else. Grab someone's hand, a big stick of "candy floss" (cotton candy), and stroll.

Blackpool needs no reservations. It's in the business of accommodating people who can't afford to holiday in Spain. Simple B&Bs and hotels abound. The classy expensive hotels are, predictably, along the waterfront. Countless lackluster budget alternatives cluster, very handy and central, around Albert Road, near the Central Pier and the tower. These B&Bs almost all have the same design—minimal character and

British trying to have fun in the sun at the beach, Blackpool

maximum number of beds. Double rooms (in the six or seven places I visited) are all the same small size with a small double bed, your basic English breakfast and a decent shower down the hall. Prices range from $14 (dingy) to $25 (cheery) per person.

Arriving at midday, you should have no trouble finding a place. July 15 to August 15 and summer weekends are most crowded. I stayed at the Belmont Private Hotel (299 Promenade, Blackpool South, FY1 6AL, tel. 0253/45815, $16 per person, clean, friendly, and cheery enough and right on the waterfront).

Visit Blackpool, Britain's fun puddle where every Englishman goes. But none will admit it.

9. Europe's Best-Preserved Little Towns

Every once in a while as you travel, you stumble onto a town that somehow missed the twentieth-century bus. Ironically, many of these "wonderfully" preserved towns are so full of Old World charm because, for various reasons, their economies failed. They became so poor that no one even bothered to tear them down to build more modern towns. Trade patterns changed (Cotswolds), their ports silted up (Brugge), the sea around them was reclaimed, leaving the former fishing port high and dry (several Dutch towns), or the capital was moved to keep up with the modern world (Toledo).

Today, many of these towns enjoy a renewed prosperity as quaint "tourist dreams come true." Others slumber on, quietly keeping their own secrets. When the Old World is not performing on big-city stages, it huddles in the pubs and chats in the markets of Europe's villages. Here are a few of my favorites. (Hotels are listed in the Appendix.)

Obidos, Portugal's medieval walled gem, is just a short drive north of Lisbon. Its perfectly preserved city wall circles a clutter of cobbled paths, alleys, flower-decked homes, and a castle, now one of Portugal's popular *pousadas* (historic government-run hotels). While several queens used the town as a dowry, today's Obidos is a tourist's prize.

Toledo, so historic and so well preserved that Spain declared the entire city a national monument, is Spain's historic, artistic, and spiritual capital. Toledo is filled with tourists day-tripping down from Madrid, 90 minutes to the north. By all means, miss the bus and spend the night! After dark, Toledo is much more medieval—almost haunted in some corners. Explore its back streets, see the art and "home" of El Greco, and marvel at the great cathedral with its sacristy full of El Greco masterpieces. End your day with a roast-suckling pig feast somewhere in the dark tangle of nighttime Toledo.

Brugge (pronounced BROOZH) is Belgium's medieval wonderland. Along with Colmar and Toledo, Brugge has more art than any other small town. Let a local guide show you Brugge's treasures. Brugge has some fun modern art, an impressive collection of Flemish paintings, a leaning tower of its own, and the only finished Michelangelo statue in Northern Europe. Like many of these small-town wonders, Brugge is so well pickled because its economy went sour. Formerly a rich textiles trading center riding high on the prosperity of the Northern Renaissance, its harbor silted up, the shipping was lost, and Brugge was forgotten—until the tourists of our day rediscovered it. Once again, Brugge thrives. Just 15 minutes from Oostende, where boats from Dover dock, Brugges makes a fine first night on the Continent for those coming over from England.

The Netherlands will tempt you with splashy tourist towns where the woman with the ruddiest cheeks is paid to stand on her doorstep wearing wooden shoes, a lace apron, and a smile. A local boy peels eels, and there's enough cheese to make another moon. These towns (such as Volendam, Monnickendam, and Marken) are designed to be fun, and they are. But make an effort to find a purely Dutch town that is true to itself, not to tourism. Rent a bike and enjoy exploring this tiny and flat country with your own wheels. In Holland, you can rent a bike at one train station and leave it at nearly any other one. My favorite Dutch village is little Hindeloopen. Silent behind its dike, it's right out of a Vermeer painting—hardcore Holland. The towns of Haarlem, Delft, and Edam are pleasant small-town bases for side-tripping into often sleazy Amsterdam, just a few minutes away by train or bus.

England loves quaintness. Every year she holds most-beautiful-town contests, and from Land's End to John O'Groats cobbles are scrubbed, flowers are planted, and hedges shaved. With such spirit, it's not surprising that England is freckled with more small-town cuteness than any country in Europe. The cobbles, flowers, pubs, and markets, combined with the townspeople, make the perfect Old English setting to enjoy tea and scones or a pint of beer.

While you're likely to find a small prize-winning town just about anywhere, the Cotswold Hills and the southeast coast are where some of the best are tucked away. Both regions were once rich, but shifting seas and industrial low tides left them high and dry. Today, their chief export is cozy cuteness with a British accent. The southeast coast has five former ports, the "Cinqueports," that now moor tourists for a living. One of them, Rye, is commonly overrated as England's most photogenic village. England's many moors are havens for time-passed villages that seem to have intentionally ducked out of our modern parade. Don't miss Staithes, Captain Cook's boyhood town, which is just north of Whitby near the York Moors. It's a salty tumble of ancient buildings bunny-hopping down a ravine to a cramped little harbor.

Europe has many more towns that time forgot. Passau in Germany, Hall in Tirol, Rouen in France, Chefchaouen in Morocco (among hundreds of others), Sighisoara in Romania, and Erice in Sicily are just a few. Remember, Europe is becoming a scavenger hunt for tourists, and most of the prizes have been found. Even with tourist crowds, which are now a standard feature in the summer months, the smaller towns of Europe give the traveler the best look at Europe's old culture.

10. Bad Towns and Tourist Traps

It's generally not considered "in good style" to write negatively about tourist destinations. But since I'm the kind of guy who burps at the dinner table anyway, I'd like to give you one man's opinion on Europe's dullest places. These are the places that may be nice to live in, but I wouldn't want to visit.

Zurich and Geneva are two of Switzerland's largest and most sterile cities. Both are pleasantly situated on a lake—like Buffalo and Duluth. And both are famous, but name familiarity is a rotten reason to go somewhere. If you want a Swiss city, see Bern, but it's almost criminal to spend a sunny Swiss day anywhere but high in the Alps.

Bordeaux must mean boredom in some ancient language. If I were offered a free trip tomorrow to that town, I'd stay home and clean the fridge. People go there for the wine, but Bordeaux wine country and Bordeaux city are as different as night and night soil. There's a wine tourist information bureau in Bordeaux which, for a price, will bus you out of town and into the more interesting wine country nearby.

Andorra, a small country in the Pyrenees between France and Spain, is as scenic as any other chunk of those mountains. People from all over Europe flock to Andorra to take advantage of its famous duty-free shopping. As far as Americans are concerned, Andorra is just a big Spanish-speaking Radio Shack. There are no great bargains here that you can't get at home.

Germany's famous Black Forest disappoints more people than it excites. If that's all Germany offered, it would be worth seeing. For Europeans, any large forest in a country the size of Oregon with 65 million people is a popular attraction. But I'd say the average American visitor who's seen more than three trees in one place would prefer Germany's Romantic Road and Bavaria to the east, the Rhine and Mosel country to the north, the Swiss Alps to the south, and France's Alsace region to the west—all high points that cut the Black Forest down to stumps.

Stavanger, famous for nearby fjords and its new status as oil boom town, is a large Norwegian port that's about as exciting as, well, put it this way—emigrants left there in droves to move to the wilds of Minnesota. Extra time in western Norway is much better spent in and around Bergen.

Bucharest, the capital of Romania, has very little to offer. Its top-selling postcard is of the Intercontinental Hotel. Belgrade, Yugoslavia's capital, is another stop that is best not started. It's one of the few things I can think of that is more boring than the long train ride through the center of Yugoslavia. Stay on board until you're in Greece or else meander down Yugoslavia's Dalmatian Coast. If you're heading from Yugoslavia to Greece, skip Thessaloníki, which deserves its chapter in the Bible but doesn't belong in travel guidebooks.

Athens, while well worth visiting, is probably the most overrated city in Europe. A hundred years ago, Athens was a sleepy town of 8,000 people with a pile of ruins in its backyard. Today it's a giant mix of concrete, smog, noise, tourists, and four million Greeks. See the four major attractions (the Acropolis, the Agora, the Plaka, and the great National Archaeological Museum), spend an evening at the delightful Dafni wine festival on the edge of town (open nightly mid-July through the end of August), and get out to the islands or countryside.

Extra caution is merited in southwest England, a minefield of tourist traps. The British are masters at milking every conceivable tourist attraction for all it's worth. Here are some booby traps that weren't worth the time or money:

Cornwall, England's southernmost region, has more than its share of cotton-candy fluff when it comes to tourism. I'll never forget driving down the road passing signs prepping me for the "Devil's Toenail." "Only five miles—The Devil's Toenail." Then, "The Devil's Toenail— next left!" Well, I figured I'd only be here once, so I better check it out. I pulled into the parking lot—paid a dollar to park. Paid two more dollars to pass through the turnstile. Walked to the bottom of the ravine. And there it was, a rock the size of a watermelon, that looked just like. . .a toenail. Disappointed, and a bit embarrassed, I took a quick picture and hiked back to my car, promising myself never again to fall for such a sly snare.

Predictably, Land's End, the far southwest tip of England, is geared up to attract—and does attract—hordes of tourists. You pay to park, pay again to enter, walk out to the point for a photo to prove you were there, grab a postcard, and leave.

Just down the coast, Penzance is enjoying a tourist boom of its own, capitalizing on the popularity of Gilbert and Sullivan's *Pirates of Penzance*. While you won't see any salty seafarers in Penzance, you will find plenty of commercial pirates ready to pillage your pocketbook; restaurants, pubs, and ye olde shoppes just bursting with smugglers' atmosphere and pirates' decor.

On the north Cornwall coast, above Land's End, are two more tourist magnets. Tintagel is famous for its castle—the legendary birthplace of King Arthur. The castle's exciting windswept and wave-beaten ruins are well worth exploring. Meanwhile, the town does everything in its little power to exploit the profitable Arthurian legend. There's even a pub in town called the Excali Bar.

Just up the coast is Clovelly. It's one of the towns I had circled in my guidebook years before I ever got there. It sounded so cute—"daintily clinging to the rocky coast desperately trying not to plunge into the wicked seas." But when you arrive, reality rules. You'll park your car for a price 100 yards away and join the crowds funneling into the little town's one street. You can shop your way down one side to the waterfront and up the other side past cute knickknack shops, all selling just about the same goodies—like "clotted cream that you can mail home."

England has so much to offer in so many ways. Be careful not to waste your time on worthless tourist traps.

The towns and places I've mentioned here are worth skipping only because they're surrounded by so many places much more worthy of the average traveler's limited vacation time. If you have a villa in Bucharest or a cuckoo clock shop in the Black Forest, no offense is meant. Just remember to distinguish carefully between entrepreneurial ventures and legitimate sightseeing attractions.

Natural Nooks and Undeveloped Crannies

11. Cinque Terre: Italy's Traffic-free Riviera

"A sleepy, romantic, and inexpensive town on the Riviera without a tourist in sight." That's the mirage travelers chase in busy Nice and Cannes. Pssst! Paradise sleeps just across the border in Italy's Cinque Terre.

With larger and larger tourist crowds trampling Europe's towns and resorts every summer, it's more important than ever to trade those long lines and "no vacancy" signs in on a more real and relaxed alternative. The Cinque Terre, between Pisa and Genova, is too rugged to develop.

Cinque Terre, meaning "five lands," is five pastel villages clinging to the rugged coast of the Italian Riviera. The villagers go about their business as if the surrounding vineyards were the very edges of the earth. An Italian syrup soaks every corner of this world, and it's yours to sop up.

Each town is a character. Monterosso al Mare, happy to be appreciated, boasts a great beach and plenty of fine hotels and restaurants. Its four little sisters are content to be overlooked—forgotten in their Old World puddle. Little Manarola rules its ravine and drinks its wine while its sun-bleached walls slumber on. The Via dell' Amore (walkway of love) leads from Manarola to Riomaggiore. With a beauty that has seduced famed artists to move in, Riomaggiore is well worth a wander.

Corniglia sits smug on its hilltop, proudly victorious in its solitary game of king of the mountain. Most visitors are lured to Corniglia by the Cinque Terre's best swimming and never tackle the winding stairs to the actual town. Those who make the Corniglian climb are rewarded by the Cinque Terre's finest wine and most staggering view— simultaneously. Ducking into a cellar with a grape-stained local, we

Vernazza, on Italy's Riviera

dipped long straws furtively into dark kegs. Wine tasting drowns the language barrier.

Vernazza is my favorite village. Its one street connects the harbor with the train station and meanders farther inland, melting into the vineyards. Like veins on a maple leaf, paths and stairways connect this watercolor huddle of houses with Main Street. Every day is a parade. A rainbow of laundry flags fly over barrel women wheeling fresh fish past the old men who man the bench. Little varnished boats are piled everywhere, and sailors suckle salty taverns while the Old World marches on to the steady beat of the crashing waves. The sun sets unnoticed—except by tourists.

The Cinque Terre is best seen on foot. A scenic trail leads you through sunny vineyards from Riomaggiore to Monterosso. The Vernazza-Monterosso trail is as rugged as the people who've worked the terraced vineyards that blanket the region. Flowers and an ever-changing view entertain every step of your hike. As you make your sweaty way high above the glistening beaches and approach each time-steeped village, you'll be glad you brought your camera.

When you run out of time or energy, simply catch a train back to your home base. While these towns are barely accessible by car, a tunnel-train blinks open at each village and provides a quick and easy way to explore the region. Trains connect all five towns nearly hourly for less than $1.

For a great day in the Cinque Terre, start by walking the Via dell' Amore from Riomaggiore to Manarola. Buy a picnic in Manarola and walk to the Corniglia beach. Swim, enjoy the shady bar, shower, picnic, and take the train to Monterosso al Mare for a look at the local big town. Enjoy its sandy beach before hiking home to Vernazza. The best bar is the umbrella-shaded balcony halfway between the castle and the surf.

While the Cinque Terre is unknown to the international mobs that ravage the Spanish and French coasts, plenty of Italians come here, so getting a room can be tough. August and weekends are bad. Avoid weekends in August altogether. (For rooms, see the Appendix.)

Five towns and the rocky surf are all that interrupt the peaceful vineyard greens and Mediterranean blues of this Riviera. The tourists are looking for it but have yet to find Italy's Cinque Terre.

12. Salema on Portugal's Sunny South Coast

The Algarve, Portugal's south coast, has long been famous as Europe's last undiscovered tourist frontier. Any place that's famous as a "last undiscovered tourist frontier" no longer is. Portugal's south coast is a disappointment to most who come looking for fun in the sun on undeveloped beaches. Most of the Algarve is whitewashed houses, sandy beaches, vacant lots, and tourists—most sunburned—all simmered in carbon monoxide and traffic noises.

But with energy, you can find places that lack fame and crowds. There are a few towns where colorful boats share the beach with a colony of sun worshipers who relax with gusto far from the tacky souvenir racks and package-tour rat race.

The Algarve of your dreams survives—just barely. To catch it before it goes, find a fringe. It took me three tries. West of Lagos, I tried Lux and Burgano, both offering only a corpse of a fishing village, bikini-strangled and Nivea-creamed. Then, just as darkness turned couples into lonely silhouettes, I found Salema. Any Algarve town with a beach will have tourism, but few mix tourism and realism as well as little Salema—tucked away where a dirt road hits the beach between Lagos and Cape Sagres on Portugal's southwestern tip. Salema is an easy 15-mile bus ride or hitch from the closest train station in Lagos. Beware of the Lagos con-ladies who'll try to talk you into their "quartos."

Salema is a whitewashed old town of scruffy dogs, wide-eyed kids, and fishermen who've seen it all. The other half was built for tourists.

Salema, catch the Algarve before it's gone

The parking lot that separates the jogging shorts from the black shawls becomes a morning market with the arrival of the trucks: a fruit and veggies mobile, a rolling meat and cheese shop, and the clothing van. The two worlds pursue a policy of peaceful coexistence. Tractors pull in and push out the fishing boats, two-year-old sand people flop in the waves, topless women read German fashion mags, and old men really do mend the nets. Tourists laze in the sun while locals grab the shade. Dogs roam like they own the place, and a very dark granny shells almonds with a railroad spike.

Salema is my kind of beach resort—four restaurants specializing in fresh fish and vinho verde, three hotels, lots of *quartos* (Portuguese for "bed and breakfast"), the beach and sun. It's quietly discovered by British and German connoisseurs of lethargy.

So often tourism chases away quaint folksiness—while the quaint folks can only survive with the help of tourist dollars. One way a fishing family speeds up the trickle-down theory, with a direct shot in the pocketbook, is to rent out a spare bedroom to the ever-growing stream of tan fans from the drizzly north. I arrived at 7:00 p.m. with nine people and saw no "B&B" signs anywhere. I asked the gang on the street corner. "Quarto?" Eyes perked, nods OK, and nine beds in three homes at $6 per person were arranged. I didn't feel like bargaining, but I'm sure the price was flexible downward. You'll find plenty of quartos along the road running left from the village center as you face the beach. For specifics, study your Appendix, or you can ask at the bar. We got simple rooms, showers, fine beds, glorious views of pure paradise, and friendly people whose smiles assured us that this was the place to be. This was the cheapest place we stayed, and after a month on the road, each member of my group called it his favorite.

In the distance, a man catches short fish with a long pole. Behind him is Cape Sagres—the edge of the world 500 years ago; as far as the gang sipping Port and piling olive pits in the beachside bar is concerned—it still is.

13. Crete's Gorge of Samaria

Swarms of tourists flock to the Greek island of Crete. Many leave disappointed. Their problem was that they failed to leave the crowded cities behind and hike through the rugged interior and enjoy a bit of the south coast. One surefire remedy is to take the 10-mile hike through the Gorge of Samaria.

Your home base for this circular excursion is Hania (pronounced "HAWN-yah"), a city on Crete's north coast serviced frequently by the overnight boat from Athens. Catch the earliest bus (6:00 to beat the heat and crowds, clarify if your ticket includes the return Chora Sfakion-Hania segment) from Hania past Omalos to Xyloskalo. By 7:00 a.m. after a very scenic 25-mile bus ride, you'll be standing high above the wild Gorge of Samaria. Xyloskalo is a small lodge, the end of the road and the beginning of the trail. The bus will be full of hikers; no one else would come here at this hour. The air is crisp, the fresh blue sky is cool, and most of the gorge has yet to see the sun. Before you lies a downhill, 10-mile trek from 5,000 feet to sea level, through some of the most spectacular scenery anywhere in Greece. This four- to six-hour hike down Europe's longest gorge is open from May through October.

Pack light for this hike, but bring a hearty picnic lunch and a water bottle. Food can't be bought in this wonderfully wild gorge. Water is no problem, since there are several springs and you follow a pure mountain stream through much of the gorge. Wear light clothes, but bring a jacket for the cool morning at the top of the gorge. Come prepared to swim in one of the stream's many refreshing swimming holes. Photographers go through lots of film on this hike.

Descend to the floor of the gorge down steep switchbacks for about an hour until you come to the stream, a great place for your picnic brunch. A leisurely meal here will do three things: bolster your energy, lighten your load, and bring you peace, as this break will let most of the other hikers get ahead of you.

Between you and the Libyan Sea on Crete's southern shore are about eight miles of gently sloping downhill trails. You'll pass an occasional deserted farmhouse, one occupied only by two lazy goats and a small ghost town with a well. In the middle of the hike, you'll come to the narrowest (and most photographed) point in the gorge, where only three yards separate the 1,000-foot-high cliffs. Keep your eyes peeled for the nimble cliff-climbing agrimi, the wild Cretan mountain goats.

The cool creek trickles at your feet, reminding you that a little farther downstream, you can take a cool dip in one of the stream's natural swimming holes. Find one without other hikers and jump into your own private tub, complete with waterfall. It's wonderfully refreshing.

Finally, by midafternoon, signs of Greek civilization begin peeking through the bushes. An oleander chorus cheers you along the last leg of your hike to the coast. You'll find a tiny community with a small restaurant and a few cheap places to stay. The town, Agia Roumeli, is accessible only by foot or by boat. Three times a day, a small boat picks up the hikers and ferries them to Chora Sfakion (about six a day, last ride around 6:00 p.m.). Before you begin your hike, confirm when the last boat leaves so you can plan accordingly.

While you're waiting for the boat (after you buy your ticket), take a dip in the bathtub-warm, crystal-clear waters of the Libyan Sea. Africa is out there somewhere. The black sand beach is beautiful, but it absorbs the heat, so wear your shoes right to the water's edge. A free shower is available on the beach.

The hour-long boat ride to Chora Sfakion passes some of Crete's best beaches and stops at the remote, touristy, but pleasant fishing village of Loutro (with several pensions). It's a rugged but breathtaking eight-hour hike to Chora Sfakion for those who find the boat too easy. Buses meet each boat at Chora Sfakion to return you to Hania. In crossing the island of Crete, the bus goes through some lovely land and several untouched villages inhabited by high-booted, long-mustachioed, espresso-drinking Cretans, returning you to Hania by 8:30 p.m.

This day is, in every sense of the word, gorgeous.

Thrill-seeking hang-gliders are a common sight on Alpine peaks. Here, an absent-minded hang-glider prepares for his last take-off.

14. The Berner Oberland: The Alps in your Lap

In Switzerland, you'll find Europe's most spectacular mountain scenery. There was a time when the only thing higher than those Alpine peaks was the prices you had to pay to see them. Switzerland has enjoyed a very low inflation rate, and today, it is no more expensive than its neighbors. Switzerland does suffer from tourist crowds, however, and you should keep this in mind when you choose your Swiss destination. How do you see the best of the Swiss Alps without enduring traffic jams and congested trails? The answer is twofold: Kleine Scheidegg and Gimmelwald.

Kleine Scheidegg — The Mona Lisa of Mountain Views

I had always considered Interlaken overrated. Now I understand that Interlaken is only a jumping-off point — the gateway to the Alps. Stop in Interlaken for shopping, banking, post, and telephone chores and to pick up information on the area. Then head for the hills. Get an early start and catch the private train (not covered by your Eurailpass) to Grindelwald. Avoid the common mistake of making heavily touristed Grindelwald your final destination. Take advantage of its friendly and very helpful tourist information office. Browse through the expensive tourist shops, if you like. Buy a first-class mountain picnic at the Co-op grocery store. Then ascend into a wonderland of powerful white peaks by train to Kleine Scheidegg or even higher by gondola to Männlichen. It's an easy hour walk from Männlichen down to Kleine Scheidegg.

Now you have successfully run the gauntlet of tourist traps and reached the ultimate. Before you towers Switzerland's greatest mountain panorama. The Jungfrau, the Mönch, and the north face of the Eiger boldly proclaim that they are the greatest. You won't argue.

Kleine Scheidegg has a lodge (with cheap dorm bunks) and an outdoor restaurant. People gather here to marvel at tiny rock climbers dangling by ropes—many of them quite dead—halfway up the icy Eiger. If money is not something you're trying to conserve, you can take the expensive ride from here to the towering Jungfraujoch ($30 R/T from Kleine Scheidegg, early and late rides are discounted). It's impressive, but I couldn't have asked for a more spectacular view than what Kleine Scheidegg gave me.

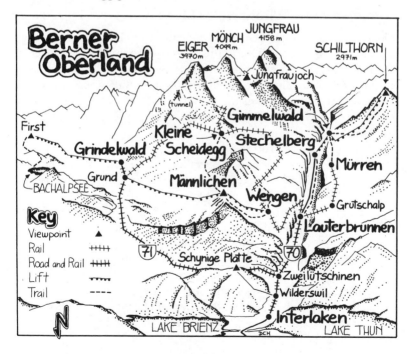

From Kleine Scheidegg, you hike into the next valley, the less-touristed Lauterbrunnen Valley. The hike is not difficult. My gear consisted only of short pants (watch the mountain sun), tennis shoes, a tourist brochure map, and a bib to catch the drools. If you have packed light and all your luggage is on your back, then you have the good feeling that it doesn't really matter where you spend the night.

It's lunchtime as you hike into your own peaceful mountain world. Find a grassy perch and your picnic will have atmosphere—the sun, flowers, and view—that no restaurant could match. Continuing downhill, you may well be all alone and singing to the rhythm of your happy footsteps. (The walk is steep in places, and some may opt to abbreviate it by catching the train early at one of two stations you'll pass along the way.) As the scenery changes, new mountains replace the ones you've already seen. After two hours, you enter the traffic-free town of Wengen. Avoid the steep and relatively dull hike from Wengen to Lauterbrunnen by taking the $3 train down to the valley floor, where you can continue by bus/gondola or funicular/train to the village of Gimmelwald. (Note: this was the scenic but very roundabout way to Gimmelwald. For a much more direct route, skip the hike and take the train direct from Interlaken-East to Lauterbrunnen.)

Gimmelwald—Where Heidi Lives

The traffic-free village of Gimmelwald hangs nonchalantly on the edge of a cliff high above the floor of the Lauterbrunnen Valley. It's a sleepy village with more cows ringing bells than people. The sounds of small avalanches on the almost touchable mountain wall across the valley, birds, waterfalls, and the crunchy march of happy hikers constantly remind you why they say, "If Heaven isn't what it's cracked up to be, send me back to Gimmelwald."

When told you're visiting Gimmelwald, Swiss people assume you mean the famous resort in the next valley, Grindelwald. When assured that Gimmelwald is your target, they lean forward, widen their eyes, and ask, "How do you know about Gimmelwald?"

This ignored station on the spectacular Schilthorn gondola (of James Bond fame) should be built up to the hilt. But it's classified "avalanche zone"—too dangerous for serious building projects. So while developers gnash their teeth, sturdy peasants continue milking cows and making hay, surviving in a modern world only by the grace of a government that subsidizes such poor traditional industries. The few travelers who figure there won't be an avalanche for a few nights enjoy the Alps in their laps in a Swiss world that looks and lives the way every traveler dreams it might.

Since it allows no cars, there are only two ways to get to Gimmelwald. Drivers park (free and safe) in Stechelberg at the far end of Lauterbrunnen Valley and catch the $3 gondola. Others can catch the bus to Stechelberg (best in the rain) or take the Lauterbrunnen-Grutschalp funicular (a small train) up the steep wall and catch the scenic train (called the "panorama fahrt" in German) to Mürren. From there, Gimmelwald is a pleasant 45-minute walk downhill.

Sleep in Gimmelwald's very rugged youth hostel ($4/bed) or at the storybook chalet called Hotel Mittaghorn ($30/double with breakfast).

Gimmelwald's shacky hostel is the loosest and friendliest hostel I've ever fallen in love with. Every day its Alps-happy family of hostelers adopts newcomers and fills them with spaghetti and mountain stories. High in the Alps, this relaxed hostel is struggling to survive. Please treat it with loving care, respect its rules (and elderly Lena, who runs the place), and leave it cleaner than when you found it (tel. 036/551704). Bring in some food since the village grocer keeps sporadic hours.

Downtown, traffic-free Gimmelwald. "If Heaven isn't what it's cracked up to be, send me back to Gimmelwald."

Up the hill is the treasure of Gimmelwald. Walter Mittler, the perfect Swiss gentleman, runs a creaky chalet called Hotel Mittaghorn. It's a classic Alpine-style place with a million-dollar view of the Jungfrau Alps. Walter is careful not to let his place get too hectic or big and enjoys sensitive Back Door travelers. He's a magnificent but occasional cook, runs his hotel alone, keeping it simple but with class. Call Walter in advance at 036/551658. (More rooms are listed in the Appendix.)

Evening fun in Gimmelwald is found in the hostel (lots of young Alpaholic hikers and a good chance to share information on the surrounding mountains) and up at Walter's. If you're staying at Walter's, don't miss his dinner or his coffee schnapps. Then sit on his porch and watch the sun lick the mountaintops to bed as the moon rises over the Jungfrau.

From Gimmelwald, you can ride the gondola up to the Schilthorn ($25 round-trip). A revolving restaurant caps this 10,000-foot peak, and I make a point to enjoy bacon, eggs, and Alps at least once a year. The early gondola is discounted and includes a great continental breakfast. (Walter has special tickets.)

Frolic on the ridge. If you want to hike down, the first 300 yards are the most difficult. The easiest descent is just to the right of the cable car as you face down. The three-hour hike drops 5,000 feet. If this is too thrilling, ride the gondola back down to Birg (the midway station), and enjoy an easier (but still steep) hike back to Gimmelwald from there. To leave this Alpine wonderland, take the lift back down to Stechelberg, and catch a bus to Interlaken.

If you're interested in the heart of Switzerland, it's best seen from Kleine Scheidegg. If you're looking for Heidi and an orchestra of cow bells in a Switzerland that most people think exists only in dreams and storybooks—spend some time in Gimmelwald.

15. From France to Italy over Mt. Blanc

Europe's ultimate mountain lift towers high above the car- and tourist-choked French resort town of Chamonix. Get as high as you can get mechanically by riding the Aiguille du Midi telepherique (gondola) to the dizzy 12,600-foot-high tip of a rock needle. Remind yourself that this thing has been going back and forth now since 1954; surely it'll make it one more time and get in. Chamonix shrinks as trees fly by, soon replaced by whizzing rocks, ice, and snow until you reach the top. Up there, even sunshine is cold. The air is thin. People are giddy. Fun things can happen if you're not too winded to join locals in the Halfway-to-Heaven tango.

Before you spread the Alps. In the distance is the bent little Matterhorn, and looming just over there is Mont Blanc, at 15,781 feet, Europe's highest point. Next, for your own private glacial dreamworld, and Europe's most exciting border crossing, get into the tiny red gondola and head south. Dangle silently for 40 minutes as you glide over the glacier to Italy. Squeeze out your porthole, exploring every corner of your view. You're sailing a new sea.

Just keep telling yourself, "It'll make it one more time."

Show your passport at Helbronner point (11,000 feet) and descend into the remote Italian Valle d'Aosta. It's a whole different world.

Your starting point for this adventure is Chamonix, a convenient overnight train ride from Paris. Chamonix is a resort town—packed and pricey. Like Interlaken, it's a springboard for mountain-worshipers. The town has an efficient and energetic tourist information center and plenty of reasonable beds, including four chalets offering $10-a-night dorm beds. The newly renovated youth hostel, the former barracks of the diggers of the six-mile long Mont Blanc Tunnel, is a good place to stay for even less.

From Chamonix, there are enough hikes and cable car rides to keep you busy for days. If you came only to take the ultimate ride, get on that telepherique to the Aiguille du Midi. This lift (about $20 round-trip, running daily from 6:00 to 5:00 in the summer, shorter hours off-season) is Europe's highest and most spectacular. If the weather is good, forget your budget. (The youth hostel gives 25% discount coupons.) Afternoons are most likely clouded and crowded. In August, the busiest time, ride by 7:00 to avoid miserable delays. If you plan to dilly-dally, go directly to your farthest point and do so on your return.

A good plan to save a little money and enjoy a hike at the same time is to buy a ticket all the way up, but only halfway back down. This gives you a chance to look down at the Alps and over at the summit of Mont Blanc from your lofty 12,600-foot lookout. Then you descend to the halfway point, where you're free to frolic in the glaciers and hike back to Chamonix at your leisure. (But there are much better hikes on the valley's other side, where lifts zip you high to what's called the Gran Balcon Sud, a world of hikes, pristine lakes, and great Mont Blanc range views. From the midway station on the Brevant, lift para-sailors lunge off the cliff every few sunny minutes. A thrilling spectator sport. Probably the best easy hike—two hours each way—is from the top of the la Flegere lift to Lac Blanc.)

France to Italy—At 11,000 Feet

From the top of Aiguille du Midi, you can continue over the mountain to Italy. It's a long trip; the last departure is at 4:00 p.m. The descent from Helbronner Point (about $14) takes you into the remote Italian Valle d'Aosta, where a dash of France and a splash of Switzerland blend with the already rich Italian flavor and countless impressive castles to create an easy-to-like first taste of Italy.

The town of Aosta, your best valley home base, is a two-hour bus ride (hourly departures, change in Courmeyeur) from the base of the lift (La Pallud). To save time and money and to give your experience an extra dimension, try catching a ride straight to Aosta with a fellow cable

Alps from atop the Aiguille du Midi, 12,600 feet up

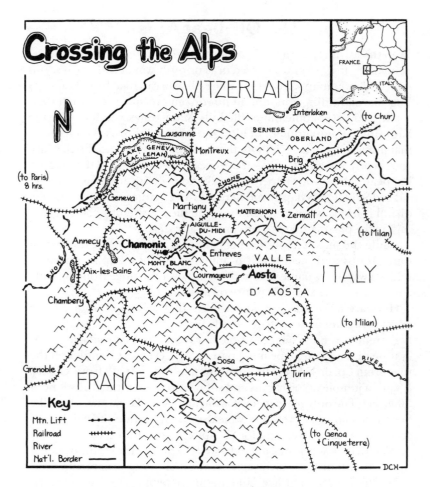

Crossing the Alps

SWITZERLAND

FRANCE

ITALY

Interlaken   (to Chur)

BERNESE
OBERLAND

Lausanne

LAKE GENEVA
(LAC LEMAN)   Montreux

Brig

RHONE

(to Paris)
8 hrs.

Geneva

Martigny

MATTERHORN   Zermatt

AIGUILLE-
DU-MIDI

(to Milan)

Annecy   **Chamonix**

Entreves   VALLE

MONT BLANC   road

Courmayeur   **Aosta**   ITALY

Aix-les-Bains

D' AOSTA

RHONE

Chambery

(to Milan)

PO RIVER

Grenoble   FRANCE   Sosa   Turin

Key

Mtn. Lift   ·—·—·

Railroad   ┼┼┼┼┼

River   ∿∿∿

Nat'l. Border   ——

(to Genoa
+ Cinque terre)

DCH

car passenger who has a car parked in La Pallud.

Historic Aosta is the valley's capital and the best place to spend the night and maybe the next day. "The Rome of the Alps," as Aosta is called, has many Roman ruins and offers a great introduction to the fine points of Italian life—cappuccino, gelati, and a busy evening *passegio* (strolling time, like American cruising without cars). Sleep at Hotel Rosini (see Appendix). The popular and inexpensive Ulisse Restaurant at Via Ed. Aubert 58 has great pizza. An evening here watching Italy stroll by is a fine way to ease into la dolce vita. And their rest room provides the uninitiated with a pleasant first footprint toilet experience.

Chamonix, Aiguille du Midi, and the Valle d'Aosta—surely a high point in anyone's European vacation.

16. Off-beat Alps

Even those who know a Rocky Mountain high find something special about the Alps. They are civilized in a curiously wonderful way. It seems man and mountain shared the same crib. You can hike from France to Yugoslavia, finding a mountain hut or remote village for each over-night, and never come out of the hills. Many times, you'll walk to the haunting accompaniment of long and legato alphorns. And it seems that just when you need it most, there will be a mechanical lift to whisk you silently and effortlessly—if not cheaply—to the top of that stagger-ing peak, where your partner can take your photo, looking very, very rugged. You'll pass happy yodelers, sturdy grannies, and pony-tailed, dirndl-skirted and singing families. And the consistently cheery greet-ings make passing hikers a fun part of any trek.

While the most famous corners are now solidly in the domain of tour groups and mass tourism, much of the best Alpine charm is folded away in no-name valleys, often just over the ridge from the Holi-day Inns and the canned culture on stage.

Here are a few places and activities that will make your Alpine adventures much more than a lovely hike.

Extremely remote but accessible by car (barely) is the village of Tav-eyanne in the French-speaking part of Switzerland, two miles off the road from Col de la Croix to Villars (or take the footpath from Villars). It's just a jumble of log cabins and snoozing cows stranded all alone at 5,000 feet. The only place in town is the Refuge de Taveyanne, where the Siebenthal family serves hearty meals—great fondue and a delicious croute au fromage avec oeuf for $7—in a prize-winning, rustic setting: no electricity, low ceilings, huge charred fireplace with a cannibal-sized cauldron, prehistoric cash register, and well-hung ornamental cow-bells. This is French Switzerland, but these people speak a little Eng-lish. For a special experience, consider sleeping in their primitive loft—it's never full, six mattresses, access by a ladder outside, $5, tel. 025/681947.

In western Austria, south of Reutte, lies a special treat for those who suspect they may have been Kit Carson in a previous life. Fallerschein is a very isolated log cabin village, smothered in Alpine goodness. Drop into its flower-speckled world of serene slopes, cowbells, and musical breezes. Thunderstorms roll down this valley like it's God's bowling alley, but the blissfully simple pint-sized church on the high ground seems to promise that this huddle of houses will remain standing. The people sitting on benches are mostly Austrian vacationers who've rented cabins—or lovers who, for whatever reason, must do it secretly. Fallerschein is notorious as a hideaway for those having affairs. For a rugged chunk of local Alpine peace, spend a night in the local Matratzen lager (simple dorm loft) "Almwirtscheft Fallerschein" (open June-September, $5 per night, 27 beds and one outhouse, good meals, tel. 05678-5142). Fallerschein is 4,000 feet high at the end of a miserable one-mile fit-for-jeep-or-rental-car-only gravel road near Namlose on the Berwang road south of Reutte in Austria's Tirol.

The Sommerrodelbahn is one of the great Alpine experiences. Several Alpine ski slopes are outfitted with concrete bobsled courses.

There's more than one way to get down an Alp.

Local speed demons spend entire summer days riding chair lifts up to "luge" down on oversized skateboards you sit in with a brake stick between your legs—push for fast, pull to stop. There's a Sommerrodelbahn at Chamonix in France and two in Tirol off the Fernpass road— one halfway between Reutte and Lermoos, the other just past Biberwier near the Shell station in the shadow of the gray and powerful Zugspitze. They are normally open daily in the summer from 8:30 a.m. to 5:00 p.m. unless it's wet. The Biberwier luge is the longest in Austria—4,000 feet. The concrete course banks on the corners and even a first-timer can go very, very fast. Most are careful their first run and really rip on their second. To avoid a slow-healing souvenir, keep both hands on your stick. You'll rumble, windblown and smile-creased, into the finish line with one thought on your mind—"Let's do it again!"

For a slower but just as invigorating activity, join the people of Bern for a midday float through their city on the Aare River. The lunchtime float is a popular tradition in the Swiss capital. Local merchants, legislators, publishers, and students, proud of their clean river and their basic ruddiness, grab every hot summer opportunity to enjoy this wet and refreshing paseo. Visitors feel very welcome joining the locals in the ritual 20-minute hike upstream from the Swiss National Parliament building, then floating playfully or sleepily back down to the excellent and free riverside baths and pool (Aarebad). If the river is a bit much, spectating is fun, and you're welcome to enjoy just the pool.

Along with staggering mountains, Switzerland is loved for its delicious chocolates. No tour of this country is complete without watching a river of molten chocolate work its way into small foil packages at a Swiss chocolate factory. The Caillers Chocolate factory in Broc, just north of Lausanne in French Switzerland, gives tours from March to October (except July) from Monday afternoon to Friday morning with departures from 9:00 to 10:00 and 1:30 to 3:00 (tel. 029/61212). Chocotours are free and finish with an all-you-can-savor sample time. Call to confirm tour schedules.

How does a fine baroque church in a Bavarian setting at a monastery that serves hearty food and the best beer in Germany in a carnival setting full of partying locals sound? That's the soon-to-be-discovered Andechs monastery, hiding happily between two lakes at the foot of the Alps, just south of Munich. Come with an appetite, because the food is great: chunks of tender pork chain-sawed especially for you, huge and soft pretzels (best I've had), spiraled white radishes, savory sauerkraut, and Andechser beer that lives up to its reputation. Everything is served in medieval proportions.

17. England's Mysterious Moors

You can get lost in England's moors. Directions are difficult to keep. It's cold. Long-haired goats and sheep seem to gnaw on grass in their sleep. The moor resists change. A castle loses itself in lush overgrowth. A church grows shorter as tall weeds eat at the stone crosses and bent tablets that mark graves.

When you tire of those disillusioning British tourist traps like Land's End and the Devil's Toenail which charge you to park after psyching you up with many roadside announcements, unclot your cream with a dip into the stark and turnstile-free world of England's moors.

There are many. Dartmoor is the wildest—a wonderland of green and powerfully quiet rolling hills just north of Plymouth. Crossed by only two or three main roads, most of the land is either unused or shared for grazing as a "common land" by its 30,000 villagers—a tradition since feudal days. Dartmoor is best toured by car, but it can be explored by bike, thumb, or on foot. Bus service is meager. Several places rent horses ($20/day). Several National Park centers provide maps and information. The key here is to make a bed and breakfast headquarters in one of the many small towns or check into a youth hostel at Steps Bridge or Bellever. This is one of England's most remote corners—and it feels that way. It is hard to believe that so many tourists so near are unaware of this inland treat.

Dartmoor, with more Bronze Age stone circles and huts than any other chunk of England, is perfect for those who dream of enjoying their own private Stonehenge sans barbed wire, policemen, parking lots, and hordes of tourists. The local Ordnance Survey maps show the moor peppered with these bits of England's mysterious past. Hator Down and Gidleigh are especially interesting.

Word of the wonders lurking just a bit deeper into the moors tempted me away from my Gidleigh B&B. Venturing in, I sank into the powerful mystical moorland. Climbing over a hill, surrounded by hateful but sleeping towers of ragged granite, I was swallowed up. Hills followed hills followed hills—green, growing gray in the murk. Where was that 4,000-year-old circle of stone?

Searching for the stones, I wandered in a world of greenery, eerie wind, white rocks, and birds singing but unseen. Then the stones appeared frozen in a forever game of statue maker. For endless centuries, they had waited, patiently, for me to come. Still and silent, they entertained. This is the way to see the puzzles left by civilizations past. You can see Stonehenge in a picture book.

Out on the moor, I sit on a fallen stone, holding the leash as my imagination runs wild, pondering the people who roamed England so long before written history was around to tell their story. Grabbing the moment to write, I take out my journal. The moor, the distant town, the chill, this circle of stones. I dip my pen into the cry of the birds and write.

18. Dingle Peninsula: A Gaelic Bike Ride

Be careful, Ireland is seductive. In many areas, the old culture seems to be winning its battle with the twentieth century. Stress is a foreign word. I fell in love with the friendliest land this side of Sicily. It all happened in a "Gaeltacht."

A Gaeltacht is a national cultural preserve, where the government is actively fostering the continued survival of the old Irish culture. Shaded green on many maps, these regions pepper the west coast of the Emerald Isle. "Gaeltacht" means Gaelic-speaking. You'll find the Gaelic culture alive, not only in the language but working the fields, singing in the pubs, and in the weathered faces of the traditionally dark-clad Irish who live there. A Gaeltacht is Ireland in the extreme.

Dingle—green, rugged, and untouched—is my favorite Gaeltacht. It's Ireland's westernmost point, quietly living the way it wants to. While nearby Killarney and the famous "Ring of Kerry" bustle with noisy tourists, Dingle Peninsula ages peacefully, offering an escape into pure Ireland.

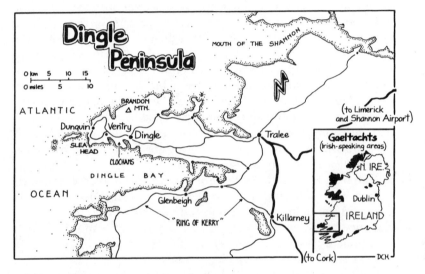

Drive, take the bus, or hitchhike to Dingle town. It's a good place to spend your first Irish night if you land at nearby Shannon airport. From the town of Tralee, you'll pass over a ruggedly scenic mountain pass. Depending on the weather, you'll be dazzled by the lush views, or you'll creep slowly through milky fog, seeing nothing past the road's dark edge.

Dingle town is quiet, salty, easygoing, and very Gaelic. A weather-beaten Dingle friendliness will warm you, even on the coldest of wet mornings.

Move in to a good bed and breakfast. I enjoy the peat-fire hospitality of Mrs. Kathleen Farrell's Corner House at Dykegate St., Dingle, County Kerry, tel. 066/51516. Any resident of Dingle should be happy and able to direct you to a good B&B, like Mrs. Farrell's. A cozy bed, a huge breakfast, and lots of tea shouldn't cost you more than $15. The cheapest beds in town ($7) are found at the Westgate/Westlodge Hostel, Dingle's friendly, private hostel (tel. 51476). The town's tourist office (tel. 51188) is helpful.

After breakfast, find a bike to rent. Your landlady knows a bike rental place. For $2 a wheel, you're mobile for the day. Pack a picnic, your camera, and a raincoat. The weather on this distant tip of Ireland is often misty, foggy, and rainy. It's as wet as it is green.

Bike around the peninsula. Follow the coastal road to the little town of Ventry. Chat with the "chatty" Irish you'll meet along the roadside. Those accents are music.

Continue along to Slea Head, the closest point in Europe to America. The rugged coastline stretches in both directions, offering smashing views of the treacherous black-rock cliffs. Crashing surf, distant boats, and the countryside (lush and barren all at once) complete this memorable picture. Sheep graze, bored, as clouds quietly cover and uncover the hills. An elfish, black-clad Gaelic man might brogue about his arthritis, point out a landmark, or sing you a song.

Be sure to explore some of the many clochans, or beehive huts. These mysterious stone huts were built without mortar by seventh-century monks in search of solitude. The huts are especially exciting when it's just you and a hut in a desolate world of dark, dank mist.

Pedal on to Dunquin. Stop by Kruger Kavanaugh's Gaelic Pub and order a pint of something very Irish. If the weather's nice, find a quiet

Ireland's top tourist attraction—the friendliest people in Europe

stream off the road a wee bit and picnic on the rocks. To complete the circle, pedal up the hill and coast back down into Dingle town.

For your evening fun, find a "singing Gaelic pub." Try O'Flaherty's, which has traditional music nearly every night, or the more ad-libbed folk music sessions at Mrs. Nelligan's Pub. (Women traveling alone need not worry—you'll become part of the pub family in no time.) Here you will enjoy traditional music that has not yet been bastardized for the tourist. A tin whistle, a fiddle, a flute, goatskin drums, and bad voices that sound better as the night goes on will awaken the leprechaun in you. Drink in the atmosphere, thick as the head on your Guinness. If an Irishman buys you a drink, you might offer him a toast in Irish. Lift your glass and say, "SLOYN-tuh!" (spelled phonetically). Before you leave, be sure to thank him by saying, "Go ra MA hagut."

Live Gaelic music, plenty to drink, and a robust crowd can be a great way to end your Dingle day. If Ireland tries to seduce you, let it.

19. Aero, Denmark's Ship-in-a-Bottle Island

Few visitors to Scandinavia even notice Aero, a sleepy, 22-by-6-mile island on the south edge of Denmark. Aero has a salty charm. Its tombstones say things like, "Here lies Christian Hansen at anchor with his wife. He'll not weigh until he stands before God." It's a peaceful and homey island, where baskets of new potatoes sit in front of houses— for sale on the honor system.

Aero's capital, Aeroskobing, Denmark's only entirely protected town, makes a fine home base. Temple Fielding said it's "one of five places in the world that you must see." The many Danes, who wash up the cobbled main drag in waves with the landing of each ferry, agree.

Aeroskobing is a town-in-a-bottle kind of place. Wander down lanes right out of the 1680s, when it was the wealthy home port of over 100 windjammers. The post office dates to 1749, and cast-iron gas lights still shine each evening. Windjammers gone, the harbor now caters to German and Danish holiday yachts. On midnight low tides, you can almost hear the crabs playing cards.

The Hammerich House is full of old junk, a turn-of-the-century garage sale open daily in the summer. The "Bottle Peter" museum on Smedegade is a fascinating house with a fleet of 750 different bottled ships. Old Peter Jacobsen died in 1960 (probably buried in a glass coffin) leaving a lifetime of his tedious little creations for us visitors to marvel at.

Touring Aero by car is like sampling chocolates with a snow shovel. Enjoy a breezy 18-mile tour of Aero's subtle charms by bike. Your hotel may loan you one, or you can rent one from the Esso station on the road behind the tourist office. On Aero, there are no deposits and no locks. If you leave in the morning, you'll hit the Kro Inn in time for a hearty lunch. Ready? As I think the old biker's blessing goes, "May the wind always be at your back, and if it's not, make some."

Leave Aeroskobing west on the road to Vra past many U-shaped farms, typical of this island. The three sides block the wind and are used for storing cows, hay, and people. *Gaard* (meaning "farm") shows up on many local names. Bike along the coast in the protection of the dike, which made the once-salty swampland to your left farmable. Pedal past a sleek modern windmill and Borgnaes, a pleasant cluster of mostly modern summer cottages. (At this point, wimps on one-speeds can short-cut directly to Vindeballe.)

After passing a secluded beach, the best you'll see on Aero, climb uphill over the island's summit to Bregninge. Unless you're tired of thatched and half-timbered cottages, turn right and roll through Denmark's "second longest village" to the church. Peek inside. Then roll back through Bregninge past many more U-shaped gaards, heading a mile down the main road to Vindeballe, taking the Voderup exit.

A straight road leads you to a rugged bluff called Voderup Klint. If I were a pagan, I'd worship here—the sea, the wind, the chilling view. Then roll on to Tanderup, past the old farm with the cows with the green hearing aids, a lovely pond, and a row of wind-bent stumps. At the old town of Olde, you'll hit the main road. Turn right toward Store Rise—marked by its church spire in the distance. Just behind the church is a 5,000-year-old Neolithic burial place, the Tingstedet Long Dolmen. Hunker down. Aero had over a 100 of these. Few survive.

Inside the Store Rise church, notice the little boats hanging in the nave, the fine altarpiece, and Martin Luther in the stern making sure everything's theologically shipshape. Continue down the main road, with the hopeful forest of modern windmills whirring on your right, until you get to Dunkaer. How about the "midday plate" special for lunch at Dunkaer's atmospheric Kro Inn or a drink and a snack in its party-stained pub?

For the homestretch, take the small road past the topless windmill. Except for "Lille Rise," it's all downhill, as you coast home past great sea views to Aeroskobing.

After a power tour of big city Scandinavia, Aero offers a perfect time-passed island in which to wind down, enjoy the seagulls, and pedal a rental bike into the essence of Denmark. Take a break in a cobbled world of sailors who, after someone connected a steam engine to a propeller, decided "maybe building ships in bottles is more our style."

Aero Island Bike Route

Misunderstood Regions and Countries

20. Rothenburg and the Romantic Road: From the Rhine to Bavaria Through Germany's Medieval Heartland

Connect the castles of the Rhine and the lederhosen charm of Bavaria by traveling Germany's "Romantische Strasse." On the Romantic Road (and especially just off it, where no unfamiliar car drives through unnoticed and flower boxes decorate the unseen side of barns), visitors find the Germany most come to see. Church steeple masts sail seas of rich, rolling farmland, and fragrant villages invite you to slow down. At each village, ignore the signposts and ask an old woman for directions to the next town—just to hear her voice and enjoy the energy in her eyes. Thousands of tourists have passed through, yet so few stop to chat.

This Back Door is no secret. But, even with its crowds, this part of Germany, peppered with pretty towns today because it was such an important and prosperous trade route 600 years ago, is a must.

A car gives you complete freedom to explore Germany's medieval heartland—just follow the green "Romantische Strasse" signs. The most scenic sections are Bad Mergentheim to Rothenburg and Landsberg to Füssen. For those without wheels, the convenient Europabus tour opens this door to small-town Germany. Romantic Road buses leave daily in both directions connecting Frankfurt/Wiesbaden with Munich (late March through early November) and Würzburg with Füssen (June through September). Any Eurailpass or Frankfurt-Munich train ticket is good on this bus. Otherwise, the bus from Munich to Frankfurt costs about $60 (the same as a second-class train ticket). The trip takes 11 hours, including three hours off the bus to explore the fairy tale towns of Rothenburg and Dinkelsbühl. You can break your journey anywhere along the road and catch the same bus the next day.

Ticket reservations are necessary only for peak season weekends (tel. 069/7903240 three days in advance).

Whenever you're traveling, lay the groundwork for your smooth departure in advance. For instance, on arrival in Munich (or Füssen, near the famous Neuschwanstein Castle), ask at the train or tourist information office exactly where and when the bus leaves the next morning and if a reservation is advisable. Then, you'll wake up on departure morning and calmly step onto the bus to begin one of the best days of your trip.

The Romantic Road bus drivers are often characters. Twice I've had the eccentric Charlie Brown. Wearing a black top hat and blowing his whistle, he seems to know everyone he passes, waving and happily greeting people all day long. At one point, his faithful canine friend, Snoopy, hops on the bus for a short ride. At Donauwörth, as the bus crosses the baby Donau (Danube), he slips in his cassette of "The Blue Danube Waltz." The group on board loosens up, and you have time to talk to and enjoy the other travelers and build some friendships. This isn't just any bus ride.

Rothenburg

While the bus passes through many lovable little towns, Rothenburg is the most lovable. This is probably the most touristy town in Germany — and for good reason. I've yet to find a better-preserved medieval town. Rothenburg is a joy even on the most crowded day. In the Middle Ages, when Frankfurt and Munich were just wide spots in the road, Rothenburg was Germany's second-largest city with a whopping population of 6,000. Today, it's her best-preserved medieval walled town, enjoying tremendous tourist popularity without losing its charm.

For those on the bus tour (or for a general orientation), here's Rothenburg's best 90 minutes. From the bus stop, climb onto the medieval wall and hike clockwise to Rodertor (the second large gateway). From here, follow the cobbles into the town center and continue through the Market Square straight down Herrengasse to the end of the castle garden for a glorious view of the "Tauber Riviera."

By this time, any normal person will have decided that, when it comes to Germany's many cute small towns, monogamy is the best policy. Leave the bus, spend the night, and love only Rothenburg. (Rooms listed in the Appendix.) But if you've got more willpower than common sense, shop and eat your way back through the town center to your bus in time to carry on down the Romantic Road.

Europe's most exciting medieval town is worth two nights and a day. And those spending the night enjoy the city without its daily hordes of big city day-trippers and risk actually hearing the sounds of the Thirty Years War still echoing through the turrets and clock towers.

Too often, Rothenburg brings out the shopper in visitors before they've had a chance to appreciate the historic city. True, this is a great place to do your German shopping (visit friendly Anneliese Friese's shop, two doors left of the tourist office—discount with this book and the best money exchange rates in town), but first see the town. The tourist information office on the Market Square offers guided tours in English (daily at 11:30). A local historian, who's usually an intriguing character as well, will bring the ramparts alive. A thousand years of history are packed between the cobbles.

After your walking tour orientation, you'll have plenty of sightseeing ideas. Walk around Rothenburg's medieval wall. This mile-and-a-half walk offers great views—especially before breakfast or at sunset. For the best view of the town and surrounding countryside, make the

Rothenburg, Germany

rigorous but rewarding climb to the top of the Town Hall Tower. The friendly ticket taker on top speaks more Japanese than English, an interesting sign of the touristic times.

Don't miss Rothenburg's fascinating Medieval Crime and Punishment Museum. It's full of old legal bits and pieces, instruments of punishment and torture, and even a special cage—complete with a metal nag gag—all well explained in English.

St. Jacob's Church contains the one "must-see" art treasure in town, a glorious 500-year-old altarpiece by Riemenschneider, the Michelangelo of German woodcarvers (upstairs in the rear).

For a peaceful break from the crowds, take a countryside walk through the Tauber Valley. The trail leads from Rothenburg's pleasant castle gardens to the cute, skinny 600-year-old castle/summer home of Mayor Toppler, intimately furnished and well worth a look. Notice the photo of bombed-out 1945 Rothenburg on the top floor. Across from the castle, a radiantly happy lady will show you her 800-year-old water-powered flour mill called the Fuchsmuhle. From here, you can walk on past the covered bridge and huge trout to the peaceful village of Detwang, which is actually older than Rothenburg and has a church with another impressive Riemenschneider altarpiece.

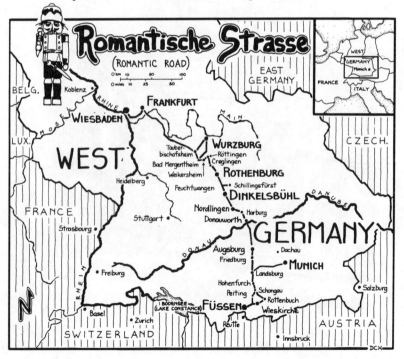

Rothenburg's little sister is Dinkelsbühl, another well-preserved medieval town an hour to the south. Old walls, towers, gateways, and the peaceful green waters of the moat protect the many medieval jewels of architecture that lie within. The bus tour stops here, giving you plenty of time for lunch at a typical restaurant (serving Franconian specialties and Dinkelsbühl beer) and for exploring, camera in hand, the old cobbled streets. Dinkelsbühl celebrates its colorfully medieval Kinderfest (Childrens' Festival) in mid-July (from the weekend before the third Monday through the weekend after).

The Romantic Road has much more. If you order now, you'll get Würzburg, with its fine baroque Prince Bishop's Residenz—the Versailles of Franconia—and its glorious chapel. You can see another lovely carved altarpiece by Riemenschneider near Creglingen. To the south is Germany's best example of baroque church architecture at the Wies Church, near Oberammergau (scaffolded through 1990), and Mad King Ludwig's Disneyesque Neuschwanstein Castle near Füssen.

The Romantic Road—a quick, comfortable, and inexpensive way to see two of Germany's most beautiful towns—is the best way to connect the Rhine and Bavaria.

21. Dungeons and Dragons: Europe's Nine Most Medieval Castle Experiences

Castles excite Americans. From Ireland to Israel and from Sweden to Spain, European castle thrills lurk in countless dark nooks and dank crannies.

In Germany, the Rhine River is lined with castle-crowned hills. There's even a castle built in the middle of the river. These can be enjoyed conveniently by train, car, or boat (the best 50-mile stretch is between Koblenz and Mainz, the best hour cruise is from St. Goar to Bacharach). To the south, Bavaria has many intriguing castles.

Castles line the Loire and seem to guard every curve of the Mediterranean. From Spain, France, Italy, and Yugoslavia to the impressive Crusader castles of Rhodes and Acre in the East, you'll find feudal fortresses in every direction.

Europe's forgotten castles, unblemished by turnstiles, postcard racks, and coffee shops, are ignored by guidebooks. The aggressive traveler will find them by tapping local information sources, like the town tourist office and the friendly guy who runs your hotel or pension.

Here are nine medieval castle experiences, where the winds of the past really howl.

Carcassonne, France

Before me lives Carcassonne, the perfect medieval city. Like a fish that everyone thought was extinct, Europe's greatest Romanesque fortress-city has somehow survived the centuries.

I was supposed to be gone yesterday, but here I sit—imprisoned by choice—curled in a cranny on top of the wall. The wind blows away the sounds of today and my imagination "medievals" me. The moat is one foot over and 100 feet down. Small plants and moss upholster my throne.

Twelve hundred years ago, Charlemagne stood below with his troops—besieging the town for several years. Just as food was running out, a cunning townsperson had a great idea. She fed the town's last bits of grain to the last pig and tossed him over the wall. Charlemagne's forces, amazed that the town still had enough food to throw fat party pigs over the wall, decided they'd never succeed in starving the people out. They ended the siege and the city was saved. Today, the walls that kept Charlemagne out open wide for visitors.

Carcassonne, a medieval fantasy of towers, turrets, and cobbled alleys, is located in southwest France near the boring little country of

Carcassonne's medieval ramparts

Andorra. It's a castle and a walled city rolled into one—and a refreshing break after the touristic merry-go-round of the French Riviera and the intensity of Paris.

Your dinner expenses are up to you. I spent $25 for a lavish feast in the Romanesque dining hall of the Hotel de la Cité one night and $3 for ravioli, melon, bread, and tea at the hostel the next. And, of course, there are the peasants who munch bread, cheese, and wine among the ramparts while tossing crumbs to moat-birds and thinking of Charlemagne.

Warwick Castle, England

From Land's End to John O'Groats, I searched for the best castle in Britain. I found it. Warwick Castle has much more than a fairy-tale exterior. It's worthwhile, even with its crowds of modern-day barbarians and its robber-baron entry fee.

Like nearby Stratford, Warwick is "upon the Avon" (which is Celtic for "river"—any river). Once you get by its moat, now a lush green park, Warwick (pronounced "war-ick") will entertain you from lookout to dungeon. There's something for every taste—a fine and educational armory, a terrible torture chamber, a knight in shining armor posing on a horse, a Madame Tussaud re-creation of a royal weekend party—an 1898 game of statue-maker, and a grand garden park patrolled by peacocks who welcome picnickers.

Eltz Castle, Germany

Germany's best medieval castle experience is the Eltz Castle, above the Mosel River between Cochem and Koblenz. One of the very few Rhine/Mosel area castles never destroyed by the French, Burg Eltz is incredibly well preserved and elegantly furnished. You'll learn here how the lives of even the Middle Age's rich and famous were "nasty, brutish, and short" (as were many of the rich themselves). The approach to Burg Eltz is part of the thrill. You'll hike from the car park through a mysterious forest long enough to really get in a medieval mood, and then all of a sudden it appears, all alone—nothing but the past engulfed in nature—Burg Eltz. (It's a steep hour's hike from the nearest train station, Moselkern.)

Rheinfels Castle, Germany

Once the mightiest of all the Rhine castles, today Rheinfels is an intriguing ruin overlooking the pleasant medieval town of St. Goar. (Rooms listed in the Appendix.) Study and follow the helpful English information sheet and map before diving in. A flashlight is handy if you want to explore some of Rheinfels' several miles of spooky tunnels. The castle museum has a reconstruction of the castle showing how it looked before the French flattened it. Louis XIV destroyed all but one of the castles that line Germany's Rhine. (That castle is Marksburg, which is great but lies on the inconvenient side of the river and allows visitors only as part of German language tours.)

Chateau Chillon, Switzerland

This wonderfully preserved thirteenth-century castle—set romantically at the edge of Lake Geneva near Montreux—is worth a side trip from anywhere in southwest Switzerland. Follow the English brochure, which takes you from tingly sit-on-the-medieval-windowsill views through fascinatingly furnished rooms. The dank dungeon, serious weapons, and 700-year-old toilets will excite even the dullest travel partner. One of Switzerland's best youth hostels is a 10-minute stroll down the lakeside promenade toward Montreux (tel. 021/9634934).

Moorish Ruins of Sintra, Portugal

Just outside Lisbon, overlooking the sea and the town of Sintra, are the ruins of an 800-year-old Moorish (Moslem) castle. Ignored by the tourists who flock to the glitzy Pena Palace, a castle capping a neighboring hilltop, the ruins of Sintra offer a unique combination of scramble-

Run with the winds of the past in Europe's countless ruined castles. Here, with a little imagination, you're under attack a thousand years ago in Portugal.

up-and-down-the-ramparts fun, atmospheric picnic perches, and desolation with a view surrounded by an enchanted forest. With a little imagination, it's 1,000 years ago, and you're under attack.

Reifenstein Castle, Italy

For an incredibly medieval kick in the pants, get off the autobahn one hour south of Innsbruck at the Italian town of Vipiteno/Sterzing. Reifenstein guards the valley with her time-pocked sister and offers castle connoisseurs the best-preserved (ugly and honest) original medieval castle interior I've ever seen. The lady who lives in Reifenstein Castle takes groups through in Italian, German, and only un poco English (tel. 0472/765879, 040/472/765879 from Austria, tours normally at 9:30, 10:30, 2:00, 3:00, and 4:00). You'll be lost in the mossy past as she explains how the cistern collected water, how drunken lords managed to get their key into the keyholes, and how prisoners were left to rot in the dungeon (you'll look down the typical only-way-out hole in the ceiling), and you'll see the only original knights' sleeping quarters (rough hewn plank boxes lined with hay) in existence. The lady of Reifenstein gave me my most intimate medieval castle experience ever.

Castle Day—Neuschwanstein (Bavaria) and the Ehrenburg Ruins (Reutte in Tirol)

Four of my favorite castles—two famous, two unknown—can be seen in one busy day. "Castle Day" takes you to Germany's "modern" Disney-like Neuschwanstein Castle and the much older Ehrenburg Ruins across the Austrian border in Reutte.

Home base is the small Tirolean town of Reutte (situated very close to the German border, three scenic hours by train west of Innsbruck). Reutte is less crowded than Füssen and has a helpful tourist information office with a room-finding service (open until 6:00 p.m., tel. 05672/2336) that can set you up in a private home "any day of the year" for $12.

From Reutte, catch the early bus across the border to Füssen, the German town nearest to Neuschwanstein. Then take a local bus to Neuschwanstein, the greatest of King Ludwig II of Bavaria's fairy-tale castles. His extravagance and romanticism earned him the title "Mad King Ludwig" (and an early death). His castle is one of Europe's most popular attractions. Get there early. The castle opens at 8:30, a good hour before the tour groups attack.

Take the fascinating (and required) English tour. This castle, only 100 years old, is a textbook example of nineteenth-century Romanticism.

"Mad" King Ludwig's Neuschwanstein Castle

To insult the Middle Ages, people who were glad they were finally out of them named that culture "Gothic" or barbarian. Then, all of a sudden, in the 1800s it was hip to be square, and neo-Gothic became the rage. Throughout Europe, old castles were restored and new ones built — wallpapered with chivalry. King Ludwig II put his medieval fantasy on the hilltop not for defensive reasons but because he liked the view.

The lavish interior, covered with damsels in distress, dragons, and knights in gleaming armor, is enchanting. (A little knowledge of Wagner's operas goes a long way in bringing these stories to life.) Ludwig had great taste — for a mad king. Read up on this political misfit — a poet, hippie king in the age of Bismarck and "realpolitik." He was found dead in a lake, never to enjoy his dream come true. After the tour, climb farther up the hill to Mary's Bridge for the best view. There is nothing quite like the crazy, yet elegant castle of Bavaria's mad king.

Ludwig's boyhood home, the Hohenschwangau Castle at the foot of the hill, offers a better look at Ludwig's life and far fewer crowds. Like its more famous neighbor, it costs about $3 and takes an hour to tour.

This is a busy day. Thinking ahead, you noted the time your bus returns to Reutte, so catching it is no problem. By lunchtime, you've crossed back into Austria and are ready for a completely different castle experience. Eurailpass users can ride the Romantic Road bus from

Füssen to the castles. It departs free at 8:15 and arrives in time to catch the first (uncrowded) castle tour.

Pack a picnic and your camera, and, with the help of some local directions, walk 30 minutes out of town to the brooding Ehrenburg Ruins. You'll see two hills: one small, crowned by its ruined castle and one larger, hiding its ruin.

The Kleine Schloss, or small castle, is on the smaller hill. It's really ruined but wonderfully free of anything from the twentieth century—except for a great view of Reutte sleeping peacefully in the valley below.

The Grosse Schloss, or large castle, is perched atop the biggest hill (you can't see it from a distance), eerily overgrown and even more ruined. This is quite a hike (possible only when the trail isn't washed out) above the small castle but worthwhile if you have time to get romantic. It's best with a cloud shroud in a spooky mist. This is especially thrilling if you've ever dreamed of medieval knights in distress and damsels in shining armor. You have your own castle—complete with sword ferns. Lower your hair; unfetter that imagination.

Back down in Reutte, you'll find your castle reconstructed on restaurant walls. Ask at your hotel where you can find a folk evening full of slap dancing and yodel foolery. A hearty dinner and an evening of local Tirolean entertainment is a fitting way to end your memorable "Castle Day."

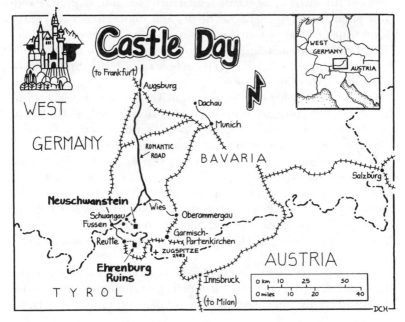

22. Alsace

The French province of Alsace stands like a flower child referee between Germany and France. Bounded by the Rhine River on the east and the softly rolling Vosges Mountains on the west, this is a lush land of villages, vineyards, ruined castles, and an almost naive cheeriness. Wine is the primary industry, topic of conversation, dominant mouthwash, perfect excuse for countless festivals, and a tradition that provides the foundation for the rest of the Alsatian folk culture.

Because of its location, natural wealth, naked vulnerability, and the fact that Germany thinks the mountains are the natural border and France thinks the Rhine River is, nearly every Alsatian generation has weathered an invasion. Centuries as a political pawn between Germany and France has given the Alsace a hybrid culture. This Gallic-Teutonic mix is evident in many things. Restaurants serve sauerkraut with fine sauces behind half-timbered Bavarian gables. If you listen carefully, you'll notice that Alsatian French is peppered with German words. On doorways of homes, you'll see mixed names like Jacques Schmidt or Dietrich Le Beau. Most locals who swear do so bilingually, and many of the towns have German names.

Alsace's wine road, the Route du Vin, is an asphalt ribbon tying 90 miles of vineyards, villages, and feudal fortresses into an understandably popular tourist package. The dry and sunny climate makes for good wine and happy tourists. It's been a wine center since Roman days. Driving through 30,000 acres of vineyards blanketing the hills from Marleheim to Thann, you'll see how vinocentric this source of some of France's finest wine is.

During the October harvest season, all Alsace erupts into a carnival of colorful folk costumes, traditional good-time music, and Dionysian smiles. I felt as welcome as a local grape picker, and my tight sightseeing plans became as hard to follow as a straight line.

Wine tasting is popular throughout the year. Roadside "degustation" signs invite you into the wine "caves," where a local producer will serve you all seven Alsatian wines from dry to sweet with educational commentary if requested. Be sure to try the Alsatian champagne, Cremant. Cave-hopping is a great way to spend an afternoon on the Route du Vin. With free tasting and fine $5 bottles, French wine tasting can be a poor man's sport.

The small caves are fun, but be sure to tour a larger wine coop. Beer-drinking Germans completely flattened many Alsatian towns in 1944. The small family-run vineyards of these villages sprang back as large,

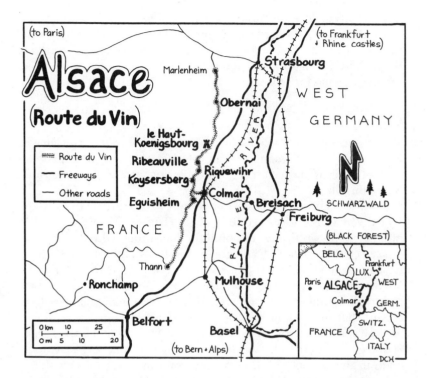

modern, and efficient cooperatives. Little Bennwihr is a coop of 211 people. They are proud to show you their facilities, which can crush 600 tons of grapes a day and turn out 14,000 bottles an hour. No tour finishes without taking full advantage of the tasting room. Bennwihr has a wine tradition going back to Roman times. Its name is from the Latin "Benonis Villare" or Beno's estate—and Beno served up a great Reisling. If you can pick grapes you can get a job in October. For a hard day in the vineyards, you'll get room and board, $30, and an intimate Alsatian social experience lubricated liberally, logically, by the leading local libation. (Sorry, I won't do that again.) There's more to Alsace than meets the palate. Those centuries of successful wine production built prosperous and colorful villages. Countless castles capped hilltops to defend the much invaded plain, and wine wasn't the only art form loved and patronized by local connoisseurs.

Alsatian towns are unique, historic mosaics of gables, fountains, medieval bell towers and gateways, cheery old inns, churches, and ancient ramparts. Geared for the tourist trade, they offer plenty of budget one- and two-star hotels (around $25 per double) and ample opportunity to savor the Alsatian cuisine. Colmar is the best home base town. Riquewihr, Kaysersberg (home of Dr. Albert Schweitzer), and Eguisheim are the best of these storybook towns. Several Alsatian castles are also worth touring. Climb the tallest tower and survey Alsace, looking as it has for centuries—the endless vineyards of the Route du Vin.

Colmar

My favorite city in Alsace, Colmar, sees very few American tourists. Popular with German and French travelers, this well-preserved old town of 70,000 is the perfect base for exploring the villages, castles, and Route du Vin.

Historic beauty was usually a poor excuse to be spared the ravages of World War II. But it worked for Colmar. The American and British military were careful not to bomb the half-timbered old burghers' houses, characteristic red- and green-tiled roofs, and cobbled lanes of Alsace's most beautiful city (and the hometown of the man who made our Statue of Liberty). Today, Colmar not only survives, it thrives—with historic buildings, impressive art treasures, and the popular Alsatian cuisine that attracts eager palates from all over Europe. And Colmar has that special French talent of being great but cozy at the same time. Schoolgirls park their rickety horse carriage in front of the city hall, ready to give visitors a $3 clip-clop tour of the old town. Antique shops welcome browsers, and hotel managers run down the sleepy streets to pick up fresh croissants in time for breakfast.

Colmar offers heavyweight sights in a warm, small-town package. By the end of the Middle Ages, the walled town was a thriving trade center filled with rich old houses. The wonderfully restored tanners' quarters is a quiver of tall, narrow, and half-timbered buildings. The confused rooftops struggle erratically to get enough sun to dry their animal skins. Nearby is "La Petite Venice," complete with canals and a pizzeria.

For maximum local fun, remember that Colmar goes crazy during its August winefest and for two weekends in September called the Sauerkraut Days. Feasting, dancing, music, and wine—Alsatian-style.

Colmar combines its abundance of art with a knack for showing it off. The artistic geniuses Grunewald, Schongauer, and Bartholdi all called Colmar home.

Before Frederic Bartholdi created our Statue of Liberty a century ago, he adorned his hometown with many fine, if smaller, statues. Don't miss the little Bartholdi museum, offering a good look at the artist's life and some fun Statue of Liberty trivia.

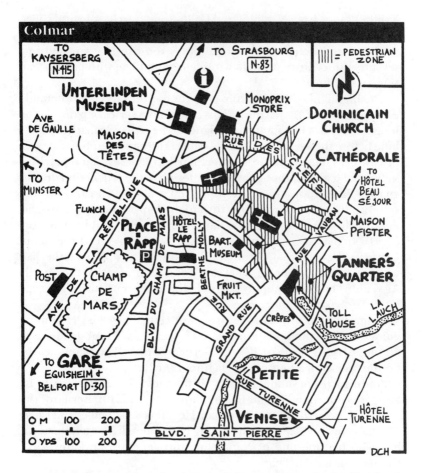

Four hundred years earlier, Martin Schongauer was the leading local artist. His _Virgin of the Rose Garden_ has given even hockey players and state troopers goose bumps. Looking fresh, crisp, and new, it's set magnificently in a Gothic Dominican church. I sat with a dozen people, silently, as if at a symphony, as Schongauer's Madonna performed solo on center stage, lit by fourteenth-century stained glass, with a richness and tenderness that could only come from another age—a late-Gothic masterpiece. Even if your sightseeing has worked you to the point where you "never want to see another Madonna and Child," give this one a chance.

The Unterlinden Museum is one of my favorite small museums in Europe. Housed in a 750-year-old convent next to the Tourist Office, it's the best collection anywhere of Alsatian art and folk treasures.

Exhibits range from Neolithic and Gallo-Roman archaeological collections to the modern art of Monet, Renoir, Braque, and Picasso. It's a medieval and Renaissance "homeshow." You can lose yourself in a seventeenth-century Alsatian wine cellar complete with presses, barrels, and tools.

The highlight of the museum (and for me, the city) is Grunewald's gripping Isenheim Altarpiece. This is actually a series of paintings on hinges that pivot like shutters. Designed to help people in a hospital—long before the age of painkillers—suffer through their horrible skin diseases, it's one of the most powerful paintings ever. Stand petrified in front of it and let the agony and suffering of the crucifixion drag its gnarled fingers down your face. Just as you're about to break down and sob with those in the painting, turn to the happy ending—a psychedelic explosion of resurrection happiness. It's like jumping from the dentist's chair directly into a Jacuzzi. We know very little about Grunewald except that, through his paintings, he's played tetherball with human emotions for 500 years. For a reminder that the Middle Ages didn't have a monopoly on grief, stop at the museum's cloth copy of Picasso's famous *Guernica.*

Colmar's helpful tourist information center provides city maps, guides, and accommodations help. They can also suggest side trips around Alsace's "wine road," into Germany's Black Forest and nearby Freiburg or even a tour of the Maginot Line.

Finding a room should be easy. My favorite is Hotel-Restaurant Le Rapp, downtown at 16 rue Berthe-Molly (tel. 416210). Bernard, the owner, is a perfect French gentleman. He offers $30 doubles and classy Alsatian cuisine in an elegant dining hall. Named after a hometown boy who became one of Napoleon's top generals, Le Rapp—like Colmar—is hard to beat.

23. French Cuisine

Cultures express themselves differently around the world. Switzerland is savored in the mountains. Music is Austria's forte, and Italy immerses you in great art. Japan tunes you in to the beauties of sensuality and simplicity. France is the world's great taste treat.

A visitor to the Alps needs a book of hikes. Those going to Italy will find an art history book handy. And, if you're going to France, you should have a list of regional culinary specialties. This section tastes better than it reads. It's basically a checklist of each region's most exciting dishes, cheese, and wines. Use it and consider each item a local art form—a Botticelli for your belly—that should be experienced next time you're eating your way through France.

Provence (the Rhone Valley) and the Côte d'Azur (the French Riviera) are famous for bouillabaisse, a fish and shellfish stew in white wine, garlic, saffron, and olive oil. Other popular dishes include the onion and anchovy tart with black olives called pissaladiere; an eggplant, tomato, pepper, onion, and garlic stew served hot or cold called ratatouille; and brandade de morue, a blend of puréed fish with olive oil and spices. Banon cheese is made locally from goat or cow milk. A popular sweet is Nougat, made from sugar and almonds. The most important regional wines to sample are Côtes de Provence (rose), Tavel (rose), Côtes du Rhone (red, rose, or white), and Chateauneuf du Pape (red or white).

The Basque country—straddling the French-Spanish border on the Atlantic Coast—eats, speaks, and lives its own way. The poulet Basquaise chicken in a hot pepper sauce and the jambon de bayonne, a

raw, slightly salty ham, are local specialties, as are duck and goose pâtés. The Basques are proud of their fromage de Pyrenees, made from cow's milk, and their popular local wine, Jurancon.

In Bordeaux, you have, of course fine local wines and truffles. Also, try entrecôte Bordelaise, a rib-eye steak in a mushroom, red wine, shallots, and local marrow sauce. North of Bordeaux is Cognac. Bet you know what to drink there.

In Bourgogne, southeast of Paris, you'll picnic in class with escargots (snails), foie gras (goose-liver pâté with truffles), Burgundy wines, and of course, spicy Dijon mustard.

After a long day of chasing chateaus on the Loire, find a cozy restaurant and treat yourself to andouilles, a spicy tripe sausage (don't look tripe up in the dictionary, just eat it), anguilles (eel), a tarte fromagere (cheese tart), and macaroons for dessert. The Loire is famous for its wines. Try Vouvray, Muscadet, and Sancerre.

In the French Alps and Savoie, fondue and raclette are two melted cheese specialties. Arbois-Jaune is the wine to try.

In Normandy, the adventurous glutton will want to try tripes à la mode de caen (tripe cooked in the oven with calf's feet, vegetables, and apple brandy)—a meal in itself. The more timid tasters are sure to enjoy crêpes (for both dinner and dessert) here. The locals wash these tasty thin pancakes down with cider (usually alcoholic). Before turning in, have a glass of Calvados, a very powerful apple brandy.

In Brittany, sample the seafood, shellfood, and far, a sweet cake made with prunes and brandy. Crêpes are also popular here. Purists go for crêpe beurre et sucre (just butter and sugar).

In the north of France, the people eat a slimy sausage called ouillette and frites/moules (French fries and mussels). Wash everything down with local beer.

Alsace, on the German border, has an exciting cuisine of its own. Many dishes have a German twist, like choucroute garnie (sauerkraut with ham, bacon, and sausage). Try the onion tart and the rhubarb tart as well as the powerful Muenster cheese. Alsatian wine is world famous. Explore the region's "Wine Road" and taste them all. I like the Gewurztraminer and the Riesling.

In nearby Lorraine, real men eat quiche. The people of Lorraine turn small yellow plums into a dandy brandy (Mirabelle) and a tart (Tarte aux Mirabelles).

To the west is Champagne (and plenty of it), and even farther west is Paris, famous for its onion soup and Brie cheese.

This "list" is far from complete, but it's a good start. Remember: the French eat lunch from 12:00 to 2:00, and so should you. In evening time, 8:00 to 9:00 is the time to dine. Tips are included in the price unless otherwise indicated (service non-compris), and you call a waiter with a polite "garcon s'il vous plaît" or "mademoiselle." To ask for the bill, just scribble on your palm with an imaginary pencil and ask, "l'addition?" (pron: lah dee zee oh). Fast service is rude. Plan to make a good meal the focus of your evening, like the French. The Michelin Red Guide is the ultimate guide to French restaurants, and the most serious Francofoodophiles don't leave home without it. Any restaurant displaying a Relais Routiers recommendation is a truck driver's choice—magnifique! Bon appétit!

24. In the Shadow of Venice: Grado, Palmanova, Chioggia

Tourists generally zip from Munich, Vienna, or Salzburg straight to Venice and then, "logically," down to Florence or Rome. On my last visit to Italy, I enjoyed the perverse thrill of bypassing Venice and focusing on a few of its neglected neighbors.

Just south of Austria near the Italian city of Udine and a stone's throw from the scenic Salzburg-Venice autobahn, you'll find some fascinating towns.

Gemona was near the epicenter of a tragic 1976 earthquake. Broken clocks around town memorialize the awesome minute that took 300 of the townspeople and most of its buildings. Today it's a sort of Steven Spielberg Italy—rebuilt, clean, new, and sleek but according to its old Renaissance designs. Scaffolding and dusty work crews give it a backstage feeling, as the town charges forward with an impressive confidence. Wind up its main street to the parking lot, just below the newly crumbled castle. Surrounded by medieval carvings and modern rubble, the church leans, but stubbornly refuses to fall. Inside is a fascinating photo essay of the earthquake and its aftermath.

A little farther south is Palmanova—1593's planned city of the future. From the sky, this Venetian Renaissance fortress city looks like a big stone snowflake. Its moated, symmetrical outer walls contain an orderly interior. Each slice of the town has its own small square and feeds into the huge hexagonal central square. The church is a textbook example of pure Renaissance planning. Apparently, our modern world can't improve on this bold product of 400 years ago—you won't find a twentieth-century building anywhere.

On the coast, very close to the Yugoslavian border, is a town that calls itself the "Mother of Venice"—Grado. Born, like Venice, on an island, but much earlier (in Roman times), Grado is now connected to the mainland by a causeway. Hordes of Europeans flock to Grado's lovely beaches each summer, but off-season its 10,000 residents relax quietly.

Five miles inland from Grado are the very quiet and underrated Roman ruins of Aquileia. In the time of Christ, Aquileia was a busy port and a Roman provincial capital. After an illustrious 600 years, Attila the Hun descended on Aquileia and raped, pillaged, and ruined it. Today it slumbers, politely entertaining its few guests with huge chunks of a former harbor, ruins of its forum, amphitheater, and baths. Its basilica is carpeted with mosaics dating from 313 (just after Emperor Constantine legalized Christianity). In this ancient church and the fascinating underground world excavated around it, you'll wander among 700 square yards of Roman mosaic symbols and Bible stories.

Finally, for a taste of Venice without its crowds, explore Chioggia. This pleasant town, an hour's drive south of Venice (or a two-hour vaporetto cruise), is Italy's top fishing port. You'll find canals, peaceful alleys, breezy laundry, crumbly buildings, and old churches. Except for a few cars, Chioggia is Venice's shadow but without the tourist crowds and much cheaper. Ponder the canal from the summit of an ornate marble bridge. Picnic on the crusty deck of an old fishing boat and savor your cappuccino in a bar where the tourist is still an oddity.

25. Peloponnesian Highlights: Overlooked Greece

Stretching south from Athens is the Peloponnesian Peninsula. This land of ancient Olympia, Corinth, and Sparta has more than its share of historic rubble, but it also offers plenty of fun in the eternal Greek sun with pleasant fishing villages, sandy beaches, and bathtub-warm water.

Just two hours south of Athens by car or bus is the Peloponnesian port town of Nafplion. Small, cozy, and easy to know, it's a welcome relief after the black-hanky intensity of smoggy Athens. Not only is Nafplion itself fun, but it's a handy home base for exploring some of Greece's greatest ancient sights. Nafplion's harbor is guarded by two castles, one on a small island and the other capping the hill above the town. Both are wonderfully floodlit at night. The hill castle, an old Venetian outpost from the days she ruled Europe economically, is the best-preserved castle of its kind in Greece—well worth the 999-step climb. From the highest ramparts you can see several Aegean islands (great one-day side trips by boat from Nafplion) and deep into the mountainous interior of the Peloponnesian Peninsula. Below you lies an enticing beach.

Nafplion has plenty of hotels, and its harbor is lined with restaurants specializing in fresh seafood. An octopus dinner cost me $4—succulent! The next night my dinner featured snapper. He smiled through the entire meal.

The infamous resin-flavored retsina wine is a drink you'll want to experience—once. Maybe with octopus. The first glass is awful. The third glass is dangerous: it starts to taste good. If you drink any more, you'll feel it all the next day—like DMSO.

For a change, on my third night I left Nafplion's popular waterfront district and had a memorable meal in a hole-in-the-wall joint. There was no menu, just an entertaining local crowd and a nearsighted man who, in a relaxed frenzy, ran the whole show. He scurried about, greeting eaters, slicing, dicing, laughing, singing to himself, cooking, serving, and billing. Potato stew, meatballs, a plate of about 30 tiny fried fish with lime, and unlimited wine cost $8 for 2—and could have fed 4. Nafplion is just a short drive from two important classical sights: Epidavros and Mycenae.

Epidavros, 18 miles northeast, is the best-preserved ancient Greek theater. Built 2,500 years ago to seat 14,000, it's still used each summer to house a popular drama festival reviving the greatest plays of antiquity. There are also performances of ancient Greek comedies and tragedies on Friday and Saturday from mid-June through September.

Epidavros, state-of-the-art acoustics

You're a guest of honor at a Greek wedding festival.

Try to see Epidavros either early or late in the day. The marvelous acoustics are best enjoyed in near solitude. From the most distant seat you can hear the beep-beep of your partner's digital watch down on the theater floor.

Thirty minutes in the other direction from Nafplion are the ruins of Mycenae. This was the capital of the Mycenaeans of Trojan War fame who dominated Greece 1,000 years before the age of Socrates.

As you tour this fascinating fortified citadel, remember that these people were as awesome to the ancient Greeks of Socrates' day as the generation of Socrates is to us. The classical Greeks marveled at the huge stones and workmanship of the Mycenaean ruins and figured, "Man, no one could build with such colossal rocks, this must be the work of the giant Cyclopes." They called it "Cyclopian" architecture.

Visitors today can climb deep into a cool ancient cistern, explore the giant tholos tombs, and inspect reconstructed pots near the North Gate next to a pile of shards that looks like a spilled jigsaw puzzle. The tombs, built 1,500 years before Christ, stand like huge stone igloos with smooth subterranean domes 40 feet wide and 40 feet tall. The most important Mycenaean artifacts, like the golden Mask of Agamemnon, are in the National Museum back in Athens.

Finikoundas

The prize-winning Peloponnesian hideaway is the remote village of Finikoundas. Located on the southwest tip of the peninsula between the twin Venetian fortress towns of Koroni and Methoni (two hours by public bus from Kalamata), Finikoundas is big enough to have a good selection of restaurants, bed and breakfast places (dhomatia in Greek), a few shops, and a business life of its own, but not big enough to draw the typical resort buildup with its traffic, crowds, and noise. It's just right for your Greek holiday retreat.

Finikoundas has plenty of private rooms for rent. Plan to spend $15 for a simple double a few steps from the beach. The little bay just east of the rock breakwater was the best beach I found, and the swimming was fine—even in October.

After a little Apollo-worshiping, I wandered through town in search

of Dionysus, at just the right waterfront restaurant. The place I found couldn't have been more "waterfront." Since the fishing village had no dock, its Lilliputian fishing boats were actually anchored to the restaurant. I settled my chair comfortably into the sand and the salty atmosphere. I dined amid rusty four-hooker anchors, honorably retired old ropes, and peely dinghies as weak wavelets licked my table's legs. A naked 20-watt bulb dangled from the straw roof, which rotted unnoticed by Greeks and a few perpetually off-season Germans who seemed to be regulars. I couldn't help but think that if all mankind lived as simply as these Greeks, we'd have more leisure and less tension.

Cuisine in a village like this is predictable—fresh seafood, Greek salad, and local wine. After a few days in Greece, you become a connoisseur of the salad, appreciating the wonderful tomatoes, rich feta cheese, and even the olive oil drenching—er, dressing.

Almost within splashing distance of my table, Greek boys in swimsuits not much bigger than a rat's hammock gathered around a bucketful of just-caught octopuses. They were tenderizing the poor things to death by whipping them like wet rags over and over on a big flat rock. They'll be featured momentarily on someone's dinner plate—someone else's.

Evening in any Mediterranean town is a pleasant time of strolling and socializing. The streets buzz with take-it-easy action. Dice chatter on dozens of backgammon boards, entrepreneurial dogs and goal-oriented children busy themselves as a tethered goat chews on something inedible in its low-profile corner. From the other end of town comes the happy music of a christening party. Dancing women fill the building while their children mimic them in the street. Farther down, two black-clad elderly women sit like tired dogs on the curb.

Succumbing to the lure of the pastry shop, I sat down for my daily honey-soaked baklava. I told the cook I was American. "Oh," he said, shaking his head with sadness and pity, "you work too hard." I assured him, "Right, but not today."

26. Diverse Yugoslavia

Imagine a country the size of Oregon with seven distinct peoples in six republics who speak five languages, with three religions (Orthodox, Catholic, and Muslim), two alphabets (Latin and Cyrillic), and one government. That's Yugoslavia, a fascinating cultural cocktail offering the visitor as much diversity, contrast, and thrills per mile, minute, and dollar as any European country.

When the Iron Curtain was dropped, Americans filed Yugoslavia away in their minds somewhere between Bulgaria and bleak. But the 22 million Yugoslavians are pioneering an independent economic course mixing capitalism and socialism. Their success has replaced most of the dreariness that tints their eastern neighbors with signs of "prosperity" (fancy hotels, sprawling resorts, traffic jams, modern shopping centers, building projects everywhere) and a spirit of pride and determination to maintain their relative freedom and prosperity.

From a traveler's point of view, Yugoslavia is Western — not Eastern — and, with a little planning and creativity, travel here can be more exciting than travel elsewhere in Western Europe and only a little more difficult.

To appreciate this country, think of it as many little countries — Slovenia, Croatia, Kosovo, Serbia, Bosnia-Herzegovina — each with its own features, heritage, Babe Ruths, and Barbra Streisands. Cross each mini-border with fanfare. History is very close to these people. Their union was formed in 1918. One-tenth of the people were killed fighting for it in World War II. Today, parts of the land are chattering into the computer age, while others are stuck in the mud of the past. The north is prosperous, progressive, and excited about democracy, while the south is more conservative and collective in its outlook.

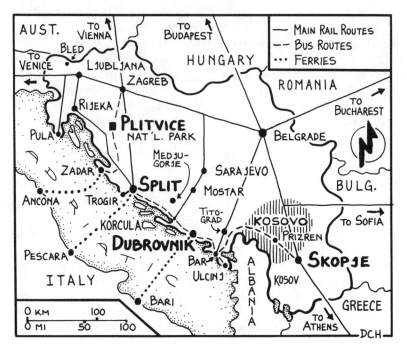

Getting around can be tedious. The trains and buses get you where you'll need to go—slowly. While they'll win no awards, they are cheap (about $1 an hour) and offer plenty of boredom or intrigue—depending on what you're looking for. Driving is easy—sparse traffic, good two-lane windy roads and $2 a gallon gas. Bringing a car in from the north or renting within requires only an American driver's license.

Driving in from Greece is trickier. Before my trip, I was told that cars with Greek plates weren't allowed in. Some on-the-spot research overcame this limitation. For $50 and my bank card's security, a large Athenian car rental agency (Inter-rent) did the necessary paperwork, got the permit, and rented me a car to take into Yugoslavia—provided I returned it to Greece.

On my last visit, I drove 1,000 trouble-free miles and took full advantage of my rental car to boldly go where no tour bus had gone before, exploring the most remote corners of Europe's last frontier, where village children mob a visitor's car out of friendly curiosity.

While Yugoslavian cuisine is simple, prices are low enough to let even budget travelers eat high on the menu in fine restaurants. Choosing from strudel and baklava on the same menu, you're constantly reminded that this is a land where East meets West. On Lake Ohrid, you'll find a tasty kind of trout found nowhere else. The south is the land of paprikas. Markets are full of colorful peppers, so you're likely to find a couple of the red, green, or yellow specialties on even your breakfast plate. In the north, you'll find entire lambs routinely roasting on festive skewers. In Muslim sections of the country, restaurants offer tasty Turkish cuisine, and on the touristic Adriatic coast, you'll find everything from fresh seafood to pizza parlors to fast-food havens for the timid tourist. Fruit and vegetables are cheap and plentiful in the markets. Beer is better than the local wine. Meals range from $2 to $10. The water is drinkable throughout the country. Yugoslavia's socialism shows through in its telltale lack of citrus fruits and its lousy ersatz chocolates.

Hotels are government regulated, generally poorly run, and not particularly cheap. Big-city and resort hotels charge up to $80 for rooms, while basic doubles cost about $30 in smaller towns. The local term for bed and breakfast is *sobe*, and, for $10 per person, these private rooms are a great deal. Shop around, since the government controls the price but not the quality. I've had the best luck skipping the local tourist board's help when it comes to landing a good value sobe.

The exchange situation is easy but crazy. The sickly Yugoslavian dinar (way over 30,000 in a dollar) is diving in value so fast that most prices are listed in German marks or U.S. dollars. You can change cash or traveler's checks for the same fair rate in hotels, banks, change desks, and even local. There is no tedious bookwork or commission fee for either, and all use (or should use) the latest rates from the local newspaper. With all the zeros and the fluid situation with the local currency, it's wise to have prices written down and confirmed before ordering anything—and count those zeros carefully! (Mentally eliminate the last three and think in thousands.) Overcharging is routine but easy to catch and correct if you're on the ball. Tourist areas (the Dalmatian coast) are relatively expensive, but the interior is very cheap.

Outside of tourist areas and big cities, few locals speak English. A little German goes a long way, since many Yugoslavians worked in Germany or had to study that language during the War. Take half an hour to learn the Cyrillic alphabet if you'll be traveling in the South. Then you'll know, for instance, "PECTOPAH" spells "Restoran."

Dubrovnik

Dubrovnik is Europe's most romantic city. Set on Yugoslavia's sparkling Dalmatian coast, laced together by a massive wall with amazing Old World architectural unity, it is indeed the "Pearl of the Adriatic." Dubrovnik is the most cosmopolitan place in Yugoslavia—and the most touristed. But it's a living fairy tale that shouldn't be missed.

Dubrovnik's present-day charm is the sleepy result of its no-nonsense past, when she was the second city of the grand Venetian Empire. Her Titian paintings and traffic-free marble avenues are the legacy of a shrewd and independent city, a trading power that bought off the Ottoman invaders and freed its slaves in the fifteenth century.

Originally, Dubrovnik was two towns: one on the mainland, the other on a tiny island. When the narrow strait separating the two was filled in and made into the main street and the towns were joined by a huge 18-foot-thick wall, a united Dubrovnik rose to prominence. Today, more visitors than merchants cross over the wooden drawbridge and under the Gothic arch into the traffic-free glory of old Dubrovnik.

Dubrovnik's individual sights are pleasant but nothing to jump ship for—several convents, a few works by famous painters, some very mediocre museums, and Europe's oldest pharmacy (1317). The attraction here is the city itself. Orient yourself with a trip up the cable car to the Napoleonic fortress, which has a grand view. Then walk around the wall. This one-mile walk culminates with a fine overall view at the Minceta Tower.

The Placa, or Main Street, cuts the circle formed by the wall in half. The Placa is the heartbeat of the city, an Old World shopping mall by day and a sprawling cocktail party after dark where everybody seems to be doing the traditional korzo, or evening stroll, flirting, ice cream licking, flaunting, and gawking. A coffee and some of Europe's best people-watching in a prime Placa café is one of travel's great $1 bargains.

The Lindo Folk Dance Company puts on Dubrovnik's "really big shoe" twice a week. A little folk dancing is often more than enough, but this group whirled, stomped, screamed, and smiled for two frenzied hours—and I still wanted more. I've never seen such a rainbow wardrobe of folk costumes and so much bubbly dancing energy packaged so atmospherically under 500-year-old stone arches.

Dubrovnik's Summer Festival (July and August) keeps its many guests well entertained. I heard the well-scrubbed Vienna Boys Choir fill a Gothic courtyard with angelic music for $5.

Those dreaming of fun in the Adriatic sun should catch the little boat to Lokrum Island. The "beaches," except for an almost tropical little saltwater pool on the island's far side (10-minute walk from boat, veer left) are solid rock. Still, the predictable sun, crystal-clear water, and showers make up for the lack of sand. Nude beaches, labeled FKK throughout the country, are very popular in Yugoslavia. If you've never worked on an all-around tan, follow the signs 300 yards to the left of the boat. First-timers get comfortable in a hurry and are never the only pink ones on the rocks.

It seems that nearly all of Dubrovnik's 60,000 people are involved in the tourist trade, either feeding, bedding, or selling. In peak season, I'd swear there are two visitors for each local person. Nevertheless, this queen of Yugoslavian tourism handles her crowds well. There always seems to be good food, enough beds, and plenty of quiet corners for those who want them.

Dubrovnik's hotels are crowded and expensive. I always go the sobe route. In the case of Dubrovnik, the room-finding service at the tourist office is a hindrance. Wander the back streets or the bus station and let it be known you're in need of a sobe. Choose between ancient, very cheap, and colorful but gloomy private rooms in the old town or remarkable comfort in more modern local-style houses just outside the wall. I found a desirable neighborhood and asked the first woman I saw, "Sobe?" She pointed to the next door. The lady there told me her rooms were all taken, but Dubrovnik is laced with sobe grapevines, and she took me down the street, where, for $10, I was finally set up—in someone's house with their 1940s wedding picture staring right down on me in that big double bed. There are countless sobes. For a cool, quiet, and bare but elegantly simple place one block from the wall and one block from the cable car, try Maja Jelic's house (Peljeska 1, tel. 050/25-061, $30 doubles).

Dubrovnik can wine and dine with the best of Mediterranean resort towns. Every restaurant in the old town is touristy. I enjoyed the Restaurant Cavtat (Ul Od Puca 29, tel. 274-99), with a traditional atmosphere and Dalmatian specialties. It's as untouristy as Dubrovnik can be and provided a tasty $10 finale to a thrilling day.

For a more Croatian and less touristic taste of the coast, stop in Split, the Dalmatian capital that grew up in the vast halls of the Roman emperor Diocletian's abandoned palace. The city has most of the color and none of the heavy tourism of Dubrovnik—easy parking, easy hotels, great evening ambience, waterfront promenade, fun modern shops woven into the incredible Roman remains.

Just 12 miles north of Split is Trogir (much more fun and less touristy than the similar town of Korcula). Trogir, a tiny art- and medieval architecture-packed town surrounded by water, has a bustling market, wonderfully carved old cathedral, and medieval ambience that can only be really appreciated from an outdoor café with a honey-drenched piece of baklava and a Turkish coffee.

Medugorje: Mary to Earth . . . Mary to Earth . . .

Since 1981, six children from the remote and windy village of Medugorje, 2 ½ hours' drive from Dubrovnik near Mostar, have been receiving messages from Mary, the mother of Jesus. A boomtown has been thrown up to accommodate the hordes of pilgrims and curious who now visit this previously unremarkable town. Of course, like Lourdes and Fatima, this pilgrimage center will have enough crass commercialism to put off those who want to be put off, but it's an interesting side trip.

Trying to keep up with its near-miraculous popularity, the ramshackle town is littered with mounds of ready-to-stack red bricks, lines of tourist stalls, fierce bees, pesky flies, and busloads of pilgrims on tour. The latest holy message, usually a call for peace and prayer, is read at mass. A day here would include: the daily 10:00 a.m. English mass, a hike to the "place of the first vision," and possibly the afternoon or evening religious activity. Just sitting in a plastic café—watching the robes, long beards, video cameras, grandmothers with freshly blessed Mary-shaped holy water bottles, and hawkers—is a vision in itself.

Kosovo—The Yugoslavian Albania

Albania, crouching between Greece and Yugoslavia, is the recluse of countries. Recently it broke relations with its only ally—China. Americans aren't allowed in, and it looks like its totalitarian rulers are doing a great job of keeping out the "evil" of Western influence.

Though we can't visit Albania we can see its people, since a third of all Albanians live in the lately troubled Yugoslavian district of Kosovo, which borders Albania on the north. Kosovo is served by several small, winding, but decent roads. Europe's most exciting bus ride connects two of its dullest cities, Skopje and Titograd. Cutting through the heart of this fascinating, most remote corner of Europe, the ride is long and exhausting. But the mountain views and intimate glimpses of village life make the time fly and the twentieth century fade. You'll see people doing their laundry on rocks grooved by their ancestors' dirty socks. Those people seem to live their entire lives up there—stranded in the past.

Stop at the entertaining Albanian-flavored town of Pritzren. The Theranda Hotel on the main square charges $16 per person, with breakfast. Sorry, you can't spend more. (There is one other hotel in town, Putnik, and no private sobes.)

The Kosovan-Albanian culture is so different from ours that even everyday things take on a fresh playfulness. I often envy wide-eyed toddlers excitedly exploring things we adults see as mundane. In this respect, Pritzren can make you a child again. You're culturally blindfolded, and they've rearranged the furniture. Everything is different, a challenge and a surprise.

Since donkey carts have no headlights, the setting sun dictates rush hour. Ox carts loaded with colorfully dressed peasant women return from the fields, and the town streets fill with people.

Turkish and Muslim influence is very strong; the Yankee impact is minimal here in the only part of Europe I've found that doesn't sing American pop music. Skullcaps and minarets, shish kebabs and rice pudding, goofy men and hidden women are all reminiscent of Turkey.

Without a list of museums and palaces to see, you have to be more creative in your "sight"-seeing. For lack of anything better to do on one particular corner, I enjoyed a shoeshine. This was an event, and a crowd gathered. One proud businessman made sure everyone knew he could speak English. An English-speaking Kosovan is rare. Take advantage of this willing source of local information. Printed information is rare.

Later on, I let a barber give me an old-fashioned shave—like one you'd see on "Gunsmoke." He was a real artist, dressed in a tie and a white lab coat with two eager apprentices. He trimmed my beard lovingly and refused to accept any payment. As I left, he pointed to a painting on the wall of a similarly trim-bearded sultan and made some joke about a harem. Normally in the Muslim world, my red beard earns me the nickname Ali Baba.

Always nearby looms the border of the real Albania, with its fierce dogs, bald mountains, and no-nonsense soldiers in a desolate no-man's land. The Kosovans and all Yugoslavians have their share of economic and political problems, but with the devastation of World War II still fresh in their minds, they treasure their peace. Nestled between the muzzled peoples of Bulgaria and Albania, they enjoy relative freedom and economic success. A visit to Kosovo is a thought-provoking experience.

Plitvice—Yugoslavia's Grand Canyon

The Plitvice National Park, a scenic 2 ½ -hour bus ride south of Zagreb, is one of Europe's greatest natural wonders—imagine Niagara Falls diced and sprinkled over a heavily forested Grand Canyon. There's nothing like this lush valley of sixteen terraced lakes laced together by waterfalls and miles of pleasant plank walks. Countless cascades and strangely clear and colorful water make this park a misty natural wonderland.

You can enjoy an entire day picnicking, rowing, exploring behind "bridal veil" falls, and climbing stone stairways that are losing their battle with the busy Plitvice (pronounced: pleet-veetz-seh) waters. Children love Plitvice, and even Mom and Dad scamper and feel kind of frisky. (Admission about $10 for us capitalists.) There are two entrances: Ulaz 1 for the lower and best falls and Ulaz 2. For the best basic four hours (and that should be enough), follow the map on your ticket from: Ulaz 1, L to F along the plank-walk up to G, over to the boat dock at P and Z, where you can buy great homemade strudel from the old ladies across from the shop and grab a large coffee to go for the half-hourly boat trip to the upper half. Get off at A and hike: A-B groups-only trail to T-C-E-F-R-G-H-I-L-K and to the bus at M, which takes you back to Ulaz 1, where you'll be hungry and ready for an atmospheric meal in the great Licka Kuca restaurant—lamb roasting on an open spit to the rhythm of a fun local folk band. Try the mixed meat grill Lika-style, a plum brandy finale with sweet, cooked-right-there fritters, $15 for two (but check your bill). Shuttle buses and boat connections are included in your ticket. If you are now or have ever been a member of the Communist party, you could probably rationalize entering without the ticket—which costs Westerners six times what they charge tourists from Eastern Europe—and skip the boat, which is where they check. Plitvice is closed in the winter.

Those sleeping in Plitvice National Park have two options: a private home (rustic, friendly, cheap, look for the sobe signs) or, for a hotel experience Stalin would love, a $70 double in any of the giant lodges.

Plitvice National Park, Yugoslavia

The local tourist offices and bus companies make a Plitvice day easy. Tourist offices in Zadar and Zagreb organize inexpensive one-day tours with round-trip bus transportation. Do-it-yourselfers can catch hourly buses from Zadar (3 ½ hours) or Zagreb (2 ½ hours).

These three highlights of Yugoslavia—Plitvice, Dubrovnik, and the bus ride through Kosovo—can be part of your trip from Central Europe to Greece or vice versa. The boring marathon train ride through Yugoslavia via its dull capital, Belgrade, may be the fastest way to Athens (short of flying), but it will seem like a million years.

A more interesting one-week plan would be: take the train from Central Europe to Ljubljana (a Yugoslavian Salzburg without Mozart and the tourist crowds, skip the overrated Postojna Caves). Then on to Split or Trogir via Plitvice. Then to Dubrovnik by bus, spending two nights there before taking the bus to Titograd where, the following day, you venture by bus into Kosovo. From Skopje, you can catch the night train to Athens. This trip can also be done in the opposite direction. This isn't Eurail country, and transportation across Yugoslavia will cost $40 or $50. There are also plenty of reasonable boats from ports like Split and Dubrovnik to Italy. ($50 per person in a stateroom, less for deck class, tickets through any travel agency in Italy or Yugoslavia or just show up. Except for a few August days, there's always room.) Whichever way you do it, you can be sure you've seen the best of Yugoslavia.

27. Eastern Europe: Melting the Iron

Europe has an eastern half—a whole different world filled with 120 million people and a rich and fascinating culture. Most tourists get within two or three hours of the East, but few venture in. Those who do find a uniquely modern side to Europe and, in some places, more old Europe than they ever dreamed possible.

The East, as rich culturally as Europe's West, is less flashy and, frankly, less appealing to the average American tourist. The new society is almost by definition dreary, gray, and stony-faced. At least, that's the impression one gets coming into this advertising-free society from our Pepsi ad world. But things are changing. A few years ago, only people on society's lowest rung could be openly warm and close to a Western visitor. I was told, "They choose to live that way so nothing can be taken from them." Today, there's a new openness. A taste for Western styles is hip. And even well-placed proponents of the socialist status quo wave their flags in new Levis.

Travel in Eastern Europe is a package deal with rewards and pitfalls. The wonders of so many families struggling to make do in a Soviet-dominated system that basically ignores what we call "free market forces" can't help but impress and forever broaden the visitor. You'll

find an admirable strength, enviable warmth, and a resilient nationalism in the local people as soon as you break through the bureaucratic
and official crust.

Eastern Europe is a challenge to the Western tourist traveling without a tour. Independent travel is bourgeois. To the socialist, individuality is a vice. The masses matter most. A socialist holiday is when all
workers go to the prescribed best beach or mountain resort (and each
country has one). They become refreshed and recharged and return to
their job. Large groups get service first. The single adventurer gets
leftovers at best. If I were a Bulgarian hotel clerk, you would be a temptation, a language problem, and a hassle to me. Your business would
mean nothing. I wouldn't work to accommodate you. But I would wonder how you got so much money. (The bold price list behind hotel
reception desks puts me into the "capitalist" category—paying more
than "socialist" guests and getting less respect.)

German has been the handiest second language, spoken by many
who were in school during the Nazi years. English is the language of the
young educated and more Western-oriented people. All students must
study Russian, but few speak it. In fact, Westerners who speak Russian
find their Eastern European travels go better if they don't use it.

An enjoyable visit to Eastern Europe requires an open mind,
patience, and flexibility. The Soviet and socialist worlds are generally
misunderstood by Americans. A healthy approach to travel in this
world is to consider the Soviet subjugation of Eastern Europe as a
buffer zone that Russia perceives as necessary in a century that so far
has brought her two devastating capitalist invasions. Regardless of
what's "right" or what works, their Marxism or Leninism is not fun-
damentally wicked but an attempt at equality. For example, while some
American cities are almost sinking in rarely used backyard swimming
pools, a socialist city would have one grand people's sports pavilion. A
socialist will remind the American capitalist that if he divided the
miles he drives in his car by the hours he invests in it (buying, using,
maintaining, and so on), he travels about four miles per hour. While
America defines oil rigs in Saudi Arabia as "vital to our national
interest," the socialist accepts the fact that cars aren't for everyone and
uses effective and very cheap government subsidized public transit
system—in a world free of traffic congestion.

While travel in the USSR is more carefully controlled, you can travel
freely through most of these countries, staying where you like and
doing pretty much exactly as you please. Most of these countries
require a visa, and some have a minimum daily expenditure requirement. These policies change with the political tide, so check with your

travel agent before departing. Visas can be purchased in the United States, in any European capital, or sometimes at the border. Most East European embassies process tourist visas within two or three days. Paris and Belgrade are both good places, although I'd much rather wait for processing in Paris. For a $15 or $20 speed fee, you can often get visas issued on the spot (as I did for Bulgaria, Hungary, and Czechoslovakia in Paris). Visas for Yugoslavia are issued free and easy at the border.

Local tourist information is basically propaganda—designed to steer you into areas each government would like you to see. Be sure to take in a guidebook from the West. I find Frommer's East Europe guidebook helpful, but Fodor's not. *Let's Go: Europe* has handy but skimpy chapters on each Eastern country. The new *Real Guide* and Lonely Planet guides to Eastern Europe are the most thorough real travelers' guides to the area. These and *Let's Go* are the only ones with the guts to tell you how to function and not be manipulated in a region where you can't just follow the local tourist board's advice.

After so many Men from Uncle and Impossible Missions in our blood, Eastern European travel does offer a special James Bond thrill. Even in these glasnost days, foreign mail is screened, and, to a varying degree, an eye is kept on visiting tourists. But I've always felt completely safe in Eastern Europe. The risk and consequences of any question-

Eastern Europe would like to meet you.

able cultural exchange is willingly borne by the subjects of these governments. A lunch with you is the average Eastern European's next best
thing to a plane ticket to London or California. To dissident types, it's
a quick recharge for a very frustrated free spirit.

Demographically, Eastern Europe is a hodgepodge. Political, racial,
and linguistic boundaries only vaguely resemble each other, but the
related problems have taken a back seat to even more immediate concerns since the Soviet army "liberated" these people from the Nazis in
1945. The date the USSR freed each country from fascism marks the
beginning of the modern age and is now each country's national holiday. While many would argue that the Soviets "liberated" Eastern
Europe from the frying pan directly into the fire, many are grateful to
the Soviets for ending their Hitlerian nightmare. Every city in every
Warsaw Pact country has a central monument glorifying the Russian
"saviors" of Eastern Europe. Locals who wish their "liberators" would
go home have learned that these reminders and frustrations are most
effectively fought not with Molotov cocktails but with jokes, patience,
and pragmatism. And after 45 years of Soviet control, things seem to
be softening.

As you travel through Eastern Europe, try to find the most remote villages and regions. The same places that most successfully resist the
modern world are also least affected by whichever government happens to be in power. According to East European "hillbillies," the governmental tune is always the same—only the musicians change.

Be approachable. English-speaking, broad-minded locals will come
out of the woodwork. Universities are great places to meet multilingual
people who want to talk. Traveling alone, I've listened to the Voice of
America in attics, been interviewed for a local college newspaper, and
explained the lyrical messages of popular rock tunes to eager
teenagers. Approach very young and very old people and those on society's bottom rung—folks who aren't worried about social and official
acceptance. Break the ice. We are fairy-tale people living in a skyscraper world speeding to a Hollywood beat, the unknowing victims of
our passionate materialism. Locals will look at you and wonder about
movie star presidents, drive-in restaurants, the sexual revolution, and
how we can go anywhere if our entire country is "private property."

Sampling Glasnost—Ideas for a Week in East Berlin, Prague, and Budapest

Hungary has joined the Eurail system, visas are a snap, Bruce Springsteen screams to 80,000 Budapest rock fans that he's "Born in the USA,"
and "I Love Gorby" pins are on sale everywhere.

The warm winds of world understanding are beginning to blow away some of the tense fog that has kept half of Europe out of the average American travel dream. Although travel east of NATO is still laced with frustrations, more and more Americans are good enough travelers to enjoy Europe's other half.

How about splicing a week of East into your Western European trip plans? Here are some ideas on East Berlin, Prague, and Budapest, the region's three most interesting cities.

Sample itinerary: night train from Amsterdam, Copenhagen, or Frankfurt to Berlin (two days, one in the West and one in the East), night train from Berlin to Prague (two days), night train from Prague to Budapest (three days), three-hour train to Vienna.

East Berlin—The most interesting thing about a trip to Berlin is a chance to spend a day in East Berlin. You'll be tempted to take an organized day tour. Don't. In fact, I forbid you. For it will isolate you and nearly defeat the purpose of going. To experience the East, walk over The Wall at Checkpoint Charlie and live there for a day.

A one-day visa is simple. Staying overnight is unnecessary and a headache. The border is open daily from 8:00 a.m. to midnight, when you must cross back into West Berlin or risk turning into a cabbage (which would probably be the only fresh produce you'll see all day). Your visa costs 5 Western marks and you must change 25 more into Eastern marks at the official (and ridiculous) rate of one for one.

The black market (which thrives around the Pergamon Museum), with rates as high as seven to one, will be tempting, but any windfalls must be spent in the East, a challenge for even an American. By Western standards, the quality and selection of consumer goods is miserable. (I blow my Ostmarks on taxis, Vodka, classical records, and government-subsidized propaganda.) For a close look into the daily life of an Eastern European, visit the huge department store (Centrum Warenhaus) on Alexander Square, right downtown under the TV tower. Go upstairs for the latest records and fake Western pop stars. Then tour the dreary shelves of the nearby supermarket.

While the West seems to have embraced the modern ways and races almost mindlessly into the future, the East seems a bit less confident, reluctant to give up its past. Visit the neoclassical, templelike Memorial to the Victims of Fascism and Militarism (guards, frozen in front of the eternal flame, change on the half-hour). The nearby history museum is interesting for the Eastern slant it gives our Western understanding of twentieth-century Europe.

The Palace of the Republic is East Berlin's proud showpiece. Have about the classiest cup of coffee in town from its second-floor café overlooking a parking lot filled with "Ruski" and "Polski Fiats." These new Eastern cars are made from the outdated and sold-cheap molds of Western Fiat plants.

While a visit here is most interesting for a firsthand look at socialism in action (or in inaction), Berlin's top museums ended up there in the Soviet sector. The Pergamon Museum, one of Europe's best, has the wonderful Pergamon Altar, the Babylonian Ishtar Gate, and many more treasures from the classical world.

Join the party: for evening fun in East Berlin, hit a disco. Paying for your drink or entry in Western marks normally makes you very popular. Remember, your visa expires at midnight.

Back in the West, climb the Wall-viewing platform, tour the Haus Am Checkpoint Charlie Museum (open daily until 10:00 p.m., with a gripping display of the Wall's 30-year history, including some spine-tingling escapes), and pray that the East-West teeter-totter of understanding and tensions will balance so that this wall will no longer be considered necessary.

Prague—Prague looks more like Mozart's Vienna than Vienna does. *Amadeus* was filmed here. The only major Eastern European city to escape the bombs of the world wars, Czechoslovakia's capital is incredibly beautiful.

But urban beauty is also only skin deep, and after a day of sightseeing and a day wandering through its gorgeous baroque streets, the 1700s get old and you feel like one of the locals who seem to be prowling around in a citywide search for something to do.

Prague is exotically bland. For starters, have lunch in the local equivalent of McDonald's, the "Moscow Fast Food restaurant." Girls in dirty white T-shirts with the red and white Moscow logo serve sausage rolls, borscht, cold fries, and pink ketchup. Plopping my loaded tray onto a table, the old lady next to me sneered at my Eastern Coke, as if to say, "Yuck, it's got no vim and less vigor." The local Coke, like the food, clothes, advertising, car paint, and perhaps life in general, has no kick.

But flat and dull is a relative thing. Most tourists here are East Germans, coming down from Dresden for a wild and crazy time. Walk the streets, dodging prewar trolleys but not many cars. Many old town streets are tunnels of scaffolding, lamp lit, with clusters of people gathered as if seeking warmth around windows selling ice cream or the local burger.

Sightsee Prague in three steps: the basic half-day city bus tour, a visit to the synagogue, and the paseo from the town cathedral square to Wenceslas Square.

Hitler planned a grand postwar archives for the exterminated Jewish culture in Prague. The synagogue, museum, graveyard of 10,000 cluttered tombstones, and exhibit of children's concentration camp art is a grueling emotional experience. This is one of the few sights in town with multilingual explanations, designed I'm sure so no visitor will leave without an appropriate understanding of Europe's fascist nightmare.

Stroll with the locals between the town's two main squares and across Europe's most beautiful pedestrian bridge, Charles Bridge. On Wenceslas Square, scene of huge recent and future anti-Soviet demonstrations, Prague's prewar elegance survives in classy hotels. Hotel Europa is dressed like a flapper. Stop in for an ice cream or coffee surrounded by waiters in black and white and hushed conversations.

The city seems to live for its sports, discos, and movie houses. Every disco has a full sign with eager dancers waiting for someone to leave. The Prague stadium seats 250,000, and apparently needs to. As our guide reminded us, "Sports prowess is the mark of a great nation." As the Soviet tank on the pedestal reminded us, they don't have another choice.

The city is cheap—for a local with Western currency. Western visitors who tour by the book pay Western prices. (For instance, hotel rooms start at $60.) The exchange situation is confusing. Of course, the official bank rate is the typical socialist government-sponsored rip-off. The street rate for your dollars is five times better—easy but illegal. Now the banks are actually getting into the black market game, offering "Tuseks" crowns, only to those who ask. These "hard" Czechoslovakian crowns are legal and work like dollars to locals with Sony, Honda, or travel dreams. To get an update on the exchange mess, ask a cabbie or a young German tourist.

Finding a room is just as straightforward. Technically, you should go through Pragotur or the CEDOK national tourist board, agencies even Mother Teresa would have a hard time liking. You'll wait forever to pay too much for a bad room. Enterprising entrepreneurs hover around the tourist offices with lines on good budget rooms. Most hotels will tell the capitalist walking in off the street to go to CEDOK. Room hustlers, trench-coated widows, and many cabbies know hotels ($30 doubles) and private homes ($8 beds) that will take you legally without CEDOK and register you with the police.

Prague's smoky beer or wine cellars are as full as its nighttime streets are empty. They serve one basic meal—pork, potatoes, and kraut. Beers—good and cheap, in half-liter mugs—hit the table automatically as soon as you do. You'll get about four for a dollar, and your waiter will keep track long after you can with a stroke talley on a slip of paper he leaves at your table. The beer is very strong, giving those who have it at lunch "Czech knees" to tour on.

Locals meet and talk in bars. Under Gothic groin vaults, I shared a table with an 18-year-old and his younger-looking girlfriend. They drank beer and chain-smoked Petra cigarettes. ("A third the price and nearly as good as Marlboroughs.") Making very small talk, all I can do in the Czech language (which is so rough it makes German sound like French), I tell them our Budweiser originated in Czechoslovakia. It was clear by their reaction that they understood me and were insulted. Czech beer is their gold medalist. I say "Druzba" (friendship in Russian) and offer a toast. The girl sends a smoky river from her mouth through her nose, stands her lighter up saying, "Czech." Then sets her pack of cigarettes on top and says "Russia." Choking on my Petra, I indicate that with Gorbachev, there's hope.

Budapest—Goulash! Hungarians are proud to be the place where the economics of East and West intermingle. Budapest is Eastern Europe's fun city, THE place for Warsaw Pact decadence.

Bustling Budapest is a can of Jolt after the flat Coke of sleepy Prague. Children are still swimming in Grandpa Lenin, but in a few years they join the braless girls in "Go West" T-shirts. "I Love Gorby" pins (say it, "Yah lyub-blee-you Gor-bah-chov") are everywhere.

Budapest's pulse seems to race. Pedestrians feel like dogs trapped on a freeway. There's sex in the window displays and virgins from Warsaw to Bucharest come here for their first Big Mac. Like a seductive beacon of free enterprise, Ronald McDonald waves at children on the pedestrian mall. Speed eating on gleaming tables, surrounded by shiny chrome-framed windows, is a powerful temptation in a world of socialist precision.

Down the street, past shops filled with stereos and high-fashion dreams on hangers, a line jostles outside the Adidas store. Shoes are in.

While there's an impression that this is the Eastern land of plenty and the city's momentum seems to be West-ward, this is still far from Kansas. The hotel situation is as Kafkaesque as Prague's, Western hotels stock three-day-old *International Herald Tribune*s, they have no concept of breakfast cereal, and the burgers are very dry. While they're hip enough to treat a stadium of 80,000 rock fans to a Bruce Springsteen concert, the efficiency of socialism persists, and after the show, hordes fill the streets looking for a ride, while the taxis sit, with nothing to do, downtown.

Cover the main sights and sort out the twin cities of Buda and Pest with the $14 (Western money only) half-day city bus tour. Then zero in on the Pest's ped zone for its elegant shops in prewar buildings, great people-watching, tasty pastries, and street entertainers. Budget travelers can live high on the Budapest menu (although service is incredibly slow). You'll pay the local equivalent of a dime for a bus, trolley, or museum ticket, a quarter for a sandwich, $1 for a taxi ride, and $4 for a good dinner. And, if Bruce Springsteen happens to be passing through, you'll find tickets at the door for $5. Vienna is just three hours by train to the west. Don't leave without a $2 manicure.

28. Ignored Bulgaria

Have you ever been to Bulgaria? Known a Bulgarian? Received a letter from Bulgaria? Have you ever even had a nice thought about Bulgaria? Public relations with the United States isn't a Bulgarian priority. But there are more than nine million Bulgarian people, and most of them would love to meet you.

I stumbled into Bulgaria and returned each summer for the next five years. It grabs you in a strange melodramatic happy/sad way. The most subservient people of Eastern Europe—mind-clutched by Mother Russia—welcome the Western visitor with curious glances and a maddening bureaucracy.

Every visitor to Bulgaria needs a visa, which can be obtained before you leave home from the Bulgarian Embassy in D.C. (tel. 202/387-7969)

or in any European capital city, but it takes 10 days without the $20-to-get-it-now fee.

As a tourist, you'll experience the same frustrations that Bulgarians do as citizens. You'll see firsthand a society that looks East and dreams West. Sofia is the Paris of Eastern Europe. A quiet capital of monuments, huge churches, and wide, yellow-cobbled boulevards, the streets just separate the sidewalks. There aren't many cars.

Sofia is the "big time" in Bulgaria. Notice the fashions, the style of this society's elite; browse through the department stores; sip coffee in the most elegant café you can find. Wander through the university. Listen to the men talking sports in the park and notice gypsies and country people gawking just like you. Under the big red star lies George Dimitrov, the local Lenin, pudgy and waxed under glass and receiving visitors most days.

Plovdiv, Bulgaria's most historic town, is just a two-hour train ride away from Sofia. The stark Stalin Gothic of Sofia takes a back seat to Plovdiv's mellow wooden balconies drooping over coarse cobbled streets. Plovdiv is cozy. Its computerized fountain pulsates to the beat of watered-down pop music as teeny-boppers gather around doing their gangly best to be decadent. The older hip crowd meets on weekend nights at the disco below street level at the Roman stadium in downtown's bustling pedestrian street. The center of town is a walking mall. People browse silently at impossible luxury goods in window displays. Even with the new hope of Glasnost, it's still a sad society of healthy birds with clipped wings.

Take the bus into the hills. Find the farms and villages where those who haven't moved to the city are closer to the earth and the government fades. Restaurants fill with rough-hewn lumberjack types, smoke, and folk music. This bawdy brew is a Brueghel painting come to life. In the countryside, you walk with dancing bears, clap to gypsy bands, and find people more relaxed, open, and easygoing.

For vacation, Bulgarians are dumped into a funnel and land on the Black Sea coast. Each socialist country has its premier resort area, and none can hold a candle to the resorts of the West. As a visitor, you are interested in the country and not its escape. Skip the beach.

Gubrovo is Bulgaria's Knott's Berry Farm, offering the best peek into what's left of the rich local folk culture. Here the folk crafts are honored as endangered species, and the visitor is free to wander, observe, learn, and, of course, buy. (The Plovdiv equivalent is Strumna Street, behind and below the ethnographic museum.)

Every culture has its comic scapegoats. Americans poke fun at Poles and Norwegians at Swedes (and vice versa). Bulgarians joke about stupid, cheapskate Gubrovians who, to save money on sweeps, let a cat down the chimney. ("Where is your wedding ring?" "My wife is wearing it this week.")

Bulgaria is complex and difficult to understand without a local friend. And a local friend is one consumer item that is plentiful in Bulgaria. You are a precious window to the West, and if you're approachable, you'll never be lonely. People will stalk you for hours to establish a friendship. They collect Western comic books and rock albums and listen regularly to the Western radio broadcasts, and the new underground video culture is booming. Bulgarians play the game of freedom in their minds. Many have been to West so many times in their dreams that they talk about it like they once lived there. But they know that— for now—a trip to Paris or London can only be a fantasy.

While Americans would make lousy pawns, it's a valuable experience to spend a few days in a land where there is no alternative. Bulgaria is a battleground of old and new, East and West, full of warm people handling life's dilemmas realistically in a land of denial.

29. Nazi Sights in Europe

Fondue, sangria, Monet, Big Ben . . . gas chambers. A trip to once-upon-a-time Europe can be a fairy tale. It can also give you a glimpse at a nightmare from our recent past—fascism and its remains. While

Memorial at the Dachau concentration camp

few travelers go to Europe in order to dwell on the horrors of Nazism, most understand the value of visiting the memorials of fascism's reign of terror and of honoring the wish of its survivors—"Forgive but never forget."

Considering the devastating impact World War II had on Europe, it's surprising how little is left in the way of memorials. But anyone interested can learn more about the Nazi era and what fascism did to Europe by visiting some of these sights.

Of the countless concentration camps, Dachau, just outside of Munich, is most visited. While many visitors complain that it's too "prettied-up," it does give a powerful look at how these places worked. This first Nazi concentration camp (1933) is the most accessible to travelers and is a very effective voice from our recent but grisly past, warning and pleading "Never Again"—the memorial's theme. On arrival, pick up the miniguide and notice when the next documentary film in English will be shown. The museum, the movie, the chilling camp-inspired art, the reconstructed barracks, the ovens built (but never used) for cremations, and the memorial shrines will chisel into you the meaning of fascism. Dachau is free, open 9:00 a.m. to 5:00 p.m. and closed Mondays.

Auschwitz, or Oswiecim, near Krakow in Poland, and Mäthausen, near Linz on the Danube in Austria, are more powerful and less touristed. Mäthausen town sits cute and prim on the romantic Danube at the start of the very scenic trip downstream to Vienna. But nearby, at a now-still quarry, linger the memories of a horrible slave-labor camp. Less tourist-oriented than Dachau, Mäthausen is a solemn place of meditation and continuous mourning. Fresh flowers adorn yellowed photos of lost loved ones. The home country of each victim has erected a gripping monument, and a visitor finds himself in a gallery of artistic grief, resting on a foundation of never forget. Mäthausen, open daily from 8:00 a.m. to 5:00 p.m., offers an English booklet, a movie, and a powerful museum.

Two moving memorials that fit easily into most itineraries are the Memorial de la Deportation in Paris and Anne Frank's House in Amsterdam. To remember the 200,000 French victims of Hitler's camps, Paris has built a moving memorial on the tip of the Ile de la Cité just behind Notre-Dame. A visit to this memorial is like entering a work of art. As you walk down the claustrophobic stairs into a world of concrete, iron bars, water, and sky and see the 200,000 crystals, one for each lost person, the message of this powerful monument is etched on your mind forever.

Anne Frank's home, made famous by her diary, gives the mind-boggling statistics of fascism the all-important intimacy of a young girl who lived through it and died from it. Even those bah humbug types who are dragged in because it's raining and their partner read the diary find themselves caught up. Before you leave that behind-the-hidden-staircase world, you'll get a look at fascism today in Europe and in the United States. The people of the Anne Frank House make it clear that the only way fascism could ever happen again is if we don't think it could ever happen again.

While Hitler controlled Europe, each country had a courageous if small resistance movement. All over Europe, you'll find streets and squares named after the martyrs of the resistance. Oslo and Copenhagen have Nazi resistance museums. If you're fascinated by modern European history, as I am, you'll find these to be two of Europe's most interesting museums.

Fascist bits and Nazi pieces of Hitler's Germany survive—but only barely. In Berlin, you'll find the Reichstag building, which burned down mysteriously, giving Hitler the excuse every fascist needs to blame the commies and supersede the law; the Great Synagogue (which was burned on Krystalnacht in 1938); the site of Hitler's bunker (where he committed suicide in the last days of the war); and four small "mountains" made of saturation-bombed rubble. While you can sample some fascist architecture at the Haus der Kunst, Munich's modern art museum, the best look at a fascist building is in Rome, where you can wander through Mussolini's futuristic suburb called E.U.R. and the bold pink houses of fascist Italy's Olympic Village.

South of Rome, on the coastal road to Naples, are several towns built in the Mussolini era (such as Latina, Sabaudia, Pontinia, and Aprilia) which are interesting for their stocky colonnades and the well-planned sterility of their piazzas.

In Nuremberg, the ghosts of Hitler's showy propaganda rallies still rustle in the Rally Grounds (now Dutzendteich Park), down the Great Road and through the New Congress Hall. The local tourist office has a handy booklet called "Nuremberg 1933 to 1945."

Berchtesgaden is any German's choice for a great mountain hideaway—including Hitler's. The remains of Hitler's Obersalzburg headquarters with its extensive tunnel system thrill many a World War II buff but are so scanty that most visitors are impressed only by the view.

Knowing you can't take on the world without a great freeway system, Hitler started Germany's autobahn system. While you're zipping through Bavaria, you may pass the first autobahn rest stop right on

Herrenchiemsee between Munich and Salzburg. Now a lakeside hotel for U.S. military personnel, it's still frescoed with "Deutschland über alles" themes. Take the Feldon exit and politely wander around; the dining room has the best art.

After the war, Hitler planned a grand museum of the "decadent" Jewish culture in Prague. Today Prague's State Jewish Museum (Statni Zidovske Muzeum) is a moving look at that city's once thriving Jewish community. The cemetery is an eerie clutter of tombstones. The synagogues are now fascinating historical exhibits including many artifacts the Nazis assembled and a powerful collection of Jewish childrens' art reflecting their experience during the nightmare of the war and the Nazis.

Possibly the most powerful sight of all is the Martyr Ville, Oradour-sur-Glane in central France. This town, 15 miles out of Limoges, was machine-gunned and burned on June 10, 1944. Nazi SS troops, seeking revenge for the killing of one of their officers, left all 642 townspeople dead in a blackened crust of a town under a silent blanket of ashes. Oradour-sur-Glane has been left as an eternal reminder of the reality of war. Like so many other victims of fascism in our century, they beg for the present to learn from our past. When you visit, the only English word you'll run across is on the sign that greets every pilgrim who enters, "Souviens-toi . . . remember."

30. Northern Ireland

Make your visit to Ireland complete by including Northern Ireland. Ulster, as the six counties of Northern Ireland are commonly called, is only a two-hour train ride from Dublin and offers the tourist a very different and still very Irish world.

Most of the tourist industry ignores "wartorn" Northern Ireland. The media blow the trouble out of proportion, leading people to believe that nowhere in Ulster is there peace. That's exciting but false. The British-ruled counties of Northern Ireland are a secret enjoyed and toured mainly by its own inhabitants.

Of course, people are being killed in Northern Ireland—but not as many as in New York City. Car accidents kill more Northern Irishmen than do bombs or guns. If you want trouble, you can find it. But, with common sense, travel in Ulster is safe. You'll see signs of the violence. Armored cars, political graffiti, and bomb-damage clearance sales tell the story of the ongoing troubles. Friends you meet may show you the remains of a bombed-out customs house or the flowers that mark a spot where someone was assassinated. But no tourist has ever been injured by "the troubles." People I've sent to Ulster give it rave reviews.

Here's a three-day plan that will introduce you to a capital city of 400,000 (including the British Army's occupation forces), the best open-air folk museum in Ireland, a once prosperous and now rather sleepy beach resort, and some powerful, if subtle, mountain beauty complete with villages, ancient stone walls, and shepherds. At the same time, you'll get a firsthand look at "the Irish problem"—a tragedy in a potentially happy land. Ulster lacks the dazzle of the Riviera, but it charms more intimately. You'll meet some of the friendliest people on earth and learn firsthand about their struggle.

Pick up the free map of Northern Ireland and Belfast at the Dublin tourist office. Since trains leave from both cities several times a day, you could even make Belfast a day-trip from Dublin. (Northern Ireland is not covered by the Eurailpass. That segment of the journey costs about $10 each way.) Belfast is also a good stopover en route to Scotland, with daily bus/ferry connections to Glasgow.

A strange peace dominates Belfast. Surrounded by police checkpoints, the pedestrians-only "safe zone" in the city center bustles along, oblivious to the problem. Many streets reek of the Industrial Revolution. Buildings most tempting to the IRA are protected by heavy metal screens. Religion is preached on billboards and through bullhorns.

Belfast—barbed wire and national fire

Promises of a better life through Jesus and pacing soldiers add to this strange urban stew. Only the visitor gawks at troops in bulletproof vests. Before leaving the city center, pick up some information and a map at the tourist office on High Street.

Enjoy the walk to Queen's University past the City Hall, with its massive exterior and impressive interior. Near the university, visit the Botanical Gardens and the Ulster Museum. The museum has some interesting traditional Irish and contemporary art and a good exhibition teaching the history of Ulster—the way the North would like you to understand it.

Belfast is really just a busy industrial city (witness the world's largest cranes towering over the harbor). Plan to see Belfast quickly and get out by midafternoon, taking the 20-minute bus ride to Cultra and the Ulster Folk Museum. Buses leave twice an hour from the Oxford Street station near the train station.

The Ulster Folk and Transport Museum at Cultra is the best museum of its kind in Ireland, offering the closest look possible at old and traditional Irish life-styles. Assembled in one huge park (like the open-air

museums so popular in Scandinavia) are cottages and buildings from all over Ireland. Only here can you actually walk into an old schoolhouse, weaver's cottage, farmhouse—in fact, an entire old Irish village—with each structure traditionally furnished and warmed by a turf fire. Buy the guidebook, wander for three hours, and you'll learn a lot about the culture of old Ireland. Any questions your guidebook doesn't answer can be answered by the man who attends each building. He'll talk about leprechauns or simply chat about the weather or sports. The neighboring Transport Museum specializes in turf sleds, horse-drawn carriages, and old cars. When you've finished the museum, catch the same bus you came in on and continue on into the town of Bangor.

Formerly a stylish resort town, Bangor is a pleasant place to spend the evening. Take one of the bed and breakfast places ($15) right on the waterfront on Queen's Parade. My host made certain I knew just where to find the pubs, the dancing, and the outdoor gospel singing. I ended up discussing—and solving—the problems of the world with my new friends until 2:00 that morning. For an especially good look at the Irish, a touch of politics, and a service you can understand, go to church on Sunday morning.

After Bangor, travel south down the Ards Peninsula along the Strangford Lough, a haven for migratory birds. At Portaferry, take the little ferry across the bay and continue south to Castlewellen or Newcastle. You'll pass through Downpatrick, where St. Patrick lies under a large but unimpressive stone.

Now you have reached the mysterious and beautiful Mourne Mountains. Explore the villages and the soft, green rolling "mountains" of 3,000 feet. It's a land rich in folk history and tradition and equally rich in hospitality. Ask questions—the more you know about the Mournes, the more beautiful they become. From Dundalk, a train will zip you back to Dublin.

Now you can send home a postcard announcing that you have toured Northern Ireland, had a blast—and survived.

Front Door Cities, Back Door Angles

31. London: A Warm Look at a Cold City

I've spent more time in London than in any other European city. It lacks the grandeur of Rome, the warmth of Munich, and the elegance of Paris, but it keeps drawing me back. Its history, traditions, markets, people, museums, and entertainment combine to make it the complete city. The thrill just doesn't wear off.

Of course, London is no secret. Everybody knows to see the Halls of Parliament and the Tower of London. But for many travelers, London is their first stop, and it can be brutally overwhelming. Here are a few ideas to soften and warm this hard and cold city. (See the Appendix for budget hotel listings.)

Right off the bat, orient yourself by taking the two-hour Round London Sightseeing Tour—the best possible fast and cheap introduction to London. Buses leave hourly from Piccadilly Circus, Marble Arch, and Victoria Station. Choose the "escorted" tour, which includes a very entertaining commentary. This double-decker bus tour shows you most of the major landmarks and gives you a feel for the city.

On your first evening in London, take yourself on a brief "London-by-night" walking tour. Romantic London is seen at night when the busy twentieth century gives way to quieter streets and floodlit monuments. Walk from Piccadilly Circus to Trafalgar Square and down Whitehall past the Clarence Pub (dip inside for a drink) and the Prime Minister's residence (talk to the bobby on duty) to Westminster. Cross the bridge and turn left to view the floodlit Halls of Parliament and "Ben" from the riverside promenade. There's nothing quite like a golden Big Ben against a black night sky. With a little imagination, London will glow with this same evening charm in the days that follow. The bus tour and this London-by-night walk provide the foundation for a very successful stay in one of the world's most exciting cities. (The walk is also a great way to spend your jet-laggy first evening if you've just flown in.)

To grasp London comfortably, see it as the old town without the modern, congested, and seemingly endless sprawl. After all, most of the visitors' London lies between the Tower of London and Hyde Park—about a three-mile walk.

Another great way to cut London down to size is to nibble at it one bite at a time by taking a series of very focused, two-hour walking tours of the city. For about $4, local historians meet small groups for a good look at one page of the London story (as announced in fliers at the tourist office or in London's periodical entertainment guides). Companies such as Streets of London and London Walks will guide you through the world of London's plague, Dickens's London, Roman Londinium, or Jack the Ripper's London. "Pub Crawl" walks are also very popular.

London is, in many ways, a collection of villages. Even today, many of these corners of the city maintain their individuality. Chelsea is still very colorful. Often compared to Paris' Left Bank, this is London's

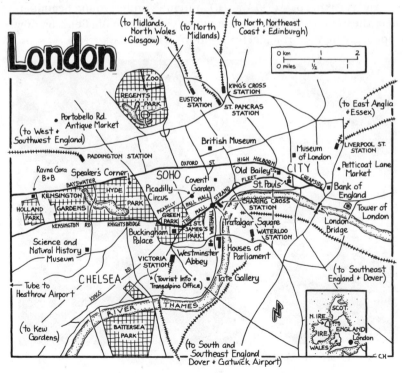

once-Bohemian, now-Yuppie quarter. Soho, which lies north of Pic-cadilly Circus, is a juicy and intoxicating combination of bustle, sleaze, markets, theater, and people—London's Greenwich Village.

The most central square mile of London—and all of Britain—is the "City" of London. This is London's Wall Street. You might want to take advantage of the interesting (and free) tours given at the Stock Exchange. Nearby, if you're interested in the traditional British system of justice, you can visit the Central Criminal Courts, nicknamed Old Bailey. Powdered wigs, black capes, and age-old courtesies, my Lord, make the public trials well worth a visit.

The Tate Gallery, with its wonderful collection of British painters (particularly Blake and Turner) and modern collection including Picasso, Moore, Rodin, van Gogh, and nearly all the major Impres-sionist and twentieth-century painters, is a must. Give yourself an art history lesson by taking one of the free tours available throughout the day.

History buffs shouldn't miss the Museum of London. It offers a well-organized chronological walk through London—from Roman Lon-dinium to World War II.

And speaking of World War II, Churchill's underground headquar-ters, the Cabinet War Rooms (about two blocks from Big Ben), are now open, giving visitors a feel for London's darkest days.

An atmospheric English public house, or "pub"

The British love their gardens, and their favorite is the peaceful and relaxing Kew Gardens. Cruise down the Thames or take the subway to Kew for a respite from the city and a good look at the British people. Don't miss the famous Palm House built of glass and filled with exotic tropical plant life. A walk through this hothouse is a veritable walk through a tropical jungle—in London.

Nearly every morning, there's a market thriving somewhere in London. There are different markets for fish, fruit, antiques, clothing, and plenty of other things. Petticoat Lane (miscellany on Sunday mornings), Portobello Road (antiques on Saturday mornings), and Camden Lock (hip crafts and miscellaneous, Saturday and Sunday 9:00 to 6:00) are just a few of the many colorful markets that offer you just one more of London's many faces (but not much in the way of bargains).

On Sunday morning, I enjoy an hour of craziness at Speaker's Corner in Hyde Park. By noon, there are usually several soapbox speakers, screamers, singers, communists, or comics performing to the crowd of onlookers. The "Round London" bus tour leaves from Speaker's Corner. If you catch it at 10:00 Sunday morning, it will drop you off at 12:00—for the prime-time action. Sundays are otherwise frustrating sightseeing days in London, as nearly all museums are only open from about 2:00 p.m. to 5:00 p.m.

When you are in London (or elsewhere in England), you will have a great opportunity to make your own brass rubbing. The tourist information people can direct you to a "brass rubbing centre" where you can be taught how to make your own rubbing. You can choose from a selection of replica memorial brasses depicting long-dead knights and ladies. You get all the necessary instruction and materials for about four dollars. Just cover the brass with your paper, grab your wax, and rub away. In twenty minutes, you'll have a meaningful souvenir that is suitable for framing. (St. Martin's in the Fields Church on Trafalgar Square has turned its crypt into a fine self-service restaurant with an adjoining brass rubbing center.)

I think one reason I never grow tired of London is its great theater. The London visitor always has a stunning array of first-class plays to choose from. I have seen many memorable performances, including _Harvey_ with Jimmy Stewart, _The King and I_ with Yul Brynner, _My Fair Lady, A Chorus Line, Cats, Starlight Express,_ and _Les Miserables._ You get the quality of Broadway at a fraction of the cost.

Try to buy your tickets several days in advance. Avoid the $2 booking charge by buying your ticket at the theater rather than from a ticket office. This is easy, since most of the theaters are located within a few

A picnic at London's Kew Gardens

blocks of each other in the area between Piccadilly Circus and Trafalgar Square. You are more likely to get the best ticket selection by buying from the theater. I generally order one of the cheaper tickets. Most theaters aren't big enough to have bad seats. Many times I've found that the people just a row or two in front of me paid nearly twice what I did. If you don't like your seat, there are ways to improve your lot. I've been in London theaters that sound like a sifter as soon as the lights go down—the people with the cheaper seats move up, filling the unsold, more expensive seats. If a performance is sold out (and many will be), you can nearly always get a ticket if you try. Ask the ticket salesperson how to get a "no-show" ticket. It will generally involve a wait, but a few tickets are usually left unclaimed just before curtain time. You may also want to ask about the availability of "standing room only" tickets.

A London play will probably cost anywhere from $10 to $50. I've chosen plays carefully, with the help of local recommendations, and have always felt that I got more entertainment than I paid for. On Leicester Square, there's a half-price day-of-show ticket booth that is popular with budget tourists. Selection here is limited, however, and I'd happily avoid it and its savings to enjoy the play of my choice.

The hottest plays in town seem to be bought up by ticket agencies who sell them at inflated prices. Save lots of money and headaches by choosing plays that people would kill to get tickets for—last year.

No visit to London would be complete without spending some time in one of London's colorful and atmospheric pubs. They are an integral part of the English culture. You'll find all kinds of pubs, each one with its own personality. Try the different beers (if you don't know what to order, ask the bartender for a half-pint of his favorite), order some "pub grub," and talk to the people—enjoy a Public House.

32. Bath, England: Elegant and Frivolous

Bath is England's most underrated city. Two hundred years ago, this city of 80,000 was the Hollywood of Britain. Today, the former trendsetter of Georgian England invites you to take the 90-minute train ride from London and immerse yourself in its elegant (and frivolous) past. Enjoy a string trio over tea and scones, discover the antique of your dreams, and trade your jungle of stress for a stroll through the garden.

If ever a city enjoyed looking in the mirror, Bath's the one. It has more government-protected buildings per capita than any town in England. The entire city is built of a warm-tone limestone it calls "Bath stone." The use of normal bricks is forbidden, and Bath beams in its cover-girl complexion.

Bath is an architectural chorus line. It's a triumph of the Georgian style, with its buildings as wrapped up in competitive elegance as the society they housed. If you look carefully, you'll see false windows built in the name of balance and classical columns that supported only Georgian egos. The rich could afford to put feathered hats atop the three-foot hairdos of their women. The very rich stretched their doors and ground floors to accommodate these women. And today, many families are nearly impoverished simply by the cost of peeling the soot of the last century from these tall walls.

Good-looking towns are not rare, but few combine beauty and hospitality as well as Bath. It is a town that makes everything easy. The town square is a quick walk from the bus and train station. This square is a bouquet of tourist landmarks including the Abbey, the Roman and medieval baths, the royal "Pump Room," and a very helpful tourist information office.

A fine way to experience the elegance of Bath is to stay in one of its top B&Bs. My favorite is Brock's Guest House. This $25 per person splurge will be the rubber ducky of your Bath time. Marian Dodd just redid her 1765 home. It's quiet and friendly and couldn't be better located at 32 Brock Street, just between the Royal Crescent and the "Circus," tel. 0225/338374.

A good day in Bath starts with a tour of the historic baths. For 2,000 years, this hot mineral water has attracted society's elite. Then enjoy a high tea with live classical music in the nearby **Pump Room** before catching the 10:30 city walking tour.

Free walking tours leave from the square nearly every morning at 10:30. There are several guides. Some are real characters, so make a quick survey and follow the most animated tour leader. These volunteers are as much a part of Bath as its architecture. A walking tour gives your visit a little more intimacy, and you'll feel like you actually have a local friend.

The afternoon should include a walk through three centuries of fashion in the Costume Museum (closed through 1991). There's an entire room for each decade, enabling you to follow the evolution of clothing styles right up to Twiggy, Charles, Princess Di, and Boy George. The guided tour is excellent—full of fun facts and fascinating trivia. For instance, haven't you always wondered what the line, "Stuck a feather in his cap and called it macaroni" from "Yankee Doodle" means?

You'll find the answer (and a lot more) in Bath—the town whose narcissism is justified.

33. York: Vikings to Dickens

Historians run around York like kids in a candy shop. But the city's sights are so well organized that even those who aren't historians find themselves exploring the past with the same fascination they'd give a hall of fun house mirrors.

Like most British tourist offices, York's takes good care of you. They find rooms, change traveler's checks, and give out road maps and pamphlets on sights, side trips, events, and organized guided walks. (Rooms listed in the Appendix.)

The guided walks, leaving morning, afternoon, and evening, offer a wonderful introduction to the city. To save museum and shopping hours and enjoy a quieter tour, try to take the evening walk. The excellent guides are usually chatty (in a fun way) and very opinionated. By the end of the walk, you'll know the latest York city gossip, which "monstrosity" the "insensitive" city planners are letting be built next, and several ghost stories.

With the introductory tour under your belt and your pockets full of exciting sightseeing brochures, you're getting the hang of York and its history. Just as a Boy Scout counts the rings in a tree, you can count the ages of York by the different bricks in the city wall—Roman on the bot-

Old World main street, York's Castle Museum

tom, then Danish, Norman, and the brand-spanking "new" addition—from the fourteenth century. On Butcher's Street you'll recognize the rusty old hooks hiding under the eaves. Six hundred years ago, bloody hunks of meat hung here dripping into the gutter that still marks the middle of the lane.

If you've read the sightseeing brochures, you know that Henry VIII, in his self-serving religious fervor, destroyed nearly everything that was Catholic—except the great York Minster. It was spared only because Henry needed a grand capital church for North England. And you know why in York a street is called a gate, a gate is a bar, and a bar is a pub. ("Gate" is a Viking word. In Norway today, streets are called _gade_. "Pub" is short for public house. And, well, I remembered two out of three.)

York's three major sights are its huge and historic church, or Minster, the York Castle Museum, and the new Jorvik Viking Museum. The Castle Museum is a walk with Charles Dickens. The England of the eighteenth and nineteenth centuries is cleverly saved and displayed in a huge collection of craft shops, old stores, living rooms, and other intimate glimpses of those bygone days. The shops are actually stocked with the merchandise of the day. For a special angle, tail English grannies as they reminisce their way through the museum's displays.

Walls bridge centuries, and each room gives you an intimate peek into a period. Three centuries of Yorkshire interiors in the Period Rooms paint a cozy picture of life centered around the hearth with a peat fire warming huge brass kettles and the aroma of fresh baked bread soaking into the heavy, open-beamed ceilings. After walking through the evolution of romantic valentines, you can trace the development of farming, milling, and brewing equipment. Early home lighting methods are fascinating, progressing from simple rush lights and candles through crude whale-oil lamps to more modern lamps and into the age of electricity. Imagine—electricity! An early electric heater has a small plaque explaining, "How to light an electric fire—switch it on!"

Musicians enjoy the museum's many historical keyboard, brass, and mechanical instruments. And everyone enjoys the glass harmonica, a group of glass bowls you massage with wet fingers to make an eerie series of notes.

Kirkgate is the museum's most popular exhibit. As towns were being modernized in the 1930s, the museum's founder, Dr. Kirk, collected whole shops intact, all fully stocked, and reassembled them here. You can wander through a Lincolnshire butcher's shop, a Bath bakery, a coppersmith's shop, a toy shop, and a barbershop. I never realized that the barber pole came from the days when a barber was a kind of surgeon. The pole's colors were symbolic of cutting not hair but skin: red for arterial blood, blue for venous blood, and white for the bandage.

The original merchandise captured my attention more than the old buildings. A general store is well stocked with groceries, candy, and haberdashery, and a sports shop has everything you'd need to fit in on a nineteenth-century archery, cricket, skittles, or tennis court. In the confectionery, you'll browse through mouth-watering "spice pigs," "togo bullets," "hum bugs," and "conversation lozenges."

York's violent past is evident as you walk through rooms and rooms of swords, centuries of firearms, and many styles of armor and military uniforms. The costume collection walks you through the closets of the last three centuries, showing each period's clothing styles incorporated into contemporary furniture and room scenes. (This is especially important, now that Bath's collection is closed for several years.)

Children of all ages are endlessly entertained by the toy collection. Dolls of the past come with porcelain heads, real hair, and fine miniature clothing. You can hear the earliest talking baby squeak "Mama." Early games are on display, including a Ping Pong set called "whiff-waff." Primitive steam and gas-driven cars are permanently parked near ancient gravity-fed petrol pumps and an early garage.

The York Castle Museum is the closest thing in Europe to a time tunnel experience, except, perhaps, for the Jorvik Viking Exhibit just down the street.

A thousand years ago, York was a thriving Viking settlement called Jorvik. While only traces are left of most thousand-year-old Viking settlements, Jorvik is an archaeologist's bonanza, the best-preserved Viking city ever excavated.

The exhibit combines the Pirates of the Caribbean cleverness of a Disney ride with the abundant harvest of this dig. First, you travel back 1,000 years in time. Rolling backward in a little train car for two, you descend past the ghosts and cobwebs of 50 generations. Cromwell . . . Shakespeare . . . Anne Boleyn . . .the mob passes and your car flips around. It's the year 990. You're in Jorvik.

Slowly you glide through the reconstructed village. Everything—sights, sounds, even smells—have been carefully re-created. You experience as closely as possible a Viking village.

Then you pass into the actual excavation site, and your time-traveling train car rolls you past the actual remains of what you just saw reconstructed. The stubs of buildings, the piles of charred wood, the broken pottery—a rotten and time-crushed echo of a thriving town.

Finally, the ride is over and you come to the museum. Glass cases display and clearly explain artifacts from every aspect of Viking life—clothing, cooking, weapons, clever locks, jewelry, even children's games.

The gift shop—the traditional final stage of English museums—capitalized nicely on my newly developed fascination with Vikings in England.

34. Lisbon

Lisbon is a wonderful mix of now and then. Old wooden trollies shiver up and down its hills, bird-stained statues mark grand squares, and people sip coffee in art nouveau cafés.

Present-day Lisbon is explained by its past. Her glory days were the fifteenth and sixteenth centuries, when explorers like Vasco da Gama opened up new trade routes, making Lisbon Europe's richest city. Later, the riches of Brazil boosted Lisbon even higher. Then, in 1755, an earthquake leveled the city, killing over 20 percent of its people.

Lisbon was rebuilt on a strict grid plan, symmetrical, with broad boulevards and square squares. The grandeur of pre-earthquake Lisbon survives only in Belem, the Alfama, and in the Bairro Alto districts.

While the earthquake flattened a lot of buildings, and its colonial empire is long gone, Lisbon's heritage is alive and well. Barely elegant outdoor cafés, exciting art, entertaining museums, the saltiest sailors' quarter in Europe and much more, all at bargain basement prices, make Lisbon an Iberian highlight. (Recommended places to stay listed in the Appendix.)

Follow me through a day in Lisbon.

After breakfast, taxi to the Alfama, the city's colorful sailors' quarter. This was the Visigothic birthplace of Lisbon, a rich district during the Arabic period and now the salty home of Lisbon's fisherfolk. One of the few areas to survive the 1755 earthquake, the Alfama is a cobbled cornucopia of Old World color. Visit during the busy midmorning market time or in the late afternoon/early evening when the streets teem with the local people.

Wander deep. This urban jungle's roads are squeezed into tangled stairways and confused alleys; bent houses comfort each other in their romantic shabbiness, and the air drips with laundry and the smell of clams and raw fish. Get lost. Poke aimlessly, sample ample grapes, avoid rabid-looking dogs, peek through windows. Make a friend, pet a chicken, read the graffiti, study the humanity ground between the cobbles. Taste the blanco seco—the local dry wine.

Gradually, work your way up the castle-crowned hill until you reach a little green square called Maradouro de Santa Luzia. Rest here and enjoy the lovely view of the Alfama below you. By now it's noon, and you should be quite hungry (unless you took more than pictures in the

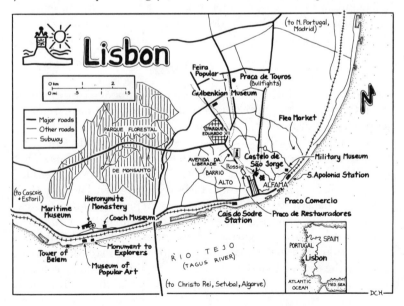

Fish market in Lisbon's Alfama

Alfama market). Across the street from Maradouro de Santa Luzia is Restaurante Farol de Santa Luzia, a busy little working-class restaurant full of babble and hungry Portuguese. Treat yourself to a huge plate of boiled clams and cockles (the house specialty).

If you climb a few more blocks to the top of the hill, you'll find the ruins of Castelo São Jorge. From this fortress, which has dominated the city for almost fifteen hundred years, you enjoy a commanding view of Portugal's capital city. For the second half of your day, grab a taxi to Torre de Belem (the Belem Tower). The Belem District, 4 miles from downtown (take trams #15, #16, or #17), is a pincushion of important sights from Portugal's Golden Age, when Vasco da Gama and company made her Europe's richest power.

The Belem Tower, Portugal's only purely Manueline-style building (the ornate Portuguese Renaissance style, built 1515, bleak interior), once protected Lisbon's harbor and today symbolizes the voyages that made her powerful. This was the last sight sailors saw as they left and the first one they'd see when they returned loaded down with gold, diamonds, and venereal diseases.

Nearby, the giant Monument to the Discoveries honors Henry the Navigator and Portugal's leading explorers. Across the street, the Monastery of Jeronimos is Portugal's most exciting building—my favorite cloisters in Europe. This giant church and cloisters are a great example of how the Manueline style combines Gothic and Renaissance features with motifs from the sea—the source of the wealth that made this art possible.

The Portuguese bullfight is a brutal affair that many enjoy because they don't kill the bull. The fight starts with an equestrian duel—fast bull against graceful horse and rider. Then the fun starts. A colorfully clad eight-man team enters the ring stringing out in a line as if to play leapfrog. The leader yells at El Toro and, with adrenalin sloshing everywhere, they charge each other. The speeding bull plows into the leader head on (the horns are wrapped so he doesn't get gored—just mashed) and—thud, thud, thud—he picks up the entire charging crew, like a hydroplane bouncing over waves.

The crew wrestles the bull, who by this time must be wondering where these lemming idiots came from, to a standstill, and one man grabs the tail. Victory is theirs when they leap off the bull and the human, still hanging onto the tail, kind of water skis behind the bull. This thrilling display of insanity is repeated with six bulls. After each round, the bruised and battered head man limps a victory lap around the ring. Portugal's top bullring is in Lisbon, and there are fights a couple of days a week throughout the summer.

These are the usual sights; cultural can-cans you can find in any guidebook. But with some imagination, your sightseeing can also include Portugal in action—live, if not on stage.

Go into a bar as if your poetry teacher sent you there on assignment. Observe, write, talk, try to understand and appreciate; send your senses on a scavenger hunt. The eating, drinking, and socializing rituals are fascinating.

My favorite Lisbon evening was at the Feira Popular. This Popular Fair rages nightly until 1:00 a.m. from May through September. Located on Ave. da Republica at the Entrecampos metro stop, it bustles with Portuguese families at play. I ate dinner surrounded by chattering

Portuguese families ignoring the ever-present TVs while great plates of fish, meat, fries, salad, and lots of wine paraded frantically in every direction. A seven-year-old boy stood on a chair and sang hauntingly emotional folk songs. With his own dogged clapping, he dragged an applause out of the less-than-interested crowd and then passed his own shabby hat. All the while, fried ducks drip, barbecues spit, and dogs squirt the legs of chairs while somehow local lovers ignore everything but each other's eyes.

35. Oslo

On May 17, Norway's national holiday, Oslo is bursting with flags, bands, parades, and blond toddlers dressed up in colorful traditional ribbons, pewter, and wool. But Oslo has plenty to offer the visitor even without its annual patriotic bash. Oslo is fresh, not too big, surrounded by forests, near mountains, and on a fjord. And Oslo's charm doesn't stop there. Norway's largest city, capital, and cultural hub is a smorgasbord of history, sights, art, and Nordic fun.

An exciting cluster of sights is just a 10-minute ferry ride from the city hall. The Bygdoy area reflects the Norwegian mastery of the sea. Some of Scandinavia's best-preserved Viking ships are on display here. Rape, pillage, and—ya sure ya betcha—plunder was the rage 1,000 years ago in Norway. There was a time when much of a frightened Western Europe closed every prayer with, "And deliver us from the Vikings, amen." Gazing up at the prow of one of those sleek time-stained vessels, you can almost hear the shrieks and smell the armpits of those redheads on the rampage.

Nearby, Thor Heyerdahl's balsa raft, the _Kon-Tiki_, and the polar ship _Fram_ exhibit Viking energy channeled in more productive directions. The _Fram_, serving both Nansen and Amundsen, ventured farther north and south than any other ship.

Just a harpoon toss away is Olso's open-air folk museum. The Scandinavians were leaders in the development of these cultural parks that are so popular around Europe now. One hundred fifty historic log cabins and buildings from every corner of the country are gathered together in this huge folk museum. Inside each house, a person in local dress is happy to answer questions about traditional life in that part of Norway. Don't miss the 1,100-year-old wooden stave church.

Oslo's avant-garde city hall, built 35 years ago, was a collective effort of Norway's greatest artists and designers. Tour the interior. Over 2,000 square yards of bold, colorful murals are a journey through the collective mind of modern Norway.

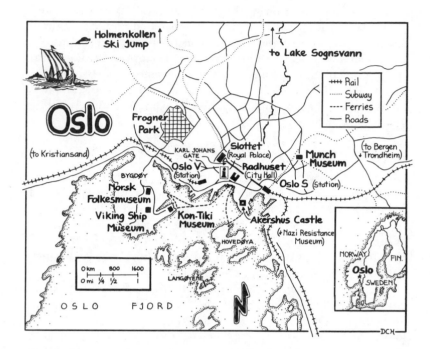

Norway has given the world two great modern artists, Edvard Münch and Gustav Vigeland. After visiting Oslo, many tourists become Vigeland fans—or even "Münchies." Frogner Park, behind the royal palace, features 150 bronze and granite sculpture groups representing 30 years of Vigeland creativity. The centerpiece of this Nordic sculpture garden is the impressive 60-foot tall totem pole of bodies known as the "Monolith of Life." This, along with the neighboring Vigeland Museum, is a must on any list of Oslo sights.

Oslo's Münch Museum is a joy. It's small, displaying an impressive collection of one man's work rather than stoning your powers of absorption with art by countless artists from countless periods. You leave the Münch Museum with a smile, feeling like you've really learned something about one artist, his culture, and his particular artistic "ism"—Expressionism. Don't miss *The Scream*, which captures the fright many feel as our human "race" does just that.

You can explore 700 years of local history in Oslo's Akershus Castle. The castle houses a fascinating Nazi resistance museum. The "Freedom Museum" shows how one country's spirit cannot be crushed, regardless of how thoroughly it's occupied by a foreign power.

Oslo has been called Europe's most expensive city. I'll buy that. Life on a budget is possible only if you have plenty of information and take advantage of money-saving options that are available. Remember: budget tricks like picnicking and sleeping in dormitory-type accommodations offer the most exciting savings in the most expensive cities—like Oslo.

Oslo is very expensive, but you're not getting less for your dollar. In Oslo you have no choice but to buy rooms that are efficient, clean, and pleasant. It's a kind of forced luxury. Know your budget alternatives, bring a little extra money, and enjoy it.

Language problems are few. The Norwegians speak better English than any people on the Continent. My cousin attends the University of Oslo. In her language studies, she had to stipulate English or American. She learned American—and knows more slang than I do.

Vigeland's Monolith of Life, Frogner Park

One Day for the Fjords?

If you go to Oslo and don't get out to the fjords, you should have your passport revoked. Take the "Norway in a Nutshell" day trip from Oslo. Every morning, northern Europe's most spectacular train ride leaves Oslo for Bergen. Cameras smoke as this super-scenic transport roars over Norway's mountainous spine. At Myrdal, a little 12-mile spur line drops you 2,800 thrilling feet to the little town of Flam for Norway's ultimate natural thrill, Sognefjord. The best of the fjord is yours as the post boat takes you up one narrow arm and down the next to the town of Gudvangen, where buses shuttle you back to the main train line at Voss.

From there, return to Oslo or carry on into Bergen for the evening (doubling back to Oslo, if necessary, on the night train). The whole trip is a snap; just follow the tourist office's brochure or my *22 Days in Norway, Sweden, and Denmark.*

36. Stalking Stockholm

If I had to call one European city "home," it would be Stockholm. Green, clean, efficient, and surrounded by as much water as land, Sweden's capital is underrated by most tourists, landing just above Bordeaux, Brussels, and Bucharest on their checklists.

While progressive and frighteningly futuristic, Stockholm respects its heritage. Daily mounted bands parade through the heart of town to the royal palace, announcing the changing of the guard and turning even the most dignified tourist into a scampering kid. The Gamla Stan (Old Town) celebrates the Midsummer Festivities (June 21, 22) with the down-home vigor of a rural village, forgetting that it's the core of a gleaming twentieth-century metropolis.

Stockholm is a place to "do" as well as see. The culture and vitality of Sweden is best felt at Skansen. An island park of traditional and historic houses, schools, and churches transplanted from every corner of the country, Skansen entertains with live folk music, dancing, pop concerts, a zoo, restaurants, peasant-craft workshops, and endless amusements. It's a smorgasbord of culture enjoyed by tourists and locals alike.

Nearby is the *Wasa*, the royal flagship that sank 10 minutes into her maiden voyage 350 years ago. While not a good example of Viking seaworthiness, the *Wasa* is incredibly intact in her super-humidified display house and is a highlight on any sailor's itinerary.

The Carl Milles Garten is a striking display of Sweden's favorite sculptor's work. Strong, pure, expressive, and Nordic, Milles' individual style takes even the most uninterested by surprise. Hanging on a cliff overlooking the city, this sculpture park is perfect for a picnic.

A sauna, Sweden's answer to support hose and a face-lift, is as important as a smorgasbord in your Swedish experience. "Simmer down" with the local students, retired folks, and busy executives. Try to cook as calmly as the Swedes. Just before bursting, go into the shower room. There's no "luke cold" and the trickle-down theory doesn't apply—

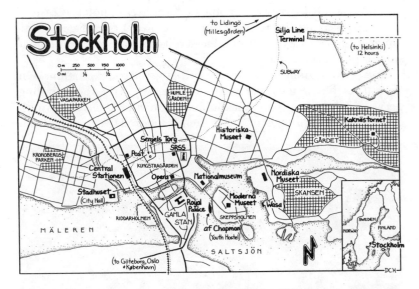

only one button bringing a Niagara of liquid ice. Suddenly your shower stall becomes the Cape Canaveral launch pad, and your body scatters to every corner of the universe. A moment later you're back together, rejoining the Swedes in the cooker, this time with their relaxed confidence and a small but knowing smile. You now know that exhilaration is just around the corner. Only rarely will you feel so good.

Consider a few side trips from Stockholm. Several interesting planned futuristic suburbs are just a subway ride away. (The TI has information.) You'll surface in the hub of a human jukebox. Apartment complexes circle you in careful formation. Department stores, parks, transportation facilities, and schools are conveniently placed, and all the people know just where to go. It makes you wonder whether such scientific packaging is the only answer as our continually more advanced society deals with ever-larger crowds.

While most visitors make side trips to the too cute town of Sigtuna, a quick visit to Helsinki is more exciting. Finland's capital, just an overnight boat ride away, is Scandinavian only by geography. Its language is completely unrelated, and culturally, there's nothing "ya sure ya betcha" about Finland. Getting to Helsinki is a joy. The daily or nightly ships (as little as $110 round-trip with smorgasbord breakfast, dinner, and a stateroom bed each way or free with a Eurailpass) feature lavish smorgasbords, dancing, and the most enchanting island scenery in Europe.

Stockholm is notoriously expensive. But with a few tips, you can manage fine on a budget. When traveling by train, try to arrive in the morning, when setting up in budget alternatives to hotels is easiest. That means taking the overnight run from Oslo or Copenhagen. (Scandinavia, always thinking ahead, located its capitals very convenient 10-hour train rides apart.)

Survey your guidebook's listing of budget accommodations. On arrival, telephone the hotel of your choice (or use the room-finding service in the station). In Stockholm, I phone the *Af Chapman* youth hostel, a classic "cutter ship" permanently moored five minutes from

Stockholm's floating youth hostel, the Af Chapman

downtown. The *Af Chapman*, with $8 bunks, is one of Europe's most popular hostels. It holds 30 beds every morning for drop-ins, and these are usually taken by midmorning.

Don't leave the Stockholm station without feasting at the ritzy Centralens Restaurant, which serves an eternal smorgasbord every morning for the price of an open-face sandwich and a cup of coffee anywhere else in town.

After this culinary smorgasm, waddle over to Europe's most energetic tourist information office, The Sweden House (Sverigehuset). Besides all the normal tourist help, this organization will do everything short of whipping you with birch twigs in the sauna. They have a "Meet the Swedes at Home" program, an English library and reading room, free pamphlets in English on any aspect of the Swedish culture you could want to study, daily walking tours through the old town, and more. Pick up the usual lists of sights and maps as well as the handy _This Week in Stockholm,_ a periodical entertainment guide in English. The Sweden House, in Kings Garden a few blocks from the station, is open daily in the summer from 9:00 a.m. to 9:00 p.m.

Finally, take advantage of tourist transportation passes. Stockholm's three-day pass gives you free run of its excellent bus and subway system as well as unlimited entrance to Skansen.

Beyond Europe: Maximum Thrills Per Mile, Minute, and Dollar

37. Morocco: Plunge Deep

Walking through the various souks of the labyrinthine medina, I found sights you could only dream of in America. Dodging blind men and clubfeet, I was blasted with a collage of smells, sounds, sights, and feelings. People came in all colors, sizes, temperaments, and varieties of deformities. Milky eyes, beggars, stumps of limbs, sticks of children, tattooed women, weather-aged old men with a twinkle behind their bristly cheeks, grabbing salesmen, inviting craftsmen, enticing scents, half-bald dogs, and little boys on rooftops were reaching out from all directions.

Ooo! Morocco! Slices of Morocco make the *Star Wars* bar scene look bland. And it's just a quick cruise from Spain. You can't, however, experience Morocco in a day trip from the Costa del Sol. Plunge deep and your journal will read like a Dali painting.

While Morocco is not easy traveling, it gets rave reviews from those who plug this Islamic detour into their European vacation.

Skip Tangiers and Tetuan, the Moroccan Tijuanas of the north coast. Tangiers is not really Morocco; it's a city full of con men who thrive on green tourists. Take the boat from Algeciras or the much more pleasant town of Tarifa in Spain to Tangiers, where you'll find the quickest connections south to Rabat. (Ticket prices have skyrocketed to around $40 for the short crossing.) Power your way off the boat, then shove through the shysters to the nearby train station. They'll tell you there's no train until tomorrow, or "Rabat is closed on Thursdays," anything to get you to stay in Tangiers. Believe nothing. Be rude if you have to. Tangiers can give you only grief, while the real Morocco lies to the south. Try to make friends with a Moroccan traveler on the boat, who won't be a con man and who'll usually be happy to help you slip through his embarrassingly stressful port of entry.

Rabat, Morocco's capital, is a good first stop. This most comfortable European city in Morocco lacks the high-pressure tourism of the towns on the north coast. Stay at the Hotel Splendid near the medina and the station, 2 rue du XVIII Juin, tel. 232-83. It's a favorite of Peace Corps workers. (Or, for a pleasant break on the beach and a relaxing way to break into Morocco, spend a day at Asilah, just far enough south of Tangiers.)

Taxis are cheap and a real bargain when you consider the comfort, speed, and convenience they provide in these hot, dusty, and confusing cities. Eat and drink carefully in Morocco. Bottled water and bottled soft drinks are safe. For safety, you might have "well-cooked" written in Arabic on a scrap of paper and order meat cooked that way. I found the couscous disappointing but the tajine and omelets uniformly good. The Arabs use different number symbols. Learn them. Morocco was a French colony, so French is more widely understood than English. A French phrase book is handy. Travel very light in Morocco. You can leave most of your luggage at your last Spanish hotel for free if you plan to spend a night there on your return from Africa.

After Rabat, pass through Casablanca (great movie, dull city) and catch the Marrakesh Express south. You'll hang your head out the window of that romantic old train and sing to the passing desert.

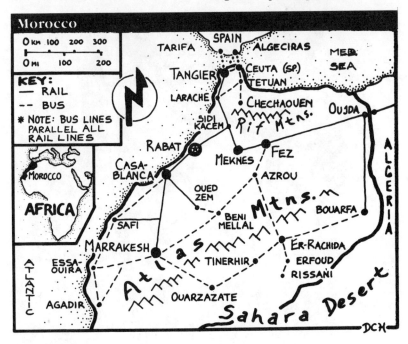

Marrakesh is the epitome of exotic. Take a horse-drawn carriage from the station to downtown where you can find a hotel near the Djemaa el Fna, the central square of Marrakesh, where the action is. Desert musicians, magicians, storytellers, acrobats, snake charmers, gamblers, and tricksters all perform, gathering crowds of tribespeople who have come to Marrakesh to do their market chores. As a tourist, you'll fit in like a clown at a funeral. Be very careful, don't gamble, and hang onto your wallet. You are not clever here. This is a trip into another world—complete with pitfalls. You can spend an entire day in the colorful medina, or marketplace. Wander aimlessly from souk to souk (there's a "souk" for each area of trade, such as the dyers' souk, the leather souk, and the carpet souk).

In the medina, you'll be badgered—or "guided"—by small boys who claim to be "a friend who wants to practice his English." They are after money, nothing else. Make two things crystal clear: you have no money for them and you want no guide. Then completely ignore them.

Remember that while you're with them, these boys get commissions for anything you buy. Throughout Morocco, you'll be pestered by these obnoxious hustler-guides.

I often hire a young and easy-to-control boy who speaks enough English to serve as my interpreter, mainly because it seems that if a tourist is "taken," the other guides leave you alone, and that in itself is worth the small price of a guide.

The market is a shopper's delight. Bargain hard, shop around, and you'll come home with some great souvenirs. Government emporiums usually have the same items you find in the market, priced fairly. If you get sick of souks, shop there and you'll get the same price—haggle-free.

From Marrakesh, consider an exciting seven-day loop to the south and ultimately to Fez. While buses are reliable and efficient throughout Morocco, this tour is best by car, and it's easy to rent a car in Marrakesh to be dropped in Fez. Do some comparative shopping.

Drive or catch the bus south, over the rugged Atlas Mountains, to a region that no longer faces the Mediterranean. This is Saharan Morocco. Explore the isolated oasis towns of Ouarzazate, Tinerhir, and Er-Rachidia. If time permits, the trip from Ouarzazate to Zagora is an exotic mud-brick pie. These towns each have a weekly "market day" when the tribespeople gather to do their shopping. Unless you enjoy goats' heads and honeydew melons, there isn't much more than pictures that a tourist would want to take. Stay in Tinerhir's Hotel du Todra and climb to the roof for a great view of the busy marketplace below.

Venture out of town into the lush fields where you'll tumble into an almost Biblical world. Sit on a rock. Dissect the silence. A bearded old man in a white robe and turban might clip-clop slowly past you. He seems to be growing side-saddle out of his weary donkey and his eyes are as wide as yours. Suddenly, six Botticelli maidens flit like watercolor confetti across your trail and giggle out of sight. Stay tuned. The show goes on.

Bus rides in this part of Morocco are intriguing. I could write for pages about experiences I've had on Moroccan buses—good and bad—but I don't want to spoil the surprise. Just ride them with a spirit of adventure—and with your fingers crossed.

Saharan Adventure

From Er-Rachidia, a long day's drive south of Fez, a series of mud-brick villages bunny hop down a lush river valley and into the Sahara. Finally, the road melts into the sand and the next stop is, literally, Timbuktu.

The strangeness of this Alice in a sandy Wonderland world, untempered, can be overwhelming—even frightening. The finest hotel in Erfoud, the region's major town, will provide a much-needed refuge, keeping the sand, heat waves, and street kids out and providing safe-to-eat and tasty local food, reliable information on the region, and a good bed ($25 doubles).

But the hotel is only your canteen and springboard. Explore! An overabundance of persistent local "wanna-be guides" may cause you to lock your car doors. Choose one you can understand and tolerate, set a price for his services, and, before dawn, head for the dunes.

You'll drive to the last town, Rissani (market days: Tuesday, Thursday, Sunday), and then farther south over 15 miles of natural asphalt to the oasis village of Merzouga. There's plenty of tourist traffic at sunrise and in the early evening, so hitching is fairly easy. A couple of places in Merzouga rent spots on their terrace for those who spend the night. Since a civil war is smoldering in the desert, you may have to show your passport.

Before you glows a chain of sand dune mountains. Climb one. It's not easy. I seemed to slide farther backward with each step. Hike along a cool and crusty ridge, observe bugs and their tracks, and watch small sand avalanches you started all by yourself. From the great virgin summit, savor the Sahara view orchestrated by a powerful silence. Your life sticks out like a lone star in a black sky. Tumble, roll, and slosh down your dune. Look back and see the temporary damage one person can inflict on that formerly perfect slope. Then get back in your car before the summer sun turns the sand into a steaming griddle. Off-season, however, the midday desert sun is surprisingly mild.

Merzouga is full of people, very poor people. The village children hang out at the ruins of some old palace. A ragtag percussion group gave us an impromptu concert. The children gathered around us tighter and tighter as the musicians picked up the tempo. The smiles, the warmth, and the sadness mixed very intimately. A little Moroccan Judy Garland saw out of one eye; the other was as cloudy as rice pudding. One gleaming six-year-old had a tiny brother slung, sleeping, on her back. His crusty little face was covered with flies, but he didn't even flinch. We had a bag of candy to share and tried to get 40 kids into an orderly line to march by one by one. Impossible. The line degenerated into a free-for-all and our bag became a piñata.

Only through the mercy of your guide can you find your way back to Rissani. Camels loiter nonchalantly—looking very lost and not caring. Cool lakes flirt from the distance—a mirage—and the black hardpan road stretches endlessly in all directions. Then with a sigh we were back in Rissani, where the road starts up again. For us, it was breakfast time, and Rissani offered little more than some very thought-provoking irony. My friends and I could find no "acceptable" place to eat. Awkwardly, we drank germ-free Cokes with pursed lips, balanced bread on upturned bottle caps, and swatted legions of flies. Funny: we were by far the wealthiest people in the valley—and the only ones unable to enjoy an abundant variety of good but strange food.

From our seats, we saw a busy girl rhythmically smashing date seeds, three stoic, robed elders with horseshoe beards, and a prophet wandering through with a message for all that he was telling to nobody.

Back at the hotel, we shared the Walkman and went for a swim, resting and recharging before our next Saharan plunge.

Saharan Nightlife

Desert dwellers and smart tourists know the value of a siesta during the hottest part of the day. But a Saharan evening is the perfect time for a traveler to get out and experience the vibrancy of African village life. We drove 10 miles north of Erfoud to a fortified mud brick oasis village. There was no paint, no electricity, no cars—only people, mud brick, and palm trees. Absolutely nothing other than the nearby two-lane highway hinted of the twentieth century.

We entered like Lewis and Clark without Sacajawea, knowing instantly we were in for a rich experience. A wedding feast was erupting. The whole town buzzed with excitement. Everyone was decked out in colorful robes and shiny smiles. We felt very welcome.

The teeming street emptied through the medieval gate and onto the field, where a band was playing squawky oboelike instruments and drums. A large circle of ornately dressed women made high siren noises with tongues flapping like party favors. Rising dust diffused the lantern light, giving everything the feel of an old photo, and the darkness focused our attention on a relay of seductively beautiful snake-thin dancers. A flirtatious atmosphere raged, cloaked safely in the impossibility of anything transpiring beyond coy smiles and teasing twists.

Then the village's leading family summoned us for dinner. Pillows, blankets, a lantern, and a large round filigreed table turned a stone cave into a warm lounge. The men of this family had traveled to Europe and spoke some English. For over two hours, the women prepared dinner and the men entertained. First the ritualistic tea ceremony. Like a mad chemist, the tea specialist mixed it just right. With a thirsty gleam in his eye and a large spike in his hand, he hacked off a chunk of sugar from their coffee can-sized master lump and watched it melt into

Morocco's basic beverage. He tested it like a fine wine, added more sugar, and let me test it. When no more sugar could be absorbed, we drank it with cookies and dates. The sweeter the better. Then the hashish pipe came out and was passed around with all the fanfare of a pack of Juicy Fruit. Our shocked look was curious to them. Next, a tape deck brought a tinny clutter of music, from Arab and tribal Berber music to James Brown, reggae, and twangy Moroccan pop. The men danced— splendidly.

Finally, the meal came. Fourteen people sat on the floor circling the round tables. Nearby, a child silently waved a palm branch fly fan. A portable wash basin and towel were passed around to start and finish the meal. With our fingers and gravy-soaked slabs of bread, we grabbed spicy meat and vegetables. Everyone dipped eagerly into the delicious central bowl of couscous.

So far, the Moroccan men dominated. Young girls took turns peeking around the corner and dashing off—much like teeny-boppers anywhere. Two older women in striking black-jeweled outfits were squatting attentively in the corner, keeping their distance and a very low profile. Then one pointed to me and motioned in charades, indicating long hair and a backpack. She held up two fingers and hand-signaled a small person. I had been in this same village in the '70s. I had longer hair and a backpack and was traveling with a very short partner. Could

Moroccan road sign: Beware of toboggans

she remember us? I scribbled "1978" on a scrap of paper. She scratched it out and wrote "1979." Wow! She remembered my 20-minute visit so long ago! I can only conclude that people in remote lands enjoy a visiting tourist and find the occasion at least as memorable as we do. So many more doors open to the traveler who takes along that assumption.

After a proud tour of their schoolhouse, we were escorted across the field back to our car, which had been guarded by a silent, white-robed man. We drove away, reeling with the feeling that the memories of this evening would be our most precious souvenir.

And Back to Europe

From Er-Rachidia, the gateway to this wondrous desert valley, return to our world by catching the bus over the Atlas Mountains to Fez or Meknes. Fez, along with Marrakesh, is a must. Both of these towns give you royal and big-city Morocco at its best.

From Fez, you can catch the air-conditioned train back to Tangiers. If you bought a round-trip boat ticket from Spain, you can just walk onto the boat. Without a ticket, you'll have to buy one at the Tangiers ticket office—no easy matter. If they will only sell you a ticket for a later boat (to prolong your stay in lovely Tangiers), you'll have to buy it. Try using that ticket for the next boat out. It will probably get you on.

After your trip, you'll always remember that swing through Morocco as the adventure that bumped the rest of your world a couple of rungs up the ladder of normalcy.

38. The Best Way from Athens to Turkey

Turkey is the last frontier of European tourism. It's a rich land. I need a slice of Turkey in each trip—but not too much of it. Like Thanksgiving leftovers, a week or so is just about right.

The best thing about Athens is the boat to Turkey. While so many people get as far east as Athens, few realize how accessible and exciting Turkey is. Those fresh back from both say Turkey has friendlier people, cheaper prices, and better food. I never visit the Greek Islands without a visit to Turkey's west coast. If you're looking for cultural thrills, remember, you travel farther culturally by taking the two-hour cruise from the Greek Isles to Turkey than you do by flying all the way from the United States to Greece.

The best way to get to Turkey from Athens is to sail. Athens is one of Europe's most notorious tourist traps; it's very crowded. See what's important (Acropolis, Agora, Plaka, and National Museum)—and leave! Catch a boat ($15, twelve hours) or plane ($50, one hour) to Samos, Rhodes, or Kos. Each of these islands is connected daily by boat ($20, two hours, must leave passport with agency for about 12 hours) to Turkey.

From any city on Turkey's historic west coast, modern buses can take you anywhere in Turkey (including Istanbul, where trains leave daily for Germany and Western Europe).

An interesting way to get to Turkey is from the visit-worthy island of Rhodes. The city of Rhodes, built by the Crusaders 1,000 years ago, is a trip back into medieval Europe. From Rhodes, you take a small Turkish boat to the enjoyable resort town of Marmaris on the southwest tip of Turkey.

Or catch a boat to the island of Samos. The 13-hour boat from Athens arrives in the morning. You can buy a sleeping berth or go deck class and sleep free under the stars or inside. Be quick to stake out a couch to sleep on. A deck-class ticket will cost about $15. Food on board is decent, or you can pack a picnic for the ride (Piraeus, Athens' port town, has a good market near the harbor).

Samos (180 square miles, 60,000 people) is my favorite Greek island: green, mountainous, diverse, and friendly. It's crowded with tourists but not as bad as other Greek islands. Bus transportation on the island is fine. Samos town (and its uphill sister, Vathi, a charming collection of narrow, winding lanes creeping up the hillside) is a fine home base. Vathi's many too-narrow-for-cars streets preserve the quiet Greek atmosphere. Learn to play backgammon with the locals—they'll love you for it.

Rent a motorbike ($10) to explore the island of Aesop. You can see the meager remains of the desolate and once mighty Temple of Hera; Pythagorian, the hometown of Pythagoras; untouched mountain towns like Pandhrosen; and forgotten old monasteries. Wild fig trees beg to be tasted, and old Greeks lead grape-laden donkeys down empty country roads. Samos has plenty of good beaches and local restaurants to enjoy as well.

This is the end of Greece; the brown mountains of Turkey dare you to cross the narrow channel, to trade the grapes of Samos for the more exotic fruits of Turkey.

Turkey is enjoyable, because it's different enough to be exciting and interesting but not so different that it's uncomfortable or stressful. The people, while most wear a Western facade in clothes, are definitely Eastern in mind. I don't know if they're bored or happy or apathetic or what, but the entire country—at least the male population, which is what the traveler sees—is "into" certain things like worry beads, drinking tea, spending a great part of their lives playing cards, dominos, or backgammon, smoking, being about two days unshaven, and keeping pictures of Ataturk on their walls.

Not only is the Turkish culture more exotic than any European culture but it's also very cheap—much cheaper than Greece. Turkey offers some of the finest classical ruins anywhere, and while it's rapidly becoming a German vacation zone, it's not overrun by tourists like the more famous corners of Greece.

Turkey has an image problem. Many Americans know Turkey only from the thrilling but unrealistic movie _Midnight Express._ The movie was paid for, produced, and acted by Armenians and Greeks (historically unfriendly neighbors). While it gives a fine impression of the Greek and Armenian bogeyman image of Turks, it says absolutely nothing about the Turks or Turkey today. Also, many visitors are put off by Turkey's "rifles on every corner" image. Turkey is not a police state.

Its NATO commitment is to maintain nearly a million-man army. Except in the far east, where they are dealing with the Kurds, these soldiers have nothing to do but "patrol" and "guard"—basically loiter, in uniform.

Unfortunately, most Turks look like someone you'd run away from on the streets of Paris. While Turks may look scary to many Americans, it's important that you step above this cultural prejudice and see Turks as the sincere and friendly people that they are. Even perfect strangers tell you, "Love is blind, but never mind."

Greek and Turkish travel agencies are more reliable and helpful than they look.

While Turkey shares its border with Iran, Syria, the USSR, and Bulgaria—nobody's idea of a fun neighborhood—its most troublesome relationship is with the Greeks. Greeks and Turks mix like Christians and Muslims. Border crossings are more difficult and expensive than they have to be. The Greek government levies a heavy tax on each Greek-island-to-mainland-Turkey ticket sold to discourage this easy exit from their country. They'd rather the tourist backtrack through Athens, contributing still more money to the industry that is Greece's No. 1 source of foreign revenue—tourism.

There's a daily boat from Samos to Kusadasi in Turkey. The two-hour ride costs around $20, which, while unfair, is still worth it. You'll land very close to what, in my opinion, is Turkey's greatest archaeological sight—Ephesus (Efes). It would be a crime to be in Samos and miss the home of the Ephesians, even if you aren't particularly interested in Roman ruins. If you're going to the Greek Islands, go to Rhodes or Samos, and for some real spice, visit Turkey.

39. Eastern Turkey

The town—I never saw a name—had one wide dusty road, lined for about 200 or 300 yards with mud-brick houses. Cow dung, dried into innocent-looking, large, rough loaves, was piled into neat mounds in every yard. Ducks, dogs, chickens, and children roamed around like they owned the place, while women loaded pails of water onto their balancing sticks at the well. Oxen pulled huge wagons of hay, and every few minutes, a proud horseman would gallop bareback down the street. This town had no electricity, no paint or advertisements on the walls, no cars or trucks, and only one small general store.

Two Yankees in town! Definitely big news. Boldly, like victorious but humane generals, we sauntered through the town, greeting people from house to house, shooting pictures, shaking hands, and faking confidence. Throngs of villagers gathered around us. We were moved to entertain. Carl sang and I danced, becoming the village stars. A cute little girl caught my eye, and she became my very embarrassed friend.

Carl found a wonderfully spunky old lady, colorfully dressed and the epitome of good health. She invited us into her spotless house, and soon half the village had crowded in after us. The window filled with faces struggling to get a look at the visitors. Our friend brought us homemade honey, still in the waxy comb, bread, stringy, powerful, and delicious cheese, and tea. By popular demand, I danced, dragging in the laughing old lady to the delight of a house full of Turks.

Most tourist maps of Turkey fill the West and leave the East empty. The only thing that eastern Turkey is empty of is organized tourism. It's a wild and fascinating land that few people even consider visiting. Here even the simplest activities become games or adventures. A walk down the street or a visit to the market becomes an exotic journey. Each meal is a first, every person an enigma, every day an odyssey.

Eastern Turkey presents the visitor with challenge after challenge. Communication is difficult. English is rarely spoken. Since many Turks have worked in Germany, German is the most valuable European language. Distances are great, and transportation, while cheap, is quite rugged. Most Western women are comfortable here only with a male partner. Where there are modern Western-style accommodations, they are often full. Arrive by midday or be ready to sleep local. There just isn't

enough demand to support lots of tourist hotels. You'll be an oddity—
the constant center of attention. People will stare and follow. Privacy
will be found only in your hotel room, if you have drapes.

Nevertheless, exploration of eastern Turkey is a special travel thrill
and those who visit scheme to return. The people are curious, basically
friendly and helpful. Communication requires creativity. A Turkish
vocabulary of 20 or 30 words is essential. Hotels and restaurants in
modest Turkish style abound, and it's impossible to spend much
money. Bus companies with modern Mercedes-Benz buses offer frequent and very cheap transportation to all corners of Turkey from all
corners of Turkey. (Varan is the best company.) Smaller, go-when-
they're-full buses called dolmuses will take you anywhere the larger
buses won't. Erzurum, eastern Turkey's major city, is only a $20 bus ride
from Istanbul. This 24-hour marathon ride drops you in a land that all
of a sudden makes Istanbul seem mild.

If you're looking for excitement and a very different culture, eastern
Turkey's cherrys are well worth its pits. There are few tourist sights as
such (museums, tours, famous buildings, and so on), but everything
about eastern Turkey combines to sweep you into a whole new world.
You're given a close look at the traditional Moslem culture in towns
with more horse traffic than cars. The streets are the man's domain,
while unliberated women appear in public only as walking gunny
sacks. A photographer will go through a lot of film.

Some Hints to Make Your Visit Easier

Good information is rare in eastern Turkey. By all means, locate some
literature on the area here in the United States. Study and know what
interests you. Take advantage of Tom Brosnahan's guidebooks to Turkey (from Lonely Planet and Frommer). Take a good map with you.

Eat carefully. Find a clean-looking restaurant and venture into the
kitchen. Choose your food personally by tasting and pointing to what
you like. Establish the price before you eat. Joke around with the cooks.
They'll love you for it. Purify your water. Bottled soft drinks and boiled
chai (tea) and coffee are cheap and safe everywhere. Watermelons are
a great source of safe liquid. If you order a glass of tea, your waiter will
be happy to "process" your melon, giving it to you peeled and in little
chunks on a big plate.

Learn to play backgammon before you visit Turkey. Backgammon,
the local pastime, is played by all the men in this part of the world. Join
in. It's a great way to make friends in a teahouse, the local hangout.

Really get away from it all. Take a minibus (dolmus) and ride into the middle of nowhere. Get off at a small village. If the men on the bus think you must be mistaken or lost to be getting off there, you've found the right place. Explore the town, befriend the children, trade national dance lessons, be a confident extrovert. Act like an old friend returning after a 10-year absence, and you'll be treated like one.

In eastern Turkey, the village children will turn out to greet you.

You'll spend a lot of time on buses. To become very popular, in fact, to become an honorary Turk and a member of all families on board, try one of these polite gestures: bring a bottle of nice cologne. When the steward makes his rounds with the bus cologne, offer yours and make it obvious it's to be shared by all. Bring a couple of current hit Turkish music cassettes. Shortly into your long bus ride offer the bus driver the tapes (they'll be returned). On the bus, offer a pack of Marlboros to someone and ask him to share them with everyone.

I make a habit of loitering near the property of a large family. Very often, the patriarch, proud to have a foreign visitor, will invite me to join him cross-legged on his large, bright carpet in the shade. The women of the household bring tea, then peer at us from around a distant corner. Shake hands, jabber away in English, play show-and-tell, take pictures of the family, and get their addresses so you can mail them a copy. They'll always remember your visit; so will you.

You'll be stared at all day long. To keep from going insane, be crazy. Keep a sense of humor. Joke with the Turks. Talk to them, even if there's no hope of communication. One afternoon, in the town of Ercis, I was waiting for a bus and writing in my journal. A dozen people gathered around me, staring with intense curiosity. I felt that they needed entertainment. I sang an old Hoagy Carmichael song, "Huggin' and a-Chalkin'." When the bus came, my friend and I danced our way on board, waving good-bye to the cheering fans. From then on, I entertained (with a terrible voice) most of eastern Turkey.

This is an exciting land—and a tremendous way to spice up your trip. Never again, in your mind, will you associate Turkey with cranberries.

40. The Treasures of Luxor, Egypt

On my rented one-speed, I pedaled through Luxor, my travel spirit flapping happily in the breeze, catching the cool shade and leaving the stifling heat with the pesky baksheesh beggar kids in the dusty distance.

Loading onto the old ferry, the man in the engine room hits the groaning motor into gear with a rock, and in a few minutes, the noisy city life is gone and the Nile has taken me back into a lush brown and green world of reeds, sugarcane, date palms, mud huts, and a village world amazingly untouched by the touristic bustle of modern Luxor.

I like the far side of the Nile. An irrigation ditch leads me into a village, where I am truly big news on two wheels. People scurry, grabbing their families to see the American who chose them over Tut. It was a royal welcome. They would have given me the Key to the Village, but

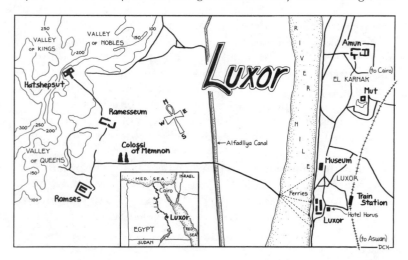

there were no locks. Smiles lit by glittering eyes kept the sunset linger-ing as a memorable evening began.

From Athens, Cairo is just a 90-minute flight or a day at sea, and you're in a whole new world. Economy or student boat and plane tickets from Athens to Egypt are reasonable at about $100 each way. For the best possible price, buy your ticket in Athens. These tickets are not advertised outside of Greece.

I spent more time in and around Luxor than in any European small town, and I could have stayed longer. On top of the village thrills, there are tremendous ancient ruins. The East Bank offers the tourist two famous temple sites: the Temples of Amun, Mut, and Khonsu at Karnak, one mile north of Luxor, and the Temple of Luxor, which dominates the town of Luxor.

And the West Bank, because of an ancient Egyptian belief, has all the funerary art, tombs, and pyramids. It was only logical to live on the East Bank, where the sun rises, and bury your dead on the West Bank, where it sets. Across the Nile from Luxor is an area rich in tombs, temples, and ruins. Be selective, buying tickets for the most important sights at the ticket office near the ferry landing. The Temple of Queen Hatshepsut, Deir el-Medina, the Ramseseum, the Colossi of Memnon, and the Val-leys of the Kings, Queens, and Nobles are just some of the many monu-ments from Egypt's ancient past that await you. You'll become jaded sooner or later, so don't waste your powers of absorption on anything mediocre.

Luxor town itself has plenty to offer. Explore the market. You can get an inexpensive custom-made caftan with your name sewed on in arty Arabic, if you like. A trip out to the camel market is always fun (and you can pick up a camel for half the U.S. price). I found the merchants who pester the tourists at the tombs across the Nile had the best prices on handicrafts and instant antiques.

Take an evening cruise on the Nile in a felucca, the traditional sail-boat of this area, for just a few dollars an hour. Lounging like Cleopatra in your private felucca in the cool beauty of a Nile sunset is a roman-tic way to end the day and start the night. For me, five days in a small town is asking for boredom. But Luxor fills five days like no town its size. Here's a good plan.

Five Days in Luxor

Day 1. Your train from Cairo arrives at 5:00 a.m. Even though it's too early to check in, leave your bags at a hotel, telling them you'll return by midmorning to inspect their rooms. Take a horse carriage to the temples at Karnak while it's still cool. The cool of these precious early hours should never be wasted. Check into a hotel by midmorning. Explore Luxor town. Enjoy a felucca ride on the Nile at sunset.

Day 2. Cross the Nile and rent a taxi for the day. It's easy to find other tourists to split the transportation costs. If you're selective and get an early start, you should be able to see everything you want at a relaxed tempo by noon. That's a lot of work, and you'll enjoy a quiet afternoon back in Luxor.

Day 3. Arrange through your hotel an all-day minibus trip to visit Aswan, the Aswan Dam, and the important temples (especially Edfu) south of Luxor. With six or eight tourists filling the minibus, this day should not cost over $12.

Day 4. Rent bikes and explore the time-passed villages on the west side of the Nile. Bring water, your camera, and a bold spirit of adventure. This was my best Egyptian day.

Day 5. Enjoy Luxor town. Tour the excellent Luxor museum. Take advantage of the great shopping opportunities here. Catch the overnight train back to Cairo.

Egypt seems distant and, to many, frightening. It's actually quite accessible, and, with a few tips, there's a reasonable chance you'll survive and even enjoy your visit.

The overnight train ride from Cairo to Luxor is posh and scenic—a fun experience itself. A second-class air-conditioned sleeping car provides comfortable two-bed compartments, fresh linen, a wash basin, and wake-up service. Make a reservation for this ride at least three days in advance, both ways. In the crazy Cairo ticket office, be patient and persistent and tip (bribe) if necessary.

In the cool months (peak season), hotel reservations are wise. Off-season, in the sweltering summer heat, plenty of rooms lay vacant. Air-conditioning is found only in the luxury hotels, and these rooms are relatively expensive at about $50 per double. Modest hotels with a private shower, fan, and balcony offer doubles for around $15. A cot in the youth hostel, for a couple of dollars, is rock bottom in price—and comfort. The Hotel Horus' central location (Maabed El Karnak Street, tel. 2165), showers, fans, good clean restaurant, friendly and helpful management, and priceless (i.e., safe to drink) cold water machine make it a real bargain (double rooms for about $20). Hotel Horus is just across the street from the impressive Temple of Luxor and a three-minute camel ride from the Nile.

Egypt is not a place where you should save money at the expense of comfort and health. A little extra expense buys a lot of comfort.

Eat well and carefully. With the terrible heat, your body will require plenty of liquids. Some Luxor water (such as water served in good restaurants) is safe to drink. Pepsi and the local cola, Sico, are safe and cheap. Watermelons are cheap, safe, and thirst-quenching. Cool your melon in your hotel's refrigerator. Choose a clean restaurant. Hotels generally have restaurants comparable to their class and price range.

One of the most interesting ways to see Egypt

Transportation in and around Luxor is a treat. The local taxis are horse-drawn carriages. These are romantic, but, as usual in Egypt, you must drive a hard bargain and settle on a price before the driver "moves 'em out." Some Egyptians will overcharge anyone who will overpay. You can cross the Nile from dawn until late at night on the very old Nile ferry. This "Tourist Fary," as the sign reads, costs only pennies. Sit on the roof and enjoy the view with the local crowd.

Transportation on the West Bank of the Nile (opposite Luxor) consists of donkeys, bicycles, and automobile taxis. You can rent donkeys for the romantic approach to the tombs and temples of West Thebes. The desert heat will melt the romance, and you may feel like a first-class ass sitting on your dusty donkey. Bikes, for the cheap and hardy, are a possibility for touring the ruins and tombs. An automobile taxi is the quickest and most comfortable way to see the sights of West Thebes. When split between four tourists, a taxi for the day is a reasonable way to go. To save money and make friends, assemble a little tour group at your hotel. You'll enjoy the quick meet-you-at-the-ferry-landing service of the taxi and, in one day, adequately cover Luxor's West Bank sights.

Survival on the Nile during the heat of summer is easier if you follow a few hints. The "day" generally lasts from 5:00 a.m. until noon. The summer heat, which they say can melt car tires to the asphalt, is unbearable and dangerous after noon. Those early hours are prime time: the temperature is comfortable, the light is crisp and fresh, and the Egyptian tourist hustlers are still sleeping. Spend afternoons in the shade. Wear a white hat (you can buy them there) and carry water. An Egypt guidebook is a shield proving to unwanted human guides that you need no "help."

You must constantly be on the budgetary defense. No tip will ever be enough. Tip what you believe is fair by local standards and ignore the inevitable plea for more. If you ever leave them satisfied—you were ripped off. Carry candies or little gifts for the myriad children constantly screaming "Baksheesh!" ("Give me a gift!") Hoard small change in a special pocket so you'll have tip money readily available. Getting change back from your large bill is like pulling teeth—on a duck.

Send Me a Postcard—Drop Me a Line

Thousands of trips are shaped by this book. That's a heavy responsibility, and I do my best to keep every page conscientious and up to date. Things do change, however, and travelers are always making new discoveries. I would really appreciate any corrections, additional ideas and discoveries, comments, criticisms, and feedback of any kind. All reader correspondence will receive a subscription to our *Back Door Travel Newsletter*.

If you would like to share your discoveries with other "Back Door" readers or help me improve the next edition of *ETBD*, please send a card to Europe Through the Back Door, 120 4th North, Edmonds, WA 98020. Thanks and happy travels!

A New Enlightenment Through Travel

Thomas Jefferson said, "Travel makes you wiser but less happy." I think he was right. And "less happy" is a good thing. It's the growing pains of a broadening perspective. After exposure to new ways of thinking and finding truths that didn't match those I always assumed were "self-evident" and "God-given," coming home gave me culture shock in reverse. I've shared with you a whole book of my love of travel. Now let me take a page to share with you some thoughts on how travel has given me a new way of thinking.

The "land of the free" has a powerful religion—materialism. Its sophisticated priesthood (business, advertising, military, and political leaders) make its goal unsustainable growth. The specter used to keep the flock in line is the threat of communism. As that fades, a new one will be needed, like drugs or terrorism. And like all religious zealotry, the result is ignorance and unquestioning obedience. And while the Golden Rule of Christianity and nearly every other major religion is "Love thy neighbor as thyself," the new Golden Rule is "Have it all!"

Sure, greater wealth would be wonderful, but the only way for 4 percent of the planet's people (the U.S.A.) to get more than the 25 percent we already take of the global economic pie (or even maintain what we already have, for that matter) is to get more and more aggressive. As individuals and as a society, I see us making bad investments. We're making serious and far-reaching personal and environmental sacrifices for more and more material wealth. While it's hard to tie it all in, especially in one page, I have a strong sense that materialism, war, poverty, and politics are interrelated.

Whoa! What happened to me? Did the young Republican with the history degree who voted for Reagan in 1980 go off the liberal deep end? Or, as Jefferson said, did I travel and become wiser but less happy?

I traveled. And travel gave me new perspectives. Like the early astronauts, I saw a planet with no boundaries. It's a tender green, blue, and white organism that will either live as one or die. I saw that I'm just one of five billion equally precious people. And by traveling, I've seen humankind as a body, which somehow must tell its fat cells to cool it because nearly half the body is starving and the whole thing is threatened.

I've found that "full utilization" of travel experience requires information that our system doesn't promote. Expose yourself to some radical thinking. You'll find a world where anchormen aren't cute and ignorance is not bliss. My ideas are from lots of travel and from books like *Small Is Beautiful* (Schumacher), *The Fate of the Earth* (Schell), *Food First* (Lappe), *The Future in Our Hands* (Dammann, $6 ppd from my office), *Bread for the World* (Simon), *War Against the Poor* (Nelson-Pallmeyer, $1 ppd from my office), and the newsletters of small peace groups.

A new enlightenment is needed. Just as the French Enlightenment led us into the modern age of science and democracy, the new Enlightenment will teach us the necessity of realistic and sustainable affluence, global understanding, peaceful coexistence, controlling nature by obeying her, and measuring success by nonmaterial wealth.

I hope that your travels will give you a fun and relaxing vacation or adventure and also that they'll make you an active patriot of the planet. The future is in our hands.

—Rick Steves

Appendix

Back Door Accommodations

This book is not written as a directory-type guidebook. My 22 Day series (published by John Muir Publications) lists nitty-gritty information on what to see, how to get there, where to eat and stay, and so on. The Let's Go series of guidebooks is also very good for Back Door-style hotel listings. Nonetheless, here are a few specific recommendations for the 40 Back Doors featured in this book. For a complete rundown on good places to eat and sleep, I've indicated which areas are covered in which 22 Day book.

1. The Hill Towns of Tuscany and Umbria

2. Città di Bagnoregio
Bagnoregio has no private rooms but two good hotels: Al Boscheto, run by Angelino and his family, Strada Monterado, tel. 0761/792369, and the new, more modern but much less colorful Hotel Fidanza, Via Fidanza 25, Bagnoregio (Viterbo), tel. 0761/793444. See *22 Days in Europe.*

3. Palermo, Sicily's Urban Carnival

4. South Spain's Pueblos Blancos: Andalusia's Route of the White Villages
Accommodations in these towns are meager. You can sleep very cheaply in any town in a private home. Just ask around for *camas* or *casas particular.* While Estepa has no hotels, you may want to spend the night in one of these places:
    Grazalema: Hostal Grazalema, $30 doubles, tel. 111342; Zahara: Hostal Marques de Zahara, $30 doubles, classy, tel. 956/137261; or the homier Pension Gonzalo next door at tel. 956/137217; Arcos: El Convento is the only reasonable place in the old town center, friendly, fine rooms, meals, and view, tel. 956/702333; the Hotel Los Olivos is a poor man's ($40) parador on the edge of town, San Miguel #2, with $40 doubles, tel. 956/700811.

Hotels are clearly rated throughout Spain. You'll see blue and white plaques on the door explaining that place's classification. The categories are, in roughly descending order of luxury and price: H (hotel), HS (hostal), HsR (hostal-residencia), P (pension), CH (casa de huespuedes), and F (fonda). Hotels and hostales are further distinguished by ratings of one to five stars (five being best). While prices correspond to the blue plaque, standards of cleanliness and comfort may vary. See _22 Days in Spain and Portugal._

5. Hallstatt, in Austria's Commune-with-Nature Lakes District
Best beds are at Gasthof Simony (moderate, 4830 Hallstatt, tel. 06134/231) right on the central square and friendly. Also good are Pension Sarstein (Gosaumuhlstrasse 83, tel. 217), Gasthof Zauner (Gosaumühlstrasse 69, tel. 06134/309), and very cheap and basic at the Naturfreunde-Hergerge (Kirchenweg 36, tel. 318) or the local youth hostel (tel. 681 or 279). See _22 Days in Germany, Austria, and Switzerland._

6. Hall, in the Shadow of Innsbruck
Sleep at Gasthof Badl (Innsbruck 4, A-6060, Hall in Tirol, tel. 05223/6784). Tourist office tel. 05223/6269. See _22 Days in Germany, Austria, and Switzerland._

7. The Cotswold Villages: Inventors of Quaint
Sleeping in Stow-on-the-Wold, the best regional home base: The Croyde B&B (Norm and Barbara Axon, Evesham Road, Stow-on-the-Wold, Nr. Cheltenham, Glos., GL54 1EJ, tel. 0451/31711) is best. Also good are: West Deyne B&B (tel. 0451/31011), The Limes (tel. 30034), and the youth hostel (right on the main square, tel. 0451/30497). For real peace and quiet, stay in Guiting Power at the Guest House (tel. 0451/850-470). See _22 Days in Great Britain._

8. Blackpool: Where England Parties
Tourist information (tel. 0253/21623) has lots of rooms listed. Try the Belmont Private Hotel (299 Promenade, Blackpool South, FY1 6AL, tel. 0253/45815). See _22 Days in Great Britain._

9. Europe's Best-Preserved Little Towns
In Brugge, stay at Hans Memling Hotel (Kuiperstr 18, 8000 Brugge, tel. 050/332096) or Hotel St. Christophe (Nieuwe Gentweg 76, tel. 050/331176). In Obidos: Casa do Poco (tel. 95358) or the Estalagem do Convente (Rua Dr. João de Orvelas, tel. 062/95217). Tourist office tel. 062/95231). In Toledo: Hostal de Cardenal (splurge, tel. 224900), Hotel Maravilla (moderate, Barrio Rey 7, tel. 223300), or Fonda Segovia (cheap, tel. 211124).

10. Bad Towns and Tourist Traps

11. Cinque Terre: Italy's Traffic-free Riviera
Vernazza Pension Sorriso, the only place in town, is my home base. ($35 per person for bed, breakfast, and dinner, 19018 Vernazza, 5 Terre, La Spezia, tel. 0187/812224, English spoken.) If that's full or too expensive, Sr. Sorriso — the godfather of local beds, who has all the business he can handle — will usually help you find a private room ($15 per person). Asking around town and at the

local bars is often cheaper. Vagabonds camp at the picnic tables on the Monterosso trail (check bags at the station for 50 cents, showers on the beach).
In Riomaggiore, Rosa Ricci runs a great youth hostel (tel. 0187/920-050) and
a small pension with 3 doubles up the hill. In Manarola, the Marina Piccola (tel.
0187/920103) and the new Albergo ca' D'Andrean (tel. 921040) are comfortable, expensive, but not very colorful. In La Spezia, the Hotel Terminus next to
the station (tel. 0187/37204) is a good ace in the hole. See *22 Days in Europe.*

12. Salema on Portugal's Sunny South Coast
Reservations normally not necessary; plenty of private rooms (quartos). The
brown tiled building up the "quartos street" has 8 doubles for $15 each (see
"Romen" on the buzzer, tel. 082/65128, no English, but their daughter in Lisbon at tel. 2533375 speaks English and can help). A British couple runs a rather
stuffy but nice place, Restaurant Pension Mare, $20 doubles, minimum three
nights, tel. 082/65165. You can camp with a low profile on the beach, showers
available in town center. See *22 Days in Spain and Portugal.*

13. Crete's Gorge of Samaria

14. The Berner Oberland: The Alps in Your Lap
Best rooms in region: Hotel Mittaghorn (Walter's place in Gimmelwald, tel.
036/551658), the Gimmelwald youth hostel (call Lena at 036/551704). The Gimmelwald Pension is the only other place in town (tel. 551730). In Lauterbrunnen, the Masenlager Stocki is a cheap and friendly dorm (tel. 551754). In Interlaken, the youthful budget place to be is Balmer's Herberge (tel. 036/221961).
See *22 Days in Europe,* or *22 Days in Germany, Austria, and Switzerland.*

15. From France to Italy over Mt. Blanc
Some specifics: train connections from Paris to Chamonix: 11:35 p.m. to 9:07
a.m., 7:24 a.m. to 1:29 p.m., or 1:12 p.m. to 7 :19 p.m. From Aosta, easy connections to Milan and Torino (and on to the Cinque Terre). Tourist information:
Chamonix—tel. 50-53-00-24, for hotels tel. 50-53-23-33, recorded weather
information tel. 50-53-0340. Aosta TI tel. 0165/40526 or 35655. Each office can
help you find a room and is open daily with long hours.
  Simple, central, clean, and inexpensive accommodations, in Chamonix:
Hôtel de l'Arve (classy, 50-53-02-31), Hôtel Marronniers (Alpine funky,
50-53-05-73), Hôtel Asia (basic, 50-55-99-25). Dorms: Les Grands Charmoz
(50-53-45-57), Ski Station (50-53-20-25), La Montagne (50-53-11-60), Le
Chamoniard (50-53-14-09), and the Youth Hostel (50-53-14-52).
  Simple budget rooms in Aosta: Hotel Rosini (friendly, modern, right in the
center at via d'Avisa 4, great value, tel. from France 19-39-165-44286, in Aosta
tel. 44286. Also, Mont Fleury (via P.S. Bernardo 26, tel. 551-926) or Mancuso (via
Voison 32, tel. 34-526, near the station).
  For castle lovers, the Fenis Castle (15 km south of Aosta, closed Tuesdays, tel.
0165/764-263) is the valley's most interesting.
  For those trying to choose between the Gimmelwald/Jungfrau region and
the Chamonix/Mont Blanc region, I'd choose Gimmelwald because it is less
touristy, offers more diverse activities, and is more fun if the weather turns bad.
With limited time in Chamonix, skip the Mer de Glace (unless you're dying to
see a dirty old glacier). See *22 Days in France.*

16. Off-beat Alps

17. England's Mysterious Moors

18. Dingle Peninsula: A Gaelic Bike Ride
For good Dingle eating, try Doyle's Seafood Bar (John St., tel. 066-51174) or the Half Door. Try a bowl of genuine Irish stew in a farmhouse café outside of Youghal.

19. Aero, Denmark's Ship-in-a-Bottle Island
In Aeroskobing, sleep at the Pension Vestergade (a quirky 200-year-old home warmly run by Bent and Phyllis Packnass, Vestergade 44, 5970 Aeroskobing, tel. 09/522298), Det Lille Hotel (a friendly and ship-shape 19th-century captain's home at Smedegade 33, tel. 09/522300), or the local youth hostel (tel. 09/521004). Tourist information tel. 09/521300. See *22 Days in Norway, Sweden, and Denmark.*

20. Rothenburg and the Romantic Road: From the Rhine to Bavaria Through Germany's Medieval Heartland
Schedule tips: best segment of Rhine Cruise (free with Eurail) is one hour from Bacharach (castle youth hostel) to St. Goar (great Rheinfels castle). The most interesting quick Germany crossing is to butt the Rhine (Koblenz to Mainz by train with above cruise spliced in) up against the Romantic Road bus tour (leaving the Frankfurt train station at 8:15 a.m.). One ridiculously early (6:00) milk run train will get you from the Rhine villages to Frankfurt's station on time. Otherwise, ride the trains to Rothenburg (3 hours, Frankfurt, changing at Würzburg, changing again at Steinach), spend the night, and catch the bus early tomorrow afternoon. The bus tour gets you into Munich at about 7:00 p.m.; no problem since the train station tourist information office is open until at least 9:00 p.m. The bus to Füssen arrives after 6:00 when its TI closes, so call ahead for a room.
    Going north, connect the Romantic Road bus tour, ending in Frankfurt with a late train into the Rhineland. It's easy to find a room in a Rhine village (I'd try Bacharach, Hotel Kranenturm, tel. 06743/1308), but it doesn't hurt to call from Rothenburg.
    Sleeping in Rothenburg: Hotel Goldener Rose, Spitalgasse 28, tel. 09861/4638, $30 double. Herr Moser's zimmer, Spitalgasse 12, tel. 5971, $25 double. Gastehaus Raidel: Wenggasse 3, tel. 3115, $30 double; Pension Poschel: Wenggasse 22, tel. 3430, $25 double. Youth hostels: tel. 4510. See *22 Days in Europe* or *22 Days in Germany, Austria, and Switzerland.*

21. Dungeons and Dragons: Europe's Nine Most Medieval
Castle Experiences
Carcassonne: right in the old center, Hôtel des Ramparts (Place de Grands-Puits, tel. 68-71-27-72) is best. The youth hostel is very good and accepts non-members (in the old town, tel. 68-25-23-16). Also good are Hotel Montmorency (tel. 68-25-19-92) and Hôtel du Donjon (tel. 68-71-08-80). See *22 Days in France.*
    Near the Rheinfels Castle, sleep in St. Goar at Hotel Landsknecht (moderate, a mile out of town on the river, tel. 06741/1693), Hotel Montag (moderate in town, tel. 1629), the private home of Frau Wolters (cheap, on the road up to

the castle, Schlosberg 24, tel. 1695), or the youth hostel, right under the castle (tel. 388).

In Reutte (tourist office tel. 05672/2336): there are two fine hostels (in town, small and modern, tel. 3039, or across the river in a more traditional old building, tel. 2644), private rooms in the Engls' home near the station (Muhlerstr. 23, tel. 41563), Hotel Goldener Hirsch (smoky Old World elegance near station, right downtown, tel. 05672/2508), Hotel Maximilian (in nearby Ehenbichl village, a classy splurge, tel. 2585), and Hotel Schluxen (rustic, in the meadow, super quiet, and traditional, tel. 05677/8452).

Closer to Ludwig's castles, you might stay in Füssen: great private rooms at the Peters Haus (near station, Augustenstr. 5 ½, tel. 08362/7171) or next door at Haus Scheicher (Augestenstr. 5, tel. 6465). The Braustuberl Hotel is a great hearty beer-stained value in Füssen (Rupprechtstr. 5, tel. 7843).
See *22 Days in Europe*.

22. Alsace
Colmar: Hôtel Le Rapp (16 rue Berthe-Molly, tel. 89-41-62-10) is my favorite. For a fine private room right downtown, call the funky and flowery Chambre d'Hôte at 12 rue de l'Ange, tel. 89-41-58-72. See *22 Days in Europe* or *22 Days in France*.

23. French Cuisine

24. In the Shadow of Venice: Grado, Palmanova, Chioggia

25. Peloponnesian Highlights: Overlooked Greece

26. Diverse Yugoslavia
To get to Plitvice, catch the hourly bus from Zagreb (2 ½ hours) or Zadar (3 ½ hours). TIs in Zadar or Zagreb organize inexpensive one-day Plitvice tours round-trip. For a fine traditional meal, eat at Plitvice's Licka Kuca restaurant near Ulaz 1; great.

27. Eastern Europe: Melting the Iron

28. Ignored Bulgaria

29. Nazi Sights in Europe

30. Northern Ireland

31. London: A Warm Look at a Cold City
All places listed are in my favorite neighborhood on the north edge of Holland Park, just west of Hyde Park. Hotel Ravna Gora, 29 Holland Park Avenue, WII, tel. 727-7725, well worn, friendly, a bit eccentric, cheapest decent rooms in town, $75 double; Holland Park Hotel, 6 Ladbrook Terrace, WII 3PG, tel. 792-0216, cozy, great value, hotelesque, $100 double; Abbey House Hotel, 11 Vicarage Gate, tel. 727-2594, $90 double, classy-cozy; Vicarage Private Hotel, 10 Vicarage Gate, tel. 229-4030, $90 double, classy-cozy, too; Alba Guest House, 53 Pembridge Villas, tel. 727-8910, funky, family run, $80; Holland House youth hostel, in Holland Park, tel. 937-0748. See *22 Days in Great Britain*.

32. Bath, England: Elegant and Frivolous
See _22 Days in Great Britain._

33. York: Vikings to Dickens
Each of these small guest houses or bed and breakfast places is a short walk from the train station, tourist office, and town center and charges from $15 to $20 per person with a huge breakfast. In York, sleep at the Airden House (snug and traditional, run by Susan Burrows, 1 St. Mary's, York YO3 7DD, tel. 0904/638915). Nearby, the Longfield House (2 Longfield Terrace, tel. 627321), and the York Lodge Guest House (64 Bootham Crescent, tel. 0904/654289) are also good. For downtown funkiness. sleep above the Golden Fleece bar, tel. 625171. The Youth Hotel (11 Bishophill Senior, tel. 625904) is a great budget value. See _22 Days in Great Britain._

34. Lisbon
Europe's cheapest capital. Decent $20 doubles abound. My favorite hotels are downtown, in the Baixa and Rossio area, and in the districts of Cheado and Bairro. Downtown: Residencia Campos, Rua Jardim do Regedor 24, tel. 320560, $15 doubles; Pensão Norte, Rua Das Douradores 159, tel. 878941, $15 doubles; Hotel Suisso Atlantico, Rua da Gloria 3-19, tel. 361713, $25 doubles. Old town districts of Chiado and Bairro (more colorful but borderline seedy): Residencial Camões, Trav. Poco da Cidade 38, tel. 367510, $20, great place; Pensão Duque, Calcada do Duque 53, tel. 363444, funky, rugged, dingy, verrry old, $13 doubles; Residencial Nova Silva, Rua Victor Cordon 11, tel. 324371, $25 doubles, great place.

Public transportation is very inexpensive and taxi rides are cheaper than bus rides in the rest of Europe. Lisbon is ten hours from Madrid by train (go overnight) and 24 from Paris. This is a fine place to end your trip. Consider an open-jaws flight plan; for instance, into London and home from Lisbon. See _22 Days in Spain and Portugal._

35. Oslo
City Hotel, Skippergatan 19, tel. 413610, $60 double with breakfast; Sjomannshjem, a "retired seaman's hotel" and a great value, Tollbugt 4, tel. 412005, $45 double; the MS Hakon Jarl Hotel, a refurbished steamer luxury hotel with one cheap room with no plumbing, the "writer's room" costs only $55 for two with breakfast, Radhusbrygge 3, tel. 424345; the Haraldsheim youth hostel, 4 Haraldsheimveien, tel. 155043, $15 per bed; St. Katarinahjemmet, a convent open to tourists in summer, Majorstuveien 21B, tel. 601370, $40 for modern doubles. See _22 Days in Norway, Sweden, and Denmark._

36. Stalking Stockholm
See _22 Days in Norway, Sweden, and Denmark._

37. Morocco: Plunge Deep

38. The Best Way from Athens to Turkey
On Samos, stay at Hotel Mariana (Kalomiris Street 22, 3 minutes from the boat dock, tel. 273/27369). In Kusadasi, stay at Hotel Altincezve, Yeni Aydin Yolu,

Kusadasi, tel. 9-636/13413. Both are very friendly. Pumakale is the best bus company for overnight rides from Kusadasi to Istanbul.

39. Eastern Turkey

40. The Treasures of Luxor, Egypt

Sample 22 Day European Regional Itineraries

22 Days in Europe

Day   1-Depart U.S. for Amsterdam
Day   2-Arrive in Amsterdam
Day   3-Amsterdam
Day   4-From Holland to the Rhine
Day   5-The Rhine to Rothenburg
Day   6-Rothenburg ob der Tauber
Day   7-Romantic Road, Dachau, Tirol
Day   8-Bavaria and Castle Day
Day   9-Drive over Alps to Venice
Day 10-Venice
Day 11-Florence
Day 12-Rome
Day 13-Rome
Day 14-Italian hill towns
Day 15-Drive the Italian Riviera
Day 16-Free on Cinque Terre beach
Day 17-Drive to the Alps
Day 18-Alps hike day, Gimmelwald
Day 19-Free in Alps; evening to France
Day 20-Colmar, Alsatian villages, wine
Day 21-Drive to Paris, stop at Reims
Day 22-Paris

22 Days in Great Britain

Day   1-Arrive and set up in London
Day   2-London
Day   3-London
Day   4-Salisbury, Stonehenge, Bath
Day   5-Bath
Day   6-Side trip to Glastonbury, Wells
Day   7-South Wales, Folk Museum
Day   8-Cotswold villages, Blenheim

Day 9-Stratford, Warwick Castle, Coventry Cathedral
Day 10-Industrial Revolution Museum
Day 11-North Wales, Snowdon National Park,
       Caenarfon Castle, Medieval Banquet
Day 12-Blackpool
Day 13-Windermere Lake District
Day 14-Hike and explore Lake District
Day 15-Loch Lomond, Scottish West Coast
Day 16-Scottish Highlands, Loch Ness
Day 17-Edinburgh
Day 18-Edinburgh
Day 19-Hadrian's Wall, Durham Cathedral, Beamish Folk Museum
Day 20-North York Moors, York
Day 21-York
Day 22-Cambridge, evening to London

22 Days in Spain and Portugal
Day 1-Arrive in Madrid and set up
Day 2-Madrid
Day 3-Madrid
Day 4-Segovia
Day 5-Salamanca to Coimbra, Portugal
Day 6-Nazaré
Day 7-Nazaré, beach day
Day 8-Obidos and on to Lisbon
Day 9-Lisbon
Day 10-Lisbon and nearby beach towns
Day 11-Salema
Day 12-Salema and nearby beaches
Day 13-Seville
Day 14-Seville
Day 15-Arcos de la Frontera, Tarifa
Day 16-Tarifa
Day 17-Morocco
Day 18-Gibraltar
Day 19-Costa del Sol and Granada
Day 20-Granada and Moorish Alhambra
Day 21-Toledo
Day 22-Madrid

22 Days in Germany, Austria, and Switzerland
Day 1-Arrive Frankfurt, to Rothenburg
Day 2-Rothenburg
Day 3-Romantic Road to Tirol
Day 4-Bavarian highlights, castle day
Day 5-Bavaria to Munich
Day 6-Munich, capital of Bavaria
Day 7-Munich to Salzburg
Day 8-Salzburg, Lakes District
Day 9-Mauthausen, Danube Valley

Day 10·Vienna—Paris' eastern rival
Day 11·Vienna to Hall in Tirol
Day 12·Innsbruck and into Switzerland
Day 13·Interlaken and up into the Alps
Day 14·Alps hike day, Gimmelwald
Day 15·Free time in Alps, French Switzerland
Day 16·Cheese and chocolate, Mürten
Day 17·Bern, drive into Germany
Day 18·Black Forest, Baden-Baden Spa
Day 19·Trier and Mosel Valley
Day 20·Mosel, Burg Eltz, Bonn
Day 21·Köln to the Rhineland
Day 22·River cruise, castle crawl, fly home from Frankfurt

22 Days in Norway, Sweden, and Denmark

Day 1·Arrive in Copenhagen
Day 2·Sightsee in Copenhagen
Day 3·Sightsee in Copenhagen
Day 4·Frederiksborg Castle, N. Zealand
Day 5·Vaxjo, Kalmar, glass country
Day 6·Pass Gota Canal to Stockholm
Day 7·Sightsee in Stockholm
Day 8·Sightsee in Stockholm, evening cruise
Day 9·Helsinki, Finland
Day 10·Stockholm, Uppsala, to Oslo
Day 11·Sightsee Oslo
Day 12·Sightsee Oslo
Day 13·Gudbrandsdalen, Peer Gynt country
Day 14·Glacier hike, Sognefjord
Day 15·Fjord cruise to Gudvangen—"Norway in a Nutshell"
Day 16·Sightsee in Bergen
Day 17·Drive from Bergen to Setesdal
Day 18·Traditional Setesdal valley, evening sail to Denmark
Day 19·Jutland, Arhus
Day 20·Aero Island
Day 21·Aero, Odense, Roskilde, Copenhagen
Day 22·Fly home from Copenhagen

22 Days in France

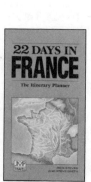

Day 1·Arrive in Paris
Day 2·Paris
Day 3·Paris
Day 4·Paris
Day 5·Into Normandy via Rouen
Day 6·Bayeux, D day beaches
Day 7·Mont St. Michel, Brittany, and to the Loire Valley
Day 8·Loire Chateau hopping
Day 9·Sarlat, the Dordogne Valley
Day 10·Dordogne Valley
Day 11·Sarlat, Albi, and Carcassonne

Day 12-From Carcassonne to Arles
Day 13-La Crême de Provence
Day 14-From the Rhone to the Riviera
Day 15-Beaches on the Côte d'Azur
Day 16-From Riviera to Alps
Day 17-Alps Admiration
Day 18-From Chamonix to Chardonnay
Day 19-A Taste of Burgundy
Day 20-From Burgundy to Alsace—Beaune to Colmar via Dijon
Day 21-Colmar and the Route du Vin
Day 22-Back to Paris, Verdun, and Reims

(Each of these itineraries is covered in a step-by-step, how to use your time most efficiently, where to eat and sleep and what to see Rick Steves guidebook by the same title from John Muir Publications.)

Eurail User's Guide

What Your Agent May Not Tell You

If you buy a train pass, read this very carefully.

Coverage and Duration

Your Eurailpass gives you unlimited travel on all the national train lines in Europe except Great Britain and Yugoslavia. That's over 100,000 miles of track!

Your pass also gives you many extras that some Eurailers never know about. Read the Eurail map and handbook (free with your pass) very carefully. These extras include international boat crossings (Denmark-Sweden, Sweden-Finland, Ireland-France, Italy-Greece), scenic river trips (Rhine, Mosel, Danube), lake rides in Switzerland, the Romantic Road bus tour in Germany, Expressway buses in Ireland, buses run by the train companies (German, Austria, Switzerland), and more.

Your pass is valid nonstop for its duration. Fifteen days would mean, for instance, from June 1 until midnight June 15. A one-month pass goes by the date number (e.g., August 8 until midnight on September 7). If you start a one-month pass in a 31-day month, you get 31 days. Starting in February leaves you short.

Starting Your Pass

Eurail passes are open-dated. You can start it on the day of your choice within six months of its date of issue, as shown stamped on the pass (e.g., a pass issued on March 1 must be validated before September 1).

The man at any train station ticket window can validate your pass (or direct you to a special Eurail window that will). Give him your pass (which you should sign in front of him), your passport, and a slip of scratch paper with the dates you figure should be entered. He will stamp the pass, enter your passport number, and fill in the dates on both the pass itself and on the connected stub. Since he may be sloppy and an error by him on your pass would cause untold problems, that slip with your dates on it is a wise precaution. (The European system of dating

is day/month/year: 3/6/90-2/7/90 is
June 3 to July 2.)

Your Validation Slip, Proof Stub, and Lost Passes

The detachable stub of your pass is
very important. Leave it intact until
your pass is validated. At that time, the
man who validates your pass should
tear it off and give it to you. Keep this
stub separate from your pass (like you
keep the proof coupon separate from
your traveler's checks). I think it's wise
for traveling partners to store their
stubs in the other person's plastic
Eurail sheath.

This validation slip has two pur-
poses. 1) A conductor may ask to see it
to substantiate any information on
your pass. If anything looks fishy, your
stub will clear or convict you. Many
people doctor the validation dates. Success in this game is nearly impossible
with the validation stubs. Also, if someone is using a stolen pass, the conductor knows they probably won't have the
stub. 2) If you lose your pass, it's replaceable if you present your stub and a sad
story to a Eurail aid office (listed on
your Eurail map). Even with the stub,
replacing a lost pass is a first-class hassle. Hang onto your pass as if it were
irreplaceable.

Refunds

Once your pass has been validated, it
cannot be refunded. Unvalidated
passes can be 85 percent refunded if
returned to the agent you bought it
from within one year of its date of issue.
If you get to Europe and decide you
don't want to use your pass, that's fine,
but it'll cost you 15 percent of the pass
price.

1st Class vs. 2nd Class

If you're 26 or older, you have a first-
class pass—forced luxury. Those under
26 can opt for the second-class Youthpass. With the Youthpass you get
exactly the same coverage with all the
extras, except you travel in the second-
class compartments. First-class people
can travel second-class freely. Second-
class pass holders must pay the difference to ride first-class. First class costs
50 percent more than second (i.e., to
upgrade a $50 second-class ride, you'd
have to give the conductor $25). First
class enjoys the special bonus of no
supplemental payments on Europe's
super trains (TGV, IC, Euro-city, Rap-
idos, etc.).

In general, trains have first- and second-class cars—all traveling at exactly
the same speed. First-class cars, marked
with a yellow line above the windows,
are less crowded, roomier, with plusher
upholstery and filled with other Eurail
travelers (mostly Yankees) and Europeans who paid 50 percent extra so
they wouldn't have to mingle with common folk. The soldiers and nuns are
partying in second-class. First-class is
most advantageous on overnight rides
(better chance to stretch out) and during peak season (July and August and
holiday periods when crowds can create problems).

Reservations

Generally, train reservations make as
much sense as calling ahead for a Big
Mac. Don't. If you want reservations
anyway, get them in the city you'll be
leaving from at the time of your arrival
there. It's easy, but you'll have to wait in
line and spend a dollar or two. Reservations are not required except in
Spain and Norway and on certain fancy
trains (IC, Euro-City, TGV, and trains
marked on the schedule with an R).
Remember, reservations must be made
at least several hours in advance. In fifteen years of Eurail travel, I think I've
made 20 or 30 reservations. On many

of those rides I walked through several empty cars to find that special seat with my number on it. Reservations from the United States are crazy.

Couchettes

Most overnight trains have sleeping cars full of beds. They range from ridiculously expensive luxury compartments to simple couchettes. A couchette (pron. "coo-SHETT") is a place in a triple bunk (6 beds per compartment or room). For about $14 you get sheets, a pillow and blankets, and up to five roommates of either sex. While couchettes can be booked well in advance, from just about anywhere, 24 hours is generally ample lead time to get a reservation. I like to book my rolling bed on the day I arrive in a town. First-class or second-class Eurailpass holders get the same simple couchette for that $14 price.

If you decide en route that you wish you had a bed, the conductor on board will set you up and take your money, if a bed is available. For maximum headroom, baggage space, and privacy, I request top bunks whenever possible.

Station Information Office and Timetables

Every station has an information desk (or at least a ticket window that will serve as one). Confirm your major travel plans here. More times than I care to admit, I've misread those easy-looking schedules. To overcome any language problem, give the man a written-out plan of your trip as you understand the schedules (e.g., Paris-Lyon 14:20-17:36, track 7?). He will affirm your plans or correct them.

There are plenty of schedules in Europe. The conductor has one, the stations are wallpapered with them, and most countries have handy national schedule booklets available for a small

price. In the stations, you'll see arrival and departure schedules. You're looking for departures. Usually, departure schedules are yellow, and arrivals are white.

The complete schedule is the _Thomas Cook Continental Timetable._ You can buy it new (expensive) or get an old one, which works just fine. It's handy (and makes you very popular on the train), but it's too bulky for me. A very handy easy-to-carry condensed Eurail timetable comes free with each pass. That is sufficient.

Basic Train Schedule Symbols

☒	Change trains
✗	Weekdays
⊶	Couchette car
⎘	Seat reservations compulsory
†	Sundays and public holidays
IC	Intercity 1st/2nd class with supplement

Any weird mark you don't understand means "Be careful, there's something funny about this particular train."

The introduction to the Cook's Timetable explains all schedule symbols very thoroughly. Schedule literacy is most helpful.

Britain

Of course, Great Britain is not covered on your Eurailpass. It's a great place to use a car with about the cheapest car rental rates in Europe— $120/week with unlimited mileage. Or you can get a Britrail pass from your travel agent at home—$179 for 8 days of unlimited second-class travel, $259 for 15 days, $389 for one month (among other durations). While you can't buy Britrail passes in Britain, it's quite easy (and often a bit cheaper than U.S.A. prices) to buy them from a travel agent on the

European continent. They can issue you one on the spot for local currency. In most ways, Britrail passes work like Eurail.

The Norway Line boat from Newcastle, England, to Bergen or Stavanger, Norway, takes about 20 hours, goes only mid-May to mid-October three times a week, and costs about $90 (or much more if you insist on buying it in the United States). It almost never fills up, but if you plan to use it, get your ticket and confirm your plans as much in advance as is convenient in London or Oslo. (In England, tel. 01/632-585555.) There's also a boat from Harwick, England, to Esbjerg, Denmark.

Off the Track—A Few Miscellaneous Tips

—Each particular car is labeled with its destination. Cars often split from the train at various locations during the journey. If you walk from car to car, remember to check your new car's travel plans.

—Your Eurail map is very handy. Bring it and use it.

—The Eurailpass is good for subway rides in Copenhagen, Hamburg, and some in Munich.

—Conductors roam the trains regularly. They are generally friendly and helpful. They can help you with connections information, arrival times, couchettes, and any train-related problems you may have. When he enters your compartment and says something in another language, he probably wants to see your ticket. Just flash your pass. Conductors growl when they see shoes on the seats.

—Many seats will be reserved. Check for reservation tags. If you sit in a reserved seat, you may be booted out at the last minute and find all previously unclaimed seats occupied. Many reservations are never used. Once you're rolling, go ahead and sit there.

Some reservations are for just a segment of the journey. This segment is usually noted on the reservations tag.

—Train toilets dump right onto the track. Don't use them in stations. They start out clean and well stocked with supplies and deteriorate as the ride progresses. First-class toilets are best. Toilet paper quality ranges from wax paper to sandpaper. Normally, lights at the end of the car tell you if the can is free.

—Whenever you take an intercity bus ride, show your pass before buying the ticket. Pleasant surprises abound.

—Make a habit of doing everything you can on arrival in a station to clear the way for a smooth and efficient departure.

—A few key mountain train lines are not covered by your Eurail pass. Since they are private lines (not national), they don't even appear on your Eurail map. The most important is in Switzerland from Brig-Goschenen-Disentis (completing the very scenic Chur-to-Martigny trip). Draw this in on your Swiss map inset. These and other private lines (shown on Swiss train maps available free at any Swiss station) cost a few dollars but are generally worthwhile.

—Irish trains are inconvenient, but many handy Irish buses are covered by your pass. Learn specifics on arrival.

—The Italy-Greece boats charge a $30 peak season supplement (from Italy—July 22 to August 15, from Greece—August 11 to September 3) and should be reserved in advance during this period. Most travel agencies in Greece and Italy can make this reservation for you. Be careful. Your trip is covered only on the Adriatica and Hellenic lines. Con men from other companies will try to lure you onto their boats and charge you when it's too late to turn back. Do what you can to avoid the peak season mobs.

—Also for safety, keep your train pass in your money belt (available at Europe Through the Back Door). If you'll be using your pass several times in a day, store it in a buttoned shirt or pants pocket.

—Nonsmoking cars are clearly marked. In many trains, red seats are for smokers, green seats are not.

—Technically, you're supposed to show your passport with your pass. Don't bother unless the conductor asks. He rarely will.

—Train water is not for drinking, and food is expensive on board. Bring a picnic with you. Window seats have small collapsible tables.

Eurail Usage Strategies

To "stretch" your pass life, consider these tips.

—When coming from London to Paris, pay to get to Paris ($22 from the coast) and start your train pass only when you leave Paris. The English Channel crossing is not covered on your pass anyway. Start or finish your Continental travels in Belgium and Holland. Distances in this region are short. Ticket prices are reasonable, and travel here rarely justifies the use of the Eurailpass.

—End your pass on completion of boat rides to either Ireland or Greece. Train travel is lousy (and cheap) in both countries. You'll do better on buses or boats. Europe's best hitchhiking is in Ireland.

—Consider an open-jaws flight plan into London and home from Athens. Or finish your Eurail time in Greece and get a cheap flight, bus, or train back to London ($150-$200 depending on your endurance, luck, and age).

—Most travel agents provide a handy pocket-sized European train schedule booklet with each pass sold. If yours doesn't, get one by sending a card to: Eurailpass, Box 10383, Stamford, CT 06904-2383.

—Eurailpasses are supposed to be purchased outside of Europe. If you need one in Europe, a friend can get one for you easily in the United States and mail it to you in Europe, or some Eurail aid offices (in major cities) issue them for an extra fee to those who can prove they reside outside of Europe.

—Choose the most scenic stopover. Many times, if you're going from B to F, you'll have to change from train B-E to train A-F. You may have a two-hour stopover options and which town offers the most entertaining layover.

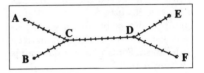

—Spend the night on the "wrong"— but less crowded—car. If you're sleeping on the popular B-E train and everyone seems to be E-bound, you may want to avoid the nocturnal crush by making a much less crowded F-bound car your rolling home for the night. Remember, one train starting in B will commonly have both E- and F- bound cars. It will split in D. The conductor can tell you what time. Let's say the train leaves B at 22:00, splits at D at 6:00, arrives in E at 8:00. You can stretch out in a less crowded F-bound car until 6:00, then move in with those E-bound sardines for the last two hours of the ride.

Beyond Eurail

While the Eurailpass gives you unlimited rail travel in seventeen countries and is far and away the most popular pass for Americans, many people are not aware that each country has special discounts and passes and those traveling extensively in that country can save a bundle by using them. Many of these passes aren't advertised in the United States. I've listed a few prices, but things are changing so fast I've left many out.

Your travel agent has up-to-date prices, variations available, and conditions for all train passes listed here.

General Europe

Interail—One month, unlimited travel in all Eurail countries plus Great Britain, Morocco, Yugoslavia, and Romania. You must be under 25 and prove at least 6 months residency in Europe. Gives only 50 percent reduction in country where purchased, so buy in a small country. A good deal if you can prove residency—difficult with a U.S. passport. It costs $250 (less than a Eurail Youthpass) but only gives 50 percent discount on ferries that are free with Eurail. For two months, Eurail is a better deal.

BIJ, Eurotrain, Transalpino, and Twen-tours tickets—Not actually a pass. One-way tickets with unlimited stops along the way. Up to 2 months to complete trip. Must be under 26. Savings of up to 50 percent on regular second-class fares. Available at student travel agencies and many train stations. Sample fare: London to Istanbul = $180. Pick up information in the Transalpino office in London's Victoria Station.

Regional Train Passes

Scandinavian Rail Pass—Denmark, Finland, Norway, Sweden. First class: 21 days, about $323. Second class: 21 days, about $214. Sold in the Scandinavian countries. The new Scanrail flexipasses offer any 4 days out of 15 for $119 second class, $159 first, or 9 of 21 for $209 or $279, or 14 of 30 for $289 or $419.

Benelux Tourrail Pass—Belgium, Netherlands, Luxembourg. Five days of travel in any 17-day period. First class: adults over 26, $107; second class: $72. Junior Pass: persons 6-26, $76 and $51, respectively. On sale in the Benelux countries and Netherlands Board of Tourism offices.

National Train Passes

Austria—Austrian Network Pass. Good on all trains and other conveyances operated by the Austrian Federal Railways (boats, cable cars, some buses). Valid for one month. First class: $355; second class: $237. Rabbit Card—Good for 4 days of travel within a 10-day period. First class: $98; second class: $68. Half Fare for Senior Citizens— Women 60 years and over, men 65 and over; half-fare passes valid for one year on the Federal Railways and many buses. A $25 Railways Senior Citizen's I.D. must be purchased. Not available in the United States.

Belgium—Belgian Tourrail. Good for 5 days out of a 17-day period. Five days, first class: adults over 26, $60; persons 6 to 26, $45. Second class: $40 and $30, respectively. 16-Day Card—Valid for 16 consecutive days of travel, year-round. First class: $110; second class: $73. Half-Fare Card—One month of unlimited train travel at half-fare, year-round, priced at $13.

Denmark—Reduced fares for groups of three or more adults traveling together and senior citizens over 60. Half-fare tickets Monday through Thursday and Saturday. Twenty-five percent discount on Friday and Sunday. See also Scandinavian Rail Pass described above.

Finland—Finnrail Pass. First class: 8 days, $135; 15 days, $203; 22 days, $249. Second class: 8 days, $90; 15 days, $135; 22 days, $166. Can be bought here. See also Scandinavian Rail Pass described above.

France—France Railpass. Two flexible passes, each of which can be used on nonconsecutive days within a specific period. Four-day pass, which must be used within 15 days. First class: $149;

children under 12, $80. Second class: $99; children under 12, $60.

Nine-day pass, which must be used within one month. First class: $249; children under 12, $130. Second class: $175; children under 12, $100.

France Rail and Drive Pass—Combines first- and second-class train travel with use of Avis rental car. It requires a minimum of two people traveling together, but an option for single travelers is available. A seven-day pass, four days of train plus three days of car, to be used within 15 days. First class: $199. Second class: $149. Fifteen-day pass, nine days of train plus six days of car, to be used within one month. First class: $329. Second class: $279. Car rental includes unlimited mileage, basic liability insurance, taxes, and free drop-offs within France.

Fly, Rail, and Drive Pass—Includes a seven-day France Rail and Drive Pass and a one-day airpass on Air Inter, the French domestic airline. The 8 transportation days can be used within a 15-day period; price is from $229 per person (based on two people traveling together). A 17-day program (nine days of rail, six days of car, and two days of air) starts from $399. Passes must be bought in the United States.

Germany—GermanRail Tourist Card. First class: 4 days, $135; 9 days, $202; 16 days, $285. Second class: 4 days, $90; 9 days, $135; 16 days, $190. GermanRail Junior Tourist Card. Second class only: 9 days, $85; 16 days, $110. Germany also offers flexipasses: 4 days in 21 for $120 second class or $180 first class, 9 in 21 for $180 or $270, 16 in 21 for $250 or $375. Available from travel agents and GermanRail offices in the United States.

Great Britain—BritRail Gold and Silver Pass. Gold (first class): 8 days, $250; 15 days, $370; 22 days, $470; one month, $540. Silver (economy): 8 days, $179; 15

days, $259; 22 days, $339; one month, $389. Children under 16 ride for half-fare.

BritRail Flexipass—Five days of rail travel out of 15 for $269 in first class or $199 in second. For ten days out of a month, you'll pay $399 first class or $299 in second.

BritRail/Drive—Combines BritRail Flexipass with use of rental car. Rates are per person for two adults traveling together, but an option for single travelers is available. An 8-day pass includes 4 days of train travel to be used within 8 days plus 4 days of car. Prices start from $185. Fifteen-day pass includes 8 days of train travel to be used within 15 days and 8 days of car. Prices start from $284. Car rental includes unlimited mileage, taxes, and car insurance.

Senior Citizen Pass (age 60 and over, first class only)—8 days, $210; 15 days, $310; 22 days, $400; one month, $460. Flexipass: 4 days, $180; 8 days, $270.

Youth Pass—Economy only. Eight days, $149; 15 days, $219; 22 days, $289; one month, $329. Flexipass: 4 days, $129; 8 days, $189.

Scottish Highlands and Islands Travel Pass—Seven days, June-September, $95; March-May, October, $60. Fourteen days, June-September, $125; March-May, October, $83. All BritRail passes must be purchased before leaving the United States.

Greece—Tourist Cards. For individual passengers, families, and groups of up to five persons; valid for 10, 20, and 30 days and entitle holder to make an unlimited number of second-class trips on every route served by the railway and buses. The prices or the card, depending on the number of passengers and the duration of validity, run from $40 for one person for 10 days to $195 for five persons for 30 days. On sale in Greece.

Ireland—Rambler Pass. Either rail or bus: 8 days of travel within a 15-day period, $74; 15 days within 30 days, $110. Combined rail and bus: 8 days within 15 days, $94; 15 days within 30 days, $135. Children under 16 half the adult fare.

Overlander Pass—Unlimited bus and train travel, including Northern Ireland. Fifteen days, $156. Passes must be purchased in the United States.

Travelsave—The Travelsave Scheme is available to holders of valid International Student Identity cards and entitles students to a discout of 50 percent off normal single adult fares on Irish Rail and Irish Bus provincial services and a 33 percent discount on 8-day return rail tickets. The student card costs $10 and can be purchased from the Council on International Educational Exchange, 205 East 42nd Street, New York, NY 10017.

Italy—Go Anywhere Train Ticket. First class: 8 days, $169; 15 days, $204; 21 days, $245; 30 days, $295. Second class: 8 days, $107; 15 days, $130; 21 days, $152; 30 days, $186.

Kilometric Ticket—Good for 20 trips. Limited to 3,000 kilometers (1,875 mi.). May be used by as many as five people traveling together. Valid two months. First class, $207; second class, $116. Both tickets can be bought here or there.

Luxembourg—Network Ticket. Second class only. One day, $6; 5 days within a period of 15 days, $18; one month, $46. Half-fare tickets for people over 65 and children 4-12. On sale in Luxembourg.

Netherlands—Rail Ranger. Three-day second-class pass, $34. Seven-day first-class pass, $69.50; second-class: $47. These passes are available at Netherlands Board of Tourism offices.

Norway—Bargain Rail Pass. Unlimited second-class train travel for seven days. Not valid on Friday, Saturday, Sunday, or Easter and Christmas holidays. About $448. On sale there.

Nordturist—Unlimited travel for 21 days. First class, $20; second class, $220. Also valid in Denmark, Finland, and Sweden. Available at Railway Travel agencies and railway stations in the Nordic countries. See also Scandinavian Rail pass described above.

Portugal—Tourist Ticket. Seven days, $74; 14 days, $119; 21 days, $169. Seniors over 65 are eligible for a 50 percent discount. On sale there.

Spain—Spain Rail Pass. First class: 8 days, $125: 15 days, $205; 22 days, $240. Second class: 8 days, $105; 15 days, $145: 22 days, $185. Available in the United States and Spain.

Sweden—Reduced fares on travel every day except Friday and Sunday. Visitors over age 60 receive a 30 percent reduction on all travel 7 days per week. Children 6-16 pay half fare; children under six, free. See Scandinavian Rail Pass.

Switzerland—Swiss Pass. Unlimited travel on the Swiss Federal Railway and on the Swiss bus network and lake steamers. First class: 4-day, $155; 8-day, $180; 15-day, $220; one month, $300. In second class, it's 8 days for $125; 15 days, $155; one month, $210. The Swiss flexipass offers 3 days in 15 for $99 in second class or $149 in first.

Swiss Card—Provides one round-trip ticket from Zurich or Geneva airports or any Swiss border point to any vacation spot in Switzerland. Also valid for unlimited number of tickets at half-price on the entire Swiss transport system. Good for one month. First class, $80; second class, $65; children 6-16, $50 and $35, respectively. Half-Fare Cards—One month, $45; one year, $65.

Sample European Train Trips

How long they take and how much they cost in 1991

From	To	2nd Class (One Way)	Journey Time (Hours)	Trains Daily (Approx.)
Amsterdam	Brussels	$ 26	3 ½	19
	Frankfurt	67	6	7
	Copenhagen	115	12	4
	Munich	125	12	7
	Paris	57	5 ½	8
	Vienna	161	15	2
	Zurich	130	11	5
Athens	Munich	122	39	2
	Beograd	52	20	3
Barcelona	Marseilles	51	8	3
	Madrid	51	8	4
	Rome	123	20	2
	Paris	101	12	3
Berlin	Hamburg	41	3 ½	3
	Brussels	108	10	3
	Warsaw	35	9	2
	Paris	137	14	4
Brindisi	Rome	45	7	4
	Patras	108	17	2
Kopenhavn	Köln	117	10	7
	Oslo	92	10	4
	Rome	271	30	4
	Paris	169	15	5
	Stockholm	77	8	7
Madrid	Lisbon	45	9	2
	Seville	41	6	3
	Paris	122	16	5
Oslo	Trondheim	76	7	5
	Stravanger	81	9	3
	Bergen	67	7	4
Paris	Marseilles	80	6	7
	Rome	142	17	4
	Venice	118	13	5
	Vienna	160	15	4
	Zurich	71	7 ½	6
Rome	Venice	43	6	10

First-class tickets cost about 50 percent more than second class. Tickets are *average* 13¢/mile second class, 10¢ in the south, 16¢ in the north.

There are faster and slower trains. These times are average.

Any journey of 6 hours or longer can be taken overnight.

From the above list you should be able to estimate the time and money required for any European train journey. Remember, times and costs of journeys per inch on the map are roughly similar to equal latitudes. So to estimate time and cost of a southern journey, compare it to a southern entry on this list. Northern trains are faster and more expensive. Don't worry about more exact information until you get to Europe. Plan with this chart, cocky confidence, and a spirit of adventure.

A Checklist of Sights

This list is very arbitrary and by no means complete. The places mentioned are just some of my favorites that I would recommend to you. In past editions, many readers have commented that they found this very helpful as a checklist for their trip plans. These are the museums and special places that have impressed me.

AUSTRIA

Wien (Vienna)
Tourist Info near Opera
Hofburg
Schloss Schobrunn
Kunsthistorisches Museum
Grinzing
Rathauskeller, City Hall
   restaurant
Danube Cruise—Melk to Krems,
   free with Eurail
Mauthausen Concentration Camp
   near Linz

Salzburg
Castle
Hellbrunn Castle, trick fountains
Baroque cathedral
Mozart's birthplace
Music festival, late July
   through August

Innsbruck
Alstadt—Old Town
Tiroler Folk Museum

Graz
  Laudeszeughaus,medieval
    armory

Reutte
  Ruins of Ehrenburg Castle

BELGIUM

Brussels
  La Grand Place
  African museum
  Kriek, Faro—local beer
  Musee d'Art Ancien, Flemish
    masters
  Place du Jeu de Balle, flea market
  Eat mussels

Brugge
  Markt, Belfry view
  Groeninge and Gruuthese
    museums, Flemish art
  Begijnhof, peaceful old "nunnery"
  Lacemaking school

Antwerp
  Cathedral
  Rubens' house
  Namur—nice town, great hostel

DENMARK

Copenhagen
  Tivoli May 1-Sept. 17 amusement
    park
  Christiania, commune
  National Museum
  Nazi Resistance Museum
  Carlsberg Brewery Tour
  Stroget—blonde-watching
    shopping street
  Nyhavn—jazz
  Walking tour by Helge Jacobsen—
    "Copenhagen on Foot"

Hesingor
  Louisiana, modern art, north
  Frederiksburg Castle

Roskilde
  Viking ships
  Cathedral

Odense
  Hans Christian Andersen land
  Billund—Legoland
  Aero Island

ENGLAND
London
  Houses of Parliament, tour
  Westminster Abbey
  Westminster Hall, oak ceiling
  #10 Downing Street
  Trafalgar Square, museums
  Piccadilly
  Soho
  British Museum
  Imperial War Museum
  Victoria and Albert Museum
  Hyde Park, Speaker's Corner
  St. Paul's Cathedral
  "The City"
  Stock Exchange
  "Old Bailey" Courthouse
  Tower of London, tour, jewels
  Museum of London
  Tate Gallery, modern art
  The theaters near
    Shaftsbury Ave.
  Kew Gardens
  Covent Garden
  Greenwich Maritime Museum
    and ships
  Antique Markets
  City walking tours,
    listed in "What's On"
  Brass Rubbing

Canterbury
  Cathedral

Cinque Ports
  Rye

Dover
  Castle

Battle
Battle (of Hastings) Abbey
Bodiam Castle

Brighton
Royal Pavilion
Palace Pier and promenade

South Downs
Beachy Head

Arundel
Castle
Mr. Potter's Curiosity Museum

Salisbury
Cathedral, Magna Carta
Stonehenge
Avebury stone circles

Bath
Roman and Medieval baths
Pump Room, tea and scones
Royal Crescent, Circus
Assembly Rooms, Costume
   Museum
Bath Abbey
Scrumpy—local cider
Walking Tours, free
American Museum

Wells
Cathedral

Glastonbury
Abbey

Tintagel
Castle, hostel, King Arthur

Oxford
University, walking tours
Blenheim Palace

Cotswold Villages
Stanton, Stanway—cutest
Stow-on-the-Wold, headquarters
Cirencester, Roman city, museum
Iron Bridge Gorge, Industrial
   Revolution

Cambridge
University, walking tours
King's College Chapel
Choose over Oxford

Durham
Norman (Romanesque) cathedral

York
Walled city, walking tours
Minster
York Castle Museum, out-
standing
Jorvik Viking Exhibit

Hadrian's Wall near Haltwistle
Once Brewed, hostel,
   museum, fort

FINLAND

Helsinki
Temppelliaukio Church
Finnish Design Center
Floating Market
Lutheran Cathedral

Scenic Stockholm-Helsinki cruise
Savonlinna Lake District
Retretti Museum

FRANCE

Paris Views
Tour Eiffel
Tour Montparnasse
Arc de Triomphe, museum and
   view on top
Notre-Dame
Sacré-Coeur
Pompidou Center
Samaritaine department store

Ile de la Cité
Notre-Dame
Ste.-Chapelle, stained glass
Conciergerie
Deportation monument

Left Bank
Sorbonne University
Latin Quarter
Les Invalides, military museum,
  Napoleon's tomb
Rodin Museum
Les Egouts (sewers tour)

Right Bank
Galeries Lafayette, shopping
American Express Co., mail
  service
Jeu de Paume, Impressionism
Palais du Louvre, greatest art
  museum
Musee d'Orsay
Sacré-Coeur, Place due Tetre
Musée de Cluny
Marmottan Museum (Monet)
Chagall ceiling in opera
  house

Side Trips
Versailles, greatest palace,
  Le Hameau
Fontainebleau, Napoleon's palace
Chantilly, great chateau
Giverny—Monet's garden
Chartres, Malcolm Miller tours,
  greatest Gothic church
Vaux-le-Vicomte

Rouen
Walking tour
Well-preserved town

Bayeaux
Tapestry, Battle of Hastings
Cathedral
Arromanches, D day landing
  museum
Omaha Beach

Mont St. Michel

Carcassonne
Europe's greatest medieval
  fortress city

Avignon
Palais des Papes

Arles, Nimes
Great Roman ruins

Nice
Chagall Museum

Loire Valley
Chateaux country
Tours—home base
Chambord, Chenenceau,
  Azay-le-Rideau, Chinon
Amboise—Close Luce (Leonardo
  exhibit)

Alsace
Route du Vin, Alsatian wine road,
  "degustation"-tasting
Riquewihr, Eguisheim,
  Kaysersberg
Colmar—Unterlinden Museum

Reims
Champagne caves
Cathedral, gothic, Chagall
  stained glass

GERMANY

Munich
Marienplatz
Residenz
Alte Pinakothek
Deutsches Museum
Stadtmuseum
Nymphenburg Palace
Mathäuser's Beerhall
Dachau
Olympic Park/BMW Museum

Oberammergau
Die Wies Church, Bavarian
  Baroque
Theater tour
Woodcarver shops

Füssen
Neuschwanstein, Mad King
  Ludwig's castle
Hohenschwangau

Berchtesgaden
Salt Mine tour
Königsee cruise
Kehlstein—Hitler's hideaway
and view

Rothenburg
Rathaus tower view
Folterkammer, torture museum
Walk the wall
Riemenschneider altarpiece
Walk to Detwang village

Bodensee
Meersburg, town and castle
Tropical island of Mainau
Lindau, Venice of the North
Boats free with Eurail

Aachen
Charlemagne's Cathedral

Köln/Cologne
Cathedral—next to station
Römisch-Germanisches Museum

Mosel Valley
Cochen Castle and town
Burg Eltz
Trier, Roman town
Overnight in Zell

Rhine Cruise
Bingen to Koblenz
St. Goar—best hour ride
St. Goar, walk to Rheinfels Castle
Bacharach, castle hostel,
nice town

Bonn
Beethoven's Haus

Würzburg
Fränkish culture museum
Residenz—Baroque palace

Berlin
Museum of the wall
(escape attempts), at Checkpoint Charlie, East Berlin over
Checkpoint Charlie

East Berlin
Pergamon Museum (East)
Brandenburg Gate
Museum for Deutsche Geschichte
(socialist view of history) (East)

GREECE

Athens
Acropolis, temples, museum
Agora, Temple of Hephaistos
Plaka, old town, shopping,
nightlife
National Archaeological Museum
Lykavittos Hill—take funicular,
sunset, view

Near Athens
Temple of Poseidon, Cape
Sounion
Dafni wine festival,
late summer, monastery,
Byzantine mosaics
Delphi ruins

Peloponnese
Old Corinth, Arco Corinth
Mycenae
Nafplion
Epidauros
Olympia
Mystra Byzantine ruins
Pirgos-Darou Caves, Mani
Finikous—best beach town,
SW coast
Back Door villages: Dimitsana,
Dafni

Islands
Mykonos, Delos
Crete, Palace and Museum of
Knossos, Gorge of Samaria
Rhodos, crusader city, boat
to Turkey
Samos
Patmos—special at Easter
Santorini
Best Athens day trip: hydrofoil
to Hydra
Corfu

Northern Greece
  Meteora Monasteries
  Metsovo—Romanian town

IRELAND

Dublin
  National Museum
  Trinity College
  General Post Office
  Hurling match, dog racing
  Guinness tour
  Kilmainham Jail

Rock of Cashel
Gaeltachts
  Gaelic pubs
  Dingle
  Aran Islands

Belfast
  Ulster Museum and Art Gallery
  Cultra Folk Museum
  Northeast coast

ITALY

Rome
  Pantheon
  Piazza Navona, nightlife
  Castel Sant Angelo
  Campidoglio Hill, Museo
    Capitollino, city history
  Forum
  Colosseum
  Mamertine Prison, St. Peter's
    Prison
  Santa Maria della Concezione,
    Cappuccin crypt, bones
  St. Peter's Cathedral
  Vatican Museum, Sistine Chapel
  National Museum, near station,
    ancient art
  Museo Etrusco
  Baths of Caracalla, open-air opera
  Tivoli, Hadrian's Villa
  Ostia Antica, ancient port town

Milan
  Duomo, cathedral, rooftop

  Santa Maria delle Grazie,
    Leonardo's _Last Supper_
  Galleria—Victorian shopping mall
  Side trip: Mantova town

Venice
  Grand Canal
  Basilica of San Marco
  Doge's Palace
  Traghetti gondola
  Campanile, bell tower
  Basilica del Frari, Donatello's
    St. John the Baptist
  Peggy Guggenheim Collection,
    modern art
  Burano, lace town

Florence
  Duomo, baptistry
  Bargello
  Palazzo Vecchio
  Uffizi Gallery
  Santa Croce
  Accademia
  Pitti Palace
  Medici Chapel
  Gelati

San Gimignano

Ravenna
  Best Byzantine mosaics

Siena

Assisi
  Basilica di San Francesco

Orvieto
  Duomo
  Etruscan Museum
  Etruscan tombs
  Bus to Bagnoregio, walk to
    Città di Bagnoregio

Naples
  Pompeii
  Herculaneum
  National Archaeological Museum

Palermo
Monreale Cathedral mosaics
Cappuccin catacombs—bones

Agrigento
Greek ruins

Syracuse
Greek ruins

NETHERLANDS

Amsterdam
Rijksmuseum, Rembrandt
Van Gogh museum
Ann Frank's House, Nazi
    Resistance
Beginhof
Red Light District
Canal tour
Leisdeplein, nightlife

Alkmaar, Edam
Cheese

Arnhem
Hoge-Veluwe National Park
Kroller-Muller museum,
    modern art

Zaandijk
Windmills

Den Haag
Peace Palace
Madurodam, mini-Holland
Torture Museum
Scheveningen beach resort town
Bali restaurant—rijstafel

NORWAY

Oslo
Radhuset, city hall tour
Nazi Resistance Museum,
    Akershus
Bygdoy—Viking ships, Fram
    Kon Titi, Ra, Open-Air Folk
    Museum
Münch Museum
Frogner Park, Vigeland
    sculptures, Vigeland Museum
Holmenkollen—ski jump, museum

Oslo-Bergen scenic train
Flam side trip, cruise
    to Gudvangen—best of fjords

Bergen
Bryggen
Hanseatic League Museum
Mt. Floien
Fantoft Stave Church
Troldhaugen, Edvard Grieg
Gamla Bergen

Trondheim
Nidaros Cathedral
Music Museum

PORTUGAL

Lisbon
Alfama, sailors' district
Castelo Sao Jorge
Belem Tower
Hieronymite Monastery
Monument to Explorers
Coach and Maritime Museum

Sintra
Moorish castle ruins
Pena Palace

Obidos
Walled town

Salema
Best town on Algarve, near Sagres

SCOTLAND

Edinburgh
Castle
Royal Mile, Robert Burns,
    Walter Scott, Robert Louis
    Stevenson
National Modern Art Gallery
Folk music in pubs
Festival—late summer

SPAIN

Madrid
Prado Museum, Bosch, Goya
Puerto del Sol
Palacio Real, royal palace
Plaza Mayor, nightlife
El Rastro, Sunday flea market

Segovia
Aqueduct, Roman
Alcazar, castle
Cathedral

Salamanca
Plaza Mayor, Spain's best square

Toledo
El Greco's House and museum
Museo de Santa Cruz,
Santo Tome
Cathedral, sacristy (take tour)

Seville
Alcazar
Cathedral, Giralda
Piazza d'Espana
Weeping Virgin alterpiece

Ronda
Pileta Caves

Estepa
Convent's hilltop chapel, excellent

Cordoba
Moorish architecture

Granada
Alhambra, Generalife

Barcelona
Picasso House, museum
Gaudi architecture
Ramblas
Montserrat Monastery

SWEDEN

Stockholm
Sverigehuset (Sweden House,
tourist info)
Gamla Stan, old town
Djurgarden, Wasa
Skansen, Grona Lund,
open-air folk museum
Historiska Museet
Kulturhuset
Sauna
Millesgarden, Carl Milles
sculpture

Planned suburbs—Farsta
Af Chapman hostel

SWITZERLAND

Bern
Modern Art Museum
Old Town
Toblerone chocolate factory tour
(tel. 031/343511)

Zurich
Kunsthaus, modern art
Swiss National Museum

Luzern
Medieval covered bridges
Rigi—mountain view

Berner Oberland
Best Alps, south of Interlaken

Murten
Walled Town
Broc Caillers chocolate factory
tour (tel. 029/61212)

Gruyeres
Walled town, cheese

Lake Geneva
Chateau de Chillon
Free Eurail cruise

WALES

Cardiff
St. Fagan's Open-Air Folk
Museum
Caerphilly, Europe's second
largest castle
St. David's Cathedral,
Welsh speaking
Aberystwyth

Caernarfon
Castle

Snowdon
National Park
Miniature railways
Slate mine tours
Ruthin Castle medieval
banquet

European Weather

Here is a list of average temperatures and days of no rain. This can be helpful in planning your itinerary, but I have never found European weather to be particularly predictable.

1st line, avg. daily low; 2nd line, avg. daily high; 3rd line, days of no rain

	J	F	M	A	M	J	J	A	S	O	N	D
AUSTRIA	26°	28°	34°	41°	50°	56°	59°	58°	52°	44°	36°	30°
Vienna	34°	38°	47°	57°	66°	71°	75°	73°	66°	55°	44°	37°
	23	21	24	21	22	21	22	21	23	23	22	22
BELGIUM	31°	31°	35°	39°	46°	50°	54°	54°	50°	44°	36°	33°
Brussels	42°	43°	49°	56°	65°	70°	73°	72°	67°	58°	47°	42°
	19	18	20	18	21	19	20	20	19	19	18	18
DENMARK	29°	28°	31°	37°	44°	51°	55°	54°	49°	42°	35°	32°
Copenhagen	36°	36°	41°	50°	61°	67°	72°	69°	63°	53°	43°	38°
	22	21	23	21	23	22	22	19	22	22	20	20
EGYPT	42°	44°	50°	59°	69°	70°	73°	73°	71°	65°	54°	45°
Luxor	74°	79°	86°	95°	104°	106°	107°	106°	103°	98°	87°	78°
	31	28	31	30	31	30	31	31	30	31	30	31
FINLAND	17°	15°	22°	31°	41°	49°	58°	55°	46°	37°	30°	22°
Helsinki	27°	26°	32°	43°	55°	63°	71°	66°	57°	45°	37°	31°
	20	20	23	22	23	21	23	19	19	19	19	20
FRANCE	32°	34°	36°	41°	47°	52°	55°	55°	50°	44°	38°	33°
Paris	42°	45°	52°	60°	67°	73°	76°	75°	69°	59°	49°	43°
	16	15	16	16	18	19	19	19	19	17	15	14
	40°	41°	45°	49°	56°	62°	66°	66°	62°	55°	48°	43°
Nice	56°	56°	59°	64°	69°	76°	81°	81°	77°	70°	62°	58°
	23	20	23	23	23	25	29	26	24	22	23	23
GERMANY	29°	31°	35°	41°	48°	53°	56°	55°	51°	43°	36°	31°
Frankfurt	37°	42°	49°	58°	67°	72°	75°	74°	67°	56°	45°	39°
	22	19	22	21	22	21	21	21	21	22	21	20
GREAT BRITAIN	35°	35°	37°	40°	45°	51°	55°	54°	51°	44°	39°	36°
London	44°	45°	51°	56°	63°	69°	73°	72°	67°	58°	49°	45°
	14	15	20	16	18	19	18	18	17	17	14	15
GREECE	42°	43°	46°	52°	60°	67°	72°	72°	66°	60°	52°	46°
Athens	54°	55°	60°	67°	77°	85°	90°	90°	83°	74°	64°	57°
	24	22	26	27	28	28	30	30	28	27	24	24
IRELAND	35°	35°	36°	38°	42°	48°	51°	51°	47°	43°	38°	36°
Dublin	47°	47°	51°	54°	59°	65°	67°	67°	63°	57°	51°	47°
	18	17	21	19	20	19	18	18	18	19	18	18
ITALY	39°	39°	42°	46°	55°	60°	64°	64°	61°	53°	46°	41°
Rome	54°	56°	62°	68°	74°	82°	88°	88°	83°	73°	63°	56°
	23	17	26	24	25	28	29	28	24	22	22	22
PORTUGAL	47°	57°	50°	52°	56°	60°	64°	65°	62°	58°	52°	48°
(Lagos/Algarve)	61°	61°	63°	67°	73°	77°	83°	84°	80°	73°	66°	62°
	22	19	20	24	27	29	31	31	28	26	22	22
	46°	47°	49°	52°	56°	60°	63°	64°	62°	57°	52°	47°
Lisbon	56°	58°	61°	64°	69°	75°	79°	80°	76°	69°	62°	57°
	22	20	21	23	25	28	30	30	26	24	20	21

1st line, avg. daily low; 2nd line, avg. daily high; 3rd line, days of no rain

	J	F	M	A	M	J	J	A	S	O	N	D
MOROCCO	40°	43°	48°	52°	57°	62°	67°	68°	63°	57°	49°	52°
Marrakesh	65°	68°	74°	79°	84°	92°	101°	100°	92°	83°	3°	66°
	24	23	25	24	29	29	30	30	27	27	27	24
	47°	48°	50°	51°	56°	60°	64°	65°	63°	59°	52°	48°
Tangiers	60°	61°	63°	65°	71°	76°	80°	82°	78°	72°	65°	61°
	21	18	21	22	26	27	31	31	27	23	20	21
NETHERLANDS	34°	34°	37°	43°	50°	55°	59°	59°	56°	48°	41°	35°
Amsterdam	40°	41°	46°	52°	60°	65°	69°	68°	64°	56°	47°	41°
	12	13	18	16	19	18	17	17	15	13	11	12
NORWAY	20°	20°	25°	34°	43°	51°	56°	53°	45°	37°	29°	24°
Oslo	30°	32°	40°	50°	62°	69°	73°	69°	60°	49°	37°	31°
	23	21	24	23	24	22	21	20	22	21	21	21
SPAIN	33°	35°	40°	44°	50°	57°	62°	62°	56°	48°	40°	35°
Madrid	47°	51°	57°	64°	71°	80°	87°	86°	77°	66°	54°	48°
	22	19	20	21	22	24	28	29	24	23	20	22
	42°	44°	47°	51°	57°	63°	69°	69°	65°	58°	50°	44°
Barcelona	56°	57°	61°	64°	71°	77°	81°	82°	67°	61°	62°	57°
	26	21	24	22	23	25	27	26	23	23	23	25
	47°	48°	51°	55°	60°	66°	70°	72°	68°	61°	53°	48°
Malaga	61°	62°	64°	69°	74°	80°	84°	85°	81°	74°	67°	62°
	25	22	23	25	28	29	31	30	28	27	22	25
SWEDEN	23°	22°	26°	32°	41°	49°	55°	53°	46°	39°	31°	26°
Stockholm	31°	31°	37°	45°	57°	65°	70°	66°	58°	48°	38°	33°
	23	21	24	24	23	23	22	21	22	22	21	22
SWITZERLAND	29°	30°	35°	41°	48°	55°	58°	57°	52°	44°	37°	31°
Geneva	39°	43°	51°	58°	66°	73°	77°	76°	69°	58°	47°	40°
	20	19	21	19	19	19	22	21	20	20	19	21
TURKEY	39°	41°	45°	51°	59°	66°	71°	72°	66°	58°	51°	43°
Antakya area	57°	59°	66°	74°	83°	89°	93°	94°	91°	84°	73°	61°
	23	21	25	25	27	28	30	30	29	28	25	24
YUGOSLAVIA	27°	27°	35°	45°	53°	58°	61°	60°	55°	47°	39°	30°
Belgrade	37°	41°	53°	64°	74°	79°	84°	83°	76°	65°	52°	40°
	23	22	24	21	22	21	25	24	24	23	23	22
	42°	43°	47°	51°	58°	64°	69°	69°	65°	58°	51°	46°
Dubrovnik	52°	53°	57°	63°	71°	78°	83°	83°	76°	69°	60°	55°
	23	21	23	23	26	26	28	28	25	23	21	21

Metric Conversion Table

1 inch	= 25 millimeters	1 ounce	= 28 grams
1 foot	= 0.3 meter	1 pound	= 0.45 kilogram
1 yard	= 0.9 meter	Temp. (F.)	= 9/5 C + 32
1 mile	= 1.6 kilometers	1 kilogram	= 2.2 lbs.
1 sq. yd.	= 0.8 square meter	1 kilometer	= .62 mile
1 acre	= 0.4 hectare	1 centimeter	= 0.4 inch
1 quart	= 0.95 liter	1 meter	= 39.4 inches

Index

Rick Steves' BACK DOOR CATALOG

All items field tested, highly recommended, completely guaranteed, discounted below retail and ideal for independent, mobile travelers. Prices include tax (if applicable), handling, and postage.

The Back Door Suitcase / Rucksack $65.00

At 9"x22"x14" this specially designed, sturdy functional bag is maximum carry-on-the-plane size (fits under the seat) and your key to foot-loose and fancy-free travel. Made of rugged water resistant Cordura nylon, it converts easily from a smart-looking suitcase to a handy rucksack. It has hide-away padded shoulder straps, top and side handles and a detachable shoulder strap (for toting as a suitcase). Lockable perimeter zippers allow easy access to the roomy (2,700 cubic inches) central compartment. Two large outside pockets are perfect for frequently used items. Also included are three net nylon stuff bags. Over 25,000 Back Door travelers have used these bags around the world. Rick Steves helped design and lives out of this bag for 3 months at a time. Comparable bags cost much more. Available in navy blue, black, grey, or burgundy.

Moneybelt $8.00

This required, ultra-light, sturdy, under-the-pants, nylon pouch just big enough to carry the essentials (passport, airline ticket, travelers checks, and so on) comfortably. I'll never travel without one and I hope you won't either. Beige, nylon zipper, one size fits nearly all, with "manual."

Catalog   FREE

For a complete listing of all the books, travel class videos, products and services Rick Steves and Europe Through the Back Door offer you, ask us for our 64-page catalog.

Eurailpasses . . .

...cost the same everywhere. We carefully examine each order and include for no extra charge a 90-minute Rick Steves VHS video Train User's Guide, helpful itinerary advice, Eurail train schedule booklet and map, plus a free 22 Days book of your choice! Send us a check for the cost of the pass(es) you want along with your legal name (as it appears on your passport), a proposed itinerary (including dates and places of entry and exit if known), choice of 22 Days book (Europe, Brit, Spain/Port, Scand, France, or Germ/Switz/Aust) and a list of questions. Within 2 weeks of receiving your order we'll send you your pass(es) and any other information pertinent to your trip. Due to this unique service Rick Steves sells more passes than anyone on the West Coast and you'll have an efficient and expertly-organized Eurail trip.

Back Door Tours

We encourage independent travel, but for those who want a tour in the Back Door style, we do offer a 22-day "Best of Europe" tour. For complete details, send for our free 32 page tour booklet.

All orders will be processed within 2 weeks and include tax (where applicable), shipping and a one year's subscription to our Back Door Travel newsletter. Prices good through 1992. Sorry, no credit cards. Send checks to:

Europe Through The Back Door • 120 Fourth Ave. N.
Box C-2009 • Edmonds, WA 98020 • (206) 771-8303

Other Books from John Muir Publications

Adventure Vacations: From Trekking in New Guinea to Swimming in Siberia, Richard Bangs (65-76-9) 256 pp. $17.95

Asia Through the Back Door, 3rd ed., Rick Steves and John Gottberg (65-48-3) 326 pp. $15.95

Being a Father: Family, Work, and Self, *Mothering* Magazine (65-69-6) 176 pp. $12.95

Buddhist America: Centers, Retreats, Practices, Don Morreale (28-94-X) 400 pp. $12.95

Bus Touring: Charter Vacations, U.S.A., Stuart Warren with Douglas Bloch (28-95-8) 168 pp. $9.95

California Public Gardens: A Visitor's Guide, Eric Sigg (65-56-4) 304 pp. $16.95

Catholic America: Self-Renewal Centers and Retreats, Patricia Christian-Meyer (65-20-3) 325 pp. $13.95

Complete Guide to Bed & Breakfasts, Inns & Guesthouses, 1991-92, Pamela Lanier (65-43-2) 520 pp. $16.95

Costa Rica: A Natural Destination, Ree Strange Sheck (65-51-3) 280 pp. $15.95

Elderhostels: The Students' Choice, Mildred Hyman (65-28-9) 224 pp. $12.95 (2nd ed. available 5/91 $15.95)

Environmental Vacations: Volunteer Projects to Save the Planet, Stephanie Ocko (65-78-5) 240 pp. $15.95

Europe 101: History & Art for the Traveler, 4th ed., Rick Steves and Gene Openshaw (65-79-3) 372 pp. $15.95

Europe Through the Back Door, 9th ed., Rick Steves (65-42-4) 432 pp. $16.95

Floating Vacations: River, Lake, and Ocean Adventures, Michael White (65-32-7) 256 pp. $17.95

Gypsying After 40: A Guide to Adventure and Self-Discovery, Bob Harris (28-71-0) 264 pp. $14.95

The Heart of Jerusalem, Arlynn Nellhaus (28-79-6) 336 pp. $12.95

Indian America: A Traveler's Companion, Eagle/Walking Turtle (65-29-7) 424 pp. $16.95 (2nd ed. available 7/91 $16.95)

Mona Winks: Self-Guided Tours of Europe's Top Museums, Rick Steves and Gene Openshaw (28-85-0) 456 pp. $14.95

Opera! The Guide to Western Europe's Great Houses, Karyl Lynn Zietz (65-81-5) 280 pp. $18.95 (Available 4/91)

Paintbrushes and Pistols: How the Taos Artists Sold the West, Sherry C. Taggett and Ted Schwarz (65-65-3) 280 pp. $17.95

The People's Guide to Mexico, 8th ed., Carl Franz (65-60-2) 608 pp. $17.95

The People's Guide to RV Camping in Mexico, Carl Franz with Steve Rogers (28-91-5) 320 pp. $13.95

Preconception: A Woman's Guide to Preparing for Pregnancy and Parenthood, Brenda E. Aikey-Keller (65-44-0) 232 pp. $14.95

Ranch Vacations: The Complete Guide to Guest and Resort, Fly-Fishing, and Cross-Country Skiing Ranches, Eugene Kilgore (65-30-0) 392 pp. $18.95 (2nd ed. available 5/91 $18.95)

Schooling at Home: Parents, Kids, and Learning, *Mothering* Magazine (65-52-1) 264 pp. $14.95

The Shopper's Guide to Art and Crafts in the Hawaiian Islands, Arnold Schuchter (65-61-0) 272 pp. $13.95

The Shopper's Guide to Mexico, Steve Rogers and Tina Rosa (28-90-7) 224 pp. $9.95

Ski Tech's Guide to Equipment, Skiwear, and Accessories, edited by Bill Tanler (65-45-9) 144 pp. $11.95

Ski Tech's Guide to Maintenance and Repair, edited by Bill Tanler (65-46-7) 160 pp. $11.95

Teens: A Fresh Look, *Mothering* Magazine (65-54-8) 240 pp. $14.95

A Traveler's Guide to Asian Culture, Kevin Chambers (65-14-9) 224 pp. $13.95

Traveler's Guide to Healing Centers and Retreats in North America, Martine Rudee and Jonathan Blease (65-15-7) 240 pp. $11.95

Understanding Europeans, Stuart Miller (65-77-7) 272 pp. $14.95

Undiscovered Islands of the Caribbean, 2nd ed., Burl Willes (65-55-6) 232 pp. $14.95

Undiscovered Islands of the Mediterranean, Linda Lancione Moyer and Burl Willes (65-53-X) 232 pp. $14.95

A Viewer's Guide to Art: A Glossary of Gods, People, and Creatures, Marvin S. Shaw and Richard Warren (65-66-1) 152 pp. $10.95

2 to 22 Days Series
These pocket-size itineraries ($4\frac{1}{2}" \times 8"$) are a refreshing departure from ordinary guidebooks. Each offers 22 flexible daily itineraries that can be used to get the most out of vacations of any length. Included are not only "must see" attractions but also little-known villages and hidden "jewels" as well as valuable general information.

22 Days Around the World, Roger Rapoport and Burl Willes (65-31-9) 200 pp. $9.95 (1992 ed. available 8/91 $11.95)

2 to 22 Days Around the Great Lakes, 1991 ed., Arnold Schuchter (65-62-9) 176 pp. $9.95

22 Days in Alaska, Pamela Lanier (28-68-0) 128 pp. $7.95

22 Days in the American Southwest, 2nd ed., Richard Harris (28-88-5) 176 pp. $9.95

22 Days in Asia, Roger Rapoport and Burl Willes (65-17-3) 136 pp. $7.95 (1992 ed. available 8/91 $9.95)

22 Days in Australia, 3rd ed., John Gottberg (65-40-8) 148 pp. $7.95 (1992 ed. available 8/91 $9.95)

22 Days in California, 2nd ed., Roger Rapoport (65-64-5) 176 pp. $9.95

22 Days in China, Gaylon Duke and Zenia Victor (28-72-9) 144 pp. $7.95

22 Days in Europe, 5th ed., Rick Steves (65-63-7) 192 pp. $9.95

22 Days in Florida, Richard Harris (65-27-0) 136 pp. $7.95 (1992 ed. available 8/91 $9.95)

22 Days in France, Rick Steves (65-07-6) 154 pp. $7.95 (1991 ed. available 4/91 $9.95)

22 Days in Germany, Austria & Switzerland, 3rd ed., Rick Steves (65-39-4) 136 pp. $7.95

22 Days in Great Britain, 3rd ed., Rick Steves (65-38-6) 144 pp. $7.95 (1991 ed. available 4/91 $9.95)

22 Days in Hawaii, 2nd ed., Arnold Schuchter (65-50-5) 144 pp. $7.95 (1992 ed. available 8/91 $9.95)

22 Days in India, Anurag Mathur (28-87-7) 136 pp. $7.95

22 Days in Japan, David Old (28-73-7) 136 pp. $7.95

22 Days in Mexico, 2nd ed., Steve Rogers and Tina Rosa (65-41-6) 128 pp. $7.95

22 Days in New England, Anne Wright (28-96-6) 128 pp. $7.95 (1991 ed. available 4/91 $9.95)

2 to 22 Days in New Zealand, 1991 ed., Arnold Schuchter (65-58-0) 176 pp. $9.95

22 Days in Norway, Sweden, & Denmark, Rick Steves (28-83-4) 136 pp. $7.95 (1991 ed. available 4/91 $9.95)

22 Days in the Pacific Northwest, Richard Harris (28-97-4) 136 pp. $7.95 (1991 ed. available 4/91 $9.95)

22 Days in the Rockies, Roger Rapoport (65-68-8) 176 pp. $9.95

22 Days in Spain & Portugal, 3rd ed., Rick Steves (65-06-8) 136 pp. $7.95

22 Days in Texas, Richard Harris (65-47-5) 176 pp. $9.95

22 Days in Thailand, Derk Richardson (65-57-2) 176 pp. $9.95

22 Days in the West Indies, Cyndy Morreale and Sam Morreale (28-74-5)136 pp. $7.95

"Kidding Around" Travel Guides for Young Readers
Written for kids eight years of age and older. Generously illustrated in two colors with imaginative characters and images. An adventure to read and a treasure to keep.

Kidding Around Atlanta, Anne Pedersen (65-35-1) 64 pp. $9.95

Kidding Around Boston, Helen Byers (65-36-X) 64 pp. $9.95

Kidding Around Chicago, Lauren Davis (65-70-X) 64 pp. $9.95

Kidding Around the Hawaiian Islands, Sarah Lovett (65-37-8) 64 pp. $9.95

Kidding Around London, Sarah Lovett (65-24-6) 64 pp. $9.95

Kidding Around Los Angeles, Judy Cash (65-34-3) 64 pp. $9.95

Kidding Around the National Parks of the Southwest, Sarah Lovett 108 pp. $12.95

Kidding Around New York City, Sarah Lovett (65-33-5) 64 pp. $9.95

Around Paris, Rebecca Clay
~-3) 64 pp. $9.95 (Available 4/91)
,ling Around Philadelphia,
...becca Clay (65-71-8) 64 pp. $9.95
Kidding Around San Francisco,
Rosemary Zibart (65-23-8) 64 pp. $9.95
Kidding Around Santa Fe, Susan York
(65-99-8) 64 pp. $9.95 (Available 5/91)
Kidding Around Seattle, Rick Steves
(65-84-X) 64 pp. $9.95 (Available 4/91)
Kidding Around Washington, D.C.,
Anne Pedersen (65-25-4) 64 pp. $9.95

Environmental Books for Young Readers

Written for kids eight years and older.
Examines the environmental issues
and opportunities that today's kids will
face during their lives.

**The Indian Way: Learning to Com-
municate with Mother Earth,** Gary
McLain (65-73-4) 114 pp. $9.95
**The Kids' Environment Book:
What's Awry and Why,** Anne Peder-
sen (55-74-2) 192 pp. $13.95
**No Vacancy: The Kids' Guide to
Population and the Environment,**
Glenna Boyd (61-000-7) 64 pp. $9.95
(Available 8/91)
**Rads, Ergs, and Cheeseburgers: The
Kids' Guide to Energy and the
Environment,** Bill Yanda (65-75-0)
108 pp. $12.95

"Extremely Weird" Series for Young Readers

Written for kids eight years of age and
older. Designed to help kids appreciate
the world around them. Each book
includes full-color photographs with
detailed and entertaining descriptions.

Extremely Weird Bats, Sarah Lovett
(61-008-2) 48 pp. $13.95 hardbound
(Available 6/91)
Extremely Weird Frogs, Sarah Lovett
(61-006-6) 48 pp. $13.95 hardbound
(Available 6/91)
Extremely Weird Spiders, Sarah
Lovett (61-007-4) 48 pp. $13.95 hard-
bound (Available 6/91)

Automotive Repair Manuals

**How to Keep Your VW Alive, 14th
ed.,** (65-80-7) 440 pp. $19.95
How to Keep Your Subaru Alive
(65-11-4) 480 pp. $19.95

**How to Keep Your Toyota Pickup
Alive** (28-81-3) 392 pp. $19.95
**How to Keep Your Datsun/Nissan
Alive** (28-65-6) 544 pp. $19.95

Other Automotive Books

**The Greaseless Guide to Car Care
Confidence: Take the Terror Out of
Talking to Your Mechanic,** Mary Jack-
son (65-19-X) 224 pp. $14.95
**Off-Road Emergency Repair & Sur-
vival,** James Ristow (65-26-2) 160 pp.
$9.95

Ordering Information

If you cannot find our books in your
local bookstore, you can order directly
from us. Please check the "Available"
date above. If you send us money for a
book not yet available, we will hold
your money until we can ship you the
book. Your books will be sent to you via
UPS (for U.S. destinations). UPS will
not deliver to a P.O. Box; please give us
a street address. Include $2.75 for the
first item ordered and $.50 for each
additional item to cover shipping and
handling costs. For airmail within the
U.S., enclose $4.00. All foreign orders
will be shipped surface rate; please
enclose $3.00 for the first item and
$1.00 for each additional item. Please
inquire about foreign airmail rates.

Method of Payment

Your order may be paid by check,
money order, or credit card. We cannot
be responsible for cash sent through
the mail. All payments must be made
in U.S. dollars drawn on a U.S. bank.
Canadian postal money orders in U.S.
dollars are acceptable. For VISA,
MasterCard, or American Express
orders, include your card number,
expiration date, and your signature, or
call (800) 888-7504. Books ordered on
American Express cards can be
shipped only to the billing address of
the cardholder. Sorry, no C.O.D.'s.
Residents of sunny New Mexico, add
5.875% tax to the total.

Address all orders and inquiries to:
John Muir Publications
P.O. Box 613
Santa Fe, NM 87504
(505) 982-4078
(800) 888-7504